Sarony & Major Lith.  117 Fulton St New York

SOI-EN-GA-RAH-TA, OR KING HENDRICK

*1740  See P. 413.*

1-60135-502-5

# NOTES

ON

# THE IROQUOIS;

OR CONTRIBUTIONS TO

# AMERICAN HISTORY, ANTIQUITIES,

AND

# GENERAL ETHNOLOGY.

## BY HENRY R. SCHOOLCRAFT,

Hon. Memb. of the Royal Soc. of Northern Antiquaries: Hon. Mem. of the Royal Geog. Soc. of London: Mem. Ordin. of the Ethnological Soc. of Paris: Vice President of the Am. Ethn. Soc. at New York: Cor. Mem of the New York Lyceum of Nat. Hist: Mem. of the Am. Philos. Soc., and of the Am. Acad. of the Nat. Sciences at Philad.: of the Am. Antiq., and of the Am. Geolog. Societies: Hon Mem. of the New York Hist. Soc: Mem. of the Hist. Soc. of Pennsylvania, Georgia, Rhode Island, Connecticut and Ohio. &c., &c., &c.

ALBANY:
ERASTUS H. PEASE & CO., 82 STATE STREET.
1847.

Entered according to act of Congress, in the year, 1847,
BY HENRY R. SCHOOLCRAFT,
In the Clerk's Office of the Northern District of New York.

J. MUNSELL, PRINTER,
ALBANY.

# PREFACE.

The aboriginal nation, whose statistics and history, past and present, are brought into discussion in this treatise, stand out prominently in the foreground of our own history. They have sustained themselves for more than three centuries, against the intruding and progressive races of Europe. During the period of the planting of the colonies, their sachems stood as independent embassadors, before the representatives of kings, and the general eloquence, diplomacy, and military exploits of the several cantons composing their confederacy, gave them a name and reputation coeval with Europe. No nation of the widely spread red race of America, has displayed so high and heroic a love of liberty, united with the true art of government, and personal energy and stamina of character, as the Iroquois. The races of the equinoctial latitudes, who obeyed respectively the sceptre of the Incas, and of the princes of Anahuac, have indeed enlisted a wider sympathy and risen to higher fame in the world's history, but it has been the fame earned by the labors and arts of subdued multitudes, and the sympathy consequent on overwhelming national misfortune; this is the difference between the empires of Peru and Mexico, and the high-toned Iroquois republic; but neither letters, Christianity, nor liberty, have cause to lament the fall of the two former empires. The policy and wisdom by which the Iroquois met and resisted the inroads of European power, and prevented the overturning of their institutions, furnishes the highest evidence of their superiority as an active, thinking race of men. They watched, as with eagle glance, encroachments upon their national rights. They kept their central council fire at Onondaga bright, and often met from all the cantons, from the east and west, to deliberate on their affairs; and when a war was resolved on against a trespassing or impinging foe, of their own race, they concentrated every effort to carry it on, and flew to the contest to root up, and tear out their name and place among men. No leading event, in fine, in the history of the colonies, has been consummated without the power, in peace or war, of the Iroquois. They were present under the British standard, at the siege of Niagara, at the overthrow of Baron Deiskau, at Lake George, and at the fall of Montcalm at Quebec. The colonies of Virginia, Maryland, and Pennsylvania, felt the strong influence of the policy of their confederacy. In any political scheme of the colonies, the course of the Iroquois, in the question at issue, was ever one of the deepest moment, and he must be a careless reader of history, who does not perceive how vital an element they became in all the interior transactions, between A. D. 1600, at the general period of the settlement of the colonies, and the close of the war of American Independence.

The stirring events of their wars are mingled, more or less, with the history of each of the colonies, and impart to them much of their interest. To extract them and set them in order, as a branch of American history, would constitute a theme of no ordinary attraction.* But the task I had taken in hand did not contemplate a his-

* It is to be regretted, that Colden, who viewed the subject in this light, drops his excellent outlines, (so essential to all who wish to study the Iroquois history), with the antique date of the peace of Ryswick, A. D. 1697, a period, when, indeed, their republic had hardly culminated.

tory. It seemed desirable that before the *modern* materials of the Iroquois history could be well employed, we should accumulate something tangible and certain of their general polity, wars, and actual statistics, and also something of the ancient period of their earlier traditions, and lore, which might help the inquirer to clear up the boundaries of historical mystery which shroud the Indian period, prior to 1492. This forms the true epoch of American ethnology.

It was a desideratum in American statistics, that a complete census, of one of the primary stocks, who had lived in our neighborhood all this time, and still preserve their nationality, should be taken. This task New York executed in 1845. It appeared desirable to the agent appointed to carry the act of the legislature into effect, that the opportunity should not be lost of making some notes of the kind here indicated; and it is in this feature indeed, if any thing in the following notes, that they aspire to the character of research, though they be intended only to shadow forth outlines, to be filled up hereafter.

In reprinting the original notes, in order to supply a demand of the public for them, which is still unabated, the occasion has been taken to revise them, and to add other portions of the original materials, which were suppressed in the publication, together with some further traditions, and biographical and historical notices and researches, which it is thought will tend to impart further interest and value to the work.

ERRATA.

Page 1, 6th line, contents of chap., for *congerity* read *longevity*.
" 14, 13th line from bottom, for *and* read *than*.
" 40, 12th line from top, for *end* read *era*.
" 48, 3rd line from top, for *literary* read *literally*.

# CONTENTS.

### CHAPTER I.

| | |
|---|---|
| Preliminary observations, | 1 |
| Obstacles opposed to statistical inquiries among the North American Indians, | 5 |
| Progressive state of agriculture, | 9 |
| Evils of the annuity system, | 12 |
| Grain and fruits raised | 14 |
| Ancient and present state of the Iroquois population compared, | 22 |
| General deductions on their longevity and effects of climate, | 27 |
| Proportion of deaf and dumb and blind, | 28 |
| Remnants of the tribes of Algonquin lineage of southern New York, | 31 |
| Abstract of census returns, | 32 |

### CHAPTER II.

#### HISTORICAL AND ETHNOLOGICAL INQUIRIES.

| | |
|---|---|
| Sketch of the Iroquois group of aboriginal tribes, | 39 |
| Ethnological suggestions, | 56 |
| Indian cosmogony, | 61 |
| Gleams of their ancient history, | 64 |

1*

## CHAPTER III.

ORIGIN AND HISTORY OF THE IROQUOIS AS A DISTINCT PEOPLE.

| | |
|---|---|
| Mohawks, | 71 |
| Oneidas and the Oneida Stone, | 75 |
| Onondagas, | 88 |
| Cayugas, | 92 |
| Senecas and their origin, | 96 |
| Tuscaroras and their flight from North Carolina, | 104 |
| Necariages, | 113 |
| St. Regis colony, | 114 |

## CHAPTER IV.

EPOCH AND PRINCIPLES OF THE IROQUOIS LEAGUE.

| | |
|---|---|
| Objects of research, | 117 |
| Era of the confederacy, | 117 |
| Principles of their government and the totemic bond, | 122 |
| Ancient worship and system of astronomy, | 137 |
| Witchcraft, and its theory and practical evils, | 139 |
| Wife's right to property; limited nature of marriage contract, | 141 |
| Idea of vampyres; traditions in reference to, | 142 |

## CHAPTER V.

EARLY WARS AND POLITICAL RELATIONS OF THE IROQUOIS WITH THE OTHER NORTH AMERICAN TRIBES.

| | |
|---|---|
| War with an ancient people called Alleghans, | 147 |
| Lenno Lenapees, or Delawares, | 148 |
| Mohegans, Munsees, Manhattans, Metöacs, | 150 |
| Adirondacks, | 152 |
| Algonquins, | 153 |
| Owegungas, | 154 |
| Shawnees, | 154 |
| Eries, | 155 |

CONTENTS.    xi

Susquehannocks, - - - - - - - 155
Massawomacs, - - - - - - - 155
Catabas, - - - - - - - - 156
Cherokees, their history and language, - - - 157
Quatoghies, or Hurons, - - - - - - 161
Wyandots, - - - - - - - - 164
Twightwies, or Miamies, - - - - - - 165
Mississagies, - - - - - - - - 168
Chippewa or Odjibwa group, - - - - - 168

## CHAPTER VI.

### ARCHÆOLOGY.

Vestiges of an ancient French fort in Lenox, - - 174
Ancient site of the Onondagas, - - - - 177
Antiquities of Pompey, - - - - - - 188
Ancient fortification of Osco, - - - - - 192
Ancient elliptical work at Canandaigua, - - - 196
Ancient entrenchments on Fort Hill, - - - 198
Ancient rock citadel of Kienuka, - - - - 207
Ancient battle field on Buffalo creek, - - - 213

## CHAPTER VII.

### ANCIENT STATE OF INDIAN ART IN NORTH AMERICA.

Architectural ruins, - - - - - - 219
Remains, sculpture and inscriptions, - - - - 220
Effect of European fabrics, - - - - - 220
Arrow heads and axes, - - - - - - 221
Pottery, - - - - - - - - 222
Architecture, - - - - - - - 224
Art of design, - - - - - - - 225
Amulets, &c., - - - - - - - 226
Clothing, &c., - - - - - - - 229

xii CONTENTS.

## CHAPTER VIII.

RELICS FOUND IN THE ANTIQUE GRAVES AND TUMULI
OF WESTERN NEW YORK.

Nabikoáguna — medals, - - - - - - 231
Medaeka — amulets, - - - - - - 235
Attajeguna — implements, &c., - - - - - 238
Opoaguna — pipes, - - - - - - 239
Minacea — beads, - - - - - - - 242
Peäga — wampums, - - - - - - 424
Mudwämina — jingling dress ornaments, - - - 244
Otoaguna — ear jewels, - - - - - - 246
Ochalisa — nose jewels, - - - - - - 247
Æsa — shells, coins, ornaments, - - - - 248

## CHAPTER IX.

ORAL TRADITIONS OF THE IROQUOIS, HISTORICAL AND
IMAGINATIVE.

Ancient shipwreck of a vessel on the North American
coast, - - - - - - - - - 251
Forays into the country of the Cherokees and Catabas, 252
Exploit of Haideoni, - - - - - - 253
Seneca embassy of peace to the Cherokees, and heroic
exploit of Awl, - - - - - - - 258
Grave yard serpent and corn giant, - - - - 259
Tradition of the siege of Fort Stanwix, - - - 261
Tradition of the defeat of the Kah-kwahs, - - - 261
Epoch of the confederacy, - - - - - 262
Some passages of their wars with monsters and giants, 262
The Iroquois Quetzalcoatl, - - - - - 270

## CHAPTER X.
### TOPICAL INQUIRIES.

| | |
|---|---|
| Who were the Eries? | 286 |
| Building of the first vessel on the upper lakes, | 289 |
| Who were the Alleghans? | 305 |
| War with the Kah-kwahs, | 318 |
| Antique inscribed stone of Manlius, | 323 |
| Original discovery of the Onondaga country by the French, | 329 |
| Burning of Schenectady, | 345 |
| Antique currency of the Manhattanese and their neighbors, | 355 |
| Cherokee tradition of the deluge, | 358 |
| Asiatic origin of the Indian race, | 360 |
| Lost colony of Kasonda, | 373 |

## CHAPTER XI.
### LANGUAGE.

| | |
|---|---|
| Structure of the class of American languages, | 382 |
| Comparative vocabulary of the Iroquois and its cognate the Wyandot, | 393 |

## CHAPTER XII.
### MORAL AND SOCIAL CONDITION AND PROSPECTS.

| | |
|---|---|
| Mission of Pyrlaus and Romeyn | 401 |
| The Jesuits, | 403 |
| Churches among the Mohawks, &c., | 406 |
| Kirkland — Conversion of Skenandoah, | 408 |
| Evil effects of the war, | 409 |
| Duties of civilized society to the Indians, | 412 |

## CHAPTER XIII.

### MISCELLANEOUS TRAITS, ETC.

| | |
|---|---|
| Soiengarahta, or King Hendrick, | 413 |
| Infant Atotarho of the Onondagas, | 421 |
| Red Jacket and the Wyandot claim to supremacy, | 423 |
| Pocahontas, | 425 |
| Anecdote of Brant, | 427 |
| Universal suffrage, the Iroquois considered, | 427 |
| County clerk and the wolf scalp, | 429 |
| Family of the Thunderers, | 429 |

### ORIGINAL NOTES.

| | |
|---|---|
| Letter from Secretary of State, | 435 |
| Indian reservations in New York, | 437 |
| Memoranda, | 438 |
| Sketches of an Indian council, | 461 |
| Indian fort at Pompey, | 468 |
| Mr. Cusick's letter on the Tuscaroras, | 473 |
| David Cusick's book, | 475 |
| Ancient work on Fort Hill, Auburn, | 479 |
| Account of Fort Hill, Le Roy, | 480 |
| Moral and religious state of Tuscaroras, | 485 |
| Tuscarora vocabulary, | 487 |
| Senecas of Cattaraugus, | 489 |
| Senecas of Alleghany, | 492 |
| Mohawk and Cayuga vocabularies, | 493 |
| Statistics of the Oneidas, | 493 |
| Iroquois laws of descent, | 495 |
| King Hendrick, | 497 |

# ILLUSTRATIONS.

| | |
|---|---|
| Portrait of Soiengarahta, | Frontispiece. |
| Oneida stone, | 77, 79, 80 |
| Atotarho, | 91 |
| Site of ancient fort in Lenox, | 175 |
| Ancient site of the Onondagas, | 178 |
| Ancient fortification of Osco, | 193 |
| Ancient elliptical work at Canandaigua, | 197 |
| Ancient entrenchments on Fort Hill, | 199 |
| Antique rock citadel of Kienuka, | 210 |
| Ancient battle field on Buffalo creek, | 215 |
| Nabikoáguna antique, | 233 |
| do Iroquois, | 234 |
| do cameo, | 235 |
| do mnemonic, | 235 |
| Medaeka Missouric, | 236 |
| do dental, | 237 |
| do okun, | 238 |
| Attajeguna Deoseowa, | 239 |
| Opoaguna Algonquin, | 240 |
| do Aztec, | 241 |
| do Iberic, | 241 |
| do Etruscan, | 242 |
| Minacea Alleghanic, | 243 |
| Peäga Iowan, | 244 |
| Mudwämina Miskwabic, | 245 |
| do Ossinic, | 245 |
| do Wassaäbic, | 245 |
| Otoaguna statuesque, | 246 |
| do pyramydal, | 246 |
| do bifurcate, | 247 |
| do quadralateral, | 247 |
| Ochalisa Odaä, | 248 |
| Æsa mariginella, | 248 |
| Manlius stone, | 324 |
| Portrait of Pocahontas, to face, | 425 |

# HISTORY OF THE IROQUOIS.

## CHAPTER I.

### VITAL AND AGRICULTURAL STATISTICS.

Preliminary Observations—Obstacles opposed to Statistical Inquiries among the North American Indians—Progressive State of Agriculture—Evils of the Annuity System—Grains and Fruits Raised—Ancient and Present State of the Iroquois Population compared—General Deductions on their Congerity, and Effects of Climate—Proportion of Deaf and Dumb Persons, Idiots and Blind—Remnants of the Tribes of Algonquin Lineage of Southern New York—Abstract of the Census Returns of the Oneidas, Onondagas, Senecas, Cayugas and Tuscaroras.

It is by the numbers of the several tribes of our North American stocks of red men, compared with their means of subsistence, and their capacity of producing the supply, that we are to judge of their advance or declension in the scale of civilization. The facts of their former history, their achievements in arms, or their attachment to peculiar modes of life and policy, retain an interest, irrespective of their present condition. But when we perceive a capacity to maintain themselves in the face of a European population, and to adopt the arts and agriculture of a higher civilization, the period of their bygone supremacy is invested with new interest. We seek with the more avidity to know by what means they have emerged from their past state, the rate of their increase, if there be any, and the general capacities they manifest for entering into the career of civilized life. Such is the condition of progress and change, under which we are led to inquire into the vital and agricultural statistics of the Iroquois.

The question of the original generic name, by which these tribes were denoted, the relation they bear to the other aboriginal stocks of America, and the probable era of their arrival, and location within the present boundaries of this state, is one, which was naturally suggested by the statistical inquiries before me. Difficult and uncertain as any thing brought forward on these subjects must necessarily be, it was yet desirable, in giving a view of the present and former condition of the people, that the matter should be glanced at. For, although nothing very satisfactory might be stated, it was still conceived to be well to give some answer to the intelligent inquirer, to the end, that it might at least be perceived the subject had not escaped notice.

A tropical climate, ample means of subsistence, and their consequence, a concentrated and fixed population, raised the ancient inhabitants of Mexico, and some other leading nations on the continent, to a state of ease and semi-civilization, which have commanded the surprise and admiration of historians. But it may be said, in truth, that, in their fine physical type, and in their energy of character, and love of independence, no people, among the aboriginal race, have ever exceeded, if any has ever equalled, the Iroquois.

Discoveries made in the settlement of New York, west of the *De-o-wain-sta*, or Stanwix Summit, have led to the belief, that there has been an ancient period of occupation of that fertile and expanded portion of the state, which terminated prior to the arrival of the Iroquois. Evidences have not been wanting to denote, that a higher degree of civilization than any of these tribes possessed, had, at a remote period, begun to develope itself in that quarter. But, hitherto, the notices and examinations of the antiquities referred to, although highly creditable to the observers, and abounding in interest, have served rather to entangle, than reveal, the archæological mystery which envelopes them. Some of these antiquarian traits, not appearing to the first settlers to be invested with the importance as industrial or military vestiges, now attached to them, have been nearly or quite obliterated by the plough. The spade of the builder and excavator has overturned others; and at the rate of increase, which has marked our numbers and industry, since the close of the revolutionary war, little or nothing of this kind will remain, in a perfect state, very long.

To gratify the moral interest belonging to the subject, by full and elaborate plans and descriptions, would require time and means, very different from any at my command at that time; but the topic was one which admitted of incidental attention, while awaiting decisions and obviating objections, which some of the tribes urged to the general principles and policy of the census. And while the subject of full archæological and ethnological survey of the state is left as the appropriate theme of future research, facts and traditions, bearing on these subjects, were obtained and minuted down, at various points.

In availing myself of the liberty extended to me in this particular, by the instructions of the legislature, I have, in fact, improved every possible means of information. Notes and sketches were taken down from the lips of both white and red men, wherever the matter itself and the trust-worthiness of the individual appeared to justify them. Many of the ancient forts, barrows and general places of ancient sepulchre were visited, and of some of them, accurate plans, diagrams or sketches made on the spot, or obtained from other hands. A general interest was manifested in the subject by the citizens of western New York, wherever it was introduced, and a most ready and obliging disposition evinced, on all hands to promote the inquiry.

The present being the first time* that a formal and full census of a nation or tribe of Indians has been called for, with their industrial efforts, by any American or European government exercising authority on this continent, the principles and policy of the measure presented a novel question to the Iroquois, and led to extended discussions. As these discussions, in which the speakers evinced no little aptitude, bring out some characteristic traits of the people, it may be pertinent, and not out of place here, briefly to advert to them.

As a general fact, the policy of a census, and its beneficial bearings on society, were not understood or admitted.† It seemed to these ancient cantons to be an infringement on that independence of condition which they still claim and ardently cherish. In truth, of all subjects upon which these people have been called on to think and act, during our proximity to them of two or three centuries, that of political economy is decidedly the most foreign and least known to them, or appreciated by them, and the census movement was, consequently, the

* It forms no contradiction to the precise terms of this remark, that the Legislature of Virginia directed the numbering of the Powhattanic tribes, within its boundaries, in 1788. *Vide Jefferson's Notes on Virginia.*

† To this remark, the Tuscaroras, who met the subject at once, in a frank and confidential manner, and the Onondagas, who appeared to be governed therein by the counsels of a single educated chief, form exceptions.

theme of no small number of suspicions and cavils and objections. Without any certain or generally fixed grounds of objection, it was yet the object of a fixed but changing opposition. If I might judge, from the scope of remarks made both in and out of council, they regarded it as the introduction of a Saxon feature into their institutions, which, like a lever, by some process not apparent to them, was designed, in its ultimate effects, to uplift and overturn them. And no small degree of pith and irony was put forth against it by the eloquent respondents who stood in the official attitude of their ancient orators. Everywhere, the tribes exalted the question into one of national moment. Grave and dignified sachems assembled in formal councils, and indulged in long and fluent harangues to their people, as if the very foundations of their ancient confederacy were about to be overturned by an innovating spirit of political arithmetic and utilitarianism. When their true views were made known, however, after many days and adjourned councils, I found there was less objection to the mere numbering of their tribes and families, than the (to them) scrutinizing demand, which the act called for, into their agricultural products, and the results of their industry. Pride also had some weight in the matter. "We have but little," said one of the chiefs, in a speech in council, "to exhibit. Those who have yielded their assent, have their barns well stored, and need not blush when you call."

Another topic mixed itself with the consideration of the census, and made some of the chiefs distrustful of it. I allude to the long disturbed state of their land question, and the treaty of compromise which has recently been made with the Ogden Company, by which the reversionary right to the fee simple of two of their reservations has been modified. In this compromise, the Tonewandas, a considerable sub-tribe or departmental band of Senecas, did not unite; yet the reservation which they occupy is one of the tracts to be given up. They opposed the census, from the mere fear of committing themselves on this prior question, in some way, not very well understood by them, and certainly not well made out by their speakers. It is known that for many years, the general question of ceding their reservations, under the provisions of an early treaty of the state with the Six Nations, had divided the Senecas into two parties. A discussion, which has extended through nearly half a century, in which Red Jacket had exhibited all his eloquence, had sharpened the national acumen in negotiation, and produced a peculiar sensitiveness and suspicion of motive, whenever, in latter times, the slightest question of interest or policy has been introduced into their councils. This spirit evinced itself in the very outset of my visit, on announcing to certain bands the requirements of the census act. Some of them were, moreover, strongly disposed to view it as the preliminary step, on the part of the legislature, to taxation. To be taxed, is an idea which the Iroquois regard with horror. They had themselves, in ancient days, put nations under tribute, and understood very well the import of a state tax upon their property.

"Why," said the Tonewanda chief, Deonehogawa, (called John Blacksmith,) "why is this census asked for, at this time, when we are in a straitened position with respect to our reservavation? Or if it is important to you or us, why was it not called for before? If you do not wish to obtain facts about our lands and cattle, to tax us, what is the object of the census? What is to be done with the information after you take it to Governor Wright, at Skenectati?"\*

Hoeyanehqui, or Sky-carrier, a Buffalo chief, in answer to a question as to their views of the abstract right of the state to tax the tribes, evaded a direct issue, but assuming the ground of policy, compared the Iroquois to a sick man, and said, "that he did not believe the state would oppress one thus weak."

Kaweaka, a Tuscarora chief of intelligence, speaking the English language very well, in which he is called William Mount Pleasant,

---

\* The aborigines are very tenacious of their geographical names. This ancient name of the seat of government I found to be used, on every occasion, among the Senecas, when it was necessary to allude to Albany. Its transference on the conquest of the province, in 1664, to the banks of the Mohawk, in lieu of the aboriginal name of *Onigarawantel*, never received, at least, their sanction.

gave a proof, in yielding to the measure promptly, that he had not failed to profit by the use of letters. "We know our own rights. Should the legislature attempt to tax us, our protection is in the Constitution of the United States, which forbids it." This is the first appeal, it is thought, ever made by an Iroquois to this instrument. The clause referred to, relates however, wholly to representation in congress, [Vide Art. 1, Sec. II, 2d.] from the privileges of which it excludes "Indians not taxed," clearly implying that such persons might be represented in that body if taxed. Civilization and taxation appear to be inseparable.

Having detailed the steps taken in procuring the census, it only remains to subjoin a few remarks, which I beg leave to add, on the general features of the statistics and the results of their agriculture upon their condition and prospects.

The printed queries being prepared exclusively for a population in a high state of prosperity and progress, embrace many items for which there was no occasion, among *pseudo* hunters, herdsmen, or incipient agriculturists. Neither privileged to vote, nor subject to taxation, nor military service, or covered by the common school system, or bearing any of the characteristic tests of citizenship, the questions designed to bring out this class of facts remained mere blanks. Others required to institute comparisons between a civilized and *quasi* savage state, were left by the tenor of the instructions, to my own discretion. I should have been, I am free to confess, happy to have extended these comparative views much more fully than I have, going further into their vital statistics, their succedaneous modes of employment and subsistence, some parts of their lexicography, besides that affecting the names of places, and a few kindred topics, had not the legislature omitted to make provision for the expenses incidental to such extended labors, and the department to which I applied giving me little encouragement that the oversight would be remedied. I have, however, proceeded to render the comparative tables effectual, and, I trust, satisfactory.

It cannot be said that the Iroquois cantons of New York have as yet any productive commerce, arts and manufactures. They are, to some extent, producers; furnish a few mechanics, and give employment to, and own a few lumber mills; but it is believed, while some of the bands, and at least one of the entire cantons, namely, the Tuscaroras, raise more grain and stock, than is sufficient for their own full subsistence, the average of the agricultural products of the whole people is not more, at the most favorable view, than is necessary for their annual subsistence. If so, they add nothing to the productive industry of the state. But it is gratifying to know that they are at least able to live upon their own means; and their condition and improvement is (certainly within the era of the temperance movement among them,) decidedly progressive and encouraging. They have reached the point in industrial progress, where it is only necessary to go forward. Numbers of families are eminently entitled to the epithet of good practical farmers, and are living, year in and year out, in the midst of agricultural affluence. That the proportion of individuals, thus advanced, is as considerable as the census columns denote it to be, is among the favorable features of the inquiry. There would appear to be no inaptitude for mechanical ingenuity, but hitherto, the proportion of their actual number who have embraced the arts, is, comparatively, very limited, not exceeding, at most, two or three to a tribe, and the effort has hitherto been confined to silversmiths,* blacksmiths, carpenters and coopers. A single instance of a wheelwright and fancy wagon maker occurs.

Viewed in its extremes, society, in the Iroquois cantons, still exhibits no unequivocal vestiges of the tie which bound them to the hunter state; and even, among the more advanced classes, there is too much dependance on means of living which mark either the absolute barbaric state, or the first grade of civilization. Hunters they are, indeed, no longer; yet it was desirable

* The Iroquois, in adopting our costume, have transferred their ancient love of silver amulets, frontlets, and other barbaric ornaments, to their guns and tomahawks, which are frequently richly inlaid with the shining metal, worked with great skill into the richest devices. They also fashion beautiful ear rings of silver for their women.

to ascertain how much of their present means of subsistence was derived from the chase. This will be found to be denoted in appropriate columns. It is gratifying to observe, that the amount is so small, nor is it less so, to the cause of Indian civilization, to remark, that the uncertain and scanty reward of time and labor which the chase affords, is less and less relied on, in the precise ratio that the bands and neighborhoods advance in agriculture and the arts. In cases where the cultivation of English grains and the raising of stock have thoroughly enlisted attention, the chase has long ceased to attract its ancient votaries, and in these instances, which embrace some entire bands, or chieftaincies, it has become precisely what it is, in civilized communities, where game yet exists, *an amusement*, and not a means of reward.

That delusive means of Indian subsistence, which is based on the receipt of money annuities from the government, still calls together annually, and sometimes oftener, the collective male population of these tribes, at an expense of time, and means, which is wholly disproportioned, both to amount actually received, and the not unimportant incidental risks, *moral* and *physical*, incurred by the assemblage. I have denoted both the gross sum of these annuities, and the distributive share to heads of families, obtained from the office of the local government agents. These are believed to be authentic in amount. Estimated at the highest rate which can be taken, the sum, per capita, of these annuities, will not, on an average of crops and prices, for a series of years, equal the cash value of seven bushels of wheat—a product, which, as a means of actual subsistence to the Indian family, would be of double or treble value. But this is far from being the worst effect of both the general and *per capita* cash distribution. Time and health are not only sacrificed to obtain the pittance, but he is fortunate who does not expend the amount in the outward or return journey to, or from the council house, or in the purchase of some showy but valueless articles, while attending there.

A still further evil, flowing from these annual gatherings for the payment of Indian annuities, is the stimulus which it produces in assembling at such places, traders and speculating dealers of various kinds, who are versed in this species of traffic, and who well know the weak points of the native character, and how best to profit by them. In effect, few of the annuitants reach their homes with a dime. Most of them have expended all, and lost their time in addition. Health is not unfrequently sacrificed by living on articles, or in a manner not customary at home. The intemperate are confirmed in intemperance; and the idle, foppish and gay, are only more enamored of idleness, foppishness and pleasure. That such a system, introduced at an early day, when it was policy for governments on this continent, *foreign* and *domestic*, to throw out a boon before wandering, hostile, and savage tribes, to display their munificence, and effect temporary interests, should have been continued to the present day, is only to be accounted for, from the accumulated duties, perpetually advancing jurisdiction, and still imperfectly organized state of that sub-department of the government, which exercises its, in some respects, anomalous administrative functions, under the name of the *Indian bureau.* So far as the Iroquois are affected by the policy adverted to, their interests demand an immediate consideration of the subject on enlarged principles. It behooves them to meditate whether, as a people, now semi-civilized, and exercising, in their internal polity, the powers of an independent government, some more beneficial appropriation of the fund could not be made. Perhaps nothing would better serve to advance and exalt them, as a people, and the application of these annuities to constitute a confederate school fund, under some compact or arrangement with the state, by which the latter should stipulate to extend the frame-work of the common school system over their reservations.

Horticulture, to some extent, and in a limited sense, was always an incident to the hunter state among these tribes, so far, at least, as we are acquainted with their history. They brought the zea maize with them, we must concede, on their early migration to the banks of the Mohawk, and the Onondaga, Oneida, Cayuga and

Seneca basins; for this grain is conceded, on all hands, to be a tropical, or at least a southern plant, and if so, it reveals the general *course* of their migration. It is of indigenous origin, and was not known in Europe before the discovery. We learned the mode of cultivation from them, and not they from us. This grain became the basis of their fixity of population, in the 14th or 15th centuries, and capacity to undertake military enterprises. It was certainly cultivated in large fields, in their chief locations, and gave them a title to agriculturists; and it is equally certain that they had a kind of bean, perhaps the same called *frijoles* by the early Spaniards, and some species of *cucurbita*. These were cultivated in gardens.

The tables will show a general and considerable advance, or any probable assumed basis of the cultivation of corn. We cannot consider this species of cultivation alone, however, as any characteristic evidence of advance in agriculture, while the more general introduction of it, and the harvesting of large fields of it, by separate families, is undoubtedly to be considered so. Taking the item of corn as the test, another and an important result will be perceived. In proportion as the cereals are cultivated, the average quantity of corn is diminished; and these are the very cases where, at the same time, the degree of civilization is most apparent in other things.

The condition of herdsmen is deemed by theorists and historians to be the first step in the progress from the hunter state. But we are in want of all evidence to show that there ever was, in America, a pastoral state. In the first place, the tribes had tamed no quadruped, even in the tropics, but the lama. The bison was never under any subjection, nor a fleece ever gathered, so far as history tells us, from the Bighorn or Rocky-mountain sheep. The horse, the domestic cow, the hog, and the common sheep, were brought over after the discovery; and the Iroquois, like most of their western brethren, have been very slow, all advantages considered, in raising them. They have, in fact, had no pastoral state, and they have only become herdsmen at the time that they took hold of the plough. The number of domestic animals now on their reservations, as shown by the tables, bears a full proportion to their other industrial field labors. It will be seen, that while horses, neat cattle and hogs are generally raised, sheep come in, at more mature periods of advance, and are found only on the largest and best cultivated farms. Sheep, therefore, like the cereals, become a test of their advance. With this stage, we generally find, too, the field esculents, as turneps, peas, &c., and also buckwheat. I have indicated, as a further proof of their advance as herdsmen and graziers, the number of acres of meadow cut. The Iroquois cultivate no flax. They probably raise no rye, from the fact that their lands are better adapted to wheat and corn.

The potato was certainly indigenous. Sir Walter Raleigh, in his efforts at colonizations, had it brought from Virginia, under the original name of *openawg*.* But none of the North American tribes are known to have cultivated it. They dug it up, like other indigenous edible roots from the forest. But it has long been introduced into their villages and spread over the northern latitudes, far beyond the present limit of the zea maize. Its cultivation is so easy and so similar to that of their favorite corn, and its yield so great, that it is remarkable it should not have received more general attention from all the tribes. With the Iroquois, the lists will denote that, in most cases, it is a mere item of horticulture, most families not planting over half an acre, often not more than a quarter of an acre, and yet more frequently, none at all.

The apple is the Iroquois banana. From the earliest introduction of this fruit into New York and New France, from the genial plains of Holland and Normandy, these tribes appear to have been captivated by its taste, and they lost no time in transferring it, by sowing the seed, to the sites of their ancient castles. No one can read the accounts of the destruction of the extensive orchards of the apple, which were cut down, on Gen. Sullivan's inroad into the Genesee country in 1779, without regretting that the pur-

* By the Algonquins of the present day, this plant is called, in the plural, *opineeg*. The inflection in *eeg* denotes the plural.

poses of war should have required this barbaric act. The census will show that this taste remains as strong now as it was 68 years ago.

Adverse to agricultural labor, and always confounding it with slavery, or some form of servitude, at least, deeming it derogatory, the first effort of the Iroquois to advance from their original corn-field and garden of beans and vines, is connected with the letting out of their spare lands to white men, who were cast on the frontiers, to cultivate, receiving for it some low remuneration in kind or otherwise, by way of rent. This system, it is true, increased a little their means of subsistence, but nourished their native pride and indolence. It seems to have been particularly a practice of the Iroquois, and it has been continued and incorporated into their present agricultural system. I have taken pains to indicate, in every family, the amount of land thus let, and the actual or estimated value received for it. These receipts, I was informed, low as they are in amount, are generally paid in kind, or in such manner as often to diminish their value and effect, in contributing to the proper sustenance of the family.

I have been equally careful to ascertain the number of families who cultivated no lands, and insert them in the tables. The division of real property among this people, appears to fall under the ordinary rules of acquisition in other societies. But it is not to be inferred in all cases, that the individual returned as without land has

## VITAL AND AGRICULTURAL STATISTICS. 19

absolutely no right to any, or having this right, has either forfeited or alienated it, although the laws of the tribes respecting property, permit one Iroquois to convey his property in fee to another. It is only to be inferred, in every case, that they are non-cultivators. In a few cases the persons thus marked are mechanics, and rely for support on their skill. In the valley of the Allegany, some of them are pilots in conducting rafts of lumber or arks down that stream. It would have relieved the industrial means of this band of the Senecas, extended as they are for forty miles along both banks of this river, could the amount received for this species of pilotage have been ascertained, together with the avails derived from several saw-mills owned by them, and from the lumber trade of that river generally. But these questions would have remained a blank in other tribes.

Not a few persons amongst the Onondagas and Tuscaroras, and the Tonewandas and other bands of Senecas, living in or contiguous to the principal wheat growing counties, labor during the harvest season as reapers and cradlers, for skill and ability in which occupations they bear a high reputation, and receive good wages in cash. There are a few engaged some parts of the year, as mariners on the lakes. It will be sufficient to denote these varied forms of incipient labor and strength of muscle and personal energy among these tribes, which it was, however, impracticable to bring into the tables.

Individual character vindicates its claims to

wealth and distinction among these tribes in as marked a manner as among any people in the world. Industry, capacity, and integrity, are strongly marked on the character and manners of numbers in each of the tribes. The art of speaking, and a facility in grasping objects of thought, and in the transaction of business, separate and distinguish persons as fully as physical traits do their faces. And it is to be observed that these intellectual traits run very much in certain families. That there are numbers, on the contrary, who are drones in the political hive, who do not labor, or labor very little; others who are intemperate; others who neither work nor own land, or would long remain proprietors of them, were new divisions and appropriations made, and all of whom are a burden and drawback upon the industrious and producing classes, it requires little observation to show. Admitting what reforms, teaching and example may accomplish among these, it is yet certain that of this number there are many who do not assimilate, or appear to constitute material for assimilation in tastes and habits, with the mass, nor appear likely to incorporate with them in any practical shape where they now reside, in their advances in agriculture, government and morals. The hunter habit in these persons is yet strong, but having nothing to stimulate it, they appear loth to embrace other modes of subsistence. Others stand aloof from labor, or at least all active and efficient labor, from a restless desire of change, or ambition to do something else than plough and raise stock; or from ill-luck, penury, or other motives. The proportion of the population who thus stand still and do not advance in civil polity, are a strong draw-back on the rest. It is conceived to be a pertinent question whether this class of the population would not find a better theatre for their progress and developement by migrating to the west, where the general government still possess unappropriated territory at their disposal. It is believed by many that their migration would result in benefit to both parties.. The question is one which has been often discussed by them in council, and is not yet, I should judge, fully settled. A point of approach for the Iroquois has already been formed in the Indian territory by the Senecas and Shawnees from Sandusky in Ohio, who, at the last accounts (vide President's Message to Congress, 1844), number in the aggregate 336 souls. They are located on the Neosho river (a branch of the Arkansas), west of the western boundary of the state of Arkansas, where the reports of the government agents represent them as raising horses, cattle and other stock, and being producers of grain. In any view, the subject of the several classes of persons represented in the accompanying tables, as semi-hunters and non-cultivators, or individuals without lands, is one entitled to attention. They should not be permitted to live within the boundaries of the state without lands. The state should cherish all who choose to remain, as vestiges of a once powerful race, to whose wisdom and bravery we owe the preservation of the domain. It would be unjust to expect the industrious and forehanded Iroquois to redivide their lands with the poor, and, to some extent, thriftless numbers of the cantons; while it may at the same time be observed, that it would be very difficult, if not impossible to provide, by legislation, suitable guards against their deterioration and depopulation in their present locations, without destroying wholly the fabric of their confederation, chieftainships and laws.

Whether the Iroquois have advanced in population since they have laid aside the character of warriors and hunters, and adopted agriculture as their only means of support, we have no accurate data for determining. That their ancient population was overrated, and *very much* overrated, at all periods of our history, there can be little question. We may dismiss many of these rude conjectures of the elder writers, as entitled to little notice, particularly that of La Houton, who estimates each canton at 14,000 souls. Still, after making every abatement for this tendency in the earlier authors to exaggerate their actual numbers, it could have been no small population which, at one time, attacked the island of Montreal with twelve hundred armed warriors, and at another (1683), marched a thousand men against the Ottagamies.*

Smith puts the whole number of fighting men

* Colden's Five Nations.

in 1756, with a moderation which is remarkable, compared to others who had touched the subject, at about twelve hundred. Giving to each warrior a home population of *five*, which is found to hold good, in modern days, in the great area of the west, we should have an aggregate of 6,000, a result which is, probably, too low. Douglass, four years afterwards, gives us data for raising this estimate to 7,500. Col. Boquet, still four years later, raises this latter estimate by 250. It must be evident that their perpetual wars had a tendency to keep down their numbers, notwithstanding their policy of aiding their natural increase by the adoption and incorporation into the cantons, in full independence, of prisoners and captives.

Mr. Jefferson estimates the population of the Powhatanic confederacy or group of tribes, at one individual to the square mile.* Gov. Clinton, who ably handled the subject in a discourse in 1811, estimates that, if this rule be applied to the domain of the Iroquois in New York, an aggregate of not less than 30,000 would be produced;† but he does not pass his opinon upon the estimate.

At a conference with the five cantons at Albany, in 1677, the number of warriors was carefully made out at 2,150, giving, on the preceding mode of computation, a population of 10,750, and this was the strength of the confederacy reported by an agent of the governor of Virginia, who

---

\* Notes on Virginia.   † Coll. N. Y. Hist. Soc., vol. 2.

had been specially despatched to the conference for the purpose of obtaining this fact. Either, then, in subsequent estimates of 1756, '60, and '64, the population had been underrated, or there had, on the assumption of the truth of the above enumeration, which is moderate, been a decline in the poulation of 3,000 souls in a period of eighty-seven years. That there was a constant tendency to decline, and that the cantons were aware of this, and made efforts to keep it up, by the policy of their conquests, is apparent, and has before been indicated.

During the American revolution, which broke out but eleven years after the expedition and estimate of Boquet, when he had put the Iroquois at 1,550 fighting men, it is estimated that the British government had in their interest and service 1,580 warriors of this confederacy. The highest number noticed of the friendly Oneidas and a few others, who sided with us in that contest, is 230 warriors, raising the number of armed men engaged in the war, to 1,810, and the gross population in 1776 to 9,050 souls. This estimate, which appears to have been carefully made, from authentic documents, is the utmost that could well be claimed. It was made at the era when danger prompted the pen of either party in the war to exhibit the military strength of this confederacy, in its utmost power; and we may rest here, as a safe point of comparison, or, at least, we cannot admit a higher population.

By the census returns herewith submitted, the

## VITAL AND AGRICULTURAL STATISTICS. 25

aggregate population of the three full, and four fragmentary cantons, namely, the Oneidas and Cayugas, &c., still residing within the state, are denoted to be as follows, namely:

| | |
|---|---|
| Senecas, | 2,441 |
| Onondagas, | 398 |
| Tuscaroras, | 281 |
| Oneidas, | 210 |
| Cayugas, | 123 |
| Mohawks, | 20 |
| St. Regis Canton, (exclusive of the number over the Canadian boundary), | 260 |

By a statement submitted to Congress, on the 3d of December, 1844,* the number of Oneidas settled in Wisconsin, is put at 722; the number of Senecas, who have removed from Ohio into the Indian territory west of the Mississippi, at 125, and the number of mixed Senecas and Shawnees, at the same general location, at 211. Deducting one-half of the latter, for Shawnees, and there is to be added to the preceding census, in order to show the natural increase of the Iroquois, 953 souls. The number of the St. Regis tribe, who are based, as a tribe, on the Praying Indians of Colden, a band of Catholic Mohawks originally located at Caughnawaga, is shewn by the census of 1845 to be 260. There are, at the village of Cornplanter, within the bounds of Pennsylvania, as numbered by me, in that year, 51 Senecas. Supposing that the Mohawks and Cayugas who fled to Canada *at* and *after* the revolutionary war, and who are now

---

* Vide Doc. No. 2, Ho. of Reps., 28th Cong., 2d Session.

settled at Brantford on the Grand river, Canada West, have merely held their own, in point of numbers, and deducting the number of Cayugas, namely, 144, found among the Senecas of Cattaraugus, and herewith separately returned, and taking Dalton's estimate of the Mohawks and Cayugas in 1776, namely, 300 warriors for each tribe, there is to be added, to the census, to accomplish the same comparative view, 2,850 souls. From this estimate, there must be deducted for a manifest error, in the original estimates of Dalton, in putting the Cayugas on the same footing of strength with the Mohawks, not less than 150 warriors or 750 souls, leaving the Canadian Iroquois at 2,106—say 2,000 souls.

Adding these items to the returns of the present census, and the rather extraordinary result will appear, that there is now existing in the United States and Canada, a population of 6,942 Iroquois, that is to say, but 2,108 less than the estimated number, and that number placed as high as it well could be, at the era of the revolution in 1776. Of this number, 4,836 inhabit the United States, and 3,843 the state of New York. I cannot, however, submit this result without expressing the opinion, that the Iroquois population has been *lower*, between the era of the revolutionary war and the present time, than the census now denotes; and that for some years past, and since they have been well lodged and clothed, and subsisted by their own labor, and been exempted from the diseases and casualties incident to savage life, and the empire of the forest, their population has recovered and IS NOW ON THE INCREASE.

I have thus brought to a close, so far as relates to their population and industrial efforts, the inquiry committed to me respecting this nation. It would perhaps have gratified statistical curiosity and philosophical theory, to have exhibited fuller data on the subject of their longevity and vital statistics generally, but it may be considered in the light of an achievement to have accomplished thus much. The general result indicates five, with a large fraction, as the average number of the Iroquois family. Throughout each canton, the number of females predominates over the males. This is a fact which has been long known to hold good with respect to wandering, predatory and warlike tribes, but was not anticipated among peaceful, agricultural communities. But few years, however, have supervened since they dropped the hatchet and took hold of the plough; and in this time, it is apparent that the proportion of males to females has approached nearer to an equilibrium. The effects on vitality of agricultural labor and a cessation from war, are likewise favorable, so far as we can judge, compared with the known results among the sparse, ill-fed, warring and erratic hunters of the western forests and prairies. The average number of the Iroquois family is not higher than the common average of the hunter state. The number of children borne by each female is a considerable fraction over four. Of a population of 312 Tuscaroras, five have reached to and passed the age of 80, or over 1¾ per cent. Among the Senecas and Cayugas of Cattaraugus, the per centage is 1½, with a smaller fraction, 12 persons in 808 having passed that limit. Local causes have diminished this to 1 per cent nearly on the Buffalo reservation. On the contrary, it is found to be increased in the valley of the Allegany to full 2 per cent. The ruling chief of that tribe, *Ten-wonny-ahs*, of Teongono, commonly called *Blacksnake*, is now in his ninety-sixth year, and is active and hale, and capable of performing journeys to the annual assemblies of his people at Buffalo.

Inquiries respecting the number of deaf and dumb, idiots, and lunatics, and blind, have not escaped my attention.

I could not learn that there ever was a child born blind among the Iroquois. The traditions of the people do not refer to any instance of the kind. They believe none has occurred. It is certain, from inquiries made on the several reservations, that no such person now exists. Yet it is a subject which, from the importance of the fact in aboriginal statistics, deserves to be further investigated.

Among the Oneidas, prior to the removal of the principal body of this tribe to Wisconsin, there was one lunatic—a young man, who was kindly taken care of, and who accompanied them on their removal to the west. There is also an instance of a deaf and dumb child, among those of the tribe who remain in the state. This person, who is a female, now under 12 years of age, was recently taken to the Onondaga reservation by her relatives, and is now at that location.

There is one idiot among the Onondagas, a young man under 21 years of age. He is supported by his relatives and friends.

I also found one idiot among the Tuscaroras.

My inquiries on the several reservations of the Senecas, at Tonawanda, Buffalo, Cattaraugus and Alleghany, did not result in detecting a single person who was either deaf and dumb, an idiot, or a lunatic. As the Senecas are sevenfold more numerous than the highest in number among the other cantons, this result, if it should be verified by subsequent and fuller inquiries, after more thoroughly explaining the object of the information sought for to each band, would offer a remarkable exemption from the usual laws of population. There are no means of instruction for this class of persons on the reservations. The care of the three individuals above designated, calls for the same disproportionate tax on time, which is elsewhere necessary, and the admission of these persons to the State Lunatic Asylum, and the Deaf and Dumb Institute at New York, free of expense, would seem to be due to them.

Among the St. Regis, which is the only tribe I did not visit and take the enumeration of, it is not known whether there be any persons of either class.

One or two additional facts may be added to the preceding statistics in this connection.

I found three saw mills, with twenty-one gangs of saws, on the Alleghany reservation, and also two council houses and two public schools, constituting public property, belonging exclusively to this reservation, which were valued by the appraisers, under the treaty of 1842, at $8,219.

On the Cattaraugus reservation, there is the church, council house, and farms, connected with the schools, being the property of the Indians, and not the missionary society, which were valued together, by the same appraisers, at $3,214.50.

There is on the Buffalo Creek reservation, a saw mill, valued at $404.75, a church built originally at an expense of $1,700, valued at $1,200, and a council house, valued at $75; making a total amount of public property, including all the preceding, of $13,113.25.

The total amount of private valuations on the Buffalo and Tonawanda reservations, under the treaty of 1842, was not exactly ascertained, but it is about $80,000. This is entirely Seneca property and funds. Its payment to individuals, in the sums awarded, is based on their removal to Cattaraugus and Alleghany, agreeably to the terms of the compromise treaty of 1842.

The Onondagas possess one saw mill, well built, and in good repair, which is of some value to them, and might be rendered more so, under a proper system of management.

It may be well here to notice the fact, that there are yet remaining in the state, some vestiges of the Algonquin race, who, under various distinctive names, occupied the southern portion of the state at the era of its discovery and colonization. As the language of the census act referred to such Indians only as lived on the *reservations*, I did not feel it to be within the scope of my appointment to search out and visit these scattered individuals, although I should have been gratified to make this inquiry. It is believed that they are comprised by about twenty of the Shinecock tribe, who yet haunt the inlets and more desolate portions of Long Island, and by a very few lingering members of the ancient Mohegans, who, under the *sobriquet* of Stockbridges, yet remain in Oneida county. The bulk of this people, so long the object of missionary care, migrated to the banks of Fox river and Winnebago lake, in Wisconsin, about 1822. They were followed to that portion of the west, about the same time, or soon after, by the small consolidated band of Nanticokes, Narragansetts, and other early coast tribes, who, in concentrating in the Oriskany valley, after the close of the revolutionary war, dropped their respective languages, learned English, and assumed the name of Brothertons. Both these migrated tribes were in an advanced state of semi-civilization, and were good farmers and herdsmen at the era of their removal.

## ABSTRACT OF CENSUS RETURNS

*Of the Indian Population on the several Reservations, with other Statistical Information.*

| Reservations. | No. of Families. | Total Population. | No. of male persons in the Reservation. | No. of female persons in the Reservation. | No. of married females, under the age of 45 yrs. in the Reservation. | No. of unmarried females between the ages of 16 and 45, in Reservation. | No. of unmarried females under the age of 16 in the Reservation. | No. of marriages during the year preceeding, in the Reservation. | No. of births in the Reservation during the year preceding. Males. | No. of births in the Reservation during the year preceding. Females. | No. of deaths in the Reservation during the year preceding. Males. | No. of deaths in the Reservation during the year preceding. Females. |
|---|---|---|---|---|---|---|---|---|---|---|---|---|
| 1. Oneida, | 31 | 157 | 71 | 86 | 24 | 3 | 47 | 5 | 8 | 5 | 1 | 12 |
| 2. Onondaga, | 56 | 368 | 173 | 195 | 63 | 19 | 73 | 6 | 6 | 10 | 11 | 3 |
| 3. Tuscarora, | 53 | 312 | 148 | 164 | 18 | 10 | 11 | 3 | 5 | 5 | 1 | 7 |
| 4. Buffalo, | 92 | 446 | 200 | 246 | 73 | 47 | 61 | 10 | 3 | 7 | 14 | 13 |
| 5. Cattaraugus, | 189 | 808 | 393 | 415 | 68 | 40 | 30 |  | 17 | 11 | 11 |  |
| 6. Cayugas on the Cattaraugus Reservation, | 20 | 114 | 56 | 58 | 16 | 6 | 5 | 2 | 4 | 1 |  | 3 |
| 7. Alleghany, | 153 | 783 | 390 | 393 | 127 | 33 | 168 | 6 | 13 | 6 | 3 | 13 |
| 8. Tonawanda, | 104 | 505 | 224 | 281 | 101 | 45 | 69 | 4 | 5 | 8 | 13 | 3 |
| 9. St. Regis, | 48 | 260 | 126 | 134 | 44 | 5 | 67 | 4 |  | 7 | 4 | 3 |
| Total, | 746 | 3,753 | 1,781 | 1,972 | 555 | 205 | 531 | 36 | 61 | 60 | 63 | 57 |

## ABSTRACT OF CENSUS RETURNS.

| Reservations. | No. of persons in the Reservation born in the State of New York. | No. of persons in the Reservation born in any of the other States | No. of persons in the Reservation born in Great Britain or its possessions | No. of children in the Reservation between the ages of 5 and 16 years. | No. of children in the Reservation attending private or select unincorporated schools. | ACRES OF LAND. No. of acres of improved land in the Reservation. | BARLEY. No. of acres of barley under cultivation. | BARLEY. Quantity of barley raised therefrom during the preceding year. | PEAS. No. of acres of peas under cultivation. | PEAS. No. of bushels raised. | BEANS. No. of acres of beans. | BEANS. Quantity raised. |
|---|---|---|---|---|---|---|---|---|---|---|---|---|
| 1. Oneida,.............. | 155 | 1 | 1 | 59 | 20 | 421 | 10 | 200 | 3½ | 35 | 3¼ | 11 |
| 2. Onondaga,.............. | 364 | .... | 1 | 169 | 40 | 2,043¼ | 2½ | 70 | 7¾ | 91 | .... | |
| 3. Tuscarora,.............. | 286 | .... | 30 | 63 | 43 | 2,079½ | 20 | 430 | 5 | 65 | .... | |
| 4. Buffalo,,.............. | 433 | 1 | 6 | 117 | 57 | 1,914 | ..... | ...... | 18½ | .... | .... | |
| 5. Cattaraugus,.............. | 789 | .... | 7 | 121 | 86 | 2,123 | 96¼ | 1,300 | ..... | 301 | .... | |
| 6. Cayugas on the Cattaraugus Reservation,.. .... | 114 | .... | .... | 21 | 14 | 316 | ..... | ...... | ..... | 23 | .... | |
| 7 Alleghany,.............. | 752 | 35 | .... | 227 | 162 | 2,163½ | 6 | 35 | 18¼ | 90 | .... | |
| 8. Tonawanda,.............. | 496 | .... | 11 | 126 | 40 | 2,216 | 42 | 550 | 30 | 200 | 1 | 15 |
| 9. St. Regis,.............. | 125 | .... | 135 | 81 | ...... | 591¼ | ¾ | ...... | 27 | 105 | 11 | 18 |
| Total,.............. | 3,514 | 37 | 191 | 984 | 462 | 13,867½ | 177½ | 2,585 | 110 | 910 | 15¼ | 44 |

## ABSTRACT OF CENSUS RETURNS.

| Reservations. | BUCKWHEAT. No. of acres of buck-wheat. | BUCKWHEAT. Quantity raised. | TURNEPS. No. of acres turneps | TURNEPS. Quantity raised. | POTATOES. No. of acres of pota-toes. | POTATOES. Quantity raised. | WHEAT. No. of acres of wheat sown. | WHEAT. No. of acres of wheat harvested. | WHEAT. Quantity of wheat raised. | CORN. No. of acres of corn sown. | CORN. Quantity harvested. |
|---|---|---|---|---|---|---|---|---|---|---|---|
| 1. Oneida, | ..... | ..... | ..... | .... | $32\frac{1}{4}$ | 841 | 14 | 13 | 325 | $60\frac{1}{2}$ | 1,458 |
| 2. Onondaga, | $2\frac{1}{2}$ | 50 | $\frac{3}{4}$ | 30 | 21 | 840 | $87\frac{3}{4}$ | $87\frac{3}{4}$ | 1,156 | $189\frac{1}{2}$ | 4,492 |
| 3. Tuscarora, | 18 | 245 | $2\frac{1}{2}$ | 55 | 31 | 1,166 | $405\frac{1}{2}$ | ..... | 4,897 | 152 | 3,515 |
| 4. Buffalo, | 3 | ..... | ..... | .... | 33 | 1,444 | ..... | ..... | ....... | $163\frac{1}{2}$ | 2,925 |
| 5. Cattaraugus, | $6\frac{1}{2}$ | 420 | $5\frac{1}{4}$ | 179 | $53\frac{3}{4}$ | 6,237 | $169\frac{1}{2}$ | ..... | 1,822 | $473\frac{1}{4}$ | 7,966 |
| 6. Cayugas on the Cattaraugus Reservation, | ..... | 227 | ..... | .... | 38 | 955 | $14\frac{1}{2}$ | 4 | 210 | $62\frac{1}{2}$ | 1,970 |
| 7. Alleghany, | $18\frac{1}{4}$ | ..... | $25\frac{3}{4}$ | 29 | $146\frac{1}{2}$ | 3,638 | 46 | ..... | 503 | 407 | 8,565 |
| 8. Tonawanda, | 5 | 112 | 3 | 60 | 40 | 1,150 | 200 | ..... | 2,400 | 170 | 3,950 |
| 9. St. Regis, | 8 | ..... | $\frac{13}{1}$ | .... | $20\frac{5}{8}$ | 410 | $42\frac{1}{2}$ | ..... | 195 | $65\frac{1}{2}$ | $658\frac{1}{2}$ |
| Total, | $61\frac{1}{4}$ | 1,054 | $38\frac{1}{16}$ | 353 | $416\frac{1}{8}$ | 16,681 | $979\frac{3}{4}$ | $104\frac{3}{4}$ | 11,508 | $1,743\frac{3}{4}$ | $35,499\frac{1}{2}$ |

## VITAL AND AGRICULTURAL STATISTICS.

## ABSTRACT OF CENSUS RETURNS.

| Reservations. | RYE. No. of acres of rye sown. | RYE. Quantity harvested. | OATS. No. of acres of oats sown. | OATS. Quantity harvested. | NEAT CATTLE. No. of neat cattle. | NEAT CATTLE. Under one year old. | NEAT CATTLE. Over one year old. | NEAT CATTLE. No. of cows milked. | NEAT CATTLE. No. of pounds of butter made during the preceding year. | HORSES. No. of horses. | SHEEP. No. of sheep. | SHEEP. No. of fleeces. | HOGS. No. of hogs. |
|---|---|---|---|---|---|---|---|---|---|---|---|---|---|
| 1. Oneida, | | | 28½ | 720 | 50 | | | 28 | 1,140 | 17 | | | 46 |
| 2. Onondaga, | | | 107 | 2,110 | 189 | | | 82 | 1,150 | 64 | 49 | 43 | 327 |
| 3. Tuscarora, | | | 205½ | 4,085 | 336 | | | 98 | 7,537 | 153 | 215 | 180 | 596 |
| 4. Buffalo, | | | 115½ | 4,251 | 270 | | | 87 | 4,888 | 123 | 41 | 30 | 369 |
| 5. Cattaraugus, | | | 58 | 8,922½ | 387 | | | 166 | 2,426 | 223 | 365 | 168 | 882 |
| 6. Cayugas on the Cattaraugus Reservation, | | | 30 | 1,622 | 63 | | | 43 | | 39 | 40 | 30 | 109 |
| 7. Alleghany, | | | 212¼ | 4,366 | 585 | | | 169 | | 149 | 79 | | 627 |
| 8. Tonawanda, | 4 | 60 | 100 | 2,500 | 305 | | | 88 | 3,200 | 130 | 50 | 40 | 390 |
| 9. St. Regis, | | | 51 | 290 | 90 | 17 | 16 | 42 | | 50 | | | 112 |
| Total, | 4 | 60 | 907 | 28,866½ | 2,275 | 17 | 16 | 803 | 20,341 | 948 | 839 | 491 | 3,458 |

## ABSTRACT OF CENSUS RETURNS.

| Reservations. | No. of acres of meadow cut. | No. of ploughs. | Value of garden and horticultural products. | LANDS LET TO OTHERS. No of acres let. | Annual value per acre received. | Total value of land let. | No. of bearing fruit trees of all descriptions. | Value of avails derived from the chase. | No. of persons who have attained the age of 50. | No. of persons who possess no lands. |
|---|---|---|---|---|---|---|---|---|---|---|
| 1. Oneida, | 17 | 8 | $173 00 | 89 | av. $2 91 | $259 00 | 44 | $85 00 | 2 | 10 |
| 2. Onondaga, | 116¼ | 17 | 1,100 00 | 1,410½ | 2 63 | 2,404 00 | 640 | 131 25 | 3 | 21 |
| 3. Tuscarora, | 195 | 59 | 61 00 | 183½ | 3 25 | 550 75 | 1,574 | 42 50 | 5 | 2 |
| 4. Buffalo, | 174½ | 53 | 210 00 | 533 | .... | .... | 259 | 61 00 | 4 | 12 |
| 5. Cattaraugus, | 201 | 87 | 399 75 | 453 | .... | 790 00 | 1,340 | 69 60 | 12 | 83 |
| 6. Cayugas on the Cattaraugus Reservation, | 50 | 17 | 37 00 | 8 | .... | 25 00 | 278 | 8 38 | 1 | 10 |
| 7. Alleghany, | 416½ | 80 | 557 00 | 238 | 2 50 | 686 68 | 1,483 | 427 00 | 15 | 15 |
| 8. Tonawanda, | 180 | 60 | 300 00 | 600 | .... | 1,500 00 | 1,250 | 50 00 | 25 | 6 |
| 9. St. Regis, | .... | .... | .... | .... | .... | .... | .... | .... | .... | .... |
| Total, | 1,350¼ | 381 | $2,837 75 | 3,515 | | $6,215 43 | 6,868 | $874 73 | 67 | 160 |

## VITAL AND AGRICULTURAL STATISTICS.

### ABSTRACT OF CENSUS RETURNS.

| Reservations. | Number of persons from other tribes. |  |  |  |  |  |  |  |  |  |  | Statistics of occupation. |  |  |  |  |  |  |  |
|---|---|---|---|---|---|---|---|---|---|---|---|---|---|---|---|---|---|---|---|
|  | Cayugas. | Undetermined tribes. | Onondagas. | Oneidas. | St. Regis. | Stockbridge or Mohegans. | Cornplanter village in Pennsylvania. | Mohawks. | Lenapees or Delawares. | Tuscaroras. | Total. | No. of farmers. | No. of mechanics. | No. of lawyers. | No. of semi-hunters, or who derive support in part from the chase. | No. of persons educated at colleges or academies. | No. of physicians. | No. of teachers, catechists or ministers. | No. of interpreters or translators of the Iroquois. |
| 1. Oneida,........... | .. | .. | .. | .. | 1 | 4 | .. | 1 | 1 | .. | 7 | 18 | 1 | .. | 6 | 1 | .. | 3 | 2 |
| 2. Onondaga,........ | 1 | .. | .. | 23 | 4 | .. | .. | 1 | .. | 4 | 33 | 47 | 2 | .. | 25 | 3 | .. | 3 | 1 |
| 3. Tuscarora,........ | 2 | .. | 13 | .. | .. | .. | .. | 18 | .. | .. | 33 | 60 | 1 | .. | 8 | 5 | 3 | 1 | 5 |
| 4. Buffalo,........... | 21 | .. | 6 | 19 | .. | .. | .. | 2 | .. | .. | 48 | 23 | 1 | 1 | 6 | 7 | 1 | 6 | 7 |
| 5. Cattaraugus,...... | 54 | .. | 42 | 1 | .. | .. | .. | .. | .. | .. | 97 | 80 | 6 | 1 | 32 | .. | .. | .. | 7 |
| 6. Cayugas on the Cattaraugus Reservation,...... | .. | .. | .. | .. | .. | .. | .. | .. | .. | .. | .. | .. | .. | .. | .. | .. | .. | .. | .. |
| 7. Alleghany,........ | 5 | .. | 3 | 29 | .. | .. | 13 | .. | .. | .. | 114 | 17 | 1 | .. | 8 | 1 | 1 | 2 | 2 |
| 8. Tonawanda,...... | .. | 64 | 3 | .. | .. | .. | .. | 1 | .. | 6 | 10 | 96 | 6 | .. | 46 | 1 | 1 | 2 | 7 |
| 9. St. Regis,......... | .. | .. | .. | .. | .. | .. | .. | .. | .. | .. | .. | 30 | 2 | .. | 20 | 2 | 1 | .. | 3 |
| Total,............. | 83 | 64 | 67 | 72 | 5 | 4 | 13 | 23 | 1 | 10 | 342 | 371 | 20 | 2 | 151 | 20 | 7 | 17 | 35 |

## ABSTRACT OF CENSUS RETURNS.

| Reservations. | Churches. | No. of persons who adhere to their native religion. | No. of church members of all denominations. | No. pledged to temperance. | Schools. | Aggregate population. | United States. | New York. | U. S. Distribution Share. | N. Y. Distribution Share. |
|---|---|---|---|---|---|---|---|---|---|---|
| | | | | | | | Annuities. | | | |
| 1. Oneida,...... | 1 | 133 | 31 | 35 | 1 | 164 | | | | |
| 2. Onondaga,... | 1 | 330 | 38 | 128 | 1 | 368 | | | | |
| 3. Tuscarora,... | 2 | 249 | 63 | 231 | 2 | 312 | | | | |
| 4. Buffalo,...... | 1 | 436 | 54 | 28 | 2 | 446 | | | $4 80 | $6 60⅓ |
| 5. Cattaraugus,.. | 1 | 768 | 40 | 75 | 4 | 808 | $12,765* | $2,430 00 | 4 80 | |
| 6. Cayugas on the Cattaraugus Reservation,.. | | 97 | 16 | 15 | 1 | 114 | | 500 00 | | |
| 7. Alleghany,.... | 1 | 603 | 117 | 158 | 2 | 783 | | 600 00 | 4 80 | |
| 8. Tonawanda,... | 1 | 465 | 40 | 200 | 1 | 505 | | | 4 80 | |
| 9. St. Regis,..... | | | | | † | 260 | | | 4 80 | 8 19 226/260 |
| Total,........... | 8 | 3,081 | 350 | 870 | 14 | 3,760 | | 2,131 69 | | |
| Deduct seven Oneidas, | | | | | | 7 | | | | |
| Total as in first column,.. | | | | | | 3,753 | | | | |

* These sums are the total annuities paid by the United States and the State of New York, to the Indians of the Tonawanda, Buffalo, Cattaraugus, including the Cayugas and Alleghany Reservations.

Note.—It has not been ascertained in what manner the $500 and $600 annuities paid to the Senecas and Cayugas are divided among themselves, whether the Senecas receive any portion of that paid to the Cayugas, and the Cayugas any part of that paid to the Senecas.

† The church of this tribe is north of the boundary line in Canada.

‡ Incomplete.

## CHAPTER II.

### HISTORICAL AND ETHNOLOGICAL INQUIRIES.

Sketch of the Iroquois Group of Aboriginal Tribes — Ethnological Suggestions — Indian Cosmogony — Gleams of their Ancient General History.

The statistical data which have been brought forward, respecting the Iroquois cantons, and their limits, may be taken as the basis of some considerations on the ancient history and antiquities, and the general ethnology of this part of North America. Much interest has been excited from time to time, and as the area of settlement and cultivation has been extended on the subject of the topics, reaching as the inquiry does, from the Gulf of Mexico to the great lakes, with extensions, at some points, laterally, *through* and *east* of the Alleghanies. By far the most striking and important of these vestiges of ancient power, and partial civilization, east of that primary range, mark their northern terminus, in the fertile area of western New York — characterized as this area is, by its numerous streams and interior lakes, and presenting a superficies abounding in all the elements of ancient subsistence. In its forest state, it was known to abound in game and fish, which yielded the hunter a ready reward for the labors of his bow and spear. Its rich valleys were favorable to the zea maize. Geographically, it possessed some very strong points to favor the prosperity of its ancient possessors, connected as it was, by water, with the Ohio valley, the upper lakes, and the Atlantic ocean; and the entire superfices appears to have been contended for, at several periods, by different tribes or confederacies, long anterior to the remotest end of the discovery of the continent.

From an early period in our history, a deep interest has been felt in the discovery of the ancient works and relics of art which characterize this area. It is evident from an examination of these curious remains, that they mark the former residence or occupancy of different races, at eras separate from each other; that there are, figuratively speaking, amidst the ruins of a darker age, traces of the footsteps of an European or advanced population, at least in small numbers, before the Columbian period; that there succeeded to this a species of psuedo-civilization, in a family of the nomadic or hunter races, who overcame the prior race, and whose descendants yet exist; that there was a subsequent decline in incipient power, and in the arts of defence, leading to a deeper state of barbarism, which marked the race on their discovery; and that evidences of each of these eras and races are to be found in the remains of art and skill in the ancient sites above mentioned.

The larger number of the class of antique, circular and elliptical works, scattered over the western and south-western part of the state, of an age anterior to the discovery, lie chiefly west of Cayuga, and upon the sources of the Susquehanna. Interspersed amid this system of common ring forts of the west, there are some of a still earlier period, which exhibit squares and parallelograms, yet without any defensive work in the nature of bastions.

The area of early French occupancy, or attempt at colonization, within the state, extends east and west between the waters of the Cayuga and Oneida lakes, as general boundaries, having the county of Onondaga as its chief and central point. This area comprehends the most striking part of the numerous remains of implements of art, and other antiquities of confessedly European origin, which have heretofore excited attention. How far these evidences extend north is not known. But any examination of either the aboriginal or foreign remains would be incomplete which did not extend also along the line of the St. Lawrence and the waters of Lake Champlain.

The valley of the Hudson, and southern part of the state generally, although it has been but little explored with this view, is known to have some antiquarian features worthy of examination. And were there none others but the artificial shell mounds and beds on the sea coast and the fossil bones of the valley, so remarkable in themselves, these would alone be entitled to the highest interest in studying the ancient history of the races of man in this area.

Geological action subsequent to the period of the habitation of the globe, has not been examined with this view, but is believed to be important in denoting eras of former occupancy; it is known that various parts of the state have yielded, at considerable depths below the surface, many curious evidences of artificial remains, along with relics of the animal and vegetable kingdoms.

There is an apparent extension of the system of works which characterize the fort and mound period of the Ohio valley, reaching from the Alleghany waters in Chautauque and Cattaraugus, along the southern shore of Lake Erie, indefinitely eastward.

To examine, describe and compare these evidences, is an object of deep historical interest. Whether the eras denoted, or the theories heretofore advanced from any quarter, be true or false, is a question of little moment as to the importance of the inquiry itself. History seeks to clear up the obscurities of time, and to enlarge the boundaries of certain knowledge. To do this, in relation to the long and obscure periods which precede the year 1492, it calls in the aid of antiquities, of ethnography, of the study of relics of early sculpture in stone or shells, and whatever other evidences exist of the former power possessed by these ancient races, to make either of the great departments of nature subservient to man.

The examinations already made, denote the field of inquiry to be one of more than the anticipated interest. Ancient works and remains cover at detached points, the larger part of western New York. They are also known to mark the valleys of the Susquehanna and Delaware, within our boundaries. They are of a different nature, and denote less energy and military skill in the sea-coast tribes, who subsisted chiefly on fish. Yet even here, the shell mounds and piles above referred to, denoting village sites, the remains of art in the fabrication of arms and utensils of stone and earthernware, and the geological mutations of the surface, and the discovery of the fossil bones of large quadrupeds, so remarkable in the valley of the Hudson, afford helps to chronology, and are worthy of being noted.

There is some evidence in the partial examinations made in the area giving rise to the Allegany and Genesee rivers, that the mound period of the Ohio valley extended, in its effects, upon the tribes which occupied those portions of the state. The barrows and places of ordinary sepulture, have yielded many ancient relics, identical in their character with those of the Ohio, the Sciota, and the Wabash. It is not probable the vast, and in part mountainous ancient hunting grounds of the northern portions of the state, were occupied to any extent with populous towns or forts. Yet even these regions of country are deserving of examination. It is confessedly, however, in respect to the fertile districts of CENTRAL AND WESTERN NEW YORK, the ancient resident domain of the Iroquois, and of which most is known, that we are still most in need of further examinations, and of exactitude and completeness in the inquiry.

Under all the circumstances, it is hoped that these references to the field of antiquities before us, while they denote its extent and probable connection with the discoveries in the Mississippi valley, may serve both to point out and justify the motive of the writer in the following observations:

On the discovery of North America, the Iroquois tribes were found seated chiefly in the wide and fertile territory of western and northern New York, reaching west to the sources of the Ohio;* north, to the banks of Lake Champlain and the St. Lawrence; and east, to the site of Albany. They had as much nationality of character, then, as any of the populous tribes, who, in the 4th century wandered over central and western Europe. They were, in a high degree, warlike, handling the bow and arrow with the

* They always denominated the Alleghany river by the name of Ohio. This I found to be the term constantly used for that river in 1845. They give the vowel *i*, in this word, the sound of *i* in machine.

skill and dexterity of the ancient Thracians and Parthians. They were confederated in peace and war, and had begun to lay the foundations of a power, against which, the surrounding nations in the Mississippi valley, and along the St. Lawrence, the Hudson, and the Delaware, could not stand. The French, when they effectually entered the St. Lawrence in 1608,* courted their alliance on the north, and the Dutch did the same in 1609, on the Hudson. Virginia had been apprised of their power at an early day, and the other English colonies, as they arrived, were soon made acquainted with the existence of this native confederacy in the north. By putting fire-arms into their hands, they doubled the aboriginal power, and became themselves, for more than a century, dependent on their caprice or friendship.

The word *Iroquois*, as we are told by Charlevoix, who is a competent and reliable witness on this point, is founded on an exclamation, or response, made by the sachems and warriors, on the delivery to them of an address. This response, as heard among the Senecas, it appeared to me, might be written *eoh;* perhaps the Mohawks, and other harsher dialects of this family, threw in an *r* between the vowels. It is recorded in the term Iroquois, on French principles of annotation, with the substantive inflection in *ois*, which is characteristic of French lexicography. It is a term which has been long and ex-

* They actually discovered this river in 1535.

tensively used, both for the language and the history of this people; and is preferable, on enlarged considerations, to any other. The term Five Nations, used by Colden, and in popular use during the earlier period of the colony, ceased to be appropriate after the Tuscarora revolt in North Carolina, and the reunion of this tribe with the parent stock, subsequent to 1712. From that period they were called the Six Nations,* and continued to acquire increased reputation as a confederacy, under this name, until the termination of the American Revolution in 1783, and the flight of the Mohawks and Cayugas to Canada, when this partial separation and breaking up of the confederacy, rendered it no longer applicable.

The term *New York Indians*, applied to them in modern days, by the eminence in their position, is liable to be confounded by the common reader, with the names of several tribes of the generic Algonquin family, who formerly occupied the southern part of the state, down to the Atlantic. Some of these tribes lived in the west, and owned and occupied lands, among the Iroquois, until within a few years. And, at any rate, it is too vague and imprecise a term to be employed in philology or history.

By the people themselves, however, neither the first nor the last of the foregoing terms appear ever to have been adopted, nor are they

* In 1723 they adopted the *Necariages*, as a seventh nation, as will be noticed under the appropriate head.

now used. They have no word to signify *New York*, in a sense more specific, than as the territory possessed by themselves—a claim which they were certainly justified in making, at the era of the discovery, when they are admitted, on all hands, to have carried their conquests to the sea.

The term *Ongwe Honwe*, or a people surpassing all others, which Colden was informed they applied proudly to themselves, may be strictly true, if limited, as they did, to mean a people surpassing all other red men. This they believed, and this was the sense in which they boastfully applied it. But it was a term older than the discovery, and had no reference to European races. The word *honwe*, as will appear by the vocabulary hereto appended, means man. By the prefixed term *ongwe*, it is qualified according to various interpretations, to mean real, as contradistinguished from sham men, or cowards; it may also mean strong, wise or expert men, and, by ellipsis, men excelling others in manliness. But it was in no other sense distinctive of them. It was the common term for the red race of this continent, which they would appear, by the phrase, to acknowledge as a unity, and is, the word as I found it, used at this day, as the equivalent for our term *Indian*.

Each tribe had, at some period of their progress, a distinctive appellation, as *Onondaga*, *Oneida*, &c., of which some traditionary matter will be stated, further on. When they came to confederate, and form a general council, they took the name of *Konoshioni*, (or as the French authors write it, *Acquinoshioni*,) meaning literary, *People of the Long House*, and figuratively a *United People*, a term by which they still denominate themselves, when speaking in a national sense. This distinction it is well to bear in mind, and not confound. This Long House, to employ their own figure, extended east and west from the present site of Albany to the foot of the great lakes, a distance, by modern admeasurement, of 325 miles, which is now traversed by rail road. An air palace, we may grant them, having beams and rafters, higher and longer than any pile of regal magnificence yet reared by human hands.

Thus much may be said, with certainty, of the name of this celebrated family of red men, by which they are identified and distinguished from other stocks of the hunter tribes of North America. Where they originated, relatively to their position on this continent, the progress of ethnology does not, at this incipient period of that science, enable us to determine, nor is it proposed, save with the merest brevity, now to inquire. Veiling their own origin, if anciently known, in allegory, or designing by fancy to supply the utter want of early history, to the intent, perhaps, that they might put forth an undisputed title to the country they occupied, the relations of their old sages affirm that they originated in the territorial area of western New York. Their traditions on this point, as put on record by the pen of one of their own people, (Cusick's historical and traditionary tract), fixes the locality of their actual origin at an eminence near the falls of the Oswego river. To cut short the narration, they assert that their ancestors were called forth, from the bowels of a mountain, by *Tarenyawagon*, the Holder of the Heavens. It represents them as one people, who moved first towards the east, as far as the sea, and then fell back, partly on their own tracks, towards the west and south-west. So far, and so far only, the tale appears credible enough, and as there is no chronology established by it, although dates are freely introduced, and consequently nothing to contradict it, their track of migration and countermigration from the Oswego, may be deemed as probable.

The diversities of language, and the separation into tribes, are represented to have taken place, according to known principles of ethnological inference.

Ondiyaka, an Onondaga sage, and the ruling chief of the confederacy, who died on an official visit to the Oneidas in 1839, at the age of ninety, confirmed these general traditions of the Tuscarora scribe. He informed Le Fort, who was with him in that journey, and at his death, that the Onondagas were created by *Neo*,\* in the

---

\* The term *Neo*, God, is generally used reverently, with a syllable prefixed in the different Iroquois dialects, as Yawa-Neo in the Tuscarora, Howai-Neo in the Seneca, Hawai-Neo, Onondaga, Lawai-Neo, Mohawk, &c.

country where they lived; that he made this island or continent, *Hawoneo*, for the red race, and meant it for them alone. He did not allude to, or acknowledge any migration from other lands. This Le Fort, himself an Onondaga, a chief, and an educated man, told me during the several interviews I had with him at the Onondaga castle.

Ondiyaka proceeded to say, as they walked over the ancient ruins in the valley of the Kasonda,* that this was the spot where the Onondagas formerly lived, before they fixed themselves in the Onondaga valley, and before they had entered into confederation. In those days they were at enmity with each other; they raised the old forts to defend themselves. They wandered about a great deal. They frequently changed their places of residence. They lived in perpetual fear. They kept fighting, and moving their villages often. This reduced their numbers, and rendered their condition one of alarms and trials. Sometimes they abandoned a village, and all their gardens and clearings, because they had encountered much sickness, and believed the place to be doomed. They were always ready to hope for better luck in a new spot. At length they confederated, and then their fortifications were no longer necessary, and fell into decay. This he believed, was

* Butternut Creek, which runs through parts of the towns of Pompey, Lafayette and De Witt, Onondaga county.

the origin of these old ruins, which were not of foreign construction.* Before the confederacy, they had been not only at war among themselves, but had been driven by other enemies.† After it, they carried their wars out of their own country, and began to bring home prisoners. Their plan was to select for adoption from the prisoners, and captives, and fragments of tribes whom they conquered. These captives were equally divided among each of the tribes, were adopted and incorporated with them, and served to make good their losses. They used the term, *We-hait-wat-sha*, in relation to these captives. This term means a body cut into parts and scattered around. In this manner, they figuratively scattered their prisoners, and sunk and destroyed their nationality, and built up their own.

At what period they confederated, we have no exact means of deciding. It appears to have been comparatively recent, judging from traditionary testimony.‡ While their advancement in the economy of living, in arms, in diplomacy and in civil polity, would lead conjecture to a more remote date. Their own legends, like

---

* This remark must be considered as applied only to the class of simple ring forts, so frequent in western New York. These forts are proved by antiquarian remains, forest growth, &c., to be the most ancient of any works, in Onondaga county, in the shape of forts.

† Colden represents them as driven by the Algonquins, on the discovery of Canada.

‡ Vide Pyrlaus.

those of some other leading stocks of the continent, carry them back to a period of wars with giants and demons and monsters of the sea, the land, and the air, and are fraught with strange and grotesque fancies of wizards and enchanters. But history, guiding the pen of the French Jesuit, describes them as pouring in their canoes through the myriad streams that interlace in western New York, and debouching, now on the gulf of the St. Lawrence, now on the Chesapeake—glancing again over the waves of Michigan, and now again plying their paddles in the waters of the turbid Mississippi. Wherever they went, they carried proofs of their energy, courage, and enterprise.

At one period we hear the sound of their war cry along the straits of the St. Mary's, and at the foot of Lake Superior. At another under the walls of Quebec, where they finally defeated the Hurons, under the eyes of the French. They put out the fires of the Gahkwas and Eries. They eradicated the Susquehannocks. They placed the Lenapes, the Nanticokes, and the Munsees under the yoke of subjection. They put the Metoacks and the Manhattans under tribute. They spread the terror of their arms over all New England. They traversed the whole length of the Appalachian chain, and descended, like the enraged yagisho and megalonyx, on the Cherokees and the Catawbas. Smith encountered their warriors in the settlement of Virginia, and La Salle on the discovery of the Illinois. Nations trembled when they heard the name of the *Konoshioni*.

They possessed a physical structure, and they lived in a climate which imparted energy to their motions. They used a sonorous and commanding language, which had its dual number, and its neuter, masculine, and feminine genders. They were excellent natural orators, and expert diplomatists. They began early to cherish a national pride, which grew with their conquests. They had, like the Algonquins, in the organization of the several clans, or families, which composed each tribe, a curious *heraldic* tie, founded on original relationship, which exercised a strong influence, but which has never been satisfactorily explained. They were governed by hereditary chieftaincies, like others of the aboriginal stocks, but contrary to the usage of these other stocks, the claims of their chiefs were subjected to the decision of a national council. The aristocratic and democratic principles were thus both brought into requisition, in candidates for office. But in all that constituted national action, they were a pure republic. So far was this carried, that it is believed the veto of any one chief, to a public measure, was sufficient to arrest its adoption by the council.

In the development of their nationality, they have produced several men of energy and ability, who were equal, in natural force of character, to some of the most shining warriors and orators of antiquity. Few war captains have exceeded

Hendrick, Brant, or Skenandoah. The eloquence and force of Garangula, Logan, and Red Jacket, in their public speeches, have commanded universal admiration. Mr. Jefferson considered the appeal of Logan to the white race, after the extirpation of his family, as without a parallel; and it has been imitated in vain, by distinguished poets and orators.

Such were the aboriginal people who occupied western New York, and their memory will forever live in the significant names which they have bestowed upon the streams and mountains which beautify and adorn the land. Viewed as one of the Indo-American stocks, they possessed some very striking traits.

Few barbarous nations have ever existed on the globe, who have shown more native energy, and distinctiveness of character. Still fewer who have evinced so firm a devotion to the spirit of independence. Yet all their native manliness, and energy of character and action, would have failed, or become inoperative, had they not abandoned the fatal Indian principle of tribal supremacy, or independent chieftainships, and made common cause in a national confederacy. The moment this was done, and each of the component clans or tribes had surrendered the power of sovereignty to a general council of the whole, the foundation for their rise was laid, and they soon became the most powerful political body among the native tribes of North America, this side of the palace of Montezuma.

In visiting the descendants of such a people, after a lapse of more than two centuries and a quarter from the discovery, it was the impulse of the commonest interest, to make some inquiries into their former history and antiquities. These were pursued under favorable circumstances, for the most part, at all points of my journey, and have been resumed, when broken off, whenever practical. The only method pursued, was to obtain all the facts possible, from red or white men, of reliable testimony. Another time and place was required to digest them into a connected history. They were collected in the pauses which intervened, in the obtaining of the statistics of the census, and they are contributed herewith, in the simple garb and freshness of the original minutes. Those who related the traditions, doubtless supposed themselves to be delivering the important lore of their history. They were related, along the road, or seated around the evening circle, as the current belief of the people. Sometimes the fields or hills, disclosing the localities of old forts, were the scene of the narrations; sometimes the Indian burial ground; sometimes more formal interviews. He who gleans popular traditions among this race, must have his ear ever open, and his pen or pencil ever ready.

Historical and biographical notices, names of places, and sketches of antiquarian remains, were thus acquired, as time or occasion prompted. To make minutes of what occurred, was all that time permitted me; but it was a rule, to make them promptly, and on the spot. This much seemed necessary in despatching this portion of my researches, with the miscellaneous details accompanying them; and having accomplished this object, my present task is terminated.

Where we have nothing else to rely upon, we may receive the rudest traditions of an Indian nation, although they be regarded as mere historical phenomena, or materials to be considered. Whether such materials are to be credited or disbelieved, wholly or in part, is quite another thing. Our Indians, like some of the ancient nations of Asia, whom they resemble in many points of character, were prone to refer their origin to myths and legends, under which they, doubtless, sometimes meant to represent truths; or, at least, to express opinions. The Indian tribes, very much like their ancient prototypes of the old world, seemed to have felt a necessity for inventing some story of their origin, where it is sometimes probable there was little or nothing of actual tradition to build it upon. They were manifestly under a kind of self-reproach, to reflect that they had indeed no history; nothing to connect their descent from prior races; and if they have not proved themselves men of much judgment in their attempts to supply the deficiency in their fabrications and allegories, they must often come in, it must be confessed, for no little share of imagination.

There appears, throughout the whole race, to be the vestiges of a tradition of the creation and the deluge, two great and striking points in the history of man, which, however he wandered, he would be most likely to remember. They uniformly attribute their origin to a superior and divine power. They do not suppose that they came into existence without the act of this pre-existing almighty power, who is called *Neo*, or *Owaneo*. This is the third great and leading point in their traditions. And these three primary vestiges of the original history of the race are to be found among the rudest tribes, between the straits of Terra del Fuego and the Arctic ocean, notwithstanding the amount of grotesque and puerile matter which serves as the vehicle of the traditions.

Between the creation and the deluge and the present era of the world, there is nearly an entire blank. Ages have dropped out of their memory, with all their stirring incidents of wars and migrations, and the first reliable truth we hear is, that at such a time they lived on the banks of the Mississippi, the Ohio, the Lakes, or the St. Lawrence, &c. Nothing but this kind of *proximate* origin could indeed be expected to be retained. They acknowledge relationship to no prior race of man. We see that they are *sui generis* with, and much resemble, some of the eastern nations in color and features. Physiologists have never been able to detect a bone or muscle, more or less, than the Caucassian race possess. Philoogists listen to their speech, and admit that in one tribe or another they possess all the powers of articulate utterance known to that race. We know by this kind of evidence, physical and moral, that they are a branch of the original Adamic stock, without reference to the pages of revelation, where we learn the same truth, and are told in so many words, that "God out of one flesh, formed all men." And we must *per force* infer, that the Indian race is of foreign origin, and must have crossed an ocean to reach the continent. Ask not the red sage to tell you how, or when, or where. He knows it not, and if he should pretend to the knowledge, it would be the surest possible evidence, philosophically considered, that his responses were fabulous. Three hundred and fifty-three years only has America been known to Europe, and yet should we strike our history out of existence, what should we know of the leading facts of the discovery and the discoverer from Indian tradition? Still the inquisitive spirit of research leads us to ask, where were this race eighteen hundred and forty-five years ago? or at the invasion of Britain by Julius Cæsar? or at the out pouring of the Gothic hordes under Alaric or Brennus? Scandinavian research tells us they were here in the 10th century. The Mexican picture writings inform us that some of them reached the valley of Mexico in the 11th century. Welsh history claims to have sent one of her princes among them in the 12th century. The mounds of the

Mississippi valley do not appear to have had an origin much earlier. The whole range of even historical conjecture is absolutely limited within eight or nine hundred years. Nothing older, of their presence certainly in the northern hemisphere, is known, than about the time of the crowning of Charlemagne, A. D. 800, unless we take the Grecian tradition of Atalantis.

In Mexico we can ascend to higher dates. But it is altogether doubtful, where the great Indian monarchy of Mexico, can be traced higher than ninety years before the conquest in 1521. At that epoch, the princes of Mexico and Tezcuco, united and prevailed against the other petty monarchies of the Mexican valley. Clavigero traces the Aztec rule to 1051. Bastamenti to 1116. Sahagan to 1200. The Toltec empire, which preceded it, is generally supposed to have been dismembered in 958. The next year they fled into distant provinces, carrying with them their peculiar religion in the worship of the sun. This empire is vaguely traced to A. D. 677. There is a single tradition which reached to A. D. 299; and another by which Quetzalcoatl, the great personage of their mythology, religion and government, is made to correspond, by the Indian chronologists, to the advent of Christ.

That we have nothing in the way of tradition older than the dates referred to, is no positive proof that the tribes were not upon the continent long prior. There are some considerations, in the very nature of the case, which argue a remote continental antiquity for these tribes. It is hardly to be supposed that large numbers of the primitive adventurers landed at any one time or place; nor is it more probable that the epochs of these early adventurers were very numerous. The absolute conformity of physical features renders this improbable. The early migrations must have been necessarily confined to portions of the old world peopled by the *red race*— by a race, not only of red skins, black hair and eyes, and high check bones, who would reproduce these fixed characteristics, *ad infinitum*, but whose whole mental as well as physiological developement assimilates it, as a distinct unity of the species. While physiology, however, asserts this unity, in the course of the dispersion and multiplication of tribes, their languages, granting all that can be asked for on the score of original diversity, became divided into an infinite number of dialects and tongues. Between these dialects, however, where they are even the most diverse, there is a singular coincidence in many of the leading principles of concord and regimen, and polysynthetic arrangement. Such diversities in sound, amounting, as they do in many cases, for instance, in the stocks of the Algonquin and Iroquois, to an almost total difference, must have required many ages for their production. And this fact alone affords a proof of the continental antiquity of the American race.

Iroquois tradition opens with the notion that there were originally two worlds, or regions of space, namely, an upper and lower world. The upper was inhabited by beings similar to the human race; the lower by monsters, moving in the waters. When the human species were transferred below, and the lower sphere was about to be rendered fit for their residence, the act of their transference or reproduction is concentrated in the idea of a female, who began to descend into the lower world, which is depicted as a region of darkness, waters and monsters. She was received on the back of a tortoise, where she gave birth to male twins, and expired. The shell of this tortoise expanded into the continent, which, in their phraseology, is called an island; and is named by the Onondagas, *Aoneo*.\*  One of the infants was called *Inigorio*, or the Good Mind; the other, *Inigohatea*, or the Bad Mind. These two antagonistical principles, which are such perfect counterparts of the Ormuzd and Ahriman of Zoroaster, were at perpetual variance, it being the law of one to counteract whatever the other did. They were not, however, men, but gods, or existences, through whom the Great Spirit, or Holder of the Heavens, carried out his purposes. The first labor of Inigorio

---

\* From this word, the term *Aonic*, has been employed to give a definite sense to discussions which relate to topics within the territorial area of the United States, particularly its mounds, inscriptions and monuments, and the Indian stocks of the northern hemisphere.

was to create the sun out of the head of his dead mother, and the moon and the stars out of other parts of the body. The light these gave, drove the monsters into the deep water, to hide themselves. He then prepared the surface of the continent, and fitted it for human habitation, by diversifying it with creeks, rivers, lakes and plains, and by filling these with the various species of the animal and vegetable kingdoms. He then formed a man and woman out of the earth, gave them life, and called them *Ea-gwe-ho-we*, or, as it is more generally known to Indian archæologists, *Ong-we-Hon-we;* that is to say, a real people.

Meanwhile the Bad Mind created mountains, waterfalls, and steeps, and morasses, reptiles, serpents, apes, and other objects supposed to be injurious to, or in mockery of mankind. He made attempts also to conceal the land animals in the ground, so as to deprive man of the means of subsistence. This continued opposition to the wishes of the Good Mind, who was perpetually busied in restoring the effects of the displacements and wicked devices of the other, at length led to a personal combat, of which the time and instruments of the battle were agreed on. They fought for two days, the one using deer's horns, and the other flag roots, as arms.*

* By reference to the Algonquin story of the combat between Manabozho and his father, the West Wind, as given in *Algic Researches*, vol. i., p. 134, it will be seen that the weapons chosen by the parties were the same as those employed by Inigorio and Inigohatea, namely, deer's horns and flag roots.

Inigorio, who had chosen horns, finally prevailed; his antagonist sunk down to a region of darkness, and became the Evil Spirit, or Kluncolux,* of the world of despair. Inigorio having obtained this triumph, retired from the earth.

This piece of ingenuity, or philosophy of the Indian mind, much of which is pure allegory, under which truths are hid, stands in the remote vista of Iroquois tradition, and it seemed necessary to notice it, in preparing to take up their more sober traditions. It is picked out of a mass of incongruous details, published by a native, which only serve, peradventure, to denote its genuineness; for divested of absurdity, in the original, we should not ascribe much antiquity to it, or be prone to attribute it to an ignorant, superstitious, pagan people, living in all their earlier times without arts, letters or civilization. Futile as it is, it will be found veritable philosophy, compared with most of the earlier theories of the renowned nations of antiquity. Take, as an instance, the account Sanchoniathus gives of the theology of the Phœnicians.†

The Iroquois believe, with the Algonquins, that the earth is a plain with four corners; and that the sky, or visible heavens, that is, hemisphere, resting on this plain, is of a substance which can be indented or broke through. They believe that the planets shine through this hemi-

---

* Oneida.

† Gowan's Ancient Fragments, 2 vol. 8vo., N. Y., 1835.

sphere, and that the sun and moon perform their orbits daily, around it.

They observe, it is believed, the autumnal and vernal equinoxes, by their effects on meteorological phenomena. They have a lunar year of about 365 days, but they make no intercalations for the true length of the year,—which never was, apparently, known to them,

When we come to draw the minds of the sages and chroniclers of the Iroquois cantons to the facts of their early history and origin, they treat us with legendary fables, and myths of gods and men, and changes and freaks in elementary matter, which indicate that such ideas were common to their progenitors, whatever part of the world they occupied. We have adverted to their notions on this head, in the preceding remarks on their cosmogony, tinctured, as it strongly is, with the old Persian philosophy.

They deny, as do all the tribes, a foreign origin. They assert that America, or *Aonco*, was the place of their origin. They begin by laying down the theory, that they were the peculiar care of the Supernal Power who created all things, and who, as a proof of his care and benevolence of a race whom he had marked by a distinct color, created the continent for their especial use, and placed them upon it. None of the tribes pretend to establish dates, nor have they any astronomical data, to fix them. But they all give to the story of their origin, or creation, a locality, which is generally fixed to some prominent geographical feature near to their present respective place of abode, or at least a spot well known. This spot, among the Iroquois cantons, is located in the northern hemisphere.

The term Ongwe Honwe, is used by these tribes, very much in the manner in which the ancient Teutons called themselves Allamanna, or Ghermann, from which we have the modern terms, Allemand and German. If they did not literally call themselves *all-men*, as did these proud tribes, they implied as much, in a term which is interpreted to mean, *real men*, or a people surpassing all others. It is the common term for the red race, as contradistinguished from all other races, and the true equivalent of the phrase Indian.

By their earliest traditions, we are told that a body of the Ongwe Honwe encamped on the banks of the St. Lawrence, where they were invaded by a nation few in number, but of giant stature, called Rononweca.* After a war, brought on by personal encounters and incidents, and carried on with perfidy and cruelty, they were delivered at length, by the skill and courage of Yatontea,* who, after retreating before them, raised a large body of men and defeated them, after which they were supposed to be extinct. They next suffered from the malice, perfidy, and lust of an extraordinary person called Shotrowea,* who was finally driven across

---

*I abbreviate these words from the originals, for the sole purpose of making them readable to the ordinary reader.

the St. Lawrence, and came to a town south of the shores of Lake Ontario, where, however, he only disguised his intentions, to repeat his cruel and perfidious deeds. This person, who assassinated many persons, and violated six virgins, they point to as a fiend in human shape.

At this time the Big Quisquis* invaded the country, who pushed down the houses of the people, and created great consternation and disturbance. After making ineffectual resistance, they fled, but were at length relieved by a brave chief, who raised a body of men to battle him, but the animal himself retired. In this age of monsters, their country was invaded by another monster called the Big Elk, who was furious against men,† and destroyed the lives of many persons; but he was at length killed after a severe contest. A great horned serpent next appeared on Lake Ontario, who, by means of his poisonous breath, produced diseases, and caused the death of many, but he was at last compelled to retire by thunderbolts. This fourth calamity was not forgotten, when a fifth happened. A blazing star fell into a fort situated on the banks of the St. Lawrence, and destroyed the people. Such a phenomenon caused great panic and dread, and they regarded it as ominous of their entire destruction. Prior to this, a confederation had taken place among these northern tribes situated north of and along the banks of the great lakes, and they had a ruling chief over all. This

\* Kwis Kwis is the name of a hog in modern Iroquois.
† Carnivorous—but this is not a characteristic of the elk.

ruler repaired to the south to visit a ruler of great fame and authority, who resided at a great town in *a lodge of gold.* But it only proved to be an embassy of folly, for this great ruler, exercising an imperial sway, availing himself of the information thus derived, of a great country full of resources, built many forts throughout the country, and almost penetrated to the banks of Lake Erie. The people who had confederated on the north resisted. A long war of a hundred years standing ensued, but the northern people were better skilled in the use of the bow and arrow, and were more expert woodsmen and warriors. They at length prevailed, and taking all these towns and forts, left them a heap of ruins. But the prediction of the blazing star was now verified. The tribes who were held together by feeble bands, fell into disputes, and wars among themselves, which were pursued through a long period, until they utterly destroyed each other, and so reduced their numbers, that the land was again overrun by wild beasts.

## CHAPTER III.

### ORIGIN AND HISTORY OF THE IROQUOIS, AS A DISTINCT PEOPLE.

MOHAWKS—ONEIDAS, AND THE ONEIDA STONE—ONONDAGAS —CAYUGAS—SENECAS, AND THEIR ORIGIN—TUSCARORAS, AND THEIR FLIGHT FROM NORTH CAROLINA—NECARIAGES— ST. REGIS COLONY.

THE first period of Indian history having thus terminated in discords, wars, and the mutual destruction of each other, tradition does not denote how long the depopulation of the country continued. It begins a second period by recollections of the Konoshioni, or Iroquois. They do not indicate what relation they bear to the ancient, broken down confederacy, glanced at in the preceding pages; but leave us to suppose that they may have been fragmentary descendants of it. That such a conclusion should not be formed, however, and in order to prove themselves an original people in the land, they frame a new myth to begin their national existence. They boldly assert, that they were, through some means, confined in a mountain, from whose subterraneous bowels they were extricated by Tarenyawagon, the Holder of the Heavens.

They point to a place at or near the falls of the Oswego river, where this deliverance happened, and they look to this divine messenger, who could assume various shapes, as the friend and patron of their nation.*

As soon as they were released, he gave them instructions respecting the mode of hunting, matrimony, worship, and other points. He warned them against the Evil Spirit, and gave them corn, beans, squashes, and potatoes and tobacco, and dogs to hunt their game. He bid them go towards the east, and personally guided them, until they entered a valley called Tenonanatchi, or the Mohawk. They followed this stream to its entrance into the Sanatatea, or as called by the Mohawks, Kohotatea, which they pursued to the sea. From this point they retraced their steps towards the west, originating as they went, in their order and position, the Mohawks, the Oneidas, the Onondagas, the Cayugas, and the Senecas. They do not omit the Tuscaroras, whom they acknowledged, after a long period of wandering, and a considerable

* Where the Indian dwelt for a long time, it is customary for them to affirm in their metaphorical language, that they originated, or were created. When they date from such a spot, we find they frame a story, saying that they came out of a hill, &c., at that spot. In 1791, an extensive work, consisting of ditches, &c., was found about forty miles south of Oswego, which is not remote from the probable place of origin, their traditions refer to; and it may be worthy of examination with this particular view. Some account of this old fort appeared in the *New York Magazine*, 1792.

change of language, and admitted as the sixth tribe of the confederacy.

The Tuscaroras affirm, that after reaching the lake waters, they turned south-west, to the Mississippi river, where a part of them crossed on a grape vine, but it broke, leaving the remainder east. Those who went west, have been lost and forgotten from their memory. The remainder, or eastern Tuscaroras, continued their wanderings, hunting, and wars, until they had crossed the Alleghanies and reached the sea again, at the mouth of the Cautoh, or Neus river, in North Carolina.

Each tribe was independent of the others. They increased in numbers, valor and skill, and in all sorts of knowledge necessary in the forest. But they began to fight and quarrel among themselves, and thus wasted and destroyed each other. They lived a life of perpetual fear, and built forts to defend themselves, or to protect their women and children. Besides this, the country was wide, and covered with large forests and lakes, and it gave shelter to many fierce wild animals and monsters, who beset their paths and kept them in dread. The evil spirit also plagued them with monstrous visitations. They were often induced to change their villages, sometimes from the fear of such enemies, and sometimes from sickness or bad luck. In this manner, and owing to their perpetual hostility, their population was often reduced. How long they wandered and warred, they do not know.

## AS A DISTINCT PEOPLE. 71

At length it was proposed by some wise man that they should no longer fight against each other, but unite their strength against their enemies, the Alleghans, the Adirondacks, the Eries, and other ancient and once powerful tribes, who figure in the foreground of their early history, and who, if accounts be true, once greatly excelled them both in war and arts, the skill of making implements, canoes and utensils, &c.

To this league, which was formed on the banks of Onondaga lake, they in time gave the name of the Long House, using the term symbolically, to denote that they were tired and braced together by blood and lineage, as well as political bonds. This house, agreeably to the allusion so often made by their speakers, during our colonial history, reached from the banks of the Hudson to the Lakes. At its eastern door stood the Mohawks, at the west the Senecas, who guarded it with vigilance.

The *Mohawks* are supposed to be the eldest brother, in the symbolical chain of the Six Nations. Their own tradition assigns them this rank, and it appears to be consonant to other traditions.

When Tarenyawagon, their liberator from their subterranean confinement, bid them travel east, he gave them his personal conduct and care until they had entered the Mohawk valley. Some of their western brethren call this stream Tenonanatche, or a river flowing through a mountain. In due time, they went on into the valley of the Hudson, and thence, if we credit their annals, to the sea. The seat of their power and growth was, however, in the genial valley where they had at first located. Here they lived when the county was discovered, and here they continued to live and flourish until the events of the American revolution, and the determined cruelty which they exercised, under the authority and influence of the British crown, drove them out of it, and lost them the inheritance.

It does not appear, from any thing history or tradition tells us, or from any monumental remains in the valley or its immediate vicinity, that it had before been occupied by other nations. They do not speak of having driven out or conquered any other tribe. There are no old forts or earthern walls, or other traces of military or defensive occupancy, of which we have heard. Their ramparts were rather their own brawny arms, stout bodies and brave hearts. From the earliest notices of them, they were renowned for wielding the war club and arrow with great dexterity. They raised corn on the rich intervales, and pursued the deer, bear and elk in the subjacent forests. Their dominion extended from the head waters of the Susquehanna and Delaware to Lake Champlain. They had pursued their forays into the territorial area of New England, as far, at least, as the central portions of the Connecticut, and had made their power felt, as temporary invaders, among the small independent tribes who lived about the region of the present city and harbor of New York. Wherever they went, they carried terror. Their very name, as we learn from Colden, was a synonyme for cruelty and dread.* No tribe, perhaps, on the continent, produced better warriors, or have ever more fully realized, as a nation, the highest measure of heroism and military glory to which hunter nations can reach.

In passing over the country which they once occupied, there is little to stimulate historical interest, beyond the general idea of their power and military renown, Their history is connected with the rise and influence of one of our most distinguished anti-revolutionary citizens, Sir William Johnson. The influence he obtained over them was never exceeded, if equalled, by that of any other man of European lineage. He moulded them to his purposes in peace and war. They followed him in his most perilous expeditions, and sustained him manfully, as we know, in the two great contests to whose successful issue he owed his laurels, namely,

* The word Mohawk itself, is not a term of Mohawk origin, but one imposed upon them, as is believed, by the Mohegan race, who inhabited the borders of the sea. Among this race the Dutch and English landed, and they would naturally adopt the term most in vogue for so celebrated a tribe. The Dutch, indeed, modified it to Maaquas—a modification which helps us to decipher its probable origin, in *mauqua* (by kindred tribes, *mukwa*, &c.) a bear. By others, it may be traced to *mohwa*, a wolf, and *awki*, a country. The Mohawk sachems, who presented their condolence at Albany in 1690, on the taking of Schenectady, said, "We are all of the race of the bear, and a bear you know never yields, while one drop of blood is left. We must all be bears."—*Colden.*

Lake George and Niagara. So completely identified were they in feeling and policy with this politic and brave man, that after his death, which happened at the crisis of '76, they transferred their attachment to his family, and staking their all on the issue, abandoned their beloved valley and the bones of their fathers, and fled to the less hospitable latitudes of Canada, from which they have never permanently returned.

Some twenty or more persons of this tribe are mingled as residents of the villages of their brethren, the Senecas, Tuscaroras, and Oneidas. A much greater number exist with intermixture of other kindred tribes, in the St. Regis canton of St. Lawrence county; but the greater number of the parent tribe reside on lands appropriated for their use by the British government, at Brantford, on the Grand river of Canada West. To this place at the close of the war, they followed their distinguished leader, Thayendanegea, the Jeptha of his tribe, who, against the custom of birth and descent, and every other obstacle, after the failure of the line of wise and brave chiefs to lead them to battle, was made their *tekarahogea* and leader, and displayed a degree of energy and firmness of purpose, which few of the aboriginal race in America have ever equalled.

What light the examination of the ancient places of burial of this tribe in the valley would throw on their ancient history or arts, by entombed articles, cannot be told without examinations which have not been made. Probably the old places of Indian interment about Canajoharie, Dionderoga, and Schenectady, would reveal something on this head, conforming at least, in age and style of art, with the stone pipes, tomahawks and amulets of the Onondaga and Genesee countries. The valley of the Schoharie and that of the Tawasentha, or Norman's kill, near Albany, might also be expected to reward this species of research. A human head, rudely carved in stone, apparently aboriginal, was sent to the New York Historical Society early in 1845, which was represented to have been found in excavating a bank at Schenectady. If this piece of sculpture, which denoted more labor than art, be regarded as of Mohawk origin, it would evince no higher degree of art, in this respect, than was evinced by similar outlines cut in the rock, but not detached, by some of the New England tribes.*

The *Oneida* canton of the Iroquois nation, deduces its origin in a remote age, from the Onondagas, with the language of which, the Oneida has the closest affinity. According to a tradition which was related to me, and which is believed to be entitled to respect, they are descended from two persons, who, in their obscure ages, and before a confederation had been thought of,

* Rude carvings of this kind are represented to exist on the banks of the Connecticut, at Bellows' Falls, &c.

went out from the people at Onondaga, and first dwelt at the head of the Oneida river. After increasing in numbers, they removed to the outlet of the Oneida creek, which flows into Oneida lake. Here they fortified themselves, and farther increased in numbers and power. Remains of this fortification are said still to exist. Their next removal was up the Oneida creek valley, to the storied locality of the Oneida stone, from which, by a figure of speech, they represent themselves to have sprung. This stone is in the town of Stockbridge, Madison county. It lies on a very commanding eminence, from which the entire valley, as far as the Oneida lake, can be seen in a clear atmosphere. The day of my visit being hazy at a distance, the lake could not be seen, although the view down the valley was both magnificent and picturesque. This eminence was formerly covered with a butternut grove. Old and partly decayed trees of this species still remain in a few places. The ancient town extended in a transverse valley, south of this ridge of land, covered as it was with nut wood trees, and was completely sheltered by it, from the north winds. A copious and clear spring of water issued at the spot selected for their wigwams. Here in seclusion from their enemies, the tribe expanded and grew in numbers. When it was necessary to light their pipes, and assemble to discuss their national affairs, they had only to ascend the hill, through its richly wooded grove, to its extreme summit, at the site of the Oneida stone. The following cut represents the stone, which became the national altar.

Standing at its side, at a probable elevation of 400 or 500 feet above the Stanwix summit, they could survey the whole valley of the Oneida; and a beacon fire lighted here, was the signal for assembling their warriors from all the surrounding lateral plains and valleys. Time and usage rendered the object sacred, and as they expanded into nationality and power, while located around it, their sages asserted with metaphorical truth, that they sprang from this rock. Stone, in this language, is *onia*. They called themselves Oniota-aug, people of, or who sprung from, the stone. There is some variety in the pronunciation. The Mohawks call them Onéota. The French wrote it Aneyoute, and the English and Dutch, Oneida, which latter has prevailed. Neither retained the plural inflection in *aug*, which carries the idea of people.

With a knowledge of these traditions, I approached the spot with deep interest. It occupies the extreme summit, as shown in the print. The first feeling, on approaching it, was one of disappointment at its size, but this feeling soon subsided in the interest of its antiquity and national associations. It is a large, but not enormous boulder of syenite,* of the erratic block groupe, and, consequently, geologically foreign to the location. There are no rocks of this species *in situ*, I believe, nearer to it, in a northerly or easterly direction, than the Kayaderosseras or the Adirondack mountains.† The summit upon which, partly embedded, it reposes, is now a cleared field, in grass. A few primitive and secondary boulders, all of lesser size, are strown about the ridge, and several of weight and magnitude rest upon its flanks, and in the valleys at its base. One of the largest of these is the white stone at the spring, which has been spoken of, I think, in some early notices of the Oneidas, as the true Oneida stone; but this opinion is erroneous, by the concurrent testimony of red and white men, cognizant of the facts, whom I consulted. This white stone, represented on the succeeding page, has been removed by the proprietor of the land, from its ancient position near the spring, to constitute part of a stone fence; it is a carbonate of lime.

*A specimen of the rock before me, brought thence, consists of flesh-colored feld-spar, quartz, and hornblende.

† If the passage of the Mohawk through the Astorenga or Astogan hills, at Little Falls, discloses syenite, I am not aware of the fact.

*Tshejoana*, one of the Oneidas, who served as my guide in visiting this interesting location, took me to see still another stone, of note, lying a mile or more distant, in a southerly direction, on a farm of Gen. Knox. This stone, of which a figure is given on the next page, I found to be a large boulder of dark, compact limestone, with organic remains.

It was observable that the encrinites contained in this mass, were red. My Indian guide would have this color to be the result of the ancient Indian war paint. But the most striking characteristic of this rock, aside from its massy and flattened size, and channelled centre, consists in the evidences it affords of the action of water, in rounding and polishing it. In several places, my guide would have this wearing effect to have been produced by the rubbing and sharpening of the Indian war axes; for he averred that it was customary for war parties who went out south against the Cherokees, to come and sharpen their axes upon this stone, and paint themselves for war. Whatever there was in this custom, I think he was probably mistaken in his locality; yet it is a question in which others may differ. At any rate, geology had been quite beforehand

with the Oneida legendary and philosopher, in producing and accounting for these two phenomena, namely, the red color and smoothed and channelled surfaces. Geology having been

## AS A DISTINCT PEOPLE.

mentioned, I may add the following incident. I told Skanawadi, one of my guides, while standing at the Oneida stone, lying on its proud ancient elevation, that there was no stone like this, in place, till we went north to the Adirondacks, or Tehawas, or great lakes, and that this block of syenite had been brought here by the ocean, when it covered the whole land, and left on its recession. He replied, after a moment's reflection, that "he believed this."

At the time the Oneidas came to fix their location at this stone, the Konoshioni or Iroquois had not confederated. This people, in the early eras of their history, like the Algonquins, sent out individuals and bands, who became powerful, and assumed the character of separate and independent tribes, making war and peace *ad libitum*. If this mode of multiplication be compared to the lower orders of creation, it had some striking analogies with it. Like the bear and the hawk, the moment the young member was ready to quit the parent lair or nest, it had not only to forage for subsistence, but to defend itself against other bears and hawks, and all other claimants to the food of the forest. To make war, is in fact the first and the last act of sovereignty of the pettiest of all our aboriginal tribes. War is with them the road, and the only road to fame, and the readiest way to secure a supply of spontaneous food. They fight to increase or defend the boundaries of their hunting grounds. Thus, doubtless, arose the first difficulties between the

Oneidas and the other branches of the Iroquois. As soon as they were important enough to be noticed, and bold enough to defend themselves, they had to raise barriers around their villages, and when these were carried, as they probably were, or were threatened to be, at two points, on the Oneida waters, they fled to the hill country, at the site of the Oneida stone. How long they abode here, and made it the seat of their council fire, we can only conjecture. They cannot and do not pretend to tell. Wisdom, at length, taught the Iroquois sages, that they had enemies enough without fighting with each other, and the idea of a confederation was suggested. Tradition has preserved the name of Thaunowaga as the original suggestor; but it has preserved nothing more of his biography. The delegate from the Oneidas, was Otatschechta. That he came from, and lived *at*, the locality of the stone, and was renowned for his deeds and wisdom, is probable. This comprises the brief biography of two celebrated aboriginal sages and statesmen. Three periods of transference, of their council fire, have been named, all of which were probably prior to the confederation. Their fourth remove was down the valley to the present site of Oneida Castle — a place, which then, as now, they called *Kunawaloa*, meaning a man's head on a pole. At this place they lived and held their council fire, when the Dutch, in 1609, discovered and ascended the Kohatatea, or Hudson river. Such are the accounts of their sachems and wise men. It is a general confirmation of them, that the other members call them Younger Brother.

By another and older Indian tradition, an earlier date is assigned to the Oneida canton, which is regarded as one of the original subdivisions of the generic stock. It represents this stock as moving from the west to the east, and at another period, returning to the point of sunsetting, leaving the several separate tribes, or cantons, in their order as they passed. In this migration, the Oneidas are named as the second in geographical position and order of chronology.

They located themselves, says the Tuscarora annalist,* at a' stream called *Kaw-nah-taw-te-ruh*, or, Pineries, a tributary of the Susquehanna, which originates, according to this authority, in Allen's lake, ten miles south of Oneida Castle. They were called Ne-haw-retahgo,† or Bigtree, a name, it may be remarked, which does not occur as the patronymic for this tribe in other authors, nor has it been retained by them. The distance and course denoted, coincide very nearly with that of the Oneida stone. It is not known, however, that any tributary of the Susquehanna exists in that vicinity.

The two traditions may indeed be reconciled to truth, by supposing the latter the more ancient one, and that the Onondaga families before mentioned, constituted a subsequent accession to, and union with a band who had seated them-

---

\* Cusick. † In Tuscarora.

selves at a prior era, at the spot denoted; or this band may have remained there, on the general passage of the people eastward, and thus been the nucleus of the tribe, on the general return of the people west. In any view, however, they were called and are still called by the Iroquois, Younger Brother, which must be considered conclusive, that their nationality is of a period subsequent to that of the Mohawks, Onondagas, Cayugas and Senecas. This fact too, is adverse to the theory, which has too much the aspect of a mere theory, that the remigration of the Iroquois westward from the Atlantic, proceeded like a marching army, leaving tribes here and there as they went, in a regular chronological order, each of which took a name, and altered, as his phrase is, the language. The writer seems all along to have had the Jewish tribes in his mind. The truth is, ethnologically speaking, no tribe or nation alters, by an authoritative decision, or pre-thought, its language or idioms. Such alterations flow from time and circumstances. Least of all, do wandering savage tribes gravely determine to alter their dialects. Accident, usage, or caprice, little by little, and at long intervals, is the parent of new dialects and languages.

A few deductions may be added. By data before introduced, it will have been seen that it is probable the present confederation, whatever had preceded it, did not take place till about 1539, or seventy years before the arrival of Hudson. It may be considered as probable, that the Oneidas did not remove from the Oneida stone, into the valley and plains of Oneida Castle, until after the event of the final confederation between the five tribes, gave them security against internal enemies. The date of this transfer of the council fire, is rather remote, but not very ancient. A new forest has grown upon the old corn fields, which were once cultivated at their ancient settlement at the Oneida stone. The appearance of corn hills in rows, is still clearly perceptible in some parts of this forest. To an inquiry how such a preservation of the outlines of corn hills could be possible, my informant, who was an Oneida, answered, that in ancient times, the corn hills were made so large, that three clusters of stalks or sub-hills were raised on each circle or hill. There being no ploughs or other general means of turning up the earth, the same hill was used year after year, and thus its outlines became large and well defined. In a black walnut tree, standing on the site of one of these ancient corn fields, which was partly cut, and partly broken off, I counted on the cut part, one hundred cortical layers, and measuring the broken part, estimated it to have one hundred and forty more. Allowing a year for each ring, the commencement of the growth was in 1555, or sixteen years after the supposed date of the confederacy, and two hundred and ninety years from the present date.

The remaining history of the Oneidas can

only be glanced at, but has some points of peculiar interest. They are the only tribe of the ancient Konoshioni who adhered to us, at least the better part of them, in our life and death struggle of the revolutionary war, saving some portion of the Tuscaroras; whose aid, however, is justly due to the Oneida influence. It was by the Oneidas that the Tuscaroras were brought off from the south. The Oneidas had long distinguished themselves in their war excursions against the southern Indians. Their traditions are replete with accounts of these war parties against the Oyada, or Cherokees. They had found allies at the south in the Tuscaroras, who were themselves engaged in desperate wars, at various periods, against the Catabas, and Cherokees, and others. Besides this, Iroquois tradition claims the Tuscaroras as one of their original cantons, or rather as a band of the original Eagwe Heowe, who had, in early times gone south.\* And when a crisis happened in their affairs, they nobly went to their relief, and seated them on their western confines, between themselves and the Onondagas, where they remained during the revolution. The Oneidas bore their full share in the long and bloody wars waged by the Iroquois for more than two centuries, against the French in the Canadas, and aganist the distant Algonquins, Hurons and Illinese. And he who scans the ancient records of treaties and councils, will find that their sachems were

---

\* Vide Cusick's pamphlet.

represented in the conferences assembled on this continent, by the kings and potentates of Europe, who planted colonies at various times, between the respective gulfs of Mexico and the St. Lawrence. After the flight of the Mohawks, in 1776, they were in the van of the Konoshioni, and to use their symbolic phraseology, stood in the eastern door of the Long House. When the mixed Saxon population of New York and New England began, after the war of 1776, to move westward, the Oneidas first felt the pressure upon their territory. By siding with the colonists, they had secured their entire ancient domain, from which they ceded to the state, from time to time, such portions as they did not want for cultivation, taking in lieu money annuities. Nor did they fail to profit, in a measure, by the example of industry set before them in agriculture and the arts. For a while, it is true, they reeled before the march of intemperance, and sunk in numbers, but many of them learned the art of holding the plough. From the earliest times they were noted, along with their more western brethren, for the cultivation of Indian corn, and the planting of orchards. They also became tolerable herdsmen, and raised in considerable numbers, neat cattle, horses and hogs.

To preserve their nationality, their sachems, about the year 1820, sent delegates west to look out a location for their permanent residence. They purchased a suitable territory from the Monomonees of Wisconsin, a wandering and non-industrious race, seated about Green bay, and expended a part of their annuities in the payment. This turned out a wise measure. They soon began to remove, and have at this time a very flourishing settlement on Duck river, in that territory. At that location they have established schools, temperance societies and a church. They bear a good reputation for morals and industry, and are advancing in civilization and the arts.

By an official return of the date of 1844, they numbered 722 persons at that settlement. Two hundred and ten are still seated within the boundaries of New York, mostly in Oneida county. They are a mild people, of a good stature, and easy manners, and speak a soft dialect of the Iroquois, abounding in the liquid *l*, which, together with a mild enunciation, imparts a pleasing character to their speech.

*Onondaga* was, from the remotest times, the seat of the Iroquois government. Granting credence to the account of their own origin, on the high grounds or falls of the Oswego, they had not proceeded far up the course of the widely gathered waters of this stream, when a portion of them planted their wigwams in this fertile region. Whatever was the cause of their migrating from their primary council fire, nothing was more natural than that, by pursuing this stream upward, they should separate into independent tribes, and by further tracing out its far spread forks, gradually expand themselves, as they were found by the discoverers and first settlers, over the entire area of western New York. On reaching the grand junction of Three River point, a part went up the Seneca river, who subsequently dividing, formed the Senecas and Cayugas. The bands who took the eastern fork, or Oneida river, pushed forward over the Deowainsta or Rome summit, into the first large stream, flowing east, and became the Mohawks. The central or Onondaga fork was chosen by the portion who, from the hill country they first located in, took this name; and from them, the Oneidas, pursuing in fact the track of the Mohawks, were an off-shoot. That such was the general route, and causes of their separation, appears as evident as strong probabilities, in coincidence with their own traditions and modern discovery, can make it. That the whole of the original number who started from the south banks of Lake Ontario, did not keep together till they reached the valley of the Hudson and the sea, and then go back to the west—for so their general tradition has it—is also both reasonable and probable to suppose. Large bodies of hunters cannot keep long together. They must separate to procure food, and would separate from other causes. The first effect of their separation and spread into various rich valleys, abounding in game, nuts and fish, was a rapid increase in population. The next, to become overbearing, quarrel about territory, and fight. They were compelled to build forts to defend their stations, or secure their women and children, at night, and, by this system, kept down their population to about its first point of increase. It is altogether probable that they did not more than maintain, for ages, a stationary population, which occasionally went down by disease and other calamities, and again revived, as we know that natural causes, in the laws of vitality, will revive a people quickly, after the scourge of pestilence.

The idea of a confederation was, it is believed, an old one with this people, for the very oldest traditions speak of something of this kind, among the lake and St. Lawrence tribes of older days. When the present league was formed, on the banks of the Onondaga lake, this central tribe had manifestly greatly increased in strength, and distinguished itself in arms, and feats of hunting and daring against giants and monsters, for in such rencontres their traditions abound.

Most distinguished, however, above all others, east or west, was a leader of great courage, wisdom and address, called Atotarho; and when they proposed to form a league, this person, who had inspired dread, and kept himself retired, was anxiously sought. He was found by the Mohawk embassy, who were charged with the matter, as he is represented in the annexed specimen of picture writing, composedly sitting in a swamp, smoking his pipe, and rendered completely invulnerable, by living serpents. These

animals extended their hissing heads from all parts of his head and body. Every thing about him, and the place of his residence, was such as to inspire fear and respect. His dishes and spoons were made of the skulls of enemies, whom he had slain in battle. Him, when they had duly approached with presents and burned tobacco in friendship, in their pipes, by way of frankincense, they placed at the head of their league, as its presiding officer. They collected a large quantity of wampum, and invested him with a broad belt of this sacred article. I found the original drawing of this personage, from which the above is reduced, in the summer of 1845, in the house of a Seneca on the Cattaraugus reservation. The owner of this curious pictorial relic, on being asked, proceeded to a chest and carefully took it from its envelope, and allowed me to make a copy. It represents Atotarho, at the moment of his discovery, by the Mohawk delegation.

The right thus awarded to the Onondagas, to furnish a presiding officer for the league, has ever been retained, and is still possessed by that canton. To the Mohawks, at the same time, was awarded the *tekarahogea*, or chief war-captain; an office, however, of the general recognition of which, there is a disagreement amongst interpreters.

A singular tradition may be here added. It is said that the thirteenth Atotarho reigned at Onondaga when America was discovered.

Giving to each Atotarho a rule of fifteen years, and taking Hudson's voyage as the period the Indians allude to, we should have A. D. 1414, as the era of the present confederacy, in place of 1539, before mentioned on the authority of a general tradition recorded by Pyrlaus. We cannot, however, place much reliance upon Cusick's chronology.

The history of the *Cayugas* does not stand out prominently among the Iroquois, while it will be found that as one of the inclusive tribes who carried their name and fame so high among the aborigines, they have performed their due part, and produced warriors, sages and speakers of eminence. Were every thing else, indeed, blotted out of their history, the fact of their having

produced a Logan\* would be sufficient to rescue
their memory from oblivion. In their early
search after a place to hunt, fish and plant corn,
as an independent tribe, they, on the assumption
of their own traditions, passed up the Seneca
river, into the sylvan and beautiful lake which
bears their name. In visiting this lake the present
year, in search of their ancient sites, it was
not without a melancholy interest, that I surveyed,
within the boundaries of Aurora, the remains
of one of those apple orchards, which were ruthlessly
cut down by a detachment of the army of
Gen. Sullivan, in his severe but necessary expedition
in 1778. Many vestiges of their ancient
residence still remain in Cayuga county, nor has
local memory, in its intelligent and hospitable
inhabitants, dropped from its scroll the names
of several of its distinguished chiefs, and their
places of abode. They point to a spot at Springport,
now trenched on by the road, where lie
the remains of Karistagea, better known by his
English appellative of Steeltrap, one of their
noted chiefs and wise men, who extended the
hospitalities of his lodge to the first settlers on
the Military Tract. The nation itself, although
they had fought strenuously under the Red Cross
of St. George in the Revolutionary war, appeared
to be composed of mild and peaceable men,
of friendly dispositions toward the settlers. They
brought venison, fish and wild fruits for sale to

\* Logan was the son of Skellelimus, a Cayuga, and went
early to the Ohio valley, if he were not born there.

the doors of families, whose elder branches yet dwell upon the shores of the Cayuga.

Yet their history is a melancholy one, and their decline, on the settlement of western New York, was probably one of the most striking instances of the rapid depopulation of a tribe in modern days. Their first cession of land to the state was in 1789. This was confirmed at the general treaty of Fort Stanwix in 1790, and such had been the pressure of emigration into that quarter, that in 1795, at a treaty held at Cayuga bridge, they ceded their reserve of one hundred miles square in the valley of the Seneca outlet and the basin of Cayuga lake, reserving but four miles square. In these treaties they deemed themselves wise to change into large money annuities,* a territory which was no longer useful for hunting, and which they did not cultivate.

Experience has shown, however, throughout America, that Indian tribes, who live on annuities, and not by agricultural labor, are in the most dangerous condition of rapid decline. To render the danger eminent, it needs but the close proximity of a European population, who present the means of indulging selfish gratifications. Among these means, so seductive to the Indian mind, ardent spirits have ever been the most baneful. It proved so at least with the Cayugas, for within sixteen years after the treaty of Fort Stanwix, they had all emigrated west.

* A perpetual annuity of $2,300 was secured by one of these treaties.

Some of them had rejoined their brethren, who followed Brant and the Mohawks to Canada. Some had migrated to Sandusky, in Ohio, and others found a refuge among the Senecas, near Buffalo. With the Senecas they have ever been on the most intimate terms. Whilst they lived on the Cayuga lake, and the latter on the Seneca, they were separated by a midland range of forest, little more than sixteen miles broad. They intermingled freely in their hunting parties, and even in their villages. The inhabitants still point to a large tree near Canoga, on the banks of Cayuga lake, where the celebrated orator, Red Jacket, was born.

In investigating the Indian population of New York, under the provisions of the census act, I found 114 Cayugas residing in twenty families, on the Cattaraugus reservation. These families cultivate 316 acres of land, and during the year 1845, they raised 1,970 bushels of corn, 1,622 of oats, 210 of wheat, 955 of potatoes, and 277 of buckwheat, besides esculents and small articles. They were found to possess 43 milch cows, 39 horses, 40 sheep, and 109 hogs. Besides the Cayugas residing on the Cattaraugus, there were found, dispersed among the other cantons, 83 persons; making the whole number within the boundaries of New York, 197. The style of their dwellings is, generally, that of squared timber, plainly but comfortably furnished, with glass windows, and plain common furniture. Sixteen of the number are members of protestant churchcs. The males dress exclusively in the European fashion, and their condition and prospects are, like those of the Senecas, among whom they dwell, in a high degree encouraging to the friends of humanity. Of the number out of the bounds of the state, there have been no accurate means of judging. The vocabulary of their language denotes a close affinity with other tribes of this family.

From a remark made to me by a daughter of Brant, (the late Mrs. Kerr,) at her house near Wellington square, Canada, in 1843, I am inclined to think, that in the early wars waged by the Iroquois against the Virginia Indians, the Cayngas defeated and made prisoners the remnant of the Tuteloes, whom they brought and settled among them, in the Cayuga country.

One of the first traits which strikes an observer on entering the territory of the *Seneca* tribe, is the fact that they are called by a name which is not known in their vocabulary, and which they only recognize from having long been thus designated by others. Identical as it is in its present orthography, with the name of the Roman moralist, it is yet wholly improbable that it had any such origin; it must be regarded as an accidental coincidence of sound in some other Indian tongue. That this tongue is the Mohawk, a people who stood first in position east on the Iroquois borders, is probable, but not certain. The earlier authors spelt it with a *k*, with the *a* final, which probably had the usual broad sound. It occurs on a map of 1614, which was brought over from Holland recently, by the historical agent of the state, and has been laid, by that gentleman, before the New York Historical Society, with the proofs of its genuineness, thus bringing the use of the word within five years of the voyage of Hudson.

The term by which they call themselves is *Nundowaga*, or the People of the Hill. A name which leads us at once to consider the accounts of their own origin. Various relations of this story have been given, differing in some of their details, but all coinciding in the main events, namely, that they originated and lived on a well known hill, at the head of Canandaigua lake, where they were put in eminent peril of utter destruction by a monstrous serpent, which circled itself about the fort and lay with its mouth open at the gate. The following is given from a native source, and has some novel details to recommend it.

While the tribe had its seat and council fire on this hill, a woman and her son were living near it, when the boy one day caught a small two-headed serpent called Kaistowanea, in the bushes. He brought it home as a pet to amuse himself, and put it in a box, where he fed it on bird's flesh and other dainties. After some time it had become so large that it rested on the beams of the lodge, and the hunters were obliged to feed it with deer; but it soon went out and made its abode on a neighboring hill, where it maintained itself. It often went out and sported in the lake, and in time became so large and mischievous that the tribe were put in dread of it. They consulted on the subject one evening, and determined to fly next morning; but with the light of the next morning the monster had encircled the hill and lay with its double jaws extended before the gate. Some attempted to pass out, but were driven back; others tried to climb over its body, but were unable. Hunger at last drove them to desperation, and they made a rush to pass, but only rushed into the monster's double jaws. All were devoured but a warrior and his sister, who waited in vain expectancy of relief. At length the warrior had a dream, in which he was showed that if he would fledge his arrows with the hair of his sister, the charm would prevail over their enemy. He was warned not to heed the frightful heads and hissing tongues, but to shoot at the heart. Accordingly, the next morning he armed himself with his keenest weapons, charmed as directed, and boldly shot at the serpent's heart. The instantaneous recoiling of the monster proved that the wound was mortal. He began in great agony to roll down the hill, breaking down trees and uttering horrid noises, until he rolled into the lake. Here he slaked his thirst, and tried by water to mitigate his agony, dashing about in fury. At length he vomited up all the people whom he had eaten, and immediately expired and sunk to the bottom.* The fort was immediately deserted, and all who had escaped went with their deliverer to, and fixed their council fire on, the west shores of Seneca lake, where Geneva now stands.

The general course of the migration and conquests of the Senecas has, however, been towards the west. Taking their own general and ancient traditions of the parent stock, to wit, their origin in the valley of the Oswego, they may be supposed to have followed the Seneca branch of those outspread waters to the banks of the Seneca and Canandaigua lakes, and thence into the rich valley of the Genesee. At an early day they were limited to the region east of this capital stream, which, crossing the country in a transverse direction, formed a natural boundary. There lived west of it, in ancient times, a tribe who are known as Alleghans, Andastes and Eries, or, as the Senecas call them, Kah-kwas. They had their council fires at or near Buffalo, extending west and also east. The people called by the French the Neuter Nation, had placed themselves, so far as we can learn, on the waters of Oak-Orchard creek, which draws its tributaries in part from the fertile dis-

* If this be viewed as an allegory, it may admit of this interpretation. Internal feuds created by somebody brought up in their own lodges, originated hatred and hot blood. In a long and bloody war, the nation was nearly exterminated; at length the affections of a woman prevailed. Harmony was restored, and a new era of prosperity began, by removing the council fire to another place.

tricts of Genesee, Niagara and Orleans counties. From the accounts of the Tuscaroras, this people were governed in early times by a queen, who ruled over twelve forts in that quarter. North of them, embracing the Niagara ridge and the country below it, dwelt a branch of the Algonquin nation, who are called by the same authority, *Twankannas*. Other names occur, which are believed to be either synonymes for these, or minor divisions of the three principal tribes named, of which some further notice will be taken in a subsequent paper on the antiquarian remains of the country.

That these Trans-Genesean people were populous and warlike, not only maintaining their grounds against the Senecas, but often defeating them and driving them back, is proved not only by the traditions of the Senecas themselves, but by the striking evidences of their military strength and skill, denoted by the remains of forts and intrenchments and cemeteries, yet existing throughout the extensive area included between the Genesee and the Niagara, extending up the southern shores of Lake Erie to Chautauque and the other principal known Indian routes to the waters of the Allegany and Ohio. There is, at least, one authority (*Cusick*) for believing that the Eries themselves were remotely descended from the Senecas, and we have living tradition to prove that, at the time of their final defeat and so called extermination, some of them fled west, whilst the remainder of them, scattered, cut up and depressed, were incorporated in the Seneca canton.

To the Twankannas, the Neuter Nation, and other tribes and bands, not being Eries, who lived in this portion of the state, the Iroquois applied the general term of Adirondacks,* a bold, warlike, northern race, who spread over many degrees of latitude and longitude in former days, covering by generic affiliation with other tribes, all New England and the Atlantic coast, to North Carolina, and who are still, in their numerous and subdivided descendants, in the upper lakes and the west, the most numerous of any of the aboriginal stocks yet existing east of the Mississippi and Missouri. So long as the Iroquois remained divided, the Eries and their Algonquin allies kept their ground; and there is no reason to believe that they began to decline until a considerable period after the era of the Onondaga league. That was at first but little more than an agreement to stand by each other, and to send delegates and forward news to a central council; but it put an end to intestine wars, and its popular capacities soon developed themselves, and made it formidable to their neighbors. Thus much by way of prelude to their wars, to be noticed hereafter.

The Senecas were from the earliest times the most powerful of the Iroquois, nearly doubling, in its best estate, the Mohawks. Their population in past days has been variously estimated,

* Called Algonquins by the French.

and often exaggerated. Perhaps Dalton, who puts it at 400 warriors, or 2,000 souls, during the American war, verges to the opposite extreme, and actually underrates it. Be this as it may, I found the entire Seneca population, within the state, to be 2,383, residing on four reservations in the counties of Niagara and Genesee, Erie, Chautauque, Cattaraugus and Allegany. They were found to be divided into 538 families, who cultivated, in the aggregate, 8,416 acres of land. The produce of this land, as near as it could be obtained, as some declined stating it, was 21,341 bushels of corn, 3,745 of wheat, 20,039 of oats, and 12,469 of potatoes, besides buckwheat, turneps, peas, and smaller articles. They possess 1,537 neat cattle, 510 milch cows, 626 horses, 335 sheep and 2,269 hogs. Other details of their advance in agriculture were equally flattering. They cut large quantities of meadow land, possess an adequate supply of farming utensils, carts, wagons, including many tasty buggies and sleighs. Very little of their means of subsistence, even in the most unfavored positions, is derived from the chase. Upwards of 4,000 fruit trees were counted. The style of their buildings, fences and household furniture, as well as the dress of the males, is not essentially different, and little, often nothing at all, inferior to that of their white neighbors. Temperance and temperance societies exist in a good state in each canton. Fifteen of their youth have received a collegiate or academic education. A number

## AS A DISTINCT PEOPLE. 103

of these have studied professions. About 350 of the children attend private or missionary schools, and so far as I could obtain returns, some 250 adults are enrolled as members of protestant churches. Of this number, there are several catechists and intelligent educated translators and interpreters of the language. On the four reservations, there are fifteen native mechanics and three physicians.

Thus it appears that the energies once devoted by their ancestors to war and hunting, are in good earnest now directed to husbandry and the arts; and there is every encouragement to hope, and reason to believe, that by a continuance in the best measures, they will be wholly reclaimed and added to the number of useful, intelligent and moral citizens. In viewing the condition of such a people, hardy, well formed and active, and pressing forward, as they are, in the great experiment of civilization, humanity consoles itself with the hope, that the energy and firmness of purpose which once carried them, in pursuit of warlike glory, far and wide, will develope itself, as it has already signally commenced to do, in the labors of the field and the workshop. Their rude picture-writing upon the bark of trees, has given place to the school. Their prophets' lodges have been converted into churches; their midnight orgies, at the Indian dancing house, into societies to promote temperance. It is but applying present experience to future results, to predict that these results may become general. The eloquence thrown out by a Red Jacket, in opposition to the further curtailment of their territory, may shine out, in some of his descendants, to enlighten his people in agriculture, morals and political economy. Nor ought we to doubt that the desk and the forum are yet to resound with Seneca eloquence.

The traditions of the *Tuscarora* canton affirm, that they are descendants of the original family of Iroquois, who began their existence, or their nationality at least, at or near the falls of the Oswego. After the migration of the parent tribe towards the sea, and their return west and separation into tribes, this band went on west till they reached Lake Erie. From hence they travelled southwest till they reached the Mississippi. Part of them crossed the river, and they were thus divided. Those who went over, became, in time, the enemies of such as remained on its eastern banks, and were finally lost and forgotten from their memory.

Tarenyawagon, who was the patron of the home bands, did not fail, in this crisis, to direct their way also. After giving them practical instructions in war and hunting, he guided their footsteps in their journeys, south and east, until they had crossed the Alleganies, and reached the shores of the sea, on the coasts which are now called the Carolinas. They were directed to fix their residence on the banks of the *Cau-*

*tan-o*, that is, a pine in the water, now called Neuse river, in North Carolina. By this time their language was altered, but not so much but that they could understand each other. Here Tarenyawagon left them to hunt, increase and prosper, whilst he returned to direct the remaining Five Nations to form their confederacy. Thus far the Tuscarora annalist. History picks up the Tuscaroras precisely where tradition and fable leave them. On the settlement of Virginia and the Carolinas, they were found to be the first nation of any stability of purpose, after passing the Powhatanic tribes, in proceeding south. The intervening coast tribes were petty chieftaindoms, few in numbers, and disunited in action or policy. They were essentially ichthiophagi. They soon fell before the two-fold influence of idleness and rum, and have left little or no history, or traits, worth preserving. Such is the history of the Chowanokes,* the Maratocks, and the Mangoacks, who, in one hundred and twenty years from the date of Raleigh's patent, had dwindled from 6,000 to 46 bowmen.†

The Tuscaroras, who lived in the game country, on the skirts of the mountains, showed themselves at the mouths of Cautano or Neuse, Contentny, and Taw rivers. They were, at this

---

* Mr. Jefferson thinks (vide Notes, p. 152, London ed. of 1787), that this tribe was connected with the Tutelos, Nottaways and Meherrins of Virginia.

† Williamson.

time, numerous and warlike, and as inimical to the inhabitants of the Carolinas, as they were numerous. They were at war with the Catabas, the Cowetas, and the Cherokees. Numbers, bravery and success, and abundance of animal food, made them haughty, and they evinced the disposition of their northern brethren, by trying to subjugate and break down their neighbors. What they had done with red men, very effectually, it must be confessed at least with the Catabas, they thought they might do with the Huguenots of France, the cavaliers of England, and the Protestants of the baronetcy of Graffenried, in Germany. It is not improbable, indeed, that at a prior era, the Tuscaroras were the very people who had exterminated the colony left on Roanoke island, under the first attempts of Sir Walter Raleigh to colonize Virginia. But, if such were the fact—a mere conjecture at best— they mistook their present neighbors, and their own position, in attempting to repeat the act.

This scheme was, however, deeply laid, although it appeared to be a matter hastily executed. They had long felt a growing jealousy of the encroaching settlements, and gave vent to it, the first occasion that offered, by seizing Lawson, the surveyor-general of the province, on a trip up the Neuse, and after a kind of trial before a council, putting him to death. The Baron Graffenried, who was with him, and was also condemned, but saved, on an appeal on the ground of his being a man of rank, and not an Englishman; but they kept him a prisoner, while they proceeded to execute their ill-advised, and nefarious plot, which was nothing less than the massacre of the entire colony in one day. The day fixed for this tragedy, was the 22d of September, 1711. Williamson* thinks it was an impulsive movement arising from the killing of Lawson, who being a public officer, they felt themselves committed in a war, and resolved to proceed with the bloody work. For this purpose they divided themselves into small bands of six or seven, and entering the settlements at various points, they struck down with the tomahawk on one day, one hundred and thirty persons. To conceal their intentions, they had left their arms, and relied on their hatchets alone. In this plot, they were assisted by the sea-coast bands of Corees, Mattamuskeets, and Bear river Indians, some three or four tribes, denoting a league and maturity in the attempt. But the plan did not succeed to their wishes, for besides that the colony consisted then of nearly two thousand men, much spread, it must needs have happened that many at the time of attack, would be absent from their homes. The colonists rallied, and prepared to carry the war home to their subtle assailants. They asked the aid of South Carolina, which came gallantly to their rescue. The legislature of that province having granted four thousand pounds, placed Col. Barnwell at the

* History of North Carolina.

head of a small detachment of armed men, supported by a large body of Cherokees, Creeks and Catabas, the deadly enemies of the Tuscaroras. He killed, in various actions, thirty Tuscaroras, and fifty of the sea-coast auxiliaries, and took two hundred women and children of the latter prisoners, and returned. The war thus commenced was continued, with various results, for some few years. The aid of Virginia, as well as South Carolina, was invoked the next year. The Tuscaroras also made vigorous exertions. They were well provided with arms and ammunition, and despatched runners to the Senecas for aid. Their auxiliaries, the Mattamuskeets, Corees, and others, killed or made prisoners the next winter, forty inhabitants of the island of Roanoke or Croatan. The Tuscaroras prepared to maintain their power, by entrenching themselves behind a picketed work on the river Taw. This work, called fort *Naharuke*, stood on a plain beside a creek, and consisted of a rampart of earth, covering the whole ground occupied, defended with palisades. To protect themselves from artillery, they had dug within this wall, square pits of earth, six feet deep, covered with poles, and connected by a wall of earth. They were well provided with corn and ammunition, and had the means of standing a siege, had they made a wise provision for water. To obtain this necessary article, they relied on an artificial ditch leading to the stream.

To this aboriginal fort Col. Moore of South

Carolina, drove them from the lower country with 40 musketeers and 800 Indians, in the early part of the winter of 1713, after having been detained on his march by a deep snow. He immediately saw the mistake of the water trench, and placed cannon to rake it. He then fortified the only passage or point of land, where the Indians would be likely to escape, and began regular approaches to the work, which he entered on the 26th of March, 1713, taking 800 Tuscaroras prisoners. It is not said how many were killed. He had lost of his army, during the siege, 22 white, and 36 red men killed, and 29 of the former, and 50 of the latter wounded. The Cherokees and their allies claimed the prisoners, who were taken to the south, and sold as slaves, a part, as we are left to infer, being offered by the southern Indians, to appease the spirit of retaliation for prior losses by them.

This brought the tribe to terms, and they entered into preliminaries of peace, by which they agreed to deliver up twenty men, who were the contrivers of the plot, and who took Lawson and Graffenried; to restore all prisoners, horses and cattle, arms and other property; to treat and pursue the Mattamuskeets and their other allies, as enemies; and finally, to give two hostages for the peaceable conduct of each of their towns.

During the following summer, the chief, called King Blount, brought in thirty scalps from his miserably treated allies; "but the greater part of the nation," says the historian before quoted, "unable to contend, and unwilling to submit, removed to the northward, and joined the Seneca, and other confederate tribes on the frontiers of New York." (*Williamson.*) Those who remained, were to have settled between the Neuse and Taw rivers; but an Indian war having broken out in the southern colonies in 1715, only three months after the peace, with the Corees and their other former allies, the Tuscaroras, now the remains of a broken down tribe, feeble in numbers and power, obtained permission to settle on the *north* side of the Roanoke river, on a reservation, where some of them were living in 1803.

The whole number of Indians living in North Carolina in 1708, estimating their fighting men, were 1,608, of whom the Tuscaroras constituted 1,200, which would give them, on the ordinary principle of estimating their population, 6,000 souls. Two thirds of the whole number of their fighting men were captured at the taking of fort *Naharuke*, in 1713. How many were killed on other occasions is not certainly known; but it is probable that in this short war of but three years' duration, and owing to the desertion of families, death by sickness, want, and other casualties consequent upon the surrender of Naharuke, they sunk to almost immediate insignificance. Those who fled to their kindred in western New York, were never counted. They were estimated, perhaps high, at 200 warriors, in 1776. They were located, at first, immediately west of, and in juxtaposition to, the Oneidas; along with whom they are mentioned as being secured in their rights, by the treaty of Fort Stanwix, in 1784. But in fact they had no independent claim to territory, living merely as guests, although the confederacy had admitted them as an integral member, after their disastrous flight from North Carolina, calling themselves no longer the *Five*, but the *Six Nations*. The Senecas gave them lands on the Niagara ridge, after the American revolution; these were subsequently secured to them in a reservation made by the state, in the present bounds of Niagara county. Here they have continued to dwell, having added to their possessions, by an early purchase from the Holland Land Company, made with the avails of the sale of their reservation north of the Roanoke, in North Carolina.

But if the Tuscaroras have erred in policy, and sunk in numbers, with a rapidity and in a ratio unequalled by any other member of the confederacy, if we except the Onondagas and Cayugas, they may be said to have grown wise by experience. Low as their present numbers are, they hold an exalted rank among their brethren for industry, temperance, and their general advance in arts, agriculture and morals.

I found, on making the enumeration, 283 persons living in 53 families, of whom 151 were males and 167 females. These families cultivated the past year 2,080 acres of land, on which they raised 4,897 bushels of wheat, 3,515 of corn,

4,085 of oats, 1,166 of potatoes, besides limited quantities of peas, beans, buckwheat and turneps. They possess 336 neat cattle, 98 milch cows, making 7,537 pounds of butter, 153 horses, 215 sheep, and 596 hogs.

When it is considered that this enumeration gives an average of six neat cattle, three horses, (nearly), two milch cows (nearly), 10 hogs, and 92 bushels of wheat, and 966 of corn to each family, their capacity to sustain themselves, and their advance as agriculturists will be perceived. Fifty-nine ploughs were found amongst fifty-three families. They cut 195 acres of meadow to sustain their cattle. They had over 1,500 fruit trees, and dwelt in excellent frame or square-timber houses, well finished, and for the most part well furnished. I noticed one edifice of stone, in the process of building, seated on rising grounds, amidst shade trees, which denotes both wealth and taste. Other results of civilization are to be already observed. Among these there are no slight indications of classes of society, arranging themselves, as rich and poor, intelligent and ignorant, industrious and idle, moral and immoral.

Of the entire population, 63 are church members, and 231 members of temperance societies, which is a far higher proportion than is found in any other of the cantons.

The Tuscaroras were probably admitted into the confederacy about 1714. Nine years afterwards the Iroquois received the *Necariages*. Under this name the long expatriated Quatoghies, or Hurons, then living at Teiodonderoghie or Michilimackinac, were taken into the confederacy as the seventh tribe, or canton. This act was consummated in the reign of George II., at a public council held at Albany on the 30th May, 1723, on their own desire. A delegation of eighty men, who had their families with them, were present. Of this curious transaction but little is known. For although done in faith, it was not perceived that a tribe so far separated from the main body, although now reconciled, and officially incorporated, could not effectually coalesce and act as one. And accordingly, it does not appear by the subsequent history of the confederacy, that they ever came to recognize, permanently, the Necariages as a seventh nation. The foundation for this act of admission had been laid at a prior period by the daring and adroit policy of Adario, who had so skilfully contrived to shift the atrocity of his own act, in the capture of the Iroquois delegates on the St. Lawrence, on the governor-general of Canada.

It has been mentioned, in a preceding page, that the Iroquois recommended their political league as a model to the colonies, long before the American revolution was thought of. And it is remarkable that its typical character, in relation to our present union, should have been also sustained, in the feature of the admission, if not *annexation*, of new tribes, who became equal participants of all the original rights and privileges of the confederacy.

The *St. Regis* colony, or band, is an off-shoot of the Iroquois stock, but not a member of the confederacy. It originated in the efforts commenced about the middle of the 17th century, by the Roman catholic church of France, to draw the Iroquois into communion with that church. It was, however, but a part of the public policy, which originated in the reign of Louis XV., to colonize the Iroquois country, and wrest it from the power of the British crown. When this effort failed — replete as it was with wars, intrigues and embassies, battles and massacres, which make it the heroic age of our history — the persons who had become enlisted in the ritual observances of this church, were induced to withdraw from the body of the tribes, and settle on the banks of the St. Lawrence, in the area of the present county of St. Lawrence. It was, in effect, a missionary colony. Its members were mostly Mohawks, from Caughnawaga, with some Oneidas, and perhaps a few of the Onondagas, amongst whom there had been catholic missions and forts established, at early dates.

The exertions made to organize this new canton were, politically considered, at direct variance with the colonial policy of New York, and were therefore opposed by the person entrusted by the crown with Indian affairs, and also by the councils of the confederacy. Those persons who composed it assimilated in faith, and almost as a necessary consequence, they soon did so in politics.* They went off in small parties, secretly, and after they had become embodied and located, they were regarded, in effect, as foreign Indians, and were never recognized or admitted to a seat in the confederacy. The feeling caused by this separation, among the tribes themselves, amounted to bitterness, and it is a feeling which, I had occasion to observe on one occasion, is not forgotten by the existing cantons even at this day.

The St. Regis colony increased rapidly, but had some extra stimulants to promote its growth, its success being equally dear to the political and ecclesiastical policy of France. It became a thorn to the frontier towns and settlements of New England, during the whole of the old French war, so called, and of the American revolution. Some of the forays of this band into the Connecticut valley were productive of thrilling and heart-rending events, as those must have realized who have had their youthful sympathies excited by narrations of the touching captivities of the Howes and the Williamses, of that valley.

\* Some exceptions to this existed. The noted chief called Col. Louis, who rendered the American cause such essential service, during the siege of Fort Stanwix, in 1777, was of the St. Regis tribe, agreeably to information given to me, at Oneida Castle, the present year, by Abraham Dennie.

When the 54° parallel came to be drawn, under the provision of the treaty of Ghent, it cut the St. Regis settlement unequally in two, leaving the church and the larger portion of the Indian population within the bounds of Canada. Those who reside within the limits of New York, numbered two hundred and sixty souls in 1845.

## CHAPTER IV.

### EPOCH AND PRINCIPLES OF THE IROQUOIS LEAGUE.

OBJECTS OF RESEARCH—ERA OF THE CONFEDERACY—PRINCIPLES OF THEIR GOVERNMENT, AND THE TOTEMIC BOND—ANCIENT WORSHIP AND SYSTEM OF ASTRONOMY—WITCHCRAFT AND ITS THEORY, AND PRACTICAL EVILS—WIFE'S RIGHT TO PROPERTY: LIMITED NATURE OF MARRIAGE CONTRACT—IDEA OF VAMPYRES: TRADITIONS IN REFERENCE TO.

SOMETHING on this head appears desirable, if it be only to mitigate, in some degree, our historical ignorance, and want of accurate or precise information, touching it. The question of the principles of their social and political association, is one of equal interest and obscurity, and would justify a more extended inquiry than is here given.

Chronology finds its most difficult tasks in establishing dates among our aboriginal tribes. Pyrlaus, a missionary at the ancient site of Dionderoga, or Fort Hunter, writing between 1742 and 1748, states, as the result of the best conjectures he could form, from information derived from the Mohawks, that the alliance took place "one age, or the length of a man's life, before the white people came into the country."* He gives the following as the names of the sachems of the Five Nations, who met and formed the alliance: *Toganawita*, for the Mohawks; *Otatschechta*, for the Oneidas; *Tatotarho*, for the Onondagas; *Togahayon*, for the Cayugas; *Ganiatario* and *Satagaruyes*, for the Senecas.

The name of *Thannawage* is given as the first proposer of such an alliance. He was an aged Mohawk sachem. It was decided that these names should forever be kept in remembrance, by naming a person in each nation, through succeeding generations, after them.

Taking 1609, the era of the Dutch discovery, and estimating "a man's life," by the patriarchal and scriptural rule, we should not at the utmost have a more remote date than 1539,† as the origin of the confederacy. This would place the event eighteen years after the taking of Mexico by Cortes, and forty-seven years after the first voyage of Columbus. Cartier, who ascended the St. Lawrence to Hochelaga, the present site of Montreal, in 1535, demonstrates clearly, by his vocabulary of words, that a people who spoke a branch of the Iroquois language, was then at the place. This people is usually supposed to have been the Wyandots or Hurons.

---

* Trans. Hist. and Lit. Com. Am. Philo. Soc., vol. i., page 36.

† For other data on this topic, see the subsequent paper, in relation to the Onondagas, in which an earlier date is assigned. See also the article Oral Traditions.

But he makes no remark on a confederacy. He only denotes the attachment of the people to an old and paralytic sachem, or head chief, who wore a frontlet of dyed porcupine's skin.

Curious to obtain some clue to this era, or test of the preceding data, I made it a topic of inquiry. The Onondagas, the Tuscaroras, and the several bands, unite in a general tradition of the event of a confederacy, at the head of which they place Atotarho, (the same doubtless whose name is spelt Tatotarho above,) but amongst neither of these tribes is the era fixed. The dates employed by Cusick, the Tuscarora legendary, giving an extravagant antiquity to the confederation, are more entitled to the sympathy of the poet, than the attention of the historian, although other traditions stated by him debarring the dates, may be regarded as the actual traditions of his tribe. Were the dates moderate, which he generally employs to confer antiquity on his nation, they might inspire respect. But, like the Chinese astronomers, he loses no little as a native archæologist, by aspiring after too much.

Atotarho, who by these traditions was an Onondaga, is the great embodiment of Iroquois courage, wisdom and heroism, and in their narrations he is invested with allegoric traits, which exalt him to a kind of superhuman character. Unequalled in war and arts, his fame had spread abroad, and exalted the Onondaga nation to the highest pitch. He was placed at the head of the confederacy, and his name like that of King Arthur of the Round Table, or those of the Paladins of Charlemagne, was used after his death as an exemplar of glory and honor; while like that of Cæsar, it became perpetuated as the official title of the presiding chief. What is said by Pyrlaus respecting the mode of the transmission of the names of the first delegates to the council forming the confederacy, appears to be probable. It is true, so far as is known, but it seems that not only the name of the ruling chief, but the title of each minor officer in the council, as he who presents the message, he who stands by the chief, or *atotarho*, &c., is preserved to this day, by its being the name of an individual who exercises a similar office.

The best light I could personally obtain from tradition of the date of the event, namely, the era of the confederacy, came through a tradition handed down from Ezekiel Webster, an American, who at an early day settled among the Onondagas, learned their language, married the daughter of a chief, and became himself a man of great influence among them. Mr. Tyler, of Seneca Falls, son of one of the first settlers in the present county of Onondaga, informed me in a casual interview at Aurora, on the 13th of August, that his father had received this account from Webster's own lips, namely, that the confederation, as related by the Onondagas, took place about the length of one man's life before the white men appeared. A remarkable confirmation of the statement of Pyrlaus.* It must be admitted, however, that we cannot, without rejecting many positive traditions of the Iroquois themselves, refuse to concede a much earlier period to the first attempts of these interesting tribes to form a general political association. For eighty years before the American revolution, they, in friendly recommendation, held up their confederacy as a political model to the English colonies. (*See Colden.*) Their own first attempts to form themselves into one nation, may have borne the same relation to them and their subsequent condition as our early confederation of states bears to the present union; and this, instead of lasting a few years, as did ours, may have continued even for centuries, among so rude a people, before it could ripen into the bonds of empire.

Two elementary powers existed at an early day in the Iroquois cantons, namely, the civil and war chieftainships. There is abundant evidence, both in their own traditions, and in existing antiquarian remains, to show that they were at variance, in the early periods of their history, and fought against each other, and built fortifications to defend themselves. Partial leagues would naturally fail. League after league probably took place. When they came to see the folly of such a course, and proposed to confede-

* A Seneca tradition which is hereafter noticed, places the event of the confederation four years before the appearance of Hudson in his ship, in the bay of New York.

rate on enlarged principles, and direct their arms exclusively against others, the question doubtless arose, how they should be represented in the general council. It is clear, from the preceding remarks on the era of the confederation, whatever age we assign to the era itself, that the *rakowanas, (Mohawk,)* or leading chiefs of each of the five cantons, did not assemble. Power was assigned to, and concentrated on, one individual, who stood as the federal representative of his canton in its sovereign capacity. It was only to the Senecas that two representatives, of this senatorial dignity, were assigned; a conclusive evidence that they were, at this era, estimated at double the numerical strength of the highest of the other four cantons. By these six men, who appear rather in the capacity of embassadors, forming the principles of a treaty, or league, the modern confederacy, as known to us, was organized. Tradition says that this treaty of alliance was held at Onondaga, where the central council fire of the confederacy, organized under it, was also originally fixed, and has permanently remained.

No one has attended to the operations of the Iroquois government and polity, as they are developed in their councils and meetings for general consultation and action, without perceiving a degree of intricacy in its workings, which it is difficult to grasp. Or rather, the obscurity may be said to grow out of the little time and the imperfect opportunities which casual observers have to devote to the object. For, maturely considered, there is no inherent difficulty in the way. It seems clear that they came together as independent tribes, who, at an early age, had all proceeded from the same parental stock, but who, after an indefinite period of fightings and wars, became convinced of the short-sightedness of such a course, and fell on the plan of a confederation which should produce general action, and yet leave the several members free, both in their internal polity, and in the exercise of most of their co-tribal powers. It was clearly a confederation for common purposes of defence and offence, and not a perfect union. Each tribe, or more properly speaking, canton, was still governed by its own chiefs, civil and military. They came together in general councils, by sachems, exercising the power of delegates.

These delegates or sages came in their hereditary or elective character, as the case might be, or as the customs and laws of the tribe, in its popular character, had decided. But their voices were in all cases, either prompted by prior expressions of the warriors and wise men, or were to be ratified by these known powers. However invested with authority, they but spoke the popular will. The relative power of the cantons is denoted, and appears as a question that was already settled, at the first formal general council for the purpose of confederating. For we there see precisely the same tribal representation, which has obtained ever after and still prevails; that is to say, the Mohawks, the Oneidas, the Onondagas, and the Cayugas, had each one chief, and the Senecas two, making six supreme dignitaries or state counsellors. That their powers were merely advisory and interlocutory, and that they aimed to come to harmonious results, by the mere interchange of opinion, without any formal or solemn vote, is evident, from all that we know, or can gather from their still existing institutions. There appeared to have been no penalties—no forfeiture of rights—no binding or coercive power, to be visited on tribes or chiefs, beyond that of *opinion.* Popular disapproval was the Iroquois penalty here and elsewhere. It is equally clear, however, that a single negative voice or opinion, was of the highest efficacy. A unanimous decision, not a decision on the majority principle, was required. The latter was a refinement, and an advance in polity, which they had not certainly reached, although they seem inclined now to follow it; and herein we may perceive the great power and efficacy of their old decisions. These decisions were, in their effects, clothed with all the power of the most full popular will. For what each of the senatorial chiefs or delegates, and all the cantons, pronounced proper, there was no one, in a patriarchal community, to lisp a word against.

So little power was abstracted from each tribe, and conceded to the federative council as a fixed government, that it seems not without scrutiny, that we can perceive there is *any*. This is, however, certain. One of the six primary sachems was selected to preside over the general councils. His power was, however, exclusively of a civil character, and extended but little beyond that of a moderator, but he was a moderator for life, or during the time he retained the right and full use of his faculties, or until just cause of dissatisfaction should bring the question of a successor before the council. This head officer, had also authority to light the council fire — that is to say, he could send messengers, and was, if so desired, bound to send messengers to assemble the general council. The act, and the symbol of the act, were both in his hands. He summoned the chiefs, and actually lit the sacred fire, at whose blaze their pipes were lighted. Thus limited, and having no other administrative power, but to appoint his own *har-yar-do-ah*, aid or pipe-bearer, and messengers, he enjoyed his executive dignity; but had little more power when the sessions were closed, than belonged to every leading chief of the component tribes. He was himself bound to respect the messages of the tribal chiefs, and receive the runners who were sent to him from the frontiers with news, and he thus performed merely and exactly the will of each tribe, thus expressed. He was never in advance of the popular will. The whole hereditary machinery was made subservient to this. And he was limited to the performance of these slender, and popular duties. He might, it is true, if a man of eloquence, talents, or bravery, be also the ruling civil chief of his tribe, and furthermore, its war captain in the field. And such is known to have actually been the character and standing of Atotarho, the first presiding chief in their federative councils. He was a man of energy and high renown. And such was the estimation in which he was held in his life time, and the popular veneration for his character after death, that, as above denoted, his name became the distinctive title for the office. Thus much is preserved by tradition, and the office and title of the atotarho, as presiding sachem, is not yet extinct, although the tribes have no longer wars to prosecute, or foreign embassadors to reply to.

But how, it may be asked, is a government so purely popular, and so simple and essentially advisory in its character, to be reconciled with the laws of hereditary descent, fixed by the establishment of heraldic devices, and bringing its proportion of weak and incompetent minds into office, and with the actual power it exercised, and the fame it acquired? To answer this question, and to show how the aristocratic and democratic principles were made to harmonize, in the Iroquois government, it will be necessary to go back, and examine the law of descent among the tribes, together with the curious and intricate principles of the *totemic bond*.

Nothing is more fully under the cognizance

of observers of the manners and customs of this people, than the fact of the entire mass of a canton or tribe being separated into distinct clans, each of them distinguished by the name and device of some quadruped, bird, or other object in the animal kingdom. This device is called, among the Algonquins (where the same separation into families or clans exists), *totem*, and we shall employ the term here, as being already well known to writers. But while the Algonquins have made no other use of it, but to trace consanguinity, or at least, remote affinities of families, and while they have also separated into wild independencies and tribes, who have assumed new tribal names, and wandered and crossed each other's track and boundaries in a thousand ways, the Iroquois have turned it to account by assuming it as the very basis of their political and tribal bond. How far fixity of territorial possession and proximity of location may have favored or led to the establishment of this new bond, need not be inquired into here; but, while we express no opinion favorable to the remote antiquity of their residence in the north, it must be evident that this tie would have lost all its binding force if the Alleghanies, the great lakes, or any other very wide geographical areas, had been interposed between them, and thus interrupted frequent and full intercourse and united action. A government wholly verbal, must be conceded to have required this proximity and nearness of access. The Senecas may be selected as an example of the influence of the totemic bond. This canton is still the most numerous of the existing Iroquois tribes. By the recent census, (see p. 102 ante,) they number over two thousand four hundred souls. This population is, theoretically, separated into eight clans or original families, who are distinguished respectively by the totems of the wolf, the bear, the turtle, the deer, the beaver, the falcon, the crane and the plover. Theory at this time, founded doubtless on actual consanguinity in their inceptive age, makes these clans brothers. It is contrary to their usages that near kindred should intermarry, and the ancient rule interdicts all intermarriage between persons of the same clan. They must marry into a clan whose totem is different from their own. A wolf or turtle male cannot marry a wolf or turtle female. There is an interdict of consanguinity. By this custom the purity of blood is preserved, while the tie of relationship between the clans themselves is strengthened or enlarged.

But by far the most singular principle connected with totems, the sign manual of alliance, is the limitation of descent exclusively to the line of the female. Owing to this prohibition, a chieftain's son cannot succeed him in office, but in case of his death, the right of descent being in the chief's mother, he would be succeeded, not by one of his male children, but by his brother;* or failing in this, by the son of his sister, or by some direct, however remote, descendant of the maternal line. Thus he might be succeeded by his own grandson, by a daughter, but not by a son. It is in this way that the line of chieftainships is continually deflected or refreshed, and family dynasties broken up.

While the law of descent is fully recognized, the free will of the female to choose a husband, from any of the other seven clans, excluding only her own, is made to govern and determine the distribution of political power, and to fix the political character of the tribe. Another peculiarity may be here stated. The son of a chief's daughter is necessarily destined to inherit the honors of the chieftainship; yet the validity of the claim must, on his reaching the proper age, be submitted to and recognized by a council of the whole canton. If approved, a day is appointed for the recognition, and he is formally installed into office. Incapacity is always, however, without exception, recognized as a valid objection to the approval of the council.

Had this law of descent prevailed among the Jews, whose customs have been so often appealed to, in connection with our red race, neither David nor Solomon would ever have sat on the throne. It would be easy, did the purposes of this work require it, to show, by other references,

---

* Thus Hendrick, who fell at the battle of Lake George, in 1755, was succeeded, in the Mohawk canton, by his brother Abraham, and not by his son.

the futility of the proofs, derived from the supposed coincidence of customs, which have been brought forward with so much learning, and so little of the true spirit of research, to prove the descent of the American aborigines from that ancient and peculiar people. But if theorists have failed on this ground, what shall we say of that course of reasoning which lays much stress on the most slender evidences of nativity, in the instance of the great Mohawk sachem, to prove the superior chances of recurring talent in the line of hereditary descent, and the legitimacy of his actual claims to the chieftainship, on the score of paternal right?*

What was true of the totemic organization of the Senecas, was equally so of the Mohawks, and of each of the other cantons. Each canton consisted, like the Senecas, of the clans of the wolf, bear, turtle, beaver, deer, falcon, plover and crane. But each of these clans were increments of reorganizations of one of the eight original clans. They were brothers, and appealed to their respective totems as a proof of original

* This remark is not made to depreciate the literary merits of the esteemed and lamented author of the Life of Brant, but as being simply due to the cause of truth. Few men have better earned the respect and remembrance of the public, than William L. Stone, whose whole life was an example of what energy and talents can achieve. It was not, indeed, to be expected that the incessant duties of the diurnal press should permit historical scrutiny into a matter very obscure in itself, and of which the details are only to be gleaned after laborious search at remote points.

consanguinity. They were entitled to the same rites of hospitality, in the lodges of their affiliated totems abroad, that they were entitled to at home. The affiliated mark on the lodge was a sufficient welcome of entrance and temporary abode. It results, therefore, that there were but eight original family clans, estimating at the maximum number existing in six cantonal departments, or tribes, and that the entire six tribes were bound together, politically, by these eight family ties. As a matter of course, each clan was not equally numerous in each tribe. This would depend on accidental circumstances and natural laws; but it is an argument in favor of the antiquity of the people, or the confederacy, that each of the tribes had organized in each of the respective clans. For we cannot suppose that at first there was a systematic, far less an equal division of the clans, or that their original separation into separate tribes, or cantons, was the result of a considerate formal public act. This would be to reverse the ordinary progress of tribes and nations who, in early ages, separate from circumstances and causes wholly casual, such as the ambition or feuds of chiefs, the desire of finding better places to live, easier means of subsistence, &c.

In the condition of a people, living in a government so purely patriarchal, following game for a subsistence, and making wars to enlarge or defend their hunting grounds, the oldest and most respected man of his clan or totem, would necessarily be its sachem or political head. We must assume that to be a fixed and settled principle of their simple constitution and verbal laws, which appears, from all we know, to have been so. Letters, they had none, and their traditions on this head are to be gleaned from scattered and broken sources, which do not always coincide.

If each clan had its leading sachem or chief, there were eight principal chiefs in each canton. Consequently, when the confederacy consisted of five cantons, there were forty *rakowanas*, (*Mohawk*,) or head chiefs. These were the recognized leaders and magistrates in the villages; but in effect, in a community thus constituted, each rakowana or ruling chief of a clan, has a number of aids, *mishinawas*, (*Algonquin*,) and minor officials, who were also regarded as semi-sachems, or chiefs. This number is always indefinite and fluctuating, but may be supposed to be, in relation to the ruling rakowana, as at least five to one. This would give to each canton forty inferior chiefs, and to the five cantons, two hundred, denoting a distribution of power and civil organization, which, acting in union, must have been very efficacious; and the more so, when we consider that all their political movements were entirely of a popular cast, and carried with them the voice of every man in the canton.

This appears to have been the standing civil organization; but it was entirely independent of the military system. War chiefs appear ever to have derived their authority from courage and capacity in war, and to have risen up as they were required in each canton. The *tekarahogea*, or war captain, founded his rights and powers in the Indian camp, on former triumphs and present capacity; but the office does not appear to have been a general one, recognized by their constitution. All males were bound to render military service by custom and opinion, but by nothing else. Disgrace and cowardice were the penalties, but they were penalties more binding than oaths or bonds among civilized communities, and always kept their ranks full. All war parties were, of course, volunteers. It seems that all able bodied males over fourteen, were esteemed capable of taking the war path; the early development of martial power being considered of all traits the most honorable. No title was more honored than that of *roskeahragehte*, (*Mohawk*,) or warrior.

There was no baggage to encumber the march of an Iroquois army. The decision of Alexander and the policy of Bonaparte were alike unnecessary here. Each Iroquois warrior supplied and carried his own arms and provisions. He joined the war dance, the analagous term for enlistment, for the particular expedition in hand. If it failed, or another force was required, other captains called for other volunteers, and sung their war songs to inflame the ardor of the young. Taunts and irony of the deepest character, were, on these occasions, flung at the character of the enemy. The war chief lifted his tomahawk as if actually engaged in combat, and in imagination he stamped his enemy under foot, while he symbolically tore off his scalp, and uttered his sharp *sasakwon, (Algonquin,)* or war whoop.

If it be inquired why this people, with so comparatively small a population, carried their wars to such an extent, and acquired, probably in no great time, so wide a sway and power over the other tribes of the continent, the reply will appear, in a great measure, in this efficient war organization. It may be said that other tribes had the same principles. But these eastern and western tribes had feeble or divided counsels. Each tribe was a sovereignty by itself, and their powers were tasked by home wars, without attempts at remote conquest. There is nothing to denote that the number of war chiefs was ever settled or fixed. Time and chance determined this, as we observe it in the Algonquin and other American stocks. Fixity, in the number of the civil chiefs, was indeed rather a theory than an actuality, and the number must have been perpetually fluctuating, according to obvious circumstances.

But while the theory of the Iroquois government thus distributed its powers between two classes of chiefs, one of which ruled in the council, and the other in the field, there was a third power of controlling influence in both, which respected, it is true, this ancient theory, but which annulled, confirmed, originated, or set aside all other power. I allude to the popular will as exercised by the warriors. Whatever was proposed, had to come under the voice of the armed men, who had the free right, at all times, to assemble in council, and put their approval or veto on every measure. Practically considered, a purer democracy, perhaps, never existed. The chiefs themselves had no power in advance of public sentiment, or else it was their policy, as we see it at this day, to express no such power, but rather to keep in abeyance of, or be the mere agents of, the popular will. In all negotiations, such absolute power is disclaimed by them. Acting on principles of the highest diplomacy, they invariably defer general answers, until a reference can be had to the warriors or men. They risk nothing by taking grounds in doubtful positions in advance, and the consequence is that the results of most Indian councils are unanimous.

There was yet a reserved power in the Iroquois councils which deserves to be mentioned. I allude to the power of the matrons. This was an acknowledged power of a conservative character, which might, at all times, be brought into requisition, whenever policy required it. And it exists to-day as incontestibly as it did centuries ago. They were entrusted with the power to propose a cessation of arms. They were literally peace-makers. A proposition from the matrons to drop the war club, could be made without compromising the character of the tribe for bravery; and accordingly, we find, in the ancient organization, that there was a male functionary, an acknowledged speaker, who was called the representative or messenger of the matrons. These matrons sat in council, but it must needs have been seldom that a female possessed the kind of eloquence suitable to public assemblies; and beyond this there was a sentiment of respect due to the female class, which led the tribes, at their general organization, to create this office.

Councils, so organized, so perpetually and truly swayed by popular will, gave the greatest scope for eloquence. Eloquence, in the aborigines, takes the place entirely of books and letters. It is the only means of acting on the multitude, and we find that it was, from the earliest times, strenuously and successfully cultivated by the Iroquois. By far the best and most abundant specimens of native eloquence we possess are from this stock. And their history is replete in proofs that the chiefs employed it, not only in their internal affairs and negotiations, but in teaching their people to appreciate their rights and the principles of their government.

Notices of the manner of holding a recent council of these cantons, called for the consideration of national questions, are given, in the miscellaneous items, appended to this work.

It was a striking peculiarity of the ancient religious system of the Iroquois that, once a year, the priesthood supplied the people with sacred fire. For this purpose, a set time was announced for the ruling priest's visit. The entire village was apprized of this visit, and the master of each lodge was expected to be prepared for this annual rite. Preliminary to the visit, his lodge fire was carefully put out and ashes scattered about it, as a symbolic sign of desolation and want. Deprived of this element, they were also deprived of its symbolic influence, the sustaining aid and countenance of the supreme power, whose image they recognized in the sun.

It was to relieve this want, and excite hope and animation in breasts which had throbbed with dread, that the priest visited the lodge. Exhibiting the insignia of the sacerdotal office, he proceeded to invoke the Master of Life in their behalf, and ended his mission by striking fire from the flint, or from percussion, and lighting anew the domestic fire. The lodge was then swept and garnished anew, and a feast succeeded.

This sacred service annually performed, had the effect to fix and increase the reverence of the people for the priestly office. It acted as a renewal of their ecclesiastical fealty; and the consequence was, that the institution of the priesthood among these cantons was deeply and firmly seated. Whether this rite had any connection with the period of the solstices, or with the commencement of the lunar year, is not known, but is highly probable. That men living in the open air, who are regardful of the celestial phenomena, should not have noted the equinoxes, is not probable. They must have necessarily known the solstices by the observation of capes and mountains, which cast their shadows from points and describe angles so very diverse at the periods of the sun's greatest recession, or return. Yet we know not that the time of such extreme withdrawal and return marked and completed the circle of the year. Their year was, as in all the Algonquin tribes, a lunar year. It consisted of twelve or thirteen moons, each of which is distinctly named. Thirteen moons of 28 days each, counting from visible phase to phase, make a year of 364 days, or 12 moons of 30 days make up the old Persian year of 365 days, which is the greatest astronomical accuracy reached by the North American tribes.

That the close of the lunar series should have been the period of putting out the fire, and the beginning of the next, the time of relumination, from new fire, is so consonant to analogy in the tropical tribes, as to be probable.

The rite itself offers a striking coincidence, with that solemn performance at the close of each year, by the Aztec priests, in the valley of Mexico, and may not unreasonably be supposed to denote a common origin for the belief. The northern tribes had, however, dropped from their ritual, if it ever was in that of their remote ancestors, the horrid rite, so revolting in the Aztec annals, of *human sacrifice*. For although prisoners were burned at the stake, this was not an act of the priesthood. It was a purely popular effervescence of revenge for losses of friends in war, or some other acts done by the enemy. Such sacrifices appeased the popular cry — all classes, young and old, rejoiced in them. They were looked on alone as an evidence of their nation's power; and by it the warriors also showed their regard for the relations of the bereaved. The widow of the warrior dried her tears. The children rejoiced — they hardly knew why — it was the triumph of the nation. And they were thus educated to regard the public burning of prisoners as a proper and glorious deed. Women, indeed, rejoiced in it apparently more than men. It seemed a solace for the loss of their progeny. And all authors agree in attributing to the older females the most extravagant and repulsive acts of participation and rejoicing in these warlike rites.

The belief in witchcraft prevailed extensively among the North American tribes. It is known that even in modern times, it was one of the principal means used by the Shawnee prophet to rid himself of his opponents, and that the venerable Shawnee chief, Tarhe, and others, were sacrificed to this diabolical spirit.

Among the Iroquois the belief was universal, and its effects upon their prosperity and population, if tradition is to be credited, were at times appalling. The theory of the popular belief, as it existed in the several cantons, was this. The witches and wizzards constituted a secret association, which met at night to consult on mischief, and each was bound to inviolable secrecy. They say this fraternity first arose among the Nanticokes. A witch or wizzard had power to turn into a fox or wolf, and run very swift, emitting flashes of light. They could also transform themselves into a turkey or big owl, and fly very fast. If detected, or hotly pursued, they could change into a stone or rotten log. They sought carefully to procure the poison of snakes or poisonous roots, to effect their purposes. They could blow hairs or worms into a person.

While in Onondaga, James Gould, one of the original settlers on the Military tract, told me that he had been intimate with Webster, the naturalized Onondaga, who told him many things respecting the ancient laws and customs of this people. Amongst them there was a curious reminiscence on the subject of witchcraft. Webster had heard this from an aged Onondaga, whom he conversed with during a visit which he once made to Canada. This Onondaga said that he had formerly lived near the old church on the Kasonda creek, near Jamesville, where there was in old times a populous Indian village. One evening, he said, whilst he lived there, he stepped out of his lodge, and immediately sank in the earth, and found himself in a large room, surrounded by three hundred witches and wizzards. Next morning he went to the council and told the chiefs of this extraordinary occurrence. They asked him whether he could not identify the persons. He said he could. They then accompanied him on a visit to all the lodges, where he pointed out *this* and *that* one, who were marked for execution. Before this inquiry was ended, a very large number of persons of both sexes were killed. He said ——* hundred.

Another tradition says that about fifty persons were burned to death at the Onondaga castle for witches.

The delusion prevailed among all the cantons. The last persons executed for witchcraft among the Oneidas, suffered about forty years ago. They were two females. The executioner was the notorious Hon Yost, of revolutionary memory. He entered the lodge, according to a prior decree of the council, and struck them down with a tomahawk. One was found in the lodge; the other suffered near the lodge door.

Marriage among the Iroquois, appears to be a verbal contract between the parties, which does not affect the rights of property. Goods, per-

---

\* Having doubts, I omit to fill this blank.

sonal effects, or valuables of any kind, personal or real, which were the wife's before, remain so after marriage. Should any of these be used by the husband, he is bound to restore the property or its worth, in the event of separation. It is not uncommon at present to find a husband indebted to a wife for moneys loaned of her, derived from payments or property, which she owned, and still owns, in her own right; and it is a cause of union in some cases where, without this obligation, a separation would probably ensue.

Marriage is therefore a personal agreement, requiring neither civil nor ecclesiastical sanction, but not a union of the rights of property. Descent being counted by the female, may be either an original cause or effect of this unique law.

The idea of the *vampyre*, among the Iroquois, I first noticed, although it is but half developed, in Cusick, who in his historical tract, (p. 30,) relates the incident of a man and his wife, and another person, taking shelter for the night, in a structure called the *house of the dead*. This scene is laid in the Oneida canton. After the light was extinguished, and they sought repose, a noise as if of a person gnawing was heard. The husband got up and rekindled the fire, and found that the flesh of one of the dead persons had been eaten by a ghost. This is Tuscarora authority. To test the superstition, I made inquiries on the subject, in some of the other cantons. There was found to be a popular belief in the idea of certain carnivorous ghosts, who eat the dead, among the Senecas, and it may be found to exist among the other tribes. It was still doubtful whether living persons were attacked, and if so, by sucking their blood in nocturnal visits. A well informed Seneca stated to me, that his people had numerous stories on this general head. He related one, in which a hunter and his wife, being belated and pushed by stress of weather, took shelter in a dead house. (This dead house appears to have been an ancient custom.) Having gone to repose, the wife was alarmed by sounds, resembling drinking and mastication, as if proceeding from some invisible source, very near her. She stirred the embers, and found the blood of her husband streaming over the ground. He was dead. He had been imperceptibly devoured in part, by a vampyre. She fled, but soon heard behind her, *the war whoop of the ghost*. The chase, the arts she resorted to, and her final escape, by entering a hollow log, and her deliverance thence, are minutely detailed. The approach of daylight, and *the symbolical character of the ghost's war club*, saved her. But the incidents are of no particular interest here, except as serving to show the existence of this ancient superstition of the human mind.

Their belief on the subject is, that ghosts gorge themselves on the blood and flesh of both dead and *living* bodies, if the latter be asleep. Whether this is the disposition of all ghosts, or the power and propensity be confined to those of particular persons, who have been cannibals in life, or have otherwise come under the condemnation of public feeling, is not known. It is believed, that such doomed spirits creep into the lodges of men at night, and during sleep suck their blood, and eat their flesh. They are invisible. Farther inquiries on this subject are required. Heretofore, we have heard much of witchcraft and necromancy among the North American Indians. The belief in these, appears to be universal. I know not a tribe, east or west of the Alleghanies, where it *is* not, or *was* not, formerly common. Transformations and the doctrine of metempsychosis, are equally common. But hitherto, the horrid idea of the vampyre has not been noticed. It is a Greek idea, and contrary to the general traits of the Indian mind, and not of an *Asiatic* cast.

The nations of Europe, who are most under the influence of this belief, in modern days, appear to be the Russians, Servians, Lithuanians, and modern Greeks. Have we then, an element in the Iroquois tribes, which we are to search for among the nations who anciently bordered on the Mediterranean? This favors the early and oft-repeated idea of a Phœnician element of population in the early constituents of our western hemisphere. If there be such an element, in the history of the past, it must, like all foreign intrusions of the kind, soon have gone down by amalgamation. Yet, if there be any tribe, in the whole ample range of America, who have manifested traits of Grecian firmness and association, it is the Iroquois.

## CHAPTER V.

### EARLY WARS AND POLITICAL RELATIONS OF THE IROQUOIS WITH THE OTHER NORTH AMERICAN TRIBES.

War with an Ancient People called Alleghans — Lenno Lenapees, or Delawares — Cherokees, their History and Language — Wyandots, and the Causes of their Separation — Eries — Adirondacks — Mohegans and Munsees, Manhattans and Metöacs — Atawawas — Nipercineans, or Algonquins Proper — Illinois, and their Congeners — Miamis, in their Triune Division of Tribes — Chippewa, or Odjibwa Group, in their multiplied Bands and Sub-Tribes — Shawnees — Susquehannocks — Powhattan League on the Southern Atlantic Coasts — Catabas — Muscogees and Appalachians — Choctaws — Musquakees and Sauks, and Minor Algonquin Tribes of late Origin — Owegungas, Abenakis, and New England Tribes generally.

To detail the wars of the Iroquois with the other tribes and groups of tribes in North America, would be to write the history of the principal nations who, since our knowledge of the country, have been located east of the Rocky mountains, and north of the Gulf of Mexico. Nothing of this kind is, in fact, thought of; but it appeared proper, in adverting to the former power and position of this warlike confederacy of tribes, who have been, not inaptly, termed the Romans of the new world, to give a brief summary of the chief tribes, who, from time to time, disputed their supremacy, or incurred their ire.

Judging from the monumental remains, in the shape of forts and tumuli, left in the land, there appear to have been extensive wars and combinations of tribes, who battled for supremacy, both east and west of the Alleghanies, long anterior to our earliest knowledge of the country. We should infer this from antiquarian evidence, were there no traditions, of any kind, lingering in the minds of the successors of these antique confederacies, at the earliest recorded dates. Such traditions were, however, to be found, in early relations of several of the leading tribes, north and south. One of the traditions of this kind, which appears to be entitled to general respect, and is sanctioned by remaining names, in the geography of the country, relates to a powerful and warlike nation, variously called, by different tribes, but who are best known, and may be well distinguished, among our antique tribes, as

*Alleghans.*—This is the term which Colden preserves for them on the earliest map which accompanied his history, and it has attached itself, in one of its modified forms, by early popular usage, to the principal chain of mountains, which traverses the United States, east of the Mississippi, from south to north. Lenapee tradition *(Vide Am. Philo. Trans. Hist. series)* affirms that this ancient people were conquered and driven off, from their position *in* and *west* of the Alleghanies, by a league between themselves and the Iroquois. The question of the former military power and influence of the Alleghans, and the probability of their having erected the ancient forts and mounds in the western country, is examined cursorily, under the head of Topical Inquiries, in a subsequent page. Materials exist, in the geographical names of western Pennsylvania and New York, for denoting the probable spread of this people to the sources of several of the principal streams east of the Alleghanies; but neither time nor space permit the pursuit of the inquiry here.

*Lenno Lenapees.*—There is reason to acquiesce, to a certain extent, in both the claim to antiquity and their ancient position, in the great Algonquin family, claimed by this people. It is believed that there are no members of this generic family of tribes, certainly none of the existing tribes in the north and west, who are known to us personally, who do not acknowledge the ancient Lenapees, under the title of grandfather. Even the Cherokees, who are not of this group of languages, bestow the same title on them, if the information recently derived from a person[*] well acquainted with their language and customs, be correct. The political relations of the Iroquois

---

[*] Mr. Wheeler, a brother-in-law of the chief *Stand Watie*.

to this people, whose descendants are known to us, in modern times, under the name of Delawares, appear to have been intimate, at an ancient era. At what period they changed their relations with them, from allies to conquerors, and under what circumstances, are unknown, at least on authority which carries with it much weight. The idea put forth by the modern Delawares, that they had *voluntarily* assumed the attitude of peace-makers, and relinquished the war cry and battle lance, and thus been, as it were, "beguiled" into the condition of a conquered people, may be one that had the power to please a Delaware ear, under the mortification of defeat or humiliation; but is contrary to all known principles in the rise or fall of tribes and nations, and unworthy of historical credence. That they ceded to William Penn the lands on the banks of the Lenapiwehittuk, on which Philadelphia now stands, is matter of undisputed record, as well as some other cessions of lands within the geographical area of Pennsylvania. But it is seen, by the treaties concluded at Lancaster, which are preserved in Colden, that cessions of a subsequent date, were considered invalid without the assent of the Iroquois, and that the latter claimed and exercised the power to confirm or disannul such territorial cessions. They spoke and acted with a degree of pride and arrogance, in those councils, which nothing but conscious power, and long-admitted supremacy could have induced the Delawares, brave and expert as they were as warriors, to submit to. That they had fallen under the Iroquois power, prior to the settlement of the English colonies, is evident. No battles between them are recorded to have taken place, after the earliest plantations were made, but the rupture was still open when the Dutch built fort Orange, on the Hudson, for they used their utmost influence to bring about a permanent pacification in the noted convocation of the two parties, which assembled on the waters of the Tawasentha, near that fort, about 1630. It is believed that this treaty of amity was faithfully kept, ever afterwards, by both Delawares and Iroquois. And it is probable that the Delaware tale of peace-makers, which has been alluded to, as calculated to sooth their pride, was based on this general convocation.

*Mohegans, Munsees, Manhattans, Metöacs,* and other affiliated tribes and bands of Algonquin lineage, inhabited the banks of the Hudson and the islands, bay and seaboard of New York, including Long Island, during the early periods of the rise of the Iroquois confederacy.

We may take the opening of the 16th century, as the period to examine the state of this question. Materials for the earlier eras of it, exist in the publications of Van Der Donck and other Dutch writers, which are to be found in the libraries of Holland. The manuscript records of Beaverwyck and New Amsterdam, abound also in minor and illustrative particulars. Much has, doubtless, been lost by the sale of the papers of the Dutch West India Company in Holland in 1820. The documents rescued by Mr. Brodhead, the historical agent of New York, and now deposited in the secretary of state's office, at Albany, may be profitably examined. Other sources of information, such as the early missionary journals of the period, may throw further light on the period.

The Mohawks, who, in the symbolic language of the natives, stood at the eastern door of the confederacy, were the chief agents in carrying the Iroquois conquests towards the sea coast. From their two most southerly positions, the ancient towns of Origonewantel, the Mohawk river, and Tawasentha, on the Hudson, they pushed their conquests to the bay and islands of New York. The tribes, on both banks of the Hudson, shrank before their war cry. They invaded the little independent tribes of the Metöacs on Long Island. They put the Connecticut and Massachusetts tribes in terror. They laid the Manhattans and their allies under the annual tribute of a quantity of shells suitable for wampum — the most valuable article in the exchanges of the natives — the *native coin*, in fact, of the new world. The period is one of much interest. We have the record of many battles and ambuscades, on the Hudson and its waters. The Mohegans finally retired over the highlands east of them into the valley of the Housatonic. The Munsees and Nanticokes retired to the Delaware river, and reunited with their kindred, the

Lenapees, or modern Delawares. The Manhattans, and numerous other bands and sub-tribes, melted away under the influence of liquor, and died in their tracks. While their natural resources of game failed, they were inadequate to commence the arts of agriculture, and fell, the double victims of inanity and the love of alcohol. They possessed courage, but were weakened by internal divisions. It was on the territories held by them, that European population first and chiefly pressed; and they felt their power and population sink more surely and fully under the evils, resulting to them, from a higher type of civilization in the intruding race, than from the Iroquois war club and scalping knife.

*Adirondacks.*—This is a term bestowed by the Iroquois, in derision, on the tribes who appear, at an early day, to have descended the Utawas river, and occupied the left banks of the St. Lawrence, above the present site of Quebec, about the close of the 15th century. It is said to signify men who eat trees, in allusion to their using the bark of certain trees for food, when reduced to straits, in their war excursions. The French, who entered the St. Lawrence from the gulf, called the same people Algonquins — a generic appellation, which has been long employed and come into universal use, among historians and philologists.

According to early accounts, the Adirondacks had preceded the Iroquois in arts and attainments. They were expert hunters, and brave and enterprising warriors. They had spread wide over the northern latitudes and longitudes, and by the force of affiliation, assumed the political condition of confederates. In this view they forestalled the Iroquois, and it is clearly to this people that the Tuscarora archæologist, Cusick, alludes, in speaking of an ancient northern confederacy. Even after the first settlement of the Canadas, they were a thorn in the sides of the *Nodowas*, as they called the Iroquois, and by such incursions as those of the indomitable Piskaret, they carried terror into the territories of their still but imperfectly united cantons. Such, at least, are the accounts of the early French writers, which are, essentially, adopted by Colden, the best English colonial historian of the Iroquois.

The term *Algonquin* applies to a very wide circle of tribes, east, west, north and south, of the point on the banks of the St. Lawrence above denoted. While the French missionaries bestowed it on a remnant of the valley race, whom they gathered together at the Lake of Two Mountains on the Utawas, writers, traders, and missionaries at large, extended it to all tribes on the North American continent who spoke the same generic language, although it differed considerably, at remote points, in idioms. Thus, all the native languages in New England, except the Abenaki, were types of the Algonquin; and the farthest tribes of the Illinois and the lakes, were found to be of the same stock. The Iroquois term of Adirondack extended generally to all those tribes against whom they warred as enemies, although the events of these wars gave them specific names for particular branches of them, as the Chictagahs, Twightwies, &c., &c.

*Owegungas.*—Under this name the Iroquois denoted the Abenakis, Micmacs, and Etchemens, who occupied portions of Maine, and the portions of the northern Atlantic coasts, embracing New Brunswick, Nova Scotia and Maine.

*Shawnees.*—After the defeat of this tribe by the Cherokees, while they dwelt on the Savannah river in Georgia and South Carolina, they were received in the north by their kinsfolk and allies, the Lenapees or Delawares, and became involved in a war with the Iroquois. Expert, proud, warlike and cruel, they drew upon themselves the epithet of Satanas, by which they became known to the Dutch of New Amsterdam. In this war, Colden informs us that the Iroquois prevailed, which inspired them with fresh courage against the Adirondacks of the north. Whatever effects this defeat had on the position or numbers of the Shawnees, the latter, however, preserved their nationality, and continued to form one of the elements of opposition which the Iroquois found in the tribes west of the Alleghanies. They were seated, at an early date, in the area of country embracing the Cumberland and Tennessee rivers, and, together with the Choctaws, were the efficient cause of keeping the Iroquois war parties north of the banks of the Kanawha river.

*Eries.*—French authorities give us the year 1653 for the outbreak of the final war with this tribe. They give us to understand, also, that they were an affiliated people. The question is, cursorily, examined under the head of Topical Inquiries.

*Susquehannocks.*—Philology furnishes data for believing that this small tribe spoke the language of the Alleghans. This idea is quite reconcilable to the known ire of the Iroquois against them. By an expression in one of the printed speeches made at a treaty at Lancaster, *(vide Colden,)* the Susquehannocks were exterminated by the Six Nations, and, in their symbolical language, "their fire put out," while they lived on the Susquehannah river.

*Massawomacs.*—By this term the Iroquois denominated the confederacy of Powhattanic tribes in Virginia. The course which the early Five Nations pursued in their wars with the Catabas and Cherokees, was to keep the elevated ranges of the Alleghanies. They sometimes encountered the Virginia tribes east of these mountains, but they only claimed jurisdiction over the lands along the Ohio, lying west. The war against the southern Indians, was, indeed, rather a war of scouting parties, and partisans, than of large bodies of warriors. And these small parties owed their success, in no small degree, to the fewness of their numbers, who could thus the more easily escape detection.

*Catabas.*—Of this tribe, who were one of the most determined southern enemies of the Iroquois, but few remain. On the settlement of South Carolina, they are represented as being capable of mustering fifteen hundred warriors, which, by the same moderate principles employed to denote the strength of the Iroquois, would give them a population of about 7,000 souls. They appear to have been known in early days, by the term of Flatheads. They bore a high character among their enemies, for daring and subtil art. With the Carolinians, however, they appear to have formed early and lasting relations of friendship; they were confederates with them in their war against the Tuscaroras, and afterwards against the Cherokees. The single exception to this remark, is furnished by their joining the general league of tribes against the Carolinians in 1715, but this was a very short war, and they ever afterwards remained at peace with the colonists.

They have dwindled away, for a long period, rather from the use of ardent spirits, and the native antipathy to labor, than from early wars. From facts stated to me, in conversation with Gen. James A. Black, of North Carolina, they had, in 1845, dwindled down to about sixty souls. This tribe had formerly reserved fifteen square miles of land, in that state, which they were in the habit of leasing to white occupants, for the term of ninety-nine years. The system turned out a bad one for them, and objectionable in other respects. The legislature finally purchased the tract, and gave them a permanent annuity of $2,500, which divides, at this time, over $40 per annum, per capita.

There are analogies between the Cataba and Muscogee languages, which deserve attention.

*Cherokees.*—The traditions of the Cherokees, respecting the ancient wars between them and the Iroquois, as related to me by the chief Stand Watie, in 1846, form a perfect counterpart to those of the Iroquois, on the same subjects. It was a perpetual war of individual exploits, and the parties seldom came into contact in large parties. The journey itself was so long, that large parties were subject to be discovered, and in danger of starvation. Individual Cherokees often traversed the entire route to western New York, to strike a blow, or retaliate a foray. Many incidents of such exploits are yet remembered, although he remarks, that the present number of persons who have traditions of their early history is but few, and fast diminishing. The whole nation has been so long and essentially engaged in the arts of peace and civilization, that their early traditions have become faint, or are forgotten.

One of the most prominent of their traditions of a public nature still retained is, according to Watie, the formation of an extensive alliance and general peace, among the southern and western tribes. In this alliance, the Iroquois themselves figure, as proposers, by a delegation, of the measure. Extensive invitations were given by the Cherokees to the tribes around; and after some delays, the alliance was entered into by all the tribes south and west, but the Osages. Hence it was said that the Osages should be like a wild fruit tree on the prairies, which every bird should pick at; and they have remained to our day, a predatory tribe.

This general alliance, to which, however, we have no date, put a stop to the Cherokee and Iroquois wars. Thus far Watie.

The language of this nation, although generally and fundamentally different from the Iroquois, has yet some affinities with the Mohawk. The words fire, pipe, cow, fox, flint, &c., have, apparently, the same radices. A horse they call by the name of pack, as the first animal of this kind they ever saw, was packed, carrying goods into their country. They first traded with the Spanish at St. Augustine, Florida. Philadelphia they call *Canastoga*. Americans they call by a name which signifies *Virginians*—the first men of this race, they ever saw, being Virginians. The Mississippi river they call by a name which denotes *Falling-in-banks*. The ancient Lenni Lenapees, or Delawares, they call, like the Algonquins generally, by the title of grandfather. They speak of long wars with the Six Nations, with the Shawnees, and with the Creeks. The latter they call *Coosa*, which means a creek or stream.

The following names, in this language, convey some idea of its rythmatic flow, in combination. Unicau is the Cherokee name of White river, in Arkansas and Missouri. It signifies a white river. It was to the banks of this stream that the first western Cherokee emigrant removed, from the body of the eastern Cherokees. I found them, in this position, in the year 1818. The same name, with a slight change of inflection, had been anciently applied by them to a white-capped mountain in Mississippi, which the present inhabitants of the region have accommodated to the sound of *Unicorn* mountain. In this manner a significant aboriginal name is sometimes perverted. *Amacalola* is the name of a picturesque waterfall on the river Etowah, in the ancient area of the Cherokees, in Georgia. The signification of the word, in this language is, *tumbling water*, from *ama*, water, and *calola*, sliding, rolling, or tumbling. The volume of water is not great, unless in flood, but the fall is thought to be the highest in the Union. It is seen in passing on the turnpike road from Dahlongea to the Tennessee line. *Tah-loo-lah*, a water fall of the river of the same name, sixty miles east of Amacalola, where the stream, which is one of tolerable size, is suddenly pitched into a chasm of the rock. The rock seems to have been rent asunder by some geological convulsion. To the lovers of the sublime it is a fine prospect. The etymology of the name is not certainly known. It appears from a Cherokee lady to have been derived from the precipitation of a child over the falls, whose body was suddenly and unexpectedly seen in the smooth water below. According to this incident, it means, "There lies your child." *Chatanooga,* a town on the Tennessee river, which is the proper terminus of the rail road from Charleston, South Carolina, and when completed, will connect the Atlantic and Mississippi valley, for transportation purposes. *Dahlongea,* a town selected as the site of a branch mint of the United States, in Georgia. The word is Cherokee, and means, *place of gold.*

In mentioning to Mr. Calhoun the objects of my inquiries among the Cherokees and southern Indians, in the summer of 1846, he remarked, that the tradition of the south, as given by aged gentlemen whom he names, is, that the Shawnees came from Sawanee river, in Florida, and that their first remove was to the banks of the Savannah. At this position they became involved in a war with the Cherokees. The Cherokees prevailed after a long and sanguinary contest, and drove the Shawnees north. This event they cherish as one of their proudest achievements. "What!" said an aged Cherokee chief, to Mr. Barnwell, who had suggested the final preservation of the race by intermarriage with the whites, "What! shall the Cherokees perish! Shall the conquerors of the Shawnees perish! Never!"

Mr. Calhoun observed that the Catabas were the fast friends of the whites. That they were confederates, with the Cherokees, against the Senecas and their allies. That the Senecas had conquered the country as far south as *Seneca Old Town*, or Fort Hill, the present site of his plantation, in South Carolina. From this position they were finally driven. This tradition tallies with what the Senecas told Gov. De Witt Clinton, *(vide N. Y. His. Col.)* that they had *lived* in the Cherokee country.

Mr. Calhoun further remarks, that the Creeks are called *western Indians;* that they came later than the Utchees, whom they conquered, and incorporated with themselves. The Utchees have an older language, which no one, it is said, can or has been able to obtain.

There is a historical fact, in the history of the Cherokee outbreak against the Americans, at the era of the revolutionary war, which has been generally overlooked. The Cherokees had furnished allies to the army destined to act against fort Du Quesne. On their return home, many of the Cherokees were fired upon and killed by the Virginians, who carried on a fierce frontier war with the Shawnees and Delawares; and who did not discriminate between them and the Cherokees. This furnished the first cause of offence, which was aggravated by severe measures on the Carolina frontiers, and finally led to the expedition which Gen. Montgomery conducted successfully against them.

*Quatoghies.*—This nation is the *Hurons* of the French. They call themselves Wyandots, in which they are followed by modern usage. The Wyandots have always assumed to have been originally at the head of the Iroquois group of tribes. They profess, indeed, in an original tradition which is preserved in Oneota, (p. 207,) to have been honored with the precedence as a tribe, in elder ages, and in a wider circle of nations. Whatever reliance may be placed on this tradition, or any part thereof, they are confessedly one of the leading branches of our elder North American stocks, and their traditions are worthy of record.

In mentioning the name of this tribe to Mr. J. C. Calhoun, of South Carolina, he said, that when at college at New Haven, in 1802, a Mr. Williams, a respectable and intelligent man, a half Wyandot, and a person interested in the land claims of Connecticut in Ohio, informed him, that the old forts in the Ohio valley, were erected some 150 or 200 years before, in the course of a long war which was carried on between the Wyandots (this I think, to tally with other traditions, should be Iroquois,) and the Cherokees. In this war, the northern confederates finally prevailed.

This tradition is important as bearing on the origin and history of the old western fortifications, which were found in ruins, at the period of the first settlement of the Ohio valley, and overgrown by the forest. The era denoted is believed, however, to be too recent, and it may be supposed that the parties engaged were, respectively, of a confederated character. Single tribes could not carry on a war, of this character, without involving their neighbors. Delaware tradition denotes an ancient combination between the Iroquois and themselves, for the purpose of driving a formidable foe from that valley, who had spread himself into the spurs of the northern Alleghanies. I have long been aware of the analogy which exists between the name of Tallageewy, which the Lenapees are said to have bestowed on this ancient foe, and the modern name of *Tsallakee*, which the Cherokees give to themselves. In visiting the dwellings of the Six Nations in 1845, I found that they called the Cherokees, not Tallageewy, as the modern Delawares report, (*see Heckewelder*,) but *Owaudah*, or a people who live in caves. It is still to be replied, that the name commented on, purports to be a Delaware term for this ancient people, and not Iroquois. The tradition of Mr. Williams is, at least, interesting, and deserves due consideration in any future examination of the subject. From the verbal traditions of Mr. Stand Watie, the Cherokees anciently lived at the Otter Peaks in Virginia—a noted point in the Alleghany group, which can be seen far—and they were in the habit of crossing the Ohio, with their war parties. Thus far at least, then, they are traced northwardly and westwardly, from their late position in Georgia and Alabama, and it is a fact which favors, rather than otherwise, the Wyandot tradition.

The Mr. Williams, who is noticed, understood the principles of the Wyandot language well, and proposed to have written a grammar of it. He spoke of the well known advantages of the native languages in their power of combination. You say, said he, *the sun rises — the branch bends —* we express each term by a single word. It is to be regretted that Mr. Williams has not, so far as is known, executed his intention as to the preparation and publication of a Wyandot grammar.

With regard to the war carried on by the Iroquois against their brothers, the Wyandots, from the time of the alliance of the latter with the Algonquins, in the St. Lawrence valley, it was of the most desperate, bloody, and unrelenting character. After defeating them utterly on the St. Lawrence, and driving them from their ancient site of Hochelaga and its precincts, the Wyandots fled, along with the Atawawas, or modern Ottowas, to the Manitoutine chain of islands, in the lake since called, in allusion to this migration, by their French name, *Huron.* They next occupied the island of Michilimackinac, thinking its isolated position and precipitous cliffs would prove a shelter. But the enraged enemy drove them thence. They fled into the territories of the Odjibwas in Lake Superior. But even there, their enemies attempted to follow them, until they were defeated by the Chippewas, in a battle fought at the foot of the south cape of its outlet, at a prominent elevation, which, in allusion to this incident, is still called Point Iroquois. The Indians call it, *Na-do-wa-gun-ing*, that is, place of the Iroquois bones. The incidents of this war are the most stirring and sanguinary of any which has been carried on between Indian tribes, within the period of the discovery and settlement, and if selected out, and set in order, would afford one of the most curious and striking chapters in our Indian history.

Of the original causes of the feud and separation of the Wyandots from their affiliated tribes, Father le Jeune gives the best and fullest account.

*Twightwies.*—This is the term bestowed by the Iroquois upon the Miamies. *Miami* is an Algonquin term, of which the precise meaning has not been stated. It is written agreeably to French principles of orthography, which were prevalent at the era of the discovery and settlement of Canada. The term bestowed by the Miamies upon themselves, is, *Twah! Twah!* being an attempt to imitate the cry of the crane, while in flight, and passing in the air, high over a village. Such is the etymology of the word, as given by the late noted chief *Pezho*, or Richardville.* That the Iroquois term as given above is an embodiment of the same idea, or sound, as falling on their ears, is also probable. How near are the sounds of *Twah-twah* and *Twigh-twie* to the original, and to each other? What analogy have they to the Seneca term *Kah-kwah*, the present term of that tribe for an ancient

* Rev. John F. Schermerhorn.

people whom they expelled from western New York, and who are supposed by some to be the same with the Ererions, or Eries? We may proceed from small and single facts to deeper inquiries. Etymology may not always be a safe guide, but in a class of languages so peculiar as the Indian, it is a species of research entitled to respect. The inquiry as to the fate of the Eries is equally obscure and interesting. Enough is manifest to denote that they were not exterminated by that war. Seneca tradition detailed in another part of these papers shews conclusively that the Kah-kwahs were defeated and driven off, making their escape down the Alleghany, partly by their superior dexterity in deceiving and eluding their pursuers.

That the Twah-twahs were objects of the hatred and attacks of the Iroquois, during their residence on the Miami of the lakes, and the Miami of the Ohio, is well known. According to the French missionary authors, they fell on the Miamies and Chictaghicks or Illinois, who were intimate allies, and were encamped together on the banks of the Maumee river in the year 1680, being twenty-five years after the final defeat of the Eries in western New York. In this attack they killed thirty and took three hundred prisoners. But the Illinois and Miamies rallied, and by a dexterous movement, got ahead of the retreating Iroquois, waylaid their path, and recovered their prisoners, killing many of the enemy. (*Charlevoix. La Hontan.*) As the

Miamies are, however, ethnologically of the great Algonquin family, this enmity is no proof of any alliance or connection with the Eries. The Iroquois pursued all the members of the Algonquin stock with unrelenting fury. The declaration of Le Moine in 1653, denotes clearly, that the Eries were neither Algonquins nor Hurons. That they were of the generic type of the Iroquois, seems the most probable conjecture. The tradition of the Tuscaroras, as stated by Cusick, affirm a kindredship. The elder missionary fathers also speak of the Eries as a confederacy of a language cognate with the Iroquois. They give their villages, and separate locations. The only people, of kindred stock, whom the Iroquois are certainly known to have driven west, are the Quaghtogies. Are we then to look to the descendants of these, in the west, for the defeated Kah-kwahs?

The Miamies rendered themselves conspicuous, after the close of the American revolution, and during Gen. Washington's administration, for their hostility to the United States. At successive periods, they defeated the armies under Harmer and St. Clair, and only yielded to the superior caution, intrepidity and perseverance of Gen. Wayne. During the first treaties made with them, there appeared, to their chiefs and leading counsellors, an advantage in their being recognized by the United States, under three separate divisions, and this is the true cause why we have ever since treated with portions of the very same tribe, under the name of Weas, and Piankashaws, as well as Miamies. Mr. Wells, who married the sister of the celebrated Miami chief, Little Turtle, is understood to have been conspicuous in this separation, and triorganization of the tribe, whose pecuniary interests with the government have, ever since, been kept separate.

*Mississagies.*—This tribe derive their name from their former residence on the waters of a river, which enters the north shores of Lake Huron, between Point Tessalon and La Cloche. The term is a purely geographical one, and means, literally, the *big mouth*—a characteristic feature of the said river. So little do the names of tribes often furnish to denote the lineage of the people. The Mississagies are of the Algonquin stock, and near akin, indeed, to one of the original tribes of this stock of the French era, namely, the Nepissings. The latter, like the former, affords no clue to lineage at all. It denotes the idea of *people of the water*.

*Chippewas.*—This widely scattered and numerous people, the *Odjibwas* of the north, and the *Saulteur* of the French, are of the true Algonquin type and language. They appear to have come into contact first with the Iroquois, in their lake position, by the shelter they afforded to the flying Wyandots. The principal event they refer to, in their traditions of that period, is the decisive defeat which they gave to a large war party of Iroquois, at Point Iroquois, at the outlet of Lake Superior. That the Iroquois warriors should have extended their war parties to this remote point, as well as the extreme points of their inroads and forays on the Illinois, the Miami, the Ohio, as well as the country of the Cherokees and Catabas, the bay of Chesapeake, the coasts of the Atlantic north to New England, and the river and gulf of St. Lawrence, is at once a proof of the extraordinary power and vigor of this indomitable race. Nor could we, indeed, follow historically the track of these war parties, without extending these hasty notes into a history, and embracing every North American tribe of any consequence.

The Odjibwas have some traditions of the deluge, and affirm that they came from the east. They had an institution of fire-worship, and regarded the sun as the symbol of the Great Spirit. They have many imaginative tales of giants, dwarfs and spirits, and also of witches, necromancers and sorcerers; and weave up wild stories of the lives of men, with these supernatural influences. They have a soft and copious language, which appears, originally, to have consisted of a limited stock of generic particles, or syllables, mostly monosyllables, which have been compounded and employed, so long, in their concrete state, that the Indian speakers cannot *now* separate them, or give the elementary equivalent for these original roots; while it is evident that they have retained the full meanings of these ancient stock particles.

## CHAPTER VI.

### ARCHÆOLOGY.

Vestiges of an Ancient French Fort in Lenox — Ancient Site of the Onondagas at Kasonda — Antiquities of Pompey, Manlius and Camillus — Ancient Fort of Osco at Auburn — Vestiges of an Ancient Elliptical Work at Canandaigua — Fort Hill, Genesee County — Rock Citadel of Kienuka, Niagara County — Circular Fort at Deoseowa, Erie County.

In considering the subject of American antiquities, it may facilitate the object to erect separate eras of occupancy, to which the facts may be referred. Such a division of the great and almost unknown period, which preceded the arrival of Europeans, will at least serve as convenient points to concentrate, arrange and compare the facts and evidences brought forward; and may enable the observer the better to proceed in any future attempts to generalize.

There appear to have been three eras in the aboriginal occupancy of the continent, or more strictly speaking, three conditions of occupancy, which may be conveniently grouped as eras, although the precise limits of them may be matters of some uncertainty. To make this uncertainty less than it now is, and to erect these eras on probable foundations, the proofs drawn from monuments, mounds, fortifications, ditches, earth-works, barrows, implements of art, and whatever other kind of evidence antiquity affords, may, it is thought, be gathered together in something like this shape, namely:

1. Vestiges and proofs of the era of the aboriginal migration from other parts of the globe. These, so far as arts or evidences of a material character are denoted, must necessarily be exceedingly limited, if any of undoubted authenticity shall, indeed, now be found. The departments of physiology, and philology, which have heretofore constituted the principal topics of research, are still an attractive, and by no means a closed field.

2. Proofs and vestiges of their continental migrations, wars, affinities and general ethnological characteristics, prior to the discovery of the continent. Such are the grouping of languages; the similarity or dissimilarity of arts, modes of defence, and means of subsistence.

3. Proofs and vestiges of occupancy, change, and progress, subsequent to the Columbian period.

With regard to the first era, it is almost wholly the subject of general and profound scientific and philosophical investigations, which require a union of great advantages for successful study. The second and third eras, fall within the compass of ordinary observation. Both kinds of proof may exist at the very same localities. They do not necessarily imply diverse or remote geographical positions. We know that some of the leading tribes, the Cherokees (till within a few years,) and the Iroquois, for instance, have continued to live in the very same positions in which they were found by the first explorers. As their chiefs and warriors died, they carried to their places of burial, (such was the result of ancient and general custom,) those kinds of ornaments, arms and utensils, which were the distinguishing tokens of art, of the several eras in which they lived. The coming of European races among them introduced fabrics of metal, earths, enamels, glass, and other materials more or less durable, and capable of resisting decomposition. These would necessarily take the place of the aboriginal articles of stone and shell, before employed. If then, places of sepulture were permanent, the inquirer at the present day would find the various fabrics of the second and the third eras, in the same cemeteries and burial grounds, and sometimes in the same barrows and mounds.

Modes of defence would also alter by the introduction of the second period. The simple ring-fort, with palisades, crowning a hill, which might have served as a place of excellent defence, against bows and arrows and clubs, would prove utterly useless, as the Tuscaroras found at

Naharuke in 1712, after the introduction of artillery. A trench to obtain water, from a spring or creek, leading from one of the works of the older period, might have been so covered as to afford full protection from the simple aboriginal missiles. Besides this, the combination of several tribes, as the Iroquois, the Algonquins, the Eries, Alleghans and others, might render these simple forts, defended with ditches, mounds, and otherwise, no longer necessary, in the interior of their territory, after the time of such general combinations or confederacies. And in this case, these works would be deserted and become ruins, long before the period of the discovery.

It is affirmed by their traditions, that, in the older periods of their occupancy of this continent, they were even obliged, or their fears suggested the measure, to build coverts and forts to protect themselves and families from the inroads of monsters, giants and gigantic animals. We are not at liberty to disregard this, be the recitals symbolic or true. Such places would afford convenient shelters for their women and children, at the particular times of such inroads, while the warriors collected to make battle against the common enemy. Whether this enemy carried a huge paw or a spear, we need not determine. The one was quite as much an object of aboriginal terror as the other. Whatever be the character of the antiquarian object to be examined, it will be well to bear in mind these ancient and changing conditions of the aboriginal population. If no absolute historical light be elicited thereby, we shall be the more likely to get rid of some of the confessed darkness enveloping the subject, and thus narrow the unsatisfying and historically hateful boundaries of mystery.

In applying these principles to the antiquarian remains of the area of western New York, which has been a theme of frequent allusion and description, at least since the life time of De Witt Clinton, it is merely proposed to offer a few contributions to the store of our antiquities, in the hope that other and abler hands may proceed in the investigation.

### ANCIENT FORT IN LENOX.

Some years have elapsed since I visited this work, (1812,) and the plough and spade may have further obliterated the lines, then more or less fully apparent. But in the meantime no notice of it has been published. The following outlines denote its extent and character.

A indicates the lines of a picketted work. B is an extensive plain, covered with wild grass and some shrubbery, which had once been in cultivation. The northern edge of this plain is traversed by a stream, which has worn its bed down in the unconsolidated strata, so as to create quite a deep gorge, C. This stream is joined from the west, by a small run, having its origin in a spring, D. Its channel, at the point of junction, is as deep below the level of the plain as the other.\* The point of junction itself forms a natural horn-work, which covered access to the water. The angle of the plain, thus marked, constituted the point defended. The excavations, E, may have once been square. They are now

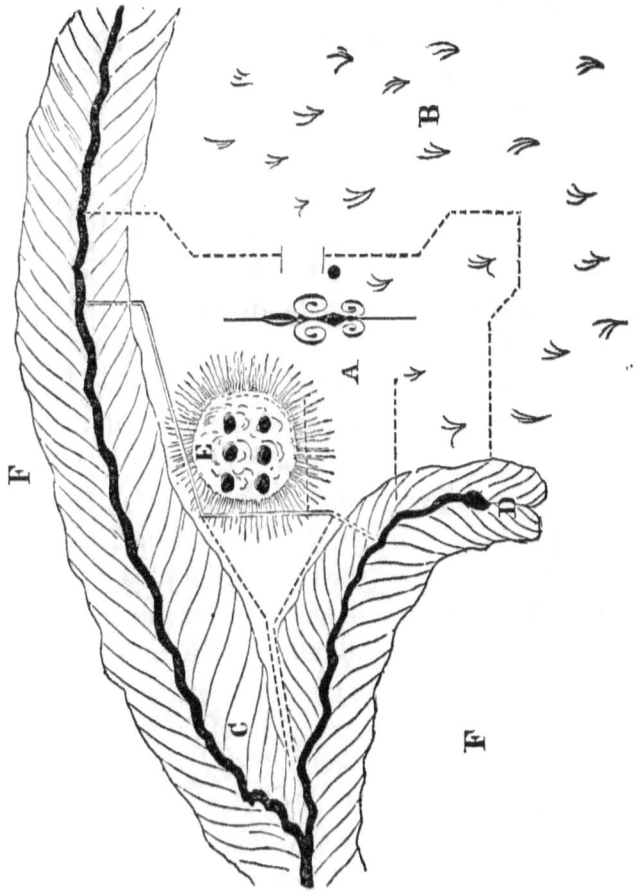

\* Some few miles below this stream is the site of an iron cupola or blast furnace, where the red or lenticular oxyde is reduced.

indentations, disclosing carbonaceous matter, as if from the decay of wood. No wood, or coal, however, existed. Their use in this position is not apparent, connected with the designated lines of palisades, unless it be supposed that they were of an older period than the latter, and designate pits, such as the aborigines used in defence. This idea is favored by the ground being a little raised at this point, and so formed that it would have admitted the ancient circular Indian palisade. If such were the case, however, it seems evident that the spot had been selected by the French, at an early period, when, as is known, they attempted to obtain a footing in the country of the Oneidas. The distance is less than ten miles northwest of Oneida Castle. It probably covered a mission. The site, which my informant, living near, called the *Old French Field*, may be supposed to have been cultivated by servants or traders connected with it. The oak and maple trees, which once covered it, as denoted by the existing forest, F F, are such, in size and number, as to have required expert axemen to fell.

With the exception of two points, in the Oneida Creek valley, where there are still vestiges of French occupation, supported by tradition, this work is the most easterly of those known, which remain to testify the adventurous spirit, zeal and perseverance which marked the attempt of the French crown to plant the flag and the cross in western New York. The bold nature of this scheme to colonize the country, and bring the

Iroquois to acknowledge their dependence upon France, and the importance of the experiment and the issue, cannot be well conceived without reference to the history of those times. Pending the famous expedition of the Chevalier de Vaudreuil, 1696, into the Iroquois country, it is known that the Jesuit Milet was stationed among the Oneidas, over whom he had so much influence, that soon after the termination of this vain display of power, thirty Oneidas deserted to the French, and desired that Milet might be appointed their pastor.*

## ANCIENT SITE OF THE ONONDAGAS.

The fact that the ruins of a square fort, with extensive sub-lines in the nature of an enclosure, had existed on the elevated grounds on the right banks of the Kasonda or Butternut creek, a mile or two from Jamesville, at the period of its first settlement, led me to visit it. There was the more interest imparted to this well attested tradition of the present inhabitants, by the accounts of the Onondagas, that this valley, in its extent above and below Jamesville, was one of their earliest points of settlement, prior to the era of their establishing their council fire at Onondaga Hollow. The subjoined sketch, although not plotted from actual measurement, will convey an idea of the relative position and former importance of the principal features, geographical and artificial, denoted.

* Colden's Five Nations, p. 193.

A indicates the site of the fort, which at the time of my visit, was covered with a luxuriant field of wheat, without a feature to denote that it had ever been held under any other jurisdiction but that of the plough. The farm which embraces it, is owned and occupied by Isaac

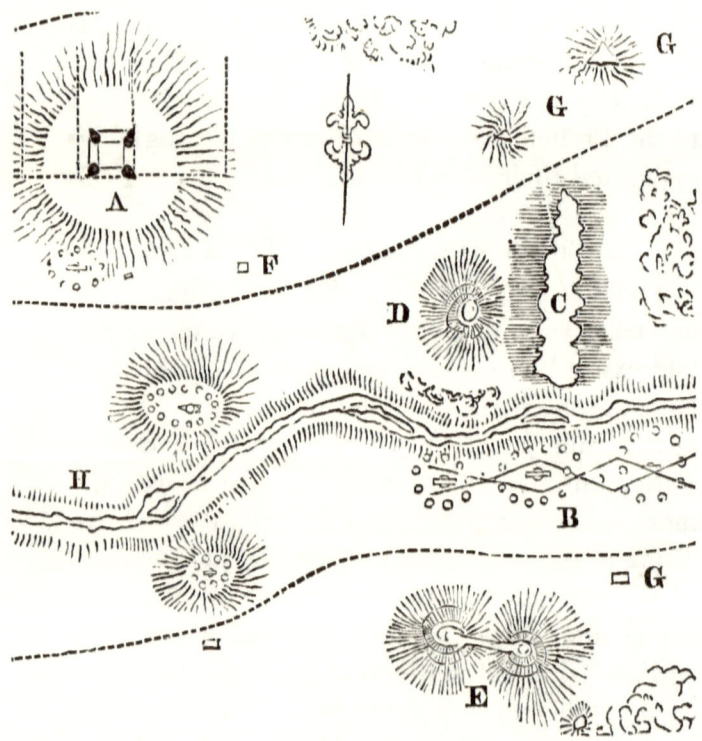

Keeler, who remarks that, at the time he came to settle here, the site of the old fort was an extensive opening in the forest, bearing grass, with some clumps of wild plum trees, and a few forest trees. On this opening, the first regiment of militia that ever paraded in Onondaga county, met. It was commanded by Major De Witt, after whom the township is now named.

About the year 1810, he felled an oak, near the site of the fort, measuring two feet six inches in diameter. In recutting it for fire wood, after it had been drawn to his door, a leaden bullet was found, covered by one hundred and forty-three cortical layers. From its position, embedded as it was in the compact wood, it was still some distance to the heart of the tree. He thinks this tree may have been a sapling when the bullet was fired. Whether this conjecture be true or not, one hundred and forty-three years appear to have elapsed since the bullet assumed its position. This would give A. D. 1667 as the era.

In 1666, the governor of Canada concluded a treaty with the Onondaga Iroquois, as is seen from the *Paris Documents* obtained by Mr. Brodhead. Colden's history of the Five Nations, which has been the principal source of information heretofore, after a brief summary of traditionary matter,* in the first chapter, opens with the transactions in 1665. This matter is more fully and satisfactorily stated by Charlevoix in his *History of New France,* from whom it is presumable Colden drew his information of the former power and preëminence of the Adirondacks.

* The States General of Holland surrendered New York to the English crown in 1664.

During this year De Traci came out as viceroy of New France, and the same year Monsieur Coursel, who is notorious for his perfidy in executing the Iroquois sachem, Agariata, arrived with the commission of governor-general of Canada. But there is little to be found bearing directly on the subject before us.

It would appear from the journal of the Jesuit, Father Le Moyne, as given in the missionary *Relacions*, that the country of the Onondagas was not discovered and explored until the year 1653. Facts disclosed by him in the same letter denote, however, prior negotiations with the French authorities, and we are probably to understand only, that as yet no missionaries, from his order, had visited, or been established amongst this tribe.* In this view, and from the incidental light which he throws on some other topics, such as the new breaking out of the war with the Eries, the discovery of the salt springs, and the existence of the buffalo in the country, this letter is important to the early Iroquois history, and a translation of it is hereto appended.† It is certain that no mission or fort had then been introduced. A footing may, however, have been gained by the French within the next fourteen years, that is, at the time of the apparent

---

\* That the Dutch traders had visited Onondaga at an earlier period is very probable. The Dutch had then been settled forty years at Albany.

† Vide chap. x., original discovery of the Onondaga country.

date of the existence of the old fort on the right banks of the Kasonda.*

Where history fails, we may appeal to tradition and to the proofs drawn from antiquarian remains. Isaac Keeler, who is before mentioned, exhibited to me one-half of the brass circle of a dial plate, three inches (less two-tenths) in diameter, which had been ploughed up by him on the site of the fort, or from that general area. This circle had engraved, in good Roman characters, the numbers II, III, IV, V, VI, VII, VIII. He likewise exhibited the box of a small brass pocket compass, with a screw lid one inch and two-tenths in diameter. From this instrument the needle had been removed and its place supplied by vermillion, the highly prized war pigment of the Indians. When ploughed up and found at the bottom of a furrow, it was encrusted with oxide, but restored by washing and friction to its original color and even surface. On being opened, it was found to contain the pigment, of which I examined a portion. It appeared to me to have been, not the Chinese vermillion of the trade, but the duller red article, which is, I believe, a peroxide of lead prepared by the Dutch.

Among the articles which he had preserved were the following:

* Fire-arms began to be first introduced among the Iroquois in 1609, the very year that Hudson explored the river now bearing his name. In this year, Champlain, heading the Algonquins, with some regular troops in Lake Corlear (since called Champlain,) defeated the Mohawks by the use of fire arms.

1. A crucifix of brass of two inches in length, ornamented by a human figure, and having a metallic loop for suspending it.

2. An octagonal medal, four-tenths of an inch, of the same material, bearing a figure with the name St. Agatha, and the Latin word *ora*, a part of the Gregorian chant.

3. A similar medal, five-tenths of an inch in length, with a figure, inscribed St. Lucia, and the same fragment of a chant.

4. A rude medal of lead, an inch and four-tenths long, ovate, with the figure of the Saviour, as is supposed, being that of a person suspended by the outstretched hands, however, and the figure of a serpent, as if this form of temptation, had been presented during his advent. On the reverse, is a sitting figure, which bears most resemblance to a common and characteristic position of one of the native priests or prophets. Should this conjecture be correct, this figure may have been intended, adopting the Indian method, to teach the office of the Saviour by a symbol. He is thus shown, however, to be merely the priest and prophet of men — an idea which does not coincide with catholic theology, and which, if not enlarged and corrected by verbal teaching, would convey no conception of his divine character and atonement, and thus leave the Onondaga neophyte as essentially in the dark as before. To figure the Saviour as the great *Josakeed* of men, as is done in this medal, is indeed the most extraordinary and audacious

act of which the history of missions among rude nations affords any parallel. The novelty of this feature in this apparently home-wrought model, gives it a claim to be hereafter figured.

5. An iron horse-shoe, four and a half inches long nearly, and five inches (lacking two-tenths) broad, with three elongated nail holes in each side, and a clumsy steel cork, partially worn. The peculiar fabric of this shoe, its clumsiness and spread, and the little mechanical skill which it evinces in the hammering and general make, denote it to be very clearly the workmanship of a Canadian blacksmith, such as a rude Canadian blacksmith is still to be witnessed, in the lake country, and to have been, at the same time, intended for the unfarried hoofs of the Canadian horse.

6. A pair of iron strap hinges, common and coarse. These my informant had turned to account, by employing them to hang the little gate which led, through a small flower plat, to his dwelling house. See figure F.

These articles have been selected for notice from many of more common occurrence, such as beads of coarse paste, enamel and glass, of various sizes and colors, which are evidently of European make. My informant further stated that a blacksmith's anvil, vice, horn, and almost every other article of a smith's shop, had been from time to time found on the site or in the vicinity, but there was nothing of this kind in his possession. On the south declivity of the hill, near the present road leading east to Pompey hill, there is a spring still sheltered with shrubbery, which he supposes furnished the fort with water.

This fort constitutes but a part of the very marked evidences of former occupancy by man in a civilized state, and in a forgotten age, which occur in this portion of Onondaga, chiefly in the present towns of Pompey, Lafayette, De Witt, Camillus and Manlius. Other observed localities and facts derived from other witnesses, illustrating the character of this fort, and of the ancient Indian settlements in the Kasonda valley, are marked H in the annexed sketch.

In this plat B denotes the site of an ancient Onondaga town or village, immediately on the banks of the stream, where water could be readily obtained for all purposes. C is the locality of the cemetery used at the period, on the ascending grounds on the north banks of the stream. It constitutes a well marked transverse ridge. Immediately west of it rises a natural mound, marked D, of large size, nearly conical in its shape, and terminating in a flat surface or plain, of an ovate border, some twelve by seventeen paces. James Gould, the proprietor of the land, who, from his residence, guided me to the spot, remarks that this conical hill was formerly covered with a hard wood forest, similar in its species to those of the surrounding country, with the exception of a spot, some four or five paces diameter, on its apex. This spot was, however, completely veiled from sight by the overtopping trees until the arcanum was entered. From the peculiar character of this eminence, and its relative position to the village and burial ground, it may be supposed to have been the site of the seer's lodge, from which he uttered his sacred responses.

Speaking of the old fort of Kasonda, this informant remarked, that when he came into the country, its outlines could still be traced; that it was a square fort, with bastions, and had streets within it. It had been set round with cedar pickets, which had been burned to the ground. Stumps of these ancient palisades were struck by the plough. It is on this testimony, which at the same time denotes a violent destruction of the work, that the geometrical figure of it, represented in A, is drawn. He had, I think, been in the revolutionary army, and drawn his bounty lands, as many of the original settlers on the military tract had done. He knew therefore, the import of the military terms he employed.

In a collection of aboriginal antiquarian articles at his house, he permitted me to make drawings of any taken from the fort grounds, or disinterred from ancient Indian graves, which appeared to me to merit it. Of these, but a few are pertinent to the present inquiry. They are as follows:

Number 1, represents an antique collar or medal, (*Nabikoágun*,) wrought out of sea shell. It is crossed with two parallel, and two horizontal lines, ornamented with dots, and dividing the surface into four equal parts. An orifice exists for introducing a string to suspend it about the neck. This species of article is found in Indian graves of the period preceding the discovery of the continent, or not extending more than one or two generations into the new period. It was probably an elegant ornament when bright and new, and exhibiting the natural color and nacer of the shell. Inhumation has so far served to decompose the surface, as to coat it with a limy or chalky exterior, which effervesces in mineral acids. By scraping deep into it, the shelly structure is detected. This kind of ornament, varying much in size, was probably soon replaced by the metallic gorget and medal introduced by the trade, and has long been unknown both to Indians and traders. I found it first in Indian cemeteries of the west, without, however, for some time suspecting its real nature, supposing it some variety of altered pottery, or enamel paste; but have since traced it over the entire area of the ancient occupation of western New York, and, so far as examined, of Canada.

No. 2. A stone ring, one inch and two-tenths in diameter, made of a dark species of somewhat hard steatite or slaty rock. Its characteristic trait is found in its adaptation to the middle finger, (of a male) and its having eleven distinct radiating lines.

No. 3. A globular bead or amulet, *(Minace,)* of sea shell one inch and a half in diameter, solid and massy, having an orifice for suspending it. It is slightly ovate. Its structure from shell, is distinctly marked. Like the flat medal-shaped Nabikoágun (No. 1.) of the same material, it has a limy coating from the effects of partial decomposition.

In the remaining features of the sketch referred to, letters G G denote ancient remains of a European character in the contiguous part of the town of Pompey, which are more particularly described elsewhere. E represents the Twin mounds, two natural formations of fine gravel and other diluvial strata, situated on the south side of the creek, on the farm of Jeremiah Gould. These mounds are conspicuous features in the landscape, from their regularity and position on elevated grounds, as well as from their connection with the ancient Indian history of the valley. These pyramidal heaps of earth are connected by a neck of earth, in the manner represented. They exhibit the appearance of having been cleared of the forest, almost entirely, at an ancient date. The surface exhibits numerous pits or holes, which excite the idea of their having served as a noted locality for the Indian *assenjigun*, or pit for hiding or putting *en cache*, corn or other articles, to preserve it from enemies, or as a place of deposit during temporary absences from the village. There can, I think, be little question that this was the true use and relation these geological eminences bore to the ancient town on the Kasonda, marked B. Such, too, is the general impression derived from local tradition. Some years ago, a skeleton was exhumed from one of these *caches.*

## ANTIQUITIES OF POMPEY.

No part of western New York has furnished a larger number of antiquarian remains, or been more often referred to, than the geographical area which constituted the original town of Pompey. There is, consequently, the less need of devoting elaborate attention to the details of this particular locality. It was first visited and described by De Witt Clinton, in 1810–11,* and the plough has since rendered it a task less easy than it then was, to examine the lines of its ancient works and its archæological remains. It is quite evident, from the objects of art disclosed at and about these antique sites of security and defence, that civilized man dwelt here in remote times, and there must be assigned to this part of the state a period of European occupancy prior to the commonly received historical era of discovery and settlement, or, at least, if falling within it, as there is now reason to believe, yet almost wholly unknown, or forgotten in its annals. Sismondi has well remarked, that only the most important events come down to posterity, and that fame, for a long flight, prepares to forget every thing which she possibly can. That no accounts should remain of obscure events, in a remote part of the country, at an

* Trans. of Philo. and Lit. Society of New York.

early date, is not surprising. As it is, we must infer both the dates and the people, from such antiquarian remains of works of art, and historical comparisons as can be obtained.

There appear to have been two or three nations who supplied very early visitors or residents to ancient Onondaga, namely, the Dutch, French and Spanish, the latter as merely temporary visitors or explorers. Both the Dutch and the French carried on an early trade here with the Iroquois. It is most probable that there are no remains of European art, or have ever been any disclosed, in this part of the country, one only excepted,* which are not due to the early attempts of the Dutch and French, to establish the fur trade among these populous and powerful tribes. To some extent, missionary operations were connected with the efforts of both nations. But whatever was the stress laid on this subject, by protestants or catholics, neither object could be secured without the exhibition of fire-arms and certain military defences, such as stockades and picketted works, with gates, afforded. No trader could, in the 16th and 17th centuries, securely trust his stock of goods, domestic animals, (if he had any,) or his own life, in the midst of fierce and powerful tribes, who acknowledged no superior, and who were, besides, subject to the temporary excitement created by the limited use of alcohol. For we can assign absolutely no date to the early European intercourse with these

* Antique stone with an inscription, Albany Institute.

tribes, in which there was no article of this kind, more or less employed. Probably we should not have been left, as we are, to mere conjectures on this subject, at least between the important dates of 1609 and 1664, had not the directors of the state paper office in Holland decided, in 1820, to sell the books and records of the Dutch West India Company, as waste paper.*

In examining the archæology of this part of New York, we are, therefore, to look for decisive proofs of the early existence of this trade in the hands of the two powers named. The Dutch were an eminently commercial people, at the epoch in question, and pursued the fur trade to remote parts of the interior, at an early date. They had scarcely any other object at the time but to make this trade profitable. Settlements and cultivation was a business in the hands of patroons, and was chiefly confined to the rich valleys and intervales of the southern parts of the state. They were, at the same time, too sagacious to let any thing interrupt their good understanding with the natives; and on this account, probably, had less need of military defences of a formidable kind than the French, who were a foreign power. It was, besides, the policy of New France,—a policy most perseveringly pursued,—to wrest this trade, and the power of the Indians, from the hands of the Dutch and their successors, the English. They sought not only to obtain the trade, but they

* Vide Mr. Brodhead's Report.

intrigued for the territory. They also made the most strenuous endeavors to enlist the minds of the Indians, by the ritual observances of the Romish church, and to propagate among the Iroquois its peculiar doctrines. They united in this early effort the sword, the cross, and the purse.

Were all the libraries of Europe and America burned and totally destroyed, there would remain incontestible evidences of each of the above named efforts, in the metallic implements, guns, sword blades, hatchets, locks, bells, horse-shoes, hammers, paste and glass beads, medals, crucifixes and other remains, which are so frequently turned up by the plough in the fertile wheat and cornfields of Onondaga.

Looking beyond this era, but still found in the same geographical area, are the antiquities peculiar to the Ante-Columbian period, and the age of intestine Indian wars. These are found in various parts of the state, in the ancient ring forts, angular trenches, moats, barrows, or lesser mounds, which constituted the ancient simple Indian system of castramentation.

This era is not less strongly marked by the stone hatchets, pestles, fleshing instruments, arrow heads and javelins of chert and hornstone; amulets of stone, bone and sea-shells, wrought and unwrought; needles of bone, coarse pottery, pipes, and various other evidences of antique Indian art. The practice of interring their favorite utensils, ornaments and amulets with the dead, renders their ancient grave yards, barrows and mounds the principal repositories of these arts. They are, in effect, so many museums of antiquity.

The field for this species of observation is so large and attractive to the antiquarian, that far more time than was at my command, would be required to cultivate it. Early in the year 1845, Mr. Joshua V. H. Clark visited some of the principal scenes mentioned. Subsequently, at my suggestion and solicitation, he revisited the same localities and extended his inquiries to others of an interesting character, in the county of Onondaga, descriptions of which are presented in a subsequent part of this work.

### ANCIENT FORTIFICATION OF OSCO.*

The eminence called Fort Hill, in the south-western skirts of the village of Auburn, has attracted notice from the earliest times. Its height is such as to render it a very commanding spot,

---

* This ancient name for the site of Auburn, was communicated to me by the intelligent Onondaga, Taht-kaht-ons, or Abraham Le Fort. It is descriptive of the ford or crossing place, which anciently existed above the falls, near the site of the present turnpike bridge. This was crossed by stepping stones, &c. The barks, which made a part of a rude Indian bridge, were, at the time the name was bestowed, nearly overflowed; the crossing was very dangerous, as it was just above the brink of the falls, and it was an act of daring to pass over. The name bestowed at this time became perpetual, although there may have been but little danger in crossing afterwards.

and crowned, as it was, with a pentagessimal work, earthern ramparts and palisades of entire efficacy against Indian missiles, it must have been an impregnable stronghold during the periods of their early intestine wars. The following diagram, drawn by James H. Bostwick, surveyor, and obligingly furnished by S. A. Goodwin, Esq., exhibits its dimensions:

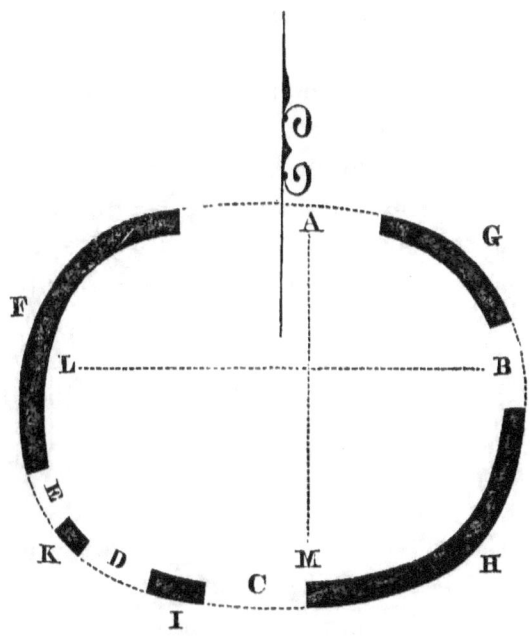

The site of this work is the highest land in the vicinity, and a visit to it affords one of the best and most varied views of the valley of the Owasco, and the thriving and beautiful inland town of Auburn, with its public buildings, prison,* and other noted public edifices. The ellipsis enclosed by the embankments, with their intervening spaces, has a circumference of 1200 feet. Its minor dimensions are as follows, namely:

From A to M, 310 feet; from B to L, 416 feet. Opening at A, 166 feet; opening at B, 66 feet, opening at C, 78 feet; opening at D, 60 feet; opening at E, 50 feet. Wall at F, 275 feet; wall at G, 145 feet; wall at H, 278 feet; wall at I, 52 feet; wall at K, 30 feet.

Viewed as a military work, the numerous breaks or openings in the wall, marked from A to C, constitute rather its characteristic trait. They are of various and irregular widths, and it seems most difficult to decide why they are so numerous. If designed for egress or regress, they are destitute of the principle of security, unless they were defended by other works of destructible material, which have wholly disappeared. The widest opening (of 166 feet,) opens directly north, the next in point of width (78 feet,) directly south; but in order to give these or any of the other spaces the character of entry or sally ports, and, indeed, to render the entire wall defensible, it must have had palisadoes.

* One of the most striking evidences of that tendency of the surface limestone stratification of western New York to assume a fissured character, marked by the cardinal points, is seen in the banks of the Owasco, a short distance below the State Prison.

Immediately below the openings at E, D, C, and a part of the embankment F, there are a series of deep ravines, separated by acute ridges, which must have made this part of the work difficult of approach. In front of the great north opening, the ground descends gradually about seventy feet, when there is a perfect acclivity. The hill has its natural extension towards the east, for several hundred yards, in the course of which a transverse depression in the surface separates the eastern terminus of the ridge from its crown at the site of the fort.

It is not known that excavations have been made for antiquarian remains, so that there is no accessory light to be derived from this source. The entire work conforms to the genius and character of the red races who occupied the Ohio valley, and who appear to have waged battle for the possession of this valuable part of the country prior to the era of the discovery of America, and ere the Iroquois tribes had confederated and made themselves masters of the soil. That the art of defence by field works was cultivated by the ancient American tribes, is denoted by their traditions, as well as by the present state of our antiquarian knowledge. This art did not aspire to the construction of bastions, at the intersection of two right angled lines, by means of which a length of wall might have been enfiladed with arrows. Even where the works were a square or parallelogram, of which there are one or two instances among the oldest class of forts, such an obvious advantage in defence does not appear to have occurred. Fire, and the coal chisel, or digger, were the ready means of felling trees, and of dividing the trunks into suitable lengths for palisades. To heap a pile of earth *within and without* such lines, was the mode adopted by the Tuscaroras at the siege of Naharuke, in 1712, and it is probable that this *then* powerful and warlike nation had inherited much of the skill in fort building possessed by their northern predecessors.

The chief point in addition to its numerous breaks in the wall, before noticed, in which this work differs from the generality of antique native forts of the oldest period in this state, is its very well preserved elliptical form. A circle is the usual form of the antique forts of Indian origin in western New York; and these works are generally placed on the apex of a hill, covered by ravines as a natural moat, or they occupy an eminence which commanded other advantages.

ANCIENT ELLIPTICAL WORK AT CANANDAIGUA.

The Senecas deduce their descent from a noted eminence, bearing the title of Fort Hill, at the head of the sylvan expanse of Canandaigua lake. The term of Fort Hill is, however, not confined to that spot, but is, as in the work under consideration, one of common occurrence, in sundry parts of the ancient and extended area of the Six Nations. The subjoined sketch, denotes the vestiges of an ancient strong-hold of the Senecas, of an elliptical form, on elevated lands about a mile northerly from the village.

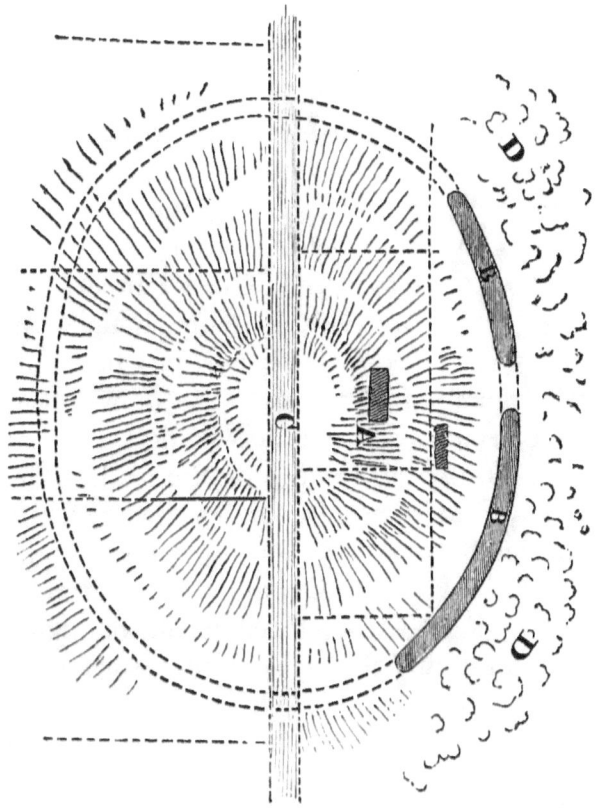

This work has been nearly obliterated by the plough. The only portions of the ancient wall yet remaining, are indicated by the letters B B. At A, a dwelling house has been erected, flanked by gardens. C, is a turnpike or rectangular town road, passing over the apex of the elevation. The dotted angular lines denote fields in cultivation, and the dotted ellipses through these grounds, are laid down from tradition, rather than from any well defined vestiges in these fields of the original wall yet visible. D D, represents a native forest. Judging from the curves of the portions of wall entire at B B, in connection with the area pointed out by the occupant, this work may have had a circumference of one thousand feet. It occupied a commanding site. The sections of the wall remaining, denote the labor of many hands, and if this rampart was crowned with palisades, and secured in the usual manner with gates, it must not only have furnished a garrison to a large body of warriors, but have been a work of much strength.

In excavating the grounds for the road, in the approach to the village, human bones were found in considerable quantities, on the descent of the hill, together with some of the usual vestiges of ancient Indian art, as evinced in the manufacture of stone and clay pipes and implements. Nothing of this kind had, however, been preserved, which appeared worthy of particular description.

ANCIENT ENTRENCHMENTS ON FORT HILL.

The following diagram of this work has been drawn from a pen sketch, forwarded by the Rev. Mr. Dewey, of Rochester.

The work occurs on an elevated point of land formed by the junction of a small stream, called Fordham's brook, with Allen's creek, a tributary of the Genesee river. Its position is about three miles north of the village of Le Roy, and some ten or twelve northeast of Batavia. The best

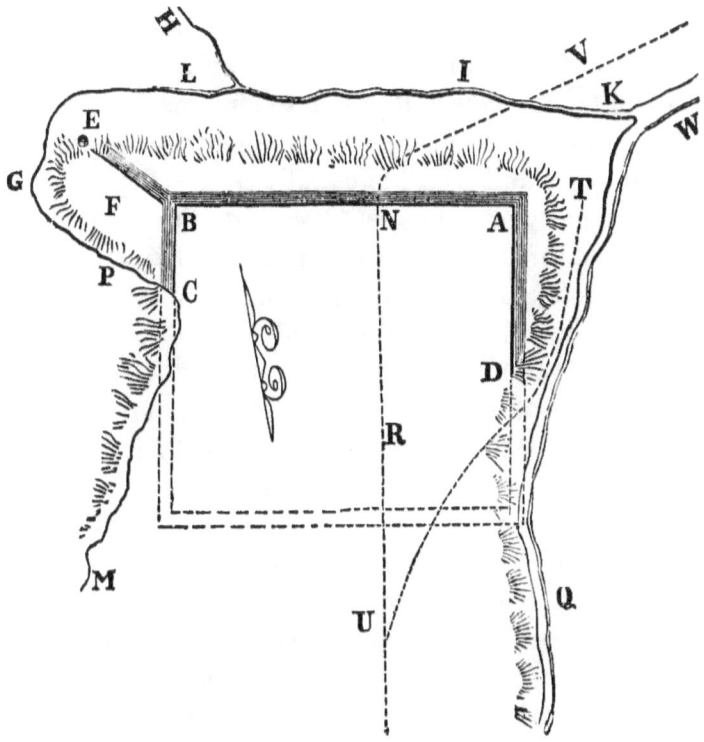

view of the hill, as one of the natural features of the country, is obtained a short distance north of it, on the road from Bergen to Le Roy.

To attain a proper conception of its susceptibilities and capacity, as the site of a work of defence, it is essential to conceive the country, for some distance, to have had the level of the extreme plain, forming the highest part of the fort. The geological column of this plain, after passing down through the unconsolidated strata, appears to be composed of various strata of corniferous limestone, Onondaga or hydraulic limestone, and perhaps Medina sandstone. Geological causes, originating, so far as we can immediately perceive, in the two streams named, have cut down this series of stratifications, on the north, east and west, unequally, to the depth of some eighty or ninety feet, isolating the original plain, on three sides, by the valleys of Allen's creek and Fordham's brook. Availing themselves of this heavy amount of natural excavation, the ancient occupants of it further strengthened its position, by casting up a wall and ditch along the brow of the two valleys, at the points of their junction, from A to B, 60 rods; from A to D, 30 rods; and from B to C, 15 rods. This is as much of the embankment as now remains; but tradition adds, that on the earliest occupancy of the country, there were evidences that the work had been continued south from the extreme points, C, D, and connected by an enclosure, parallel to A, B, which would have given it a regular quadrangular shape. The encroachments of the respective valleys, at C and D, now terminate the trench. And if we concede that geological changes of this kind must have required some time for their production, by the present power of action possessed by the streams named, it is an argument for the antiquity of the work. But, however antique, it was still the effort of a rude, and at best half civilized people, at an epoch when bows and arrows, clubs, spears and stones, and the stone *cassatete*,* were the principal weapons of defence. For these are the chief objects of antiquarian interest dug from the ground. There are also disclosed by the place or its vicinity, the amuletum archæus and other amulets of sea shell, bone and fossil stone, which were so much prized by the ancient red races of this continent, by whom they were manufactured, and exclusivly used before the era of the discovery. That the spot continued, however, whether a ruin or not, to be visited or occupied, after this era, is proved by some remains of art, which were found here and described by Mr. Follet, in a letter which constitutes a valuable part of the materials employed in this description. But the most remarkable and distinctive trait connected with its archæology is the discovery of human bones denoting

---

* I find the French word cassatete more exactly descriptive of the probable and exclusive uses of the antique stone tomahawk, than any other which has been met with. The shape of this warlike instrument resembled strongly the ancient crossbill. It presents the figure of a crescent, tapering gradually to the ends, which are rounded and proceed to a sharp point. In the concave centre of the crescent is an orifice for a helve. It is an instrument denoting skill, and the possession of some mechanical tool for carving it, harder than the dark silecious slate, from which it is generally made. One of these instruments sent to me by Mr. Follet, of Batavia, and which, from an inscription, was found " in that vicinity by Jerome A. Clark, Esq., on the 16th May, 1844," is worthy the chisel of a sculptor.

an uncommon stature and development, which are mentioned in the same communication. A humerus or shoulder bone, which is preserved, denotes a stature one-third larger than the present race, and there is also a lower jaw bone, preserved by a physician at Batavia, from the vicinity, which indicates the same gigantic measure of increase.

To supply the fort with water, a trench was continued about fifteen rods, from B, at the northeast angle, to E, in order to reach a spring below the declivity. In the isolated portion of the hill, marked F, haiks of moderate sized round stones have been found, which were probably one of the ancient means of defence. This spot, from the remains found, appears also to have been an ancient place of burial. Among the articles exhumed, were several curious pipes of stone and earthenware. One of these was formed out of granular limestone; another was of baked clay in the form of a man's head and face, the nose, eyes and other features being depicted in a style resembling some of the figures in Mr. Stephens's plate of the ruins of Central America. The top of the head is surrounded by a fillet; on the occipital part are also two fillets. The neck has a similar ornament, and there is another on the breast. The orifices of the ears are denoted, and the whole evinces no little degree of art. This is the most curious relic found.

Another pipe of reddish baked clay is ornamented with dots; two rows of which extend round it, and another in festoons, like a chain looped up.

Other parts of the topography are denoted by the plot. Q, W, is Allen's creek; H, I, K, Fordham's brook; L, P, M, a branch of Fordham's brook; R, N, V, denote the road, which passes through the centre of the work. A former road led from U down the ravine to T. There was formerly a bridge at N, to cross the ditch. This trench was estimated by early observers at from eight to ten feet deep, and as many wide. The earth in making it had been thrown either way, but much of it inwards. Forest trees were standing, both in the trench and on its sides. In size and age they appeared to be equal to the general growth of the forest. Prostrate upon the ground, there were found numerous trunks of the heart-wood of black cherry trees of large size. These were evidently the remains of a more antique forest, which had preceded the existing growth of beech and maple. They were in such a state of soundness as to be employed for timber by the first settlers.

There were no traditions among the Indians of the country respecting the use and design of this work. It was to them, as to the first settlers, an object of mystery. About half a mile below the hill, Allen's creek has a fall of some eighty feet. It is a perpendicular fall of much beauty. At this place the hydraulic limestone is seen to be the underlying rock. This rock had also been struck in excavating the north line of the trench on Fort Hill, and some portions of it had been thrown out with the earth.

Such are the interesting facts communicated to me, by the gentlemen whose names have been mentioned. The notice of the present altered state of the site, and the following just reflections naturally springing from the subject, may be stated in the exact words of Dr. Dewey:

"The forest has been removed. Not a tree remains on the quadrangle, and only a few on the edge of the ravine on the west. By cultivating the land, the trench is nearly filled in some places, though the line of it is clearly seen. On the north side the trench is considerable, and where the road crosses it, is three or four feet deep at the sides of the road. It will take only a few years more to obliterate it entirely, as not even a stump remains to mark out its line.

"From this view it may be seen or inferred,

"1. That a real trench bounded three sides of the quadrangle. On the south side there was not found any trace of trench, palisadoes, blocks, &c.

"2. It was formed long before the whites came into the country. The large trees on the ground and in the trench, carry us back to an early era.

"3. The workers must have had some convenient tools for excavation.

"4. The direction of the sides may have had some reference to the four cardinal points, though the situation of the ravines naturally marked out the lines.

"5. It cannot have been designed merely to catch wild animals, to be driven into it from the south. The oblique line down to the spring is opposed to this supposition, as well as the insufficiency of such a trench to confine the animals of the forest.

"6. The same reasons render it improbable that the quadrangle was designed to confine and protect domestic animals.

"7. It was probably a sort of fortified place. There might have been a defence on the south side by a stockade, or some similar means, which might have entirely disappeared.

"By what people was this work done?

"The articles found in the burying ground at F, offer no certain reply. The axes, chisels, &c., found on the Indian grounds in this part of the state, were evidently made of the greenstone or trap of New England, like those found on the Connecticut river in Massachusetts. The pipe of limestone might be from that part of the country. The pipes seem to belong to different eras.

"1. The limestone pipe indicates the work of the savage or aborigines.

"2. The third indicates the age of French influence over the Indians. An intelligent French gentleman says such clay pipes are frequent among the town population in parts of France.

" 3. The second, and most curious, seems to indicate an earlier age and people.

" The beads found at Fort Hill are long and coarse, made of baked clay, and may have had the same origin as the third pipe.

" Fort Hill cannot have been formed by the French as one of their posts to aid in the destruction of the English colonies. In 1689, or 156 years ago, the French in Canada made serious attempts to destroy the English colony of New York. If the French had made Fort Hill a post as early as 1660, or 185 years ago, and then deserted it, the trees could not have grown to the size of the forest generally in 1810, or in 150 years afterwards. The white settlements had extended ' only twelve miles west of Avon' in 1798, and some years after 1800, Fort Hill was covered with a dense forest. A chesnut tree, cut down in 1842 at Rochester, showed 254 concentric circles of wood, and must have been more than 200 years old in 1800. So opposed is the notion that this was a deserted French post.

" Must we not refer Fort Hill to that race which peopled this country before the Indians, who raised so many monuments greatly exceeding the power of the Indians, and who lived at a remote era?"

## ANTIQUE ROCK CITADEL OF KIENUKA.

In the preceding sketches, evidences have been presented of the readiness and good judgment of the aboriginal fort builders of western New York,* in availing themselves of steeps, gulfs, defiles, and other marked localities, in establishing works for security or defence. This trait is, however, in no case more strikingly exemplified than in the curious antique work before us, which is called, by the Tuscaroras, *Kienuka*. The term Kienuka is said to mean

* It is not without something bordering on anachronism, that this portion of the continent is called New York, in reference to transactions not only before the bestowal of the title in 1664, but long before the European race set foot on the continent. Still more inappropriate, however, was the term of New Netherlands, that is, New Lowlands, which it bore from 1609 to 1664, many parts of the state being characterized by lofty mountains, and all having an elevation of many hundreds of feet above the sea. In speaking of these ancient periods, a title drawn from the native vocabulary would better accord with the period under discussion, if not with the laws of euphony. But the native tribes were poor generalizers, and omitted to give generic names to the land. The term of *Haonao* for the continent, or island as they called it, occurs, but this would have no more pertinence applied to New York, than to any other portion of it. The geographical feature most characteristic of the state, is *Niagara*, and next in prominence, *Ontario*, and either would have furnished a better cognomen for the state, had they been thought of in season. But it is too late now to make the change, and even for the remote era alluded to, the name under which the country has grown great, is to be preferred. It is already the talismanic word for every honorable and social reminiscence.

the strong hold, or fort, from which there is a sublime view. It is situated about three and a half or four miles eastward of the outlet of the Niagara gorge at Lewiston, on a natural escarpment of the ridge.

This ridge, which rises in one massy up-towering pile, almost perpendicularly, on the brink of the river, developes itself as we follow its course eastward for a mile or two, in a second plateau, which holds nearly a medium position in relation to the altitude of the ridge. This plateau attains to a width of a thousand yards or more, extending an unexplored distance, in the curving manner of the ridge, towards Lockport. Geologically considered, its upper stratum is the Niagara limestone, which in the order of superposition, immediately overlies the red shaly sandstone at the falls. Its edges are jagged and broken, and heavy portions of it have been broken off, and slid down the precipice of red shaly undergrit, and thus assumed the character of debris. Over its top there has been a thin deposit of pebble drift, of purely diluvial character, forming, in general, not a very rich soil, and supporting a growth of oaks, maples, butternut, and other species common to the country. From the ascent of the great ridge, following the road from Lewiston to Tuscarora village, a middle road leads over this broad escarpment, following, apparently, an ancient Indian trail, and winding about with sylvan irregularity. Most of the trees appear to be of second growth; they do not, at any rate, bear the impress of antiquity, which marks the heavy forests of the country. Occasionally there are small openings, where wigwams once stood. These increase as we pass on, till they assume the character of continuous open fields, at the site of the old burying ground, orchard and play ground of the neighboring Tuscaroras. The soil in these openings appears hard, compact and worn out, and bears short grass. The burial ground is filled almost entirely with sumach, giving it a bushy appearance, which serves to hide its ancient graves and small tumuli. Among these are two considerable barrows, or small elliptic mounds, the one larger than the other, formed of earth and angular stones. The largest is not probably higher than five feet, but may have a diameter of twenty feet in the longest direction.

Directly east of this antique cemetery, commences the old orchard and area for ball playing, on which, at the time of my visit, the stakes or goals were standing, and thus denoted that the ancient games are kept up on these deserted fields by the youthful population of the adjacent Tuscarora village. A small ravine succeeds, with a brook falling into a gulf, or deep break in the escarpment, where once stood a saw mill, and where may still be traced some vestiges of this early attempt of the first settlers to obtain a water power from a vernal brook. Immediately after crossing this little ravine, and rising to the general level of the plain, we enter the old fields and rock fortress of Kienuka, described in the following diagram.

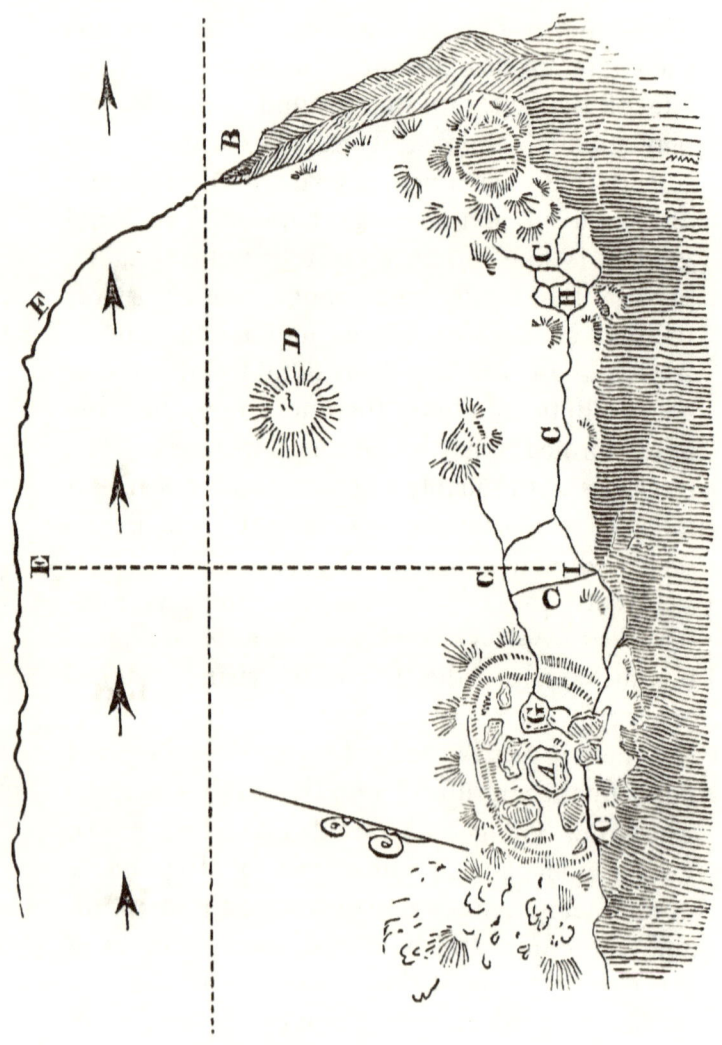

To obtain a proper conception of this plan, it is necessary to advert to geological events, in this part of the country, whose effects are very striking. The whole country takes an impress, in some degree, from the great throe which worked out a passage for the Niagara, through seven miles of solid rock, severing, at its outlet, the great coronal ridge, at its highest point of elevation. Nothing, we think, is more evident to the observer, in tracing out the Kienuka plateau, than the evidences which exist of Lake Ontario having washed its northern edge, and driven its waters against its crowning wall of limestone. The fury of the waves, forced in to the line of junction, between the solid limestone and fissile sandstone, has broken up and removed the latter, till the overlying rock, pressed by its own gravity, has been split, fissured or otherwise disrupted, and often slid in vast solid masses down the ragged precipice. Kienuka offers one of the most striking instances of this action. The fissures made in the rock, by the partial withdrawal of its support, assume the size of cavern passages; they penetrate, in some instances, under other and unbroken masses of the superior stratum, and are, as a whole, curiously intersected, forming a vast reticulated area, in which large numbers of men could seek shelter and security.

A, denotes the apex of this citadel of nature. At this point, heavy masses of the limestone rest, in part, upon the fissures, and serve as a covering. From these primary fissures, others, marked C C C C C, proceed. The distance from G to H is 227 paces. The cross fissure at I, 37 paces.

Most of these fissures, which extend in the general parallel of the brink, appear to have been narrow, and are now covered with the sod, or filled with earth and carbonaceous matter, which gives this portion of them the aspect of ancient trenches. D, denotes a small mound or barrow. E F, a brook, dry at midsummer. B, the site of an abandoned saw-mill, at the head of an ancient lake inlet or gorge. The arrow head denotes the site of habitations, which are marked by remains of pottery, pipes, and other evidences of the ancient rude arts of the occupants. The parallel dots at B mark the road, which, at this point, crosses the head of the gorge. Trees, of mature growth, occupy some portions of the brink of the precipice, extending densely eastward, and obscure the view, which would otherwise be commanding, and fully justify the original name. Directly in front, looking north, at the distance of seven or eight miles, extends the waters of Lake Ontario, at a level of several hundred feet below. The intermediate space, stretching away as far as the eye can trace it, east and west, is one of the richest tracts of wheat land in the state, cultivated in the best manner, and settled compactly, farm to farm. Yet such to the eye is the effect of the reserved woodlands on each farm, seen at this particular elevation, that the entire area, to the lake shore, has the appearance of a rich, unbroken forest, whose green foliage contrasts finely with the silvery whiteness of the lake beyond. It requires the observer, however, at this time, to ascend the crown of the ridge, to realize this view in all its beauty and magnificence.

ANCIENT BATTLE FIELD ON BUFFALO CREEK.

The following sketch of the site of an ancient battle field, and vestiges of an entrenchment and fortification on the banks of the *Deoseowa*, conveys an idea of the relative position of the several objects alluded to. Taken together they constitute the distinguishing feature in the archæology of the existing Indian cemetery, mission station, and council house on the Seneca reservation, five or six miles south of the city of Buffalo. As such, the site is one of much interest, and well worthy of further observation and study. The time and means devoted to it, in the preparation of this outline, were less than would be desirable, yet they were made use of, under favorable circumstances, as the current periodical business and deliberations of the tribe brought together a large part of them, including the chief persons of education and intelligence, as well as many aged persons who are regarded as the depositories of their traditions and lore.

Tradition, in which all concur, points out this spot as the scene of the last and decisive battle fought between the Senecas and their fierce and inveterate enemies the Kah-kwahs, a people who are generally but erroneously supposed to be the same as the Eries.* It is not proposed in this place, to consider the evidences on this point, or to denote the origin and events of this war. It is mainly alluded to as a historical incident connected with the site. It is a site around which the Senecas have clung, as if it marked an era in their national history; although the work itself was clearly erected by their enemies. It has been the seat of their government or council fire, from an early period of our acquaintance with them. It was here that Red Jacket uttered some of his most eloquent harangues against the steady encroachments of the white race, and in favor of retaining this cherished portion of their lands, and transmitting them with full title to their descendants. It was here that the noted captive, Dehewamis, better known as Mary Jemison, came to live after a long life of most extraordinary vicissitudes. And it is here that the bones of the distinguished orator, and the no less distinguished captive, rest, side by side, with a multitude of warriors, chiefs and sages. Nor can we, on natural principles of association, call in question the truthfulness or force of the strenuous objections, which, for so many years, the whole tribe has opposed to the general policy of its sale. But these events are now history; the tribe has come into arrangements to remove to

* This is a French pronunciation of a Wyandot or Huron term. Vide Hennepin, Amsterdam, ed. 1698.

reservations owned by their brethren, in more westerly parts of the state, and there will soon be no one left whose heart vibrates with the blood of a Seneca, to watch the venerated resting places of their dead.

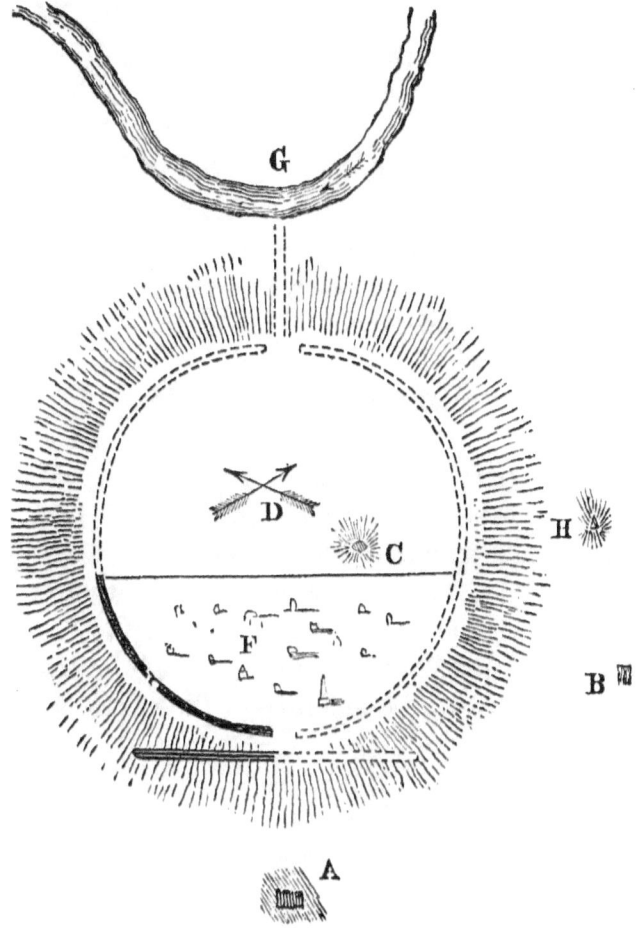

It was suitable, before the plough was put into these precints, and the last trench and mound of the tribe were obliterated, that some memorial of the locality should be preserved, and I can only regret that the labor itself has not been better or more successfully accomplished.

A, denotes the site of the mission house; B, of the council house; D, of the battle field, or that portion of it where the result was consummated; F, the grave yard. At C, there are still the remains of a mound, which tradition asserts was raised over the incinerated bodies of victor and vanquished slain in battle. These bodies were piled together, interspersed with the carcasses of deer and other game, which had been hunted with the special view that it might be offered as a sacrifice with the bodies, or to appease their spirits in the land of the dead. In making partial excavations into this mound, which has been frequently ploughed over in modern times, I procured several partially charred or blackened bones, supposed to represent parts of the human and brute species; a proof, it would seem, of the truth of this curious part of the tradition.* Mixed in the funeral pile, there were set

---

* The Indian name of Buffalo creek, which gives name to the city, has been variously written. In the treaty of 1784, at Fort Stanwix, it is called *Tehoseroron*, which is the Mohawk term, the final *n* being probably designed to convey a nasal sound. The word, as pronounced to me by the late Mrs. Carr of Wellington square, Canada, who was a daughter of the celebrated Brant, I have written *Tehoseroro*, meaning Place of the Linden tree. The letters *d* and *t* are inter-

vessels of pottery, with drinks offered as libations to the dead. And it is certain, also, that pieces of reddish coarse pottery were obtained at the same time, in making these partial examinations.

changeable between the Mohawks and Senecas. The latter, who at the same time do not use the letter *r*, and have some peculiarities in the use of the vowels, pronounce it in a manner which I thought should be written Deoseowa, as above. Mr. Wright, in his *Mental Elevator* and *Seneca Spelling Book*, makes it a word of four syllables, and uses the sound of *y* as heard in *yonder*, for the vowel *e* in his second syllable. Every practised ear is acute to satisfy its own requisitions of sound, which is not easy in unwritten languages; and there is besides a marked difference in the pronunciation of Indians from different localities, or uttered under different circumstances. Mr. Ellicott, on his original plat of Buffalo, writes it *Tushuway*. Others have spelt it still differently. The meaning of the word has excited but little difference of opinion. It denotes a locality of the linden or basswood tree, a species found upon the rich bottom lands of this stream, whose bark was highly valuable to these tribes for covering their lodges, and for the tough and fibrous inner coat, which at an early time served them to make both twine and ropes.

Whence then, it may be asked, is the origin of the word Buffalo, since it is not found in the Indian term? Tradition denotes that the range of this animal once extended to the banks of the great lakes. There was a current opinion among the early travellers along the shores of Lake Erie, that the bison had been seen and killed on this creek. Whether the impression arose from, or was traceable, in part or wholly, to a deception of certain hunters in bringing in "other flesh," under the denomination of Buffalo meat, as has been said, it would be difficult to determine. From whatever cause, it is certain that the stream acquired the popular name it now bears at an early day, whilst the aboriginal name was neglected.

The dotted lines are designed to show the probable figure and extent of the work, from the accounts of the Indians. That it was a circular work, appears to be denoted by the only parts of the wall yet remaining, which are drawn in black. The site itself was elevated moderately above the plain. There is no reason to suppose that this elevation of the surface was artificial. The relative position of the creek is denoted by G. H, marks the position of a stone, which is connected with the history of their domestic arts, before the discovery of the country. It was not practicable to obtain accurate admeasurements of distances; the design being merely to present a pencil sketch.

# CHAPTER VII.

## ANCIENT STATE OF INDIAN ART IN NORTH AMERICA.

To denote the state of art among the aboriginal race, it is necessary closely to examine such monuments of it, as exist. The word *monument* is used to denote any remains of art. Such are their relics in the form of worked shells and amulets, pottery, carved implements and utensils of stone, and other antiquarian remains found in their mounds, graves, fortifications, and other places of ancient occupancy in our latitudes. Of architectural ruins in stone, which constitute so striking a portion of aboriginal antiquities, in Central and South America, particularly in the ruins of their temples and teocalli, (the only form of such architecture indeed, which survives,) we have no remains north of the latitude of the mouth of the Mississippi, unless they shall be disclosed in some of the large mounds yet unopened, or in portions of the country north of such a line, which yet remains unexplored, west of the extreme sources of the Red river and the Rio Del Norte.

From this inquiry, we may peremptorily exclude all articles and remains of metal (not gold, silver or native copper), and all sculpture and inscriptions (not picture writing), which have been found and commented on, with an air of wonder, in various places, but which are one and all, undoubtedly of European, or to give the greatest scope to conjecture, of Trans-Atlantic origin. Such are, to begin with the highest object, the Grave creek inscription in apparently Celtiberic characters, the stone with a rude inscription in Roman letters and Arabic figures found in Onondaga county, and now deposited in the Albany Institute; the amulets of coarse enamel, colored pastes and glass, of the imperfect fabrics of the fifteenth and sixteenth centuries, found in Indian graves; or old village and fort sites, together with the flattened gun barrels, broken locks, artists' tools and other articles of iron, brass, or semi-vitrified earthenware, which are found over so considerable an extent of country in western New York. The latter are, undoubtedly, evidences of either earlier or more systematic attempts to settle, if not to found, colonies amongst the red race from abroad, than we are yet prepared fully to comprehend. But there need be no question as to the general era and character of art to which they belong; they are too clearly European in every instance to admit of scruple.

The introduction of the fabrics of European art, among the tribes of this continent, had the inevitable and speedy effect to destroy the prior Indian arts. It is astonishing to find how soon the aborigines of our latitudes lost the art of making culinary vessels of clay; of carving amulets and pipes out of steatites and other fissile mineral bodies; of perforating, dissecting and forming sea shells into the various shapes of wampum, gorgets, pendants, necklaces, belt and pouch ornaments, and other ornamental fabrics. They no sooner obtained the light brass, copper, iron, and tin kettle, than they laid aside the more clumsy and frail *akeek*, or clay pot; their women, relieved from the labor of selecting and tempering the clay, and forming it into pots and dishes, were advanced one step in the art of housewifery, and took the first lesson in European civilization.

The maker of arrow and javelin heads, for this was a distinct art, was superseded by the superior efficacy of fire arms; and his red descendant at this day, as well as the gleaner of antiquities, is alike at a loss to find where the ancient artist in chert and hornstone procured his materials, of so suitable a quality and fracture, and how he obtained the skill to chip and form them into such delicate and appropriate patterns. The small and slender axe of iron, with a steel edge, and pipe head, at once took the place of the crescent shaped stone tomahawk, which had alone been appropriated to war; while the larger half-axe, so called, supplanted the clumsy stone *agakwut*, before employed rather as a gouge to detach coal in the process of felling trees by fire, than an axe proper. By the application of the common lathe and turning chisel, those species of thick sea shells, which the natives had, with so much labor, converted into seawan and wampum, were manufactured with such superior skill, expedition and cheapness, (although this is an article which the trader always held comparatively high) that the old Indian art of the *wampum-maker*, sunk, like that of the *arrow-maker*, never to be revived. But of all the exchanges made between civilized and savage life, the gift of the steel trap in replacing the Indian trap of wood, was the most eagerly sought and highly prized by the hunter, although it hastened the period of the destruction of the whole class of furred animals, and thus in effect, brought to a speedy close the Indian dominion.

Pottery was an art known universally among all the tribes from Patagonia to the Arctic ocean, but was practised with very different degrees of skill. The northern tribes who bordered on the great lakes, and thence reached down to the Atlantic, made a rude article, which just answered the simple purposes of the culinary art. The clay, or argillaceous material used for it, was such as is common to diluvial and tertiary soils. It was tempered with silex, in the form of pounded quartz, or often quartz and feldspar, as it exists in granite, in quite coarse particles. This mixture prevented shrinkage and cracks in drying, and enabled the mass to withstand the application of heat—an art which has resulted, and would very soon result, in any given case, from experience. There were no legs to the Indian akeek, or pot. It was designed to be used, to use a chemical phrase, as a sand bath. Being set on the ashes, a fire was built around it. It might also admit of suspension, by a bark cord tied below the lip, which flared out well, and thus could be attached to the ordinary Indian cooking tackle, namely, a long-legged tripod, tied at the top with bark.

There is no evidence in the structure of any of this species of pottery, at least in these latitudes, that it had been raised or formed on a potter's wheel. The fact that prepared clay placed on a revolving horizontal circle, would rise by the centrifugal force, if resisted by the hand, or a potter's stick or former, was not known to these tribes; although it is admitted to be one of the oldest arts in the world. Some skill was consequently required to form the mass and shape the vessel, without machinery. It was essential to its utility, and to prevent unequal shrinkage in drying, that the body should be of uniform thickness; and this art was also, if we may judge from fragments, and one or two entire vessels examined, very well attained.

It is believed that this art, in this quarter, was in the hands of females; but every female or mistress of a lodge, was not adequate to it. It must have been the business of a class of persons in each village, who were professed potters. Tradition says that it was the practice to mingle some blood in wetting and tempering the clay.

It was impossible that this art, so rude and laborious, and so ill-suited to perform its offices when done, could survive and continue to be practised for any length of time after the tribes had been made acquainted with the products of the European potteries, rude as these were comparatively speaking, in the fifteenth and sixteenth centuries.

Architecture, as it existed in the north and west, was confined, we may suppose, to earthen structures, crowned with wood, in the shape of beams and posts. And it is only as it exhibited a knowledge of geometry, in the combination of squares and circles, to constitute a work of defence, that it is deserving of notice. The knowledge of the pyramid and its durability, is one of the most ancient geometrical discoveries in the world, and it is quite clear, in viewing the mounds and teocalli of North America, that the aborigines possessed, or had not forgotten it. In most of the works of defence, in the western country, the circular pyramid, or mound of earth of various sizes, formed a striking feature; whilst in relation to the mounds used for religious ceremonies, as we must suppose the larger mounds to have been, its completeness of plan and exact truncation, parallel to the plain or basis, denotes the prevalence among them, of this ancient

## ANCIENT STATE OF INDIAN ART. 225

architectural idea. We detect also, in a survey of the old works, the square, the parallelogram, the circle, and the ellipsis. And these figures were variously employed in the arrangement of masses of earth, to produce a rampart and a moat.

The domestic economy required implements to perform the arts which we express by the words sewing and weaving. The awl and needle were made from various species of animal bones of the land and water. The larger awl used to perforate bark, in sewing together the sheathing of the northern canoe, made from the rind of the betula, was squared and brought to a tapering point. A very close grained and compact species of bone was employed for the fine lodge awl used for sewing dressed skins for garments. After this skin had been perforated, a thread of deer's sinew was drawn through, from the eye of a slender bone needle. There was, besides this, a species of shuttle of bone, which was passed backwards and forwards, in introducing the bark woof of mats and bags; two kinds of articles, the work of which was commonly made from the scirpus lacustris, or larger bulrush. It was only necessary to exhibit the square and round awl, and gross and fine needle of steel, to supersede these primitive and rude modes of *seamstress-work* and *weaving*.

In an examination of Indian antiquarian articles, taken from the graves and mounds, there is some glimmering of the art of design. There is no other branch of art to which we can refer the numerous class of carved ornaments and amulets, or their skill in symbolical or representative drawing, evinced in their picture writing.

Amulets, and neck, ear and head ornaments, constituted a very ancient and very important department in the arcanum of the Indian wardrobe. They were not only a part of the personal gear and decorations which our old British writers sometimes denote *braveries*, but they were connected with his superstitions, and were a part of the external system of his religion. The aboriginal man, who had never laid aside his oriental notions of necromancy, and believed firmly in witchcraft, wore them as charms. They were among the most cherished and valued articles he could possibly possess. They were sought with great avidity, at high prices, and, after having served their office of warding off evil, while he lived, they were deposited in his grave at death. Bones, shells, carved stones, gems, claws and hoofs of animals, feathers of carnivorous birds, and above all the skin of the serpent, were cherished with the utmost care, and regarded with the most superstitious veneration. To be decked with suitable amulets was to him to be invested with a charmed life. They added to his feeling of security and satisfaction in his daily avocations, and gave him new courage in war.

But if such were the influence of pendants, shells, beads, and other amulets or ornaments, inspired by children who saw and heard, what their parents prized, this influence took a deeper hold of their minds at and after the period of the virile fast, when the power of dreams and visions was added to the sum of their experimental knowledge of divine things, so to call them. To fix it still stronger, the Indian system of medicine, which admits the power of necromancy, lent its aid. And thus, long before the period which the civilized code has fixed on, to determine man's legal acts, the aboriginal man was fixed, grounded and educated in the doctrine of charms, talismans, and amulets.

To supply the native fabric in this particular branch, was more difficult. Christianity, in a large part of Europe, certainly all protestant Europe, had, in 1600, religiously discarded all such, and kindred reliances on amulets, from its ritual and popular observances, where they had taken deep root during the dark ages; and hence the first English and Dutch voyagers and settlers who landed north of the capes of Florida, regarded the use of them as one of the strong evidences of the heathenishness of the tribes, and made light of their love of "beads and trinkets." It was necessary, however, to the success of their traffic and commerce—the great object of early voyages—that this class of articles should be noticed; and they brought from the potteries and glass houses of Europe various substitutes, in the shape of white, opaque, transparent, blue, black, and other variously colored beads, and of as many diverse forms as the genius of geometry could well devise. We see, what it is somewhat difficult as an inquiry of art otherwise to reach, that they also brought over a species of paste-mosaic, or curious oval, and elongated beads, made of a kind of enamel or paste, skilfully arranged in layers of various colors, which, viewed at their poles, represented stars, radii, or other figures. These were highly prized by the natives, (ignorant as they were of the manner of making them,) and were worn instead of the native amulets. In place of their carved pipes of steatite, or clay pipes ornamented with the heads of birds, men, or animals, they supplied them with a somewhat corresponding heavy, plain, or fluted pipe-bowl, which was designed, like the native article, to receive a large wooden stem, such as we see among the remote interior tribes at the present day. The jingling ornaments of native copper, or deer hoofs, were replaced from European work-shops, by the article of brass called hawks-bells, an article which, like that of wampum, still retains its place in the invoices of the Indian trade.

But by far the most attractive class of fabrics which the commerce of Europe supplied in exchange for their rich furs and peltries, was arm-bands, wrist-bands, ear-rings, gorgets, and other ornaments, both for the person and dress, of silver. This metal was esteemed, as it is at this day, above all others. Its color and purity led them to regard it as preëminently *the* noble metal, and its introduction at once superseded the cherished nabikoágun antique, and other forms of medals and gorgets made from compact sea-shells.

In this manner the introduction of European arts, one after another, speedily overturned and supplanted the ancient Indian arts, and transferred them, at the end of but a few generations, from useful objects to the class of antiquities.

It is unnecessary to pursue the subject to the department of clothing, in which woolens, cottons, linens and ribbons, took the place of the dressed skins of animals and birds, and the inner bark of trees, &c. Such objects are no part of the antiquities to be studied here. They are wholly perishable, and if any thing is to be gleaned from their study in the unburied cities of Pompeii and Herculaneum, where stone and marble offered objects of temporary resistance to currents of flowing lava, they offer no facts to guide the pen of the antiquarian here. The European and the Indian fabrics of the 16th century, have alike submitted to the inevitable laws of decomposition; but were it otherwise, could we disinter from the Indian graves the first duffils, strouds, osnaburgs, and blankets, that were given to the race, they would only prove that the latter quickly laid aside the inferior when they could get the superior article. It would prove that guns and gunpowder, brass-kettles and iron axes, had caused the manufacture of stone darts and clay kettles to be thrown aside and forgotten, and in like manner the labors of the spindle and loom had given the Indian, even before Columbus descended to his grave, a new wardrobe.

To denote what the Indian arts were, at the beginning of the sixteenth century, we must resort to their tombs, mounds, and general cemeteries. The melancholy tale that is told from the dust and bones of these sacred repositories is to be our teacher and schoolmaster. Its whispers are low and almost inaudible. There are pauses and lapses which it is difficult to make out. It requires great care — nice attention — examination and reëxamination. We must not hastily compose the thread of the narrative. We must doubt and reject where doubt and rejection are proper. We must discriminate the various epochs of art from the objects disinterred. If objects of various ages lie in the same cemeteries we must not confound them. Carefully to labor, patiently to study, cautiously to conclude, is the province of the antiquarian; and if, after all, he has but little to offer, it is, perhaps, because there is but little to glean.

## CHAPTER VIII.

### RELICS FOUND IN THE ANTIQUE GRAVES AND TUMULI OF WESTERN NEW YORK.

NABIKOAGUNA, (MEDALS,) — MEDAEKA, (AMULETS,) — ATTAJE-
GUNA, (IMPLEMENTS, &c.,) — OPOAGUNA, (PIPES,) — MINACEA,
(BEADS,) — PEAGA, (WAMPUMS,) — MUDWAMINA, (JINGLING
DRESS ORNAMENTS,) — OTOAUGUNA, (EAR JEWELS,) — OCHALI-
SA. (NOSE JEWELS,) — ÆSA, (SHELLS, SHELL-COINS, ORNA-
MENTS.)

It will tend to render the work of antiquarian examination exact, and facilitate comparison, if names descriptive of the general classes and species of each object of archæological inquiry be introduced. No science can advance if the terms and definitions of it be left vague. The mere inception of this design is here announced; it is not proposed, at present, to do more than submit a few specimens from a large number of antiquarian articles, the result of many years' accumulation. The figures and descriptions introduced are confined exclusively to the geographical area under examination.

To establish the classes of articles, names are introduced from the Indian vocabulary. These are qualified by specific terms, adjective or substantive, from the same class of languages, or from the English; rarely from other sources. A nomenclature derived from such sources, appeared preferable for these simple objects of savage art, to one taken from the ancient languages, whose prerogative it has, so long, been, to furnish terms for science and art.

CLASS I. NABIKOÁGUNA.*

Objects of this kind were worn as marks of honor or rank. So far as known, they were constructed from the most solid and massy parts of the larger sea shells. Few instances of their having been made from other materials, are known, in our latitudes. The ruins and tombs of Central and South America have not been explored, so far as is known, with this view. Nor have any insignia of this character been found of stone.

*Nabikoáguna Antique* (*Fig.* 1).—This article is generally found in the form of an exact circle, rarely, a little ovate. It has been ground down and repolished, apparently, from the sea conch. Its diameter varies from three-fourths of an inch to two inches. Thickness, two-tenths in the centre, thinning out a little towards the edges. It is doubly perforated. It is figured on the face and its reverse, with two parallel latitudinal, and two longitudinal lines crossing in its centre, and

* From the Algic, denoting a medal, a breast-plate or collar.

ANTIQUITIES OF WESTERN NEW YORK. 233

dividing the area into four equal parts. Its circumference is marked with an inner circle, corresponding in width to the cardinal parallels.

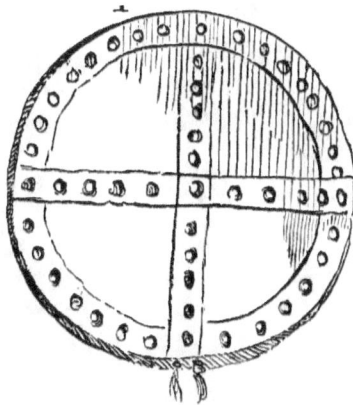

Fig. 1.

Each division of the circle thus quartered, has five circles with a central dot. The latitudinal and longitudinal bands or fillets, have each four similar circles and dots, and one in its centre, making thirty-seven. The number of these circles varies, however, on various specimens. In the one figured, they are fifty-two. The partial decomposition of the surface renders exactitude in this particular sometimes impossible. This article was first detected, many years ago, in a medal, one and a half inches diameter, found in an ancient grave on the Scioto, in Ohio, and was supposed to be a kind of altered enamel or earthernware. The structure of the shell is, however, present in all cases, in its centre. Its occurrence the present year, in the ancient fort grounds and cemeteries of Onondaga, identifies the epochs of the ancient Indian settlements of Ohio and western New York, and furnishes a hint of the value of these investigations. A medium specimen was examined, in the possession of I. Keeler, jr., Jamesville, very much obliterated; another, of the minimum size, at James Gould's, Lafayette. The largest specimen seen, is one sent by J. V. H. Clarke, from Manlius. The Indians have no traditions of the wearing of this species of shell medal, so far as known. It must be referred to the era preceding the discovery.

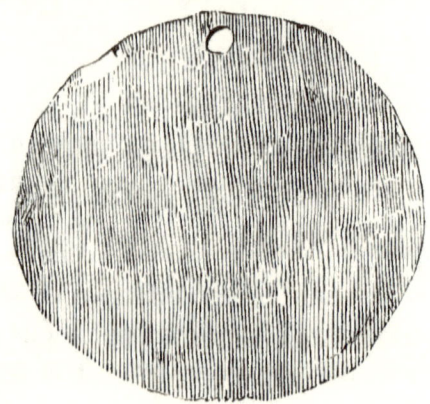

Fig. 2.

*Nabikouiguna Iroquois* (*Fig.* 2).—This article consists of a metal, which is apparently an alloy. It is slightly ovate, and is perforated in the rim, so as to have been hung transversely. Its greatest diameter is two and four-tenths inches. There are no traces of European art about it, unless the apparent alloy be such. Locality, valley of Genesee river.

ANTIQUITIES OF WESTERN NEW YORK. 235

Fig. 3.  Fig. 4.

*Nabikoáguna Cameo* (*Figs.* 3, 4).—This well sculptured article, was discovered in the valley of the Kasonda creek, Onondaga county. The material is a compact piece of sea shell. It still possesses, in a considerable degree, the smoothness and lustre of its original finish. Fig. 4 shows the prominence of the features in profile. At the angles of the temples are two small orifices, for suspending it around the neck. The entire article is finished with much skill and delicacy (*Mifflin Gould*).

Fig. 5.

*Nabikoáguna Mnemonic* (*Fig.* 5).—This is the head of an infant represented in the fine red pipe-stone from the Missouri. Locality, site of the ancient fort of the Kasonda valley (*I. Keeler, junior*).

## CLASS II. MEDÄEKA.

This class comprises the amulets proper. All the objects comprehended by it are supposed to have been worn on various parts of the person, as a defence against witchcraft, sorcery, or spells, or to propitiate good luck by superstitious means.

Fig. 6.

*Medäeka Missouric* (*Fig.* 6), with the illustration of the manner of its being worn on the breast. This article varies moderately in length, breadth and figure. It is generally the frustrum of an acute pyramid, perforated in its length, to admit being suspended from the neck, or ears. The figure exhibited is three inches in length by two-tenths in breadth at its superior, and nine-tenths at its inferior extremity. Sometimes, as in the figure given, it has a raised surface in the direction of the perforation. It is formed of the red pipe-stone of the Coteau du Prairie, west of the Mississippi; and its disinterment from Indian graves in western New York, denotes an early traffic or exchange of the article, or rather the material of its construction, with the tribes in that quarter. This stone is fissile, and easily cut or ground by trituration with harder substances to any figure. It bears a dull gloss, not a polish, which was produced by rubbing the surface with the equisitum, or rush, which has a silicious gritty surface. It is of the period anterior to the introduction of European arts. The specimen figured is from Onondaga county (*J. V. H. Clarke*). It occurred also at Oswego, in removing the elevation of the old fort (*J. McNiel*). Also, at Lower Sandusky, Ohio (*L. Cass*).

Fig. 7.

Fig. 8.

*Medäeka Dental* (*Figs.* 7, 8).—Fossil specimens of the bear's tooth. A power against charms or spells was often attributed to amulets of this kind. The two species, very different in size, and of course the age of the animal, were obtained from a single grave. Valley of the Genesee river (*Miss E. Trowbridge*).

Fig. 9.

*Medäeka Okun* (*Fig.* 9).—This species is made from a compact kind of bone, squared and perforated. Valley of the Genesee river (*Miss. E. Trowbridge*). From an ancient grave.

CLASS III. ATTAJEGUNA.*

Under this class are grouped a great variety of implements and instruments of utility, war, hunting and diversion. The material is chiefly stone. Without plates, however, it is impossible to give that exactitude to the description of this numerous class of antiquarian remains which is desired. But a single figure has been prepared—*Attajeguna Deoseowa*. This relic of Indian art was pointed out to me by Mr. Wright, missionary on the Seneca reservation, near the

---

* From the Algonquin *jeegun*, an instrument, an implement, or any artificial contrivance, or invention.

city of Buffalo. It consists of a block of limestone, having two spherical basin-shaped depres-

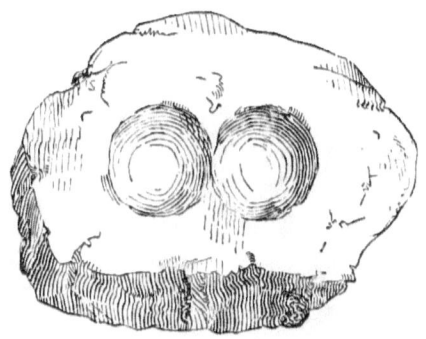

*Attajeguna Deoscowa.* Fig. 10.

sions. It is the tradition of this people that in this ancient mortar, the female potters of olden time pounded the stone material with which they tempered the clay for the ancient akeek, or cooking vessel. The original stone had been broken. From the portion of which the annexed is a figure, the entire mass must have been one of considerable weight.

## CLASS IV. OPOAGUNA.

The class of antique pipes. Smoking pipes constitute a branch of Indian art, which called forth their ingenuity by carvings of various forms of steatite, serpentine, indurated clay, limestone, sandstone and other bodies. A very favorite material was the red sedimentary compact deposit, found on the high dividing ridge between the Missouri and Mississippi, called the Coteau du Prairie. Pipes were also made from clay, tempered with some silicious or felspathique material, similar to that used in their ancient earthenware.

Fig. 11.

*Opoaguna Algonquin* (*Fig.* 11).—The composition of this pipe is a compact brown clay, tempered with a fine silicious matter, and dried in the sun, not baked in a potter's oven. The exterior is stained black, and bears a certain gloss, not a glazing. The bowl has been formed by hand, and is rude. The principal point of skill is evinced in the twist ornamenting the exterior of the bowl. Locality, Genesee river valley.

ANTIQUITIES OF WESTERN NEW YORK. 241

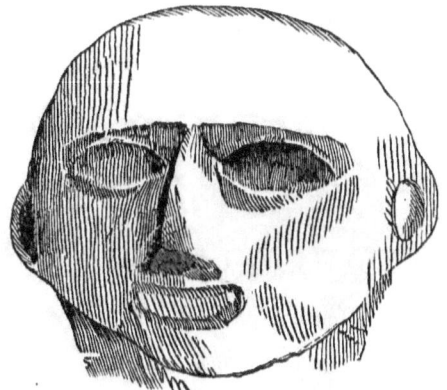

Fig. 12.

*Opoaguna Aztec* (*Fig.* 12).—The material is a species of terra cotta, or reddish earthenware. Its fracture discloses very minute shining particles, which appear to be mica. Probably the ingredient used to temper the clay, was pounded granite. The features resemble, very strikingly, those of Mexico and Central America. Onondaga county.

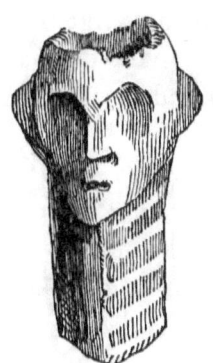

Fig. 13.

*Opoaguna Iberic* (*Fig.* 13).—Material, a slate colored ware. Features, thin and sharp. Neck,
32

acute in front, with an angular line extending from the chin downwards. Onondaga.

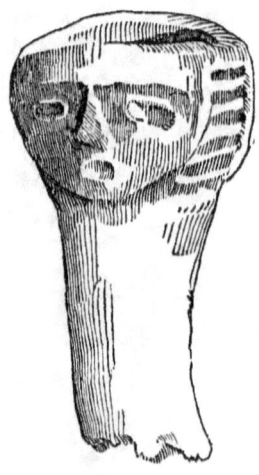

Fig. 14.

*Opoaguna Etruscan* (*Fig.* 14).—Material similar to *Opoag*. *Aztec*. Figure double headed—heads alike, placed back to back, like the Grecian deity Janus, connected by five parallel fillets,—bowl rudely formed, by hand. Onondaga.

CLASS V. MINACEA.*

Articles of this kind hold the relative character of modern beads or necklace ornaments. They are made of shells, bones, fissile minerals, sometimes pieces of calcareous or crystal. The

* From *meen*, a berry; and *ace*, a diminutive; hence minas or minace, a bead, or an ornament for the neck.

substitutes of the European period are glass and pastes.

Fig. 15.

*Minacea Alleghanic* (*Fig.* 15). — This article was first disclosed on opening the Grave-creek mound, in the Ohio valley, in 1839, and received the false designation of ivory. It is figured and described in the first volume of the Transactions of the American Ethnological Society, published at New York in 1845, where its character is determined. It has often the appearance of having been formed of solid masses of horn. It is believed to be, however, in every case, a product of massy sea-shell. Decomposition gives its surface a dead white aspect and limy feel. The powder scraped from the surface effervesces in acids. It is generally, not uniformly, an exact circle, and resembles extremely a very thick horn button-mould. It is characteristic of the orifice, that it appears to have been perforated with an instrument giving a spiral or circular line. This ancient ornament was also disclosed in my visit to the Beverly bone deposits of Canada in 1843. Its occurrence, in Onondaga, denotes the universality of the art, during the Ante-European period.

CLASS VI. PEÄGA.*

The ancient species of this article are numerous, and not exclusively confined to sea shells. The Indian cemeteries denote it in the form of bone and mineral.

Fig. 16.

*Peäga Iowan* (*Fig.* 16).—The material in this species is the red pipe stone of the west, so much valued. It is perforated longitudinally, and was evidently worn about the neck and breast like the modern article of wampum.

CLASS VII. MUDWÄMINA.

Ornament alone appears to have been the object of this numerous class of remains. Generally the object was the production of a jingling sound in walking. It was generally used to decorate some part of the dress. It assumed a great variety of shapes, and was made from as many species of material, including native copper. Another object was to inspire fear by the tread.

* From *peag*, one of the sea-coast terms of the Algonquins, for wampum.

ANTIQUITIES OF WESTERN NEW YORK. 245

Fig. 17.

*Mudwämina Miskwabic\** (*Fig.* 17).—The article figured is three-fourths of an inch in length, bell shaped, and composed of native copper, beat very thin. Onondaga.

Fig. 18.

*Mudwämina Ossinic†* (*Fig.* 18).—Material, red pipe stone, perforated. Onondaga.

Fig. 19.

*Mudwämina Wassäabic* (*Fig.* 19).—Material, a crystal, perforated. Traces of its irridescence. Probably a crystal of strontian. Onondaga.

\* Copper.  † Stone.

## CLASS VIII. OTOAUGUNA.

The name is derived from *Otowug*, meaning implements of, or relating to, the ear. It is a noun inanimate in *a*. Under this head all pendants and ornaments for the ear are comprised.

Fig. 20.

*Otoauguna Statuesque (Fig.* 20).—This pendant for the ear is made out of sea shell. It bears eight perpendicular and four transverse dots. Locality, old fort, site near Jamesville. Onondaga.

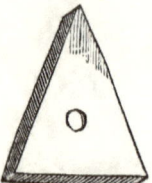

Fig. 21.

*Otoauguna Pyramidal (Fig.* 21).—This article varies in size, in the specimens examined, from nine-tenths to one and five-tenths inch, in the greatest length. It is an inequilateral triangle, generally, as here shown, varying to a very acute truncated prism reversed. Thickness from four to six lines. Perforated. Material, red pipe stone. Locality, Onondaga county.

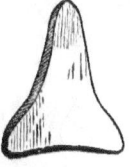

Fig. 22.

*Otoauguna Bifurcate* (*Fig.* 22).—Length eight-tenths inch. Perforated. Red pipe stone. Ondaga county.

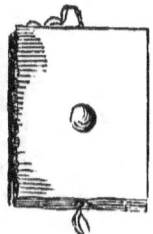

Fig. 23.

*Otoauguna Quadralateral* (*Fig.* 23).—Material red pipe stone. Onondaga county.

CLASS IX. OCHALISA*

This class of ornaments were worn as pendants from the inner cartilage of the nose. The material of nose jewels in modern times, when worn, is, generally, silver or some metal. Anciently bone or shell were the chief substances.

* From the Shawanoe word *ochalis*, a nose.

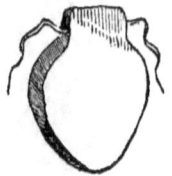

Fig. 24.

*Ochalisa Odä-ä\** (*Fig.* 24).—The material is a part of some massy species of sea shell. The outer coating is partially decomposed, exhibiting an opaque, limy appearance. Length, eight-tenths of an inch—rounded, heart-shaped. Onondaga (*J. V. H. Clarke*).

### CLASS X.  ÆSA.†

The number and variety of sea, and sometimes fresh water shells, worn by the ancient aborigines, has not been ascertained, but is large. They are uniformly found to be univalves.

Fig. 25.

*Æsa Marginella* (*Fig.* 25).—This species was first detected in the Grave-creek mound. It is a marginella. The figure is, incidentally, inexact. Onondaga.

\* Heart-shaped, or like.

† Æsa, a generic name for a shell— Algonquin.

## CHAPTER IX.

### ORAL TRADITIONS OF THE IROQUOIS, HISTORICAL AND IMAGINATIVE.

Ancient Shipwreck of a Vessel on the N. A. Coast — Forays into the Country of the Cherokees and Catabas — Exploit of Hiadeoni — Seneca Embassy of Peace to the Cherokees, and Heroic Exploit of Awl — Grave yard Serpent, and Corn Giant — Tradition of the Siege of Fort Stanwix — Tradition of the defeat of the Kah-kwahs — Epoch of the Confederacy — Some Passages of their Wars with Monsters and Giants — The Iroquois Quetzalcoatl.

This department of the inquiry constitutes one of deep and varied interest. It is found, however, that no little time is required to study, compare and arrange such parts of the matter as have claims to be considered historical, whilst those which are symbolical or fictitious, take so wide a range as hardly to justify, in this essay, the space which they would occupy. Specimens drawn from both classes of matter are introduced in the following papers, which, together with those inserted under the first head of Inquiries, will serve to convey a proper idea of this species of lore.

### ANCIENT SHIPWRECK ON THE COAST.

Whilst the northern tribes lived under the ancient confederacy before named, on the banks of the St. Lawrence and its waters, and before they had yet known white men, it is affirmed by Cusick, that a foreign ship came on the northern coasts, but being driven by stress of weather, passed southward, and was wrecked in that quarter. Most of the crew perished, but a few of them, dressed in leather, reached the shore, and were saved with some of their implements. They were received by a people called the Falcons,* who conducted them to a mountain, where, however, they remained but a short time, for their allies, the Falcons, disclosed an unfriendly and jealous spirit, and threatened them. In consequence they immediately selected another location, which they fortified. Here they lived many years, became numerous and extended their settlements, but in the end, they were destroyed by furious nations.

This tradition is divested of some of the symbolic traits which it possesses in the original, and by which the narrators may be supposed to have concealed their own acts of hostility or cruelty, in the extirpation of the descendants of the Europeans thus cast on their shores. To this end, they represent in the original, the

---

* One of the totems and clans of the Iroquois, is the hawk, or falcon.

saving of the crew to have been done through the instrumentality of carnivorous birds, and attribute the final destruction of the colony to fierce animals. It is one of the well known facts of history that none of the vessels of Columbus, Cabot, Verrizani, Sir Walter Raleigh, or Hudson, were *wrecked* on the American coasts; and there is hence a bare presumption that some *earlier* voyage or adventure from the old world is alluded to.

Can we suppose that in this dim tradition there is light cast on the lost colony of Virginia, which was first left on the island of Roanoke? The Tuscaroras,* who preserve the tradition, came to western New York from that quarter. They were a fierce, powerful and warlike nation, having in 1712 resolved on the massacre, on a certain day, of all the whites in the Carolinas. What is once done by natives, barbarous or civilized, is often the reproduction of some prior national act, and especially if that act had been attended with success; and it is by no means improbable that in this desperate and bloody resolve of 1712, the Tuscaroras meant to repeat the prior tragedy of Croatan.† Whether, however, the incident be of Ante-Columbian or Post-Columbian date, it is worthy preservation, and may be assigned its place and proper importance when we have gleaned more facts from the dark abyss of American antiquity.

\* This tribe have also the clan of the hawk or falcon.
† Vide Hackluit.

## FORAYS INTO THE COUNTRY OF THE CHEROKEES AND CATABAS.

Nothing is more distinct or better settled in the existing traditions of the Iroquois, than their wars with some of the southern tribes, particularly the Cherokees. I found this subject first alluded to among the Oneidas, who were hotly engaged in this southern war; afterwards among the Onondagas, the Senecas of Tonawanda, the Tuscaroras, and with still increasing particularity, among the Senecas of Buffalo, Cattaraugus, and Teonigono. But I was never able to fix the era of its commencement, or to find an adequate cause for it. It seems almost incredible that a war of this kind should have been carried on, at such a great distance from their central council fire at Onondaga, yet nothing is better established in their reminiscences.

They first came into contact, as Tetoyoah told me was his opinion, in the western prairies. The Iroquois are known to have hunted and warred far and wide in that quarter. The two nations seem to have been deeply and mutually exasperated. Tetoyoah spoke of an act of horrid treachery, the breaking of a peace pledge, and the murder of a peace deputation.

The war, however, instead of calling out the banded energies of the confederacy, appears to have been almost entirely one of a partizan character. It is memorable rather for partial enterprises and personal exploits, than for exhibiting the grander features of the military policy of the Iroquois. Warriors tested their bravery and heroism by going against the Cherokees. There were, it seems, no great armies, no grand battles. All was left to individual energy and courage. The great object of every young Iroquois, as soon as he was old enough to take the war path, was to go against the Cherokees. A march from the Oneida stone, the Kasonda creek, or the Genesee valley, to the southern Alleghanies, was regarded as a mere excursion or scouting trip. This long journey was performed without provisions, or any other preparation than bows, arrows and clubs. The fewer there were in one of these partizan enterprises, the greater was their chance of concealment and success. They relied on the forest for food. Thousands of miles were not sufficient to dampen their ardor, and no time could blot out their hatred. They called the Cherokees, by way of derision, *We-yau-dah*, and *O-yau-dah*, meaning a people who live in caves. These are the terms I found to be in use for the Cherokee nation, in 1845.

## EXPLOIT OF HIADEONI.

The following incident in the verbal annals of Iroquois hardihood and heroism, was related to me by the intelligent Seneca, *Tetoyoah* (William Jones of Cattaraugus), along with other reminiscences of the ancient Cherokee wars. The Iroquois thought life was well lost, if they could gain glory by it.

*Hi-a-de-o-ni,* said he, was the father of the late chief Young King. He was a Seneca warrior, a man of great prowess, dexterity, and swiftness of foot, and had established his reputation for courage and skill, on many occasions. He resolved, while the Senecas were still living on the Genesee river, to make an incursion alone into the country of the Cherokees. He plumed himself with the idea, that he could distinguish himself in this daring adventure, and he prepared for it, according to the custom of warriors. They never encumber themselves with baggage. He took nothing but his arms, and the meal of a little parched and pounded corn.* The forest gave him his meat.

Hiadeoni reached the confines of the Cherokee country in safety and alone. He waited for evening before he entered the precincts of a village. He found the people engaged in a dance. He watched his opportunity, and when one of the dancers went out from the ring into the bushes, he despatched him with his hatchet. In this way he killed two men that night, in the skirts of the woods, without exciting alarm, and took their scalps and retreated. It was late when he came to a lodge, standing remote from the rest, on his course homeward. Watching here, he saw a young man come out, and killed him as he had done the others, and took his scalp. Looking into the lodge cautiously, he

* One tablespoonful of this mixed with sugar and water will sustain a warrior twenty-four hours without meat.

saw it empty, and ventured in with the hope of finding some tobacco and ammunition to serve him on his way home.

While thus busied in searching the lodge, he heard footsteps at the door, and immediately threw himself on the bed from which the young man had risen, and covered his face, feigning sleep. They proved to be the footsteps of his last victim's mother. She, supposing him to be her son, whom she had a short time before left lying there, said, "My son, I am going to such a place, and will not be back till morning." He made a suitable response, and the old woman went out. Insensibly he fell asleep, and knew nothing till morning, when the first thing he heard was the mother's voice. She, careful for her son, was at the fireplace very early, pulling some roasted squashes out of the ashes, and after putting them out, and telling him she left them for him to eat, she went away. He sprang up instantly, and fled; but the early dawn had revealed his inroad, and he was hotly pursued. Light of foot, and having the start, he succeeded in reaching and concealing himself in a remote piece of woods, where he laid till night, and then pursued his way towards the Genesee, which, in due time he reached, bringing his three Cherokee scalps as trophies of his victory and prowess.

Such are the traditionary facts which are yet repeated by the Iroquois, to console their national pride in their decline. The incident reminds one strongly of the class of daring personal deeds of the noted Adirondack, Piskaret, as related by Colden; and it demonstrates how soon the daring traits of one ruling tribe may be adopted and even surpassed by another.

The Tonawandas, who are Senecas, appear to have preserved more distinct recollections of the origin of this war. Hohoeeyuh, (J. A. Sandford) stated to me, as did Tetoyoah, that it originated from the contact of their hunting parties on the plains of the southwest. But the latter affirms, that the Cherokees were the original offenders, by robbing and plundering a Seneca hunting party, and taking away their skins. Retaliation ensued. Tragic scenes of surprise and treachery soon followed. The Five Nations took up the matter in all their strength. They, contrary to what is above intimated, raised large war parties, and marched through the country to the Cherokee borders, and brought away scalps and prisoners. There are now, he added, descendants of the Cherokees in the third degree living on the Tonawanda reservation. Le Fort, an Onondaga chief, speaking on the same subject, said that there was, some years ago, a chief of pure Cherokee blood, by father and mother, living among them. He had been taken captive when a mere child. The fact being revealed to him after he had obtained the chieftancy, he went to seek his relatives in the south, and to live and die among them; but after every inquiry, he was unable to find them. The memory of the event of his loss was forgotten. He lingered a time, and then came back to the Senecas, and died among them—an example of that severe principle in the policy of this people, which has been before referred to, under the term of *We-hait-wa-tsha*, that is, flesh cut in pieces, and scattered amongst the tribes.

Iroquois tradition on this subject is the same now that it was in 1794. During this year, the interpreters told Col. Timothy Pickering, who was a commissioner on the part of the United States, that there were then living, warriors of the Six Nations, who had marched the whole distance to the Cherokee country, and attacked the latter. In proof of the former wars, they showed him a chief, who was a native Cherokee, born in the Cherokee country, who had been captured when a boy, and invested with this honor in mature life by the Senecas.* While the foregoing tradition of living Iroquois is strengthened by this coincidence, we are, at the same time, furnished by the latter with a proof that the Iroquois policy was favorable to the rise of talent and bravery, and that whatever be the checks provided by the totemic system, on the descent of chiefs, the elective feature was ever strongly marked upon their entire government and policy.

---

* Yates and Moulton, p. 232.

## DARING FEAT OF A SENECA.

In the course of the long and fierce war between the Six Nations and the Cherokees, it happened, said Oliver Silverheels, that eight Senecas determined to go on an embassy of peace. Among them was Little Beard the elder, and Jack Berry. They met some Cherokees on the confines of the Cherokee territories, to whom they imparted their object. Intelligence of this interview was sent forward to their village, where the embassadors were duly received, and after this preliminary reception, they were introduced to the ruling chiefs, and favorably received by the Cherokee council.

All but *one* of the Cherokee chiefs agreed to the terms of peace. He also would consent, if, prior to the treaty, the eight Seneca delegates would first consent to go to war against their enemies, situated south of them. (Who their enemies were is not mentioned.) They consented, and set out with a war party. A fight ensued in which the leader of the Senecas, called *Awl*, was taken prisoner. The other seven escaped. The fate of Awl was decided in the enemy's camp, where it was determined that he should be burned at the stake. Preparations were made for this purpose, but as they were about to bind him, he claimed the privilege of a warrior, to sing his death song and recite his exploits by striking the post. Pleased with the spirit of his request, and his noble air and words, his suit was granted, and they put a tomahawk into his hands, that he might go through the ceremony. He began by relating his exploits in the north. He recited his feats against the western Indians, adding, with the usual particularity, times and places, and the number of scalps taken. They were pleased and interested in these recitals, and quite forgot the prisoner, in the warrior. At last he came to the late battle, in which he was taken. He told how many of the Catabas, Apalaches, or Muscogees (if these were the tribes) he had killed. He kindled with redoubled ardor as he struck the post with his tomahawk, exclaiming, "so many of your own people, I have killed," and suiting his actions to his words, "so many I will yet kill." With this he struck down two men, bounded through the ring and ran. Consternation, for a moment, prevented pursuit, which gave him a start. Being swift of foot he outran his pursuers, eluded them in the woods, and reached the Cherokee camp, where he found and joined his seven companions.

They concluded the peace, and returned in safety to the Seneca country.

GRAVE YARD SERPENT, AND CORN GIANT.

Seneca tradition states that they formerly lived on the Chippewa river, near Niagara falls, Canada. One year, while thus located, they were visited by a calamitous sickness, and their corn was blighted. Their prophet dreamt, one night, that a great serpent laid under the village, with his head to the grave yard, and that it devoured all the bodies buried. This gave a most offensive breath, which was the cause of the sickness. He also dreamt that there was a great giant under the cornfield, who ate up the corn.

When he revealed these dreams to the chiefs, they determined to abandon the town, and immediately removed to Buffalo creek. The serpent soon followed them, and entered the mouth of the creek, but the Great Spirit, whose especial favorites they ever were, sent lightning to destroy it. The monster, however, proceeded up the stream, until the arrows from above fell so thick, that he was obliged to turn. His great size made him press against the shores, and break off the ground, and this is the cause of the expanse of the river three miles above its mouth. Before he reached the mouth of the stream, however, the arrows had cut him apart, and thus they escaped this scourge.

When they went back to visit their old town on the Chippewa river, they found the giant who had eaten up the corn, hanging by one leg from the crotch of a high lodge pole, with his body on the ground. He was very meagre, and had very long and thin legs, with scarcely any flesh on them (*W. I. C. Hosmer*).

If the above is to be regarded as an allegory of sickness and famine, it would have put Greek fancy to the task, to have concentrated the matter in a smaller compass, or to have exhibited it in a more striking light.

## SIEGE OF FORT STANWIX AND BATTLE OF ORISKANY.

Seneca tradition is rife on this subject. Tetoyoah says that they lost thirty-three chiefs in the battle of Oriskany.

Jacob Blacksnake adds, that he has seen a book in which it was stated that the Senecas had burned eight officers taken at this battle, in revenge for their losses. This he contradicts, on the authority of his father, Governor Blacksnake, who was there. The officers had been asked for after the battle, by the British, for the purpose of being rescued, but they were refused by the Indians, on account of their great losses. They were not, however, burned at the stake. It was decided that they should run the gauntlet, and they were killed by clubs, &c., in this ordeal.

## DEFEAT OF THE KAH-KWAHS ON BUFFALO CREEK.

Some of the Senecas affirm, that it is ninety years since the battle with the Kah-kwahs, on the site of the grave yard, on the Buffalo creek reservation, was fought. This would place the event in 1755, a date so modern, and so well known, in our colonial history, as to prove what a poor figure they make in attempts to adjust chronology. If 190 years (and, perhaps, such should be the tradition,) be taken, the event (allowing two years for their defence) would assume the precise time (1655) indicated for it, by one of Le Moyne's missionary letters, in which he says, that the war with the Eries had broken out afresh in 1653.

### ERA OF THE CONFEDERATION.

There is a tradition among portions of the Senecas, that the present confederation took place four years before Hudson sailed up the river bearing his name. This gives A. D. 1605. This question has been examined in its general bearings in a prior paper. All other authorities *indicate an earlier* date. The traditions of the Onondagas, as recorded in the account hereafter inserted, under the head of *Quetzalcoatl*, refer to the earliest period of their national existence, and render probable, a remark before made (vide Iroquois Groupe), that the last confederation was but the reconstruction of preceding ones, and that the idea of it was by no means new to them.

### TRADITIONS OF WARS WITH MONSTERS, GIANTS AND SUPERNATURAL PHENOMENA.

It is proposed to narrate a few passages of their early wars with monsters and giants, the two prominent objects in the foreground of their traditions. If it be thought, in perusing them, that mythology and superstition mingle too freely with real events or actions, to which the mind makes no exception, that is a matter upon which we have nothing to offer. Let it rather be considered as a proof of the authenticity of the narrative; for certainly there could be no stronger indication of a contrary character, than to find the Indian narrator relating a clear, consistent chain of indisputable facts and deductions to fill up the foreground of his history. What is said of such creations tallies admirably with their belief, at the present day, and harmonizes with itself, and with that state of proud heathendom, adventurous idolatry, and wild and roving independence, in which they lived. Who but an Aonaod? who but an Iroquois? could enact such a part, or believe that his ancestors ever did? To be great, and admired and feared, they roved over half America in quest of beasts and men. Surely, the man should be allowed to tell his own story in his own way, with all the witchcraft and spiritcraft he has a mind to bring to bear upon it.

No people in the world have ever, probably, so completely mingled up and lost their early history, in fictions and allegories, types and symbols, as the red men of this continent. Making no sort of distinction themselves, between the symbolic and the historical, they have left no distinctions to mark the true from the false. Their notions of a deity, founded, apparently, upon some dreamy tradition of original truth, are so subtile and divisible, and establish so heterogeneous a connection, between spirit and matter, of all imaginable forms, that popular belief seems to have wholly confounded the possible with the impossible, the natural with the supernatural. Action, so far as respects cause and effect, takes the widest and wildest range, through the agency of good or evil influences, which are put in motion alike for noble or ignoble ends—alike by men, beasts, devils or gods. Seeing some things mysterious and wonderful, he believes all things mysterious and wonderful; and he is afloat, without shore or compass, on the wildest sea of superstition and necromancy. He sees a god in every phenomenon, and fears a sorcerer in every enemy. Life, under such a system of polytheism and wild belief, is a constant scene of fears and alarms. Fear is the predominating passion, and he is ready, wherever he goes, to sacrifice at any altar, be the supposed deity ever so grotesque. When such a man comes to narrate events, he stops at nothing, be it ever so gross or puerile. He relates just what he believes, and unluckily he believes every thing that can possibly be told. A beast, or a bird, or a man, or a god, or a devil, a stone, a serpent, or a wizzard, a wind or a sound, or a ray of light—these are so many causes of action, which the meanest and lowest of the series, may put in motion, but which shall, in his theology and philosophy, vibrate along the mysterious chain through the uppermost skies; and life or death may, at any moment, be the reward or the penalty. If there be truth mingled in the man's narrations, as there sometimes is, it must be judged of by the lights of reason, common sense, science, sound philosophy, and religion. It is a

Gordian knot for the modern historian to untie; or it is a mass of traditionary chaff, from which we may perhaps, winnow a few grains of wheat. Herodotus had, probably, just such materials to work upon, and he made the best possible use of them, by letting the events stand as they were given, without exercising any inductive faculty upon them, or telling us the why and the wherefore; or if he ever deviates from the rule, as in the case of the fishes descending the Nile, it is a species of labor which might as well have been omitted.*

By the figure of a long house, the Iroquois meant to denote the confederated frame work of the league; by a great tree planted, they symbolized its deep seated natural power, one in blood and lineage, and its overshadowing influence and permanency. To assail such a combination of stout hearts, nature, they thought, must send forth the stoutest and most appaling objects of her creation.

The first enemy that apeared to question their power, or disturb their peace, was the fearful phenomenon of *Ko-nea-rau-neh-neh*, or the flying heads. These heads were enveloped in a beard and hair, flaming like fire; they were of monstrous size, and shot through the air with the velocity of meteors. Human power was not adequate to cope with them. The priests pro-

* It was designed, when these preliminary remarks were penned, to add some wilder legends than are here presented, which are, at present, withheld.

nounced them an emanation of some mysterious influence, and it remained with the priests alone to exorcise them by their arts. Drum, and rattle, and incantation, were deemed more effective than arrow or club. One evening, after they had been plagued a long time with this fearful visitation, the flying head came to the door of a lodge occupied by a single female and her dog. She was sitting composedly before the fire roasting acorns, which, as they became done, she deliberately took from the fire and eat. Amazement seized the flying head, who put out two huge black paws from beneath his streaming beard. Supposing the woman to be eating *live* coals he withdrew, and from that time he came no more among them.\*

The withdrawal of the Konearaunehneh, was followed by the appearance of the great *On-yar-he*† or lake serpent, which traversed the country, and by coiling himself in leading positions near the paths, interrupted the communication between the towns. He created terror wherever he went, and diffused a poisonous breath.

While this enemy yet remained in the land, and they were counselling about the best means of killing him, or driving him away, the country was invaded by a still more fearful enemy, namely, the *Ot-ne-yar-heh*, or Stonish Giants.

---

\* For a poetic use of this tradition of the Heads and Stonish Giants, see Hoffman's Wild Scenes, vol. 1, page 82. New York edition of 1843.

† Mohawk.

They were a powerful tribe from the wilderness, tall, fierce and hostile, and resistance to them was vain. They defeated and overwhelmed an army which was sent out against them, and put the whole country in fear. These giants were not only of prodigious strength, but they were cannibals, devouring men, women and children in their inroads.

It is said by the Shawnees, that they were descended from a certain family, which journeyed on the east side of the Mississippi, after the vine broke, and they went towards the northwest. Abandoned to wandering and the hardships of the forest, they forgot the rules of humanity, and began at first to eat raw flesh, and next men. They practised rolling themselves in the sand, and by this means their bodies were covered with hard skin, so that the arrows of the Iroquois only rattled against their rough bodies, and fell at their feet. And the consequence was, that they were obliged to hide in caves, and glens, and were brought into subjection by these fierce invaders for many winters, (or years.) At length the Holder of the Heavens visited his people, and finding that they were in great distress, he determined to grant them relief, and rid them entirely of these barbarous invaders. To accomplish this, he changed himself into one of these giants, and brandishing his heavy club, led them on, under the pretence of finding the Akonoshi-oni. When they had got near to their strong hold at Onondaga, night coming on, he bid them lie down in a hollow, telling them that he would make the attack at the customary hour, at day break. But at day break, having ascended a height, he overwhelmed them with a vast mass of rocks, where their forms may yet be seen. Only one escaped to carry the news of their dreadful fate, and he fled towards the north.

They were thus relieved, and began to live in more security, but the great Onyarhe, was yet in the country. Alarmed by what Tarenyawagon had done to relieve his people, and fearing for himself, he withdrew to the lakes, where he and his brood were destroyed with thunder bolts, or compelled to retire to deep water.

The Five Families were so much molested with giants and monsters, that they were compelled to build forts to protect themselves. The manner of doing it was this; they built fires against trees, and then used their stone axes to pick off the charred part; in this way, by renewing the fire, they soon felled them; and the fallen trunks were burned off in suitable lengths, in the same way, and then set up according to the size and plan of the fort, a bank of earth being piled outside and inside. They left two gates, one to get water, and the other as a sally port.

For some time after the great Onyarhe had left the country, they had peace; but in after years a still more terrific enemy came. It had a man's head on the body of a great serpent. This terrific foe took his position on the path between the Onondagas and Cayugas, and thus cut off all intercourse between their towns, for this was also the great thoroughfare of the Five Families, or nations. The bravest warriors were mustered to attack him with spears, darts and clubs. They approached him on all sides with yells. A terrible battle ensued; the monster raged furiously, but he was at last pierced in a vital place, and finally killed. This triumph was celebrated in songs and dances, and the people were consoled. They hunted again in peace, but after a time rumors began to be rife of the appearance of an extraordinary and ferocious animal in various places, under the name of the great *O-yal-kher*, or mammoth bear. One morning, while a party of hunters were in their camp, near the banks of a lake, in the Oneida country, they were alarmed by a great tumult breaking out from the lake. Going to see the cause of this extraordinary noise, they saw the monster on the bank rolling down stones and logs into the water, and exhibiting the utmost signs of rage. Another great animal of the cat kind, with great paws, came out of the water, and seized the bear. A dreadful fight ensued; in the end the bear was worsted and retired, horribly lamed. The next day the hunters ventured out to the spot, where they found one of the fore legs of the bear. It was so heavy that two men were required to lift it, but they found it was palatable food and made use of it, for their warriors believe that it inspires courage to eat of fierce and brave animals.

After a while, a great pestiferous and annoying creature of the insect tribe, appeared about the forts at Onondaga, in the guise of the *Ge-ne-un-dah-sais-ke*, or huge musquito. It first appeared in the Onondaga country. It flew about the fort with vast wings, making a loud noise, with a long stinger, and on whomsoever it lighted, it sucked out his blood and killed him. Many warriors were killed in this way, and all attempts made to subdue it were abortive, till Tarenyawagon, or the Holder of the Heavens, was on a visit one day to the ruler of the Onondagas. The giant musquito happened to come flying about the fort, as usual, at this time. Tarenyawagon attacked it, but such was its rapidity of flight that he could scarcely keep in sight of it. He chased it around the border of the great lakes, towards sun-setting, and round the great country at large, east and west. At last he overtook it and killed it near Gen-an-do-a, or the salt lake of Onondaga. From the blood flowing out on this occasion, the present species of small musquitoes originated.

## THE IROQUOIS QUETZALCOATL.

A TRADITION OF THE ORIGIN OF THE LEAGUE OF THE FIVE NATIONS.

It appears from the best authorities, that the first inhabitants of the ancient valley of Anahuac, or Mexico, came from the north. According to the historian Sahagun, these early inhabitants were Toltecs. They lived first at Tullantzinco, and thence migrated to Tulla. They had for their god Quetzalcoatl, whom they regarded as their teacher in arts and learning. They traced to him their progress in power and civilization; he rendered them superior to other men in war and cultivation, and as he was deemed both a god and a man, they appealed to him as a divine director, as well as their leader and founder. They also had in after times a king, or a ruling priest, of the same name. By the counsel of the former they left Tulla, and travelled eastward till they found a place called Tlapallan, or the city of the sun. This city they, in process of time, condemned and destroyed. Having done this, they went and founded the celebrated town of Cholula — still known for the ruins of its magnificent terraced pyramid.* Thus far Quetzalcoatl, under whom they had risen to power, abode with them, and, having accomplished the object of his care, it was in this quarter that he left them, and disappeared. He was, however, expected to reappear, and this belief was preserved up to the time of the conquest of the country by Cortez, whom the Aztecs, at first, mistook for their benefactor, the lost Quetzalcoatl.

It is remarkable that we find in the dim vista of Iroquois tradition, a counterpart of this story of Quetzalcoatl, differing chiefly in the name of the individual and some of the incidents, to whom the bold northern clans ascribed their early power and supremacy, and in the extent to

* This pyramid, which rises in three vast steps to the height of 177 feet, has a base of 1,423 feet.

which he was supposed to have carried them, in arts, arms and exploits.

Tarenyawagon, as the name is written by Cusick, united in one person the powers of a god and a man, and while they gave him the expressive name of the Holder of the Heavens, denoting the highest degree of sustaining power, he appeared only in the form of a man, and taught them hunting, gardening, the knowledge of medicine, and the art of war. He extricated them from the spot of their subterraneous confinement, not far inland from the borders of one of the great lakes. He imparted to them, the knowledge of the laws and government of the Great Spirit, and gave them directions and encouragement how to fulfil their duties and obligations. He gave them corn, and beans, and fruits of various kinds, with the knowledge of planting these fruits. He taught them how to kill, and roast game. He made the forests free to all the tribes to hunt, and removed obstructions from the streams. He took his position, sometimes, on the top of high cliffs, springing, if need were, over frightful chasms; and he flew, as it were, over the great lakes in a wonderful canoe of immaculate whiteness and magic power.

Having done this, he came down to closer terms of intimacy with the Onondagas, and resolved to lay aside his divine character, and live among them, that he might exemplify the maxims which he had taught. For this purpose he selected a handsome spot of ground on the southern banks of a lake called *Te-on-to*—being the same sheet of water, which, in the present area of western New York, is called Cross lake. Here he built his cabin, and from the shores of this lake he went out into the forest like the rest of his red companions, in quest of game and fish. He took a wife of the Onondagas, by whom he had an only daughter, whom he tenderly loved, and most kindly and carefully treated and instructed—so that she was known far and wide, as his favorite child, and regarded almost as a goddess. The excellence of his character, and his great sagacity and good counsels, led the people to view him with veneration, and they gave him, in his sublunary character, the name of *Hi-a-wat-ha*, signifying a very wise man. People came to consult him from all quarters, and his abode was thronged by all ages and conditions, who came for advice. He became the first chief in all the land, and whoever he made his companions and friends, were likewise clothed with the authority of chiefs in the tribe. In this manner all power came naturally into his hands, and the tribe rejoiced that they had so wise and good a man to rule over them. For in those days, each tribe was independent of all others; they had not yet formed a league, but fought and warred with each other.

Nothing that belonged to Hiawatha in his character of Tarenyawagon, was more remarkable than his light and magic canoe, which shone with a supernatural lustre, and in which he had performed so many of his extraordinary feats. This canoe was laid aside when he came to fix his residence at Teonto, and never used but for great and extraordinary purposes. When great councils were called, and he assembled the wise men to deliberate together, the sacred canoe was carefully lifted from the grand lodge, which formed its resting place; and after these occasions were ended, it was as carefully returned to the same receptacle, on the shoulders of men, who felt honored in being the bearers of such a precious burthen.

Thus passed away many years, and every year saw the people increasing in numbers, skill, arts and bravery. It was among the Onondagas that Tarenyawagon had located himself, and although he regarded the other tribes as friends and brothers, he had become identified as an adopted member of this particular tribe. Under his teaching and influence they became the first among all the original clans, and rose to the highest distinction in every art which was known to, or prized by the Akonoshioni. They were the wisest counsellors, the best orators, the most expert hunters, and the bravest warriors. They also afforded the highest examples of obedience to the laws of the Great Spirit. If offences took place, Hiawatha redressed them, and his wisdom and moderation preserved the tribe from feuds. Hence the Onondagas were early noted among all the tribes for their preeminence. He appeared to devote his chief attention to them, that he might afterwards make them examples to the others, in arts and wisdom. They were foremost in the overthrow of the Stone Giants, and the killing of the great serpent. To be an Onondaga was the highest honor.

While Hiawatha was thus living in domestic quiet among the People of the Hills, and administering their simple government with wisdom, they became alarmed by the sudden news of the approach of a furious and powerful enemy from the north of the great lakes. As this enemy advanced, they made an indiscriminate slaughter of men, women and children. The villages fled, in a short time, before them, and there was no heart in the people to make a stand against such powerful and ruthless invaders. In this emergency they fled to Hiawatha for his advice. He counselled them to call a general council of all the tribes from the east and the west. "For" said he, "our safety is not alone in the club and dart, but in wise counsels." He appointed a place on the banks of the Onondaga lake for the meeting. It was a clear eminence from which there was a wide prospect. Runners were despatched in every direction; and the chiefs, warriors, and head men forthwith assembled in great numbers, bringing with them, in the general alarm, their women and children. Fleets of canoes were seen on the bosom of the lake, and every interior war path was kept open by the foot prints of men, hurrying to obey the summons of Hiawatha. All, but the wise man himself, had been there for three days, anxiously awaiting the arrival of Hiawatha, when messengers were despatched after him. They found him gloomy and depressed. Some great burthen appeared to hang on his mind. He told them that evil lay in his path, and that he had a fearful foreboding of ill fortune. He felt that he was called to make some great sacrifice, but he did not know what it was. Least of all, did he think it was to be his daughter. Ever careful of her, he bade her kindly to accompany him. Nothing happened to hinder, or at all interrupt their voyage. The talismanic white canoe, which held them, glided silently down the deep waters of the Seneca. Not a paddle was necessary to give it impetus while it pursued the downward course of the stream till they reached Sohahee, or the point of the lake outlet. At this point Hiawatha took his paddle and gave it impetus against the current, until they entered on the bright and level surface of the Onondaga, cradled as this pure sheet of water is, among lofty and far sweeping hills. When the white canoe of the venerable chief appeared, a shout of welcome rang among these hills. The day was calm and serene. No wind ruffled the lake, and scarcely a cloud floated in the sky overhead. But while the wise man was measuring his steps towards the council ground, and up an ascent from the water's edge, a long and low sound was heard, as if it were caused by the approach of a violent, rushing wind. Instantly all eyes were turned upwards, where a small and compact mass of cloudy darkness appeared. It gathered size and velocity as it approached, and appeared to be directed inevitably to fall in the midst of the assembly. Every one fled in consternation but Hiawatha and his daughter. He stood erect, with ornaments waving in his frontlet, and besought his daughter calmly to await the issue. "For it is impossible," said he, "to escape the power of the Great Spirit; if he has determined our destruction, we cannot, by running, fly from it." She modestly assented, and they stood together, while horror was depicted in every other face. But the force of the descending body, was like that of a sudden storm. They had hardly taken the resolution to halt, when an immense bird, with long distended wings, came down, with a swoop, and crushed the daughter to the earth. This gigantic agent of the skies came with such force, that the whole assembly felt the shock, and were blown back several rods. The girl, who was beautiful in her looks and form, was completely crushed, and the head, beak and neck of the bird were buried in the ground from the mere force of the fall. The very semblance of a human being could not be recognised among the shattered remains of the daughter. These were, however, collected and buried.

But Hiawatha was inconsolable for his loss. He grieved sorely, day and night; and wore a desponding and dejected countenance. But these were only faint indications of the feelings of his heart. He threw himself on the ground, and refused to be comforted. He seemed dumb with melancholy, and the people feared for his life. He spake nothing; he made no answers to questions put to him. He laid still, like one dead. After several days the council appointed Hosee Noke, a merry-hearted chief, to make a visit to him, and to whisper a speech of consolation in his ears, and to arouse him from his stupor. The result was successful; he approached him with ceremonies, and induced him to arise, and name a time to meet the council. Yet haggard with grief, he called for refreshments, and ate. He then adjusted his wardrobe and head dress, and went to the council. He drew his robe of wolf-skins gracefully round him, and walked to his seat at the head of the assembled chiefs, with a majestic step. Stillness, and the most fixed attention, reigned in the council, while the discussion was opened and proceeded. The subject of the invasion was handled by several of the ablest counsellors and boldest warriors. Various plans were proposed to foil the enemy. Hiawatha listened with silence till all had finished speaking. His opinion was then asked. After a brief allusion to the calamity which had befallen him, through the descent of the bird of the Great Spirit, he spoke to the following effect:

"I have listened to the words of wise men, and brave chiefs. But it is not fitting that we should do a thing of so much importance in haste. It is a subject demanding calm reflection and mature deliberation. Let us postpone the decision for one day. During this time, we will weigh well the words of the speakers, who have already spoken. If they are good, I will then approve them. If they are not, I will then open to you my plan. It is one which I have reflected on, and feel confident that it will ensure safety."

When another day had expired, the council again met. Hiawatha entered the assembly with even more than the ordinary attention, and every eye was fixed upon him, when he began his address in the following words:

"Friends and brothers: You are members of many tribes. You have come from a great distance. The voice of war has roused you up. You are afraid for your homes, your wives and your children. You tremble for your safety. Believe me, I am one with you. My heart beats with your hearts. We are *one*. We have one common object. We come to promote the common interest, and to determine how this can be best done.

"To oppose these hordes of northern tribes, singly and alone, would prove certain destruction. We can make no progress in that way. We must unite ourselves into one common band of brothers. We must have but one voice. Many voices make confusion. We must have one fire, one pipe, and one war club. This will give us strength. If our warriors are united, they can defeat the enemy, and drive them from our land. If we do this, we are safe.

*Onondaga*, you are the people sitting under the shadow of the *Great Tree*, whose roots sink deep in the earth, and whose branches spread wide around. You shall be the first nation, because you are warlike and mighty.

*Oneóta*, and you the people who recline your bodies against the *Everlasting Stone*, that cannot be moved, shall be the second nation, because you always give wise counsel.

———, and you the people who have your habitations at the foot of the *Great Mountain*, and are overshadowed by its crags, shall be the third nation, because you are all greatly gifted in speech.

———, and you the people whose dwelling is in the *Dark Forest*, and whose home is every where, shall be the fourth nation, because of your superior cunning in hunting.

———, and you the people who live in the *Open Country*, and possess much wisdom, shall be the fifth nation, because you understand better the art of raising corn and beans, and making cabins.

You *Five* great and powerful nations, with your tribes, must unite and have one common interest, and no foes shall disturb or subdue you.

———, you the people who are as the *Feeble Bushes*, and you, ———, who are a *Fishing People*, may place yourselves under our protection, and we will defend you. And you of the south, and you of the west, may do the same, and we will protect you. We earnestly desire the alliance and friendship of you all.

Brothers: If we unite in this bond, the Great Spirit will smile upon us, and we shall be free, prosperous and happy; but if we remain as we are, we shall be subject to *His* frown. We shall be enslaved, ruined, perhaps annihilated forever. We may perish, and our names be lost forever.

Brothers: These are the words of Hiawatha. Let them sink deep in your hearts. I have said it."

A deep and impressive silence followed the delivery of this speech. On the following day the council assembled to act on it. Deliberation had recommended it, as founded in high wisdom. The union of the tribes into one confederacy was discussed and unanimously adopted. To denote the character and intimacy of the union, they employed the figure of a single council house, or lodge, whose boundaries were coextensive with their territories. Hence the name of *Aquinushioni*, who were called Iroquois by the French.

The great bird which fell from heaven, brought a precious gift to the warriors, in the white plumes which covered it. Every warrior, as he approached the spot where it fell, plucked a feather of snowy whiteness to adorn his brows; and the celestial visitant thus became the means of furnishing the aspirants of military fame with an emblem, which was held in the highest estimation. Succeeding generations imbibed the custom from this incident, to supply themselves with a plumage approaching it, as nearly as possible; they selected the plumes of the white heron.

Hiawatha, the guardian and founder of the league, having now accomplished the will of the Great Spirit, and the withdrawal of his daughter having been regarded by him as a sign that his mission was ended, he immediately prepared to make his final departure. Before the great council, which had adopted his advice, dispersed, he arose, with a dignified air, and addressed them in the following manner.

"Friends and Brothers: I have now fulfilled my mission below. I have taught you arts, which you will find useful; I have furnished you seeds and grains for your gardens; I have removed obstructions from your waters, and made the forest habitable by teaching you to expel its monsters; I have given you fishing grounds and hunting grounds; I have instructed in the making and use of warlike implements; I have taught how to cultivate corn. Many other arts and gifts I have been allowed by the Great Spirit to communicate to you. Lastly, I have aided you to form a league of friendship and union. If you preserve this, and admit no foreign element of power, by the admission of other nations, you will always be free, numerous and happy. If other tribes and nations are admitted to your councils, they will sow the seeds of jealousy and discord; and you will become few, feeble and enslaved.

"Friends and Brothers: Remember these words. They are the last you will hear from the lips of Hiawatha. The Great Master of breath calls me to go. I have patiently waited his summons. I am ready to go. Farewell."

As the voice of the wise man ceased, sweet sounds, from the air, burst on the ears of the multitude. The whole sky appeared to be filled with melody. And while all eyes were directed to catch glimpses of the sights, and enjoy strains of the celestial music that filled the sky, Hiawatha was seen, seated in his snow-white canoe, in the mid air, rising with every choral chant that burst out. As he rose, the sounds became more soft and faint, till he vanished in the summer clouds, and the melody ceased. Thus terminated the labors and cares of Tarenyawagon, or the Iroquois Quetzalcoatl.

## CHAPTER X.

### TOPICAL INQUIRIES.

Who were the Eries?—Building of the first Vessel on the Upper Lakes—Who were the Alleghans?—War with the Kah-kwahs—Antique Inscribed Stone of Manlius—Original Discovery of the Onondaga Country by the French—Burning of Schenectady—Antique Currency of the Manhattanese and their Neighbors—Cherokee Tradition of the Deluge—Asiatic Origin of the Indian Race.

Some interesting topics of inquiry, bearing on Iroquois history, cannot be well pursued at this time, without access to European libraries. The state of the book trade, and the importation of books into this country, but a few years ago, were such as to present still more scanty advantages to the pursuit of historical letters. There were but few libraries deserving of notice, and these were placed at remote points, spread over a very extensive geographical area, where access became often difficult or impossible. By far the largest number of American libraries were limited to a few thousand volumes, often to a few hundreds only, and these were chiefly made up of common or elementary works on arts, sciences and general literature. Writers were compelled to consult works at second hand, and could seldom get access to scarce and valuable originals; and the difficulties of making original inquiries into archæology, antiquities, philology, and other more abstruse, or less popular topics, increased at every step, and were in fact insurmountable to men of ordinary means. This state of things will sufficiently account for the low state of historical letters up to within a comparatively short period, without impugning the judgment or sagacity of early observers, on our local and distinctive history; and the fact offers the best plea why the aboriginal branch of our antiquities, and the just expanding science of ethnology, have been left enshrouded in so much darkness and historical mystery. We have, in fact, not had the means of making such inquiries. The libraries at Harvard, the public collection set on foot by Franklin at Philadelphia, the library of Congress, and that of the New York Historical society, and perhaps the growing library of the State Capitol at Albany, are some of the chief collections yet made in the Union; and these might be conveniently stowed away, *en masse*, in one corner of the Bibliotheque Royal at Paris, without exciting notice.

It is a subject of congratulation, that a class of booksellers is springing up in our cities, who are importers of antique works. The German and continental press, generally, is beginning to find access to our shores, and we may anticipate a period as not very remote, when original investigations into the most recondite topics may be made here, with every facility of this character.

## WHO WERE THE ERIES?

Louis Hennepin, who was a Recollect, remarks, in the original Amsterdam edition of his Travels, of 1698, that Canada was first discovered by the Spanish, alluding doubtless to the voyage of Cortereal, and that it received its first missionaries under the French, from the order of Recollects. These pioneers of the cross, according to this author, made themselves very acceptable to the Hurons, or Wyandots, who occupied the banks of the St. Lawrence, and who informed them that the Iroquois pushed their war parties beyond Virginia, and New Sweden,* and other parts remote from their cantons. They went, he says, in these wars, near to a lake, which they called *Erige* or *Erie*. Now, if they went "beyond Virginia and New Sweden," they were very remote from Lake Erie, and the assertion implies a contradiction or marked ignorance of the geography of the country. *Erie*, in the Huron language, he informs us, signifies the *Cat*, or *Nation of the Cat*; a name, he says, which the lake derived from

* The present area of the state of Delaware bore this designation.

the fact that the Iroquois, in returning to their cantons, brought the *Erige*, or *Erike*, captives through it. The French softened this word to *Erie*. It would appear, then, that the Eries either did not occupy the immediate banks of the lake, or else they lived on the upper or more remote parts of it. To be brought captives through it, they must have been embarked at some distance from its lower extremity. This vague mode of expression leaves a doubt as to the actual place of residence of this conquered and, so called, extinct tribe. Whether extinct or not, is not certain, nor, indeed, probable. The name is only a Wyandot name. They had others.

From inquiries made among the Senecas, some believe the Eries to be the same people whom this nation call Kah kwahs. But we do not advance much by changing one term for another. The inquiry returns, who were the Kah-kwahs? Seneca tradition affirms that they lived on the banks of Lake Erie, extending eastward towards the Genesee river, and westward indefinitely; and that they were finally conquered in a war, which was closed by a disastrous battle, the locality of which is not fixed; after which they were chased west, and the remnant driven down the Alleghany river. (See a subsequent paper, "War with the Kah-kwahs.")

Cusick, the Tuscarora archæologist, who writes the word *Squawkihows*, intimates that the Eries were an affiliated people, and that the remnant, after their defeat, were incorporated with the Senecas.

Colden states that after the war with the Adirondacks broke out, say at the end of the sixteenth century, the Iroquois, to try their courage, went to war against a nation called Satanas,* who lived on the banks of the lakes, whom they defeated and conquered, which raised their spirits so much, that they afterwards renewed the war against the Adirondacks and Hurons† on the St. Lawrence, and finally prevailed against them.‡

Satanas, it appears from the same author, is a name for the Shaouanons, Shawanoes, or Shawnees, as the term is variously written; a tribe, it may be further remarked, who are called *Chat* by the modern Canadian French. Still, we must guard against mere etymologies. There is no reason to suppose the Satanas and Eries, by any means, the same people.

A letter of the missionary Le Moyne, published in the Missionary *Relacions*, and hereto appended, proves that the war with the Eries, whatever may have been its origin or former state,

---

* This word appears to be an English *sobriquet*, derived from the Dutch language, and is from Satan, a synonyme for Duivel. (See Jansen's new Pocket Dictionary, Dortracht, 1831.) The plural inflection in *a*, if this derivation be correct, is duplicated in its meaning, by the corresponding English inflection in *s*, a practice quite conformable to English orthœpy, which puts its vernacular plural to foreign plurals, as Cherubims for Cherubim, &c.

† Called Quatoghies by the Iroquois.

‡ Hist. Five Nations, p. 23, London ed. 1767.

had newly broken out in 1653, and there are references of a subsequent date to denote that by the year 1655, this war had terminated in the disastrous overthrow of this people. They appear to have been then located where the existing traditions of the Senecas place them, namely, west of Genesee river, reaching to or near Buffalo. We may suppose that up to this period, the Senecas were limited to the eastern banks of the Genesee. And it was probably the results of this war that transferred their council fire from the present site of Geneva or Canandaigua to the Genesee valley.

When La Salle reached the Niagara river in 1679, but twenty-four years after the close of this Erie war, he found the entire country on its eastern or American banks in the possession of the Senecas. The history and fate of the Eries was then a tradition. Let it be remembered, that the early French missionaries included the Eries in the Iroquois family.

We may here drop the inquiry to be resumed at a future period.

### BUILDING OF THE FIRST VESSEL ON THE UPPER LAKES.

The enterprise of La Salle, in constructing a vessel above the falls of Niagara, in 1679, to facilitate his voyage to the Illinois and the Mississippi, is well known; but while the fact of his having thus been the pioneer of naval architecture on the upper lakes, is familiar to historical readers, the particular *place* of its construction, has been matter of various opinions. Gen. Cass, in his historical discourse, places it at Erie; Mr. Bancroft in his history, designates the mouth of the Tonawanda. Mr. Sparks in the biography of Marquette, decides to place it on the Canadian side of the Niagara. These variances result in a measure from the vague and jarring accounts of the narrators, whose works had been consulted in some instances in abridged or mutilated translations, and not from doubt or ambiguity in the missionary *Letters*.

Literary associations in America, who aimed to increase the means of reference to standard works, began their labors in feebleness. The New York Historical Society, which dates its origin in 1804, and has vindicated its claims to be one of the earliest and most efficient aids to the study of historical letters in America, published Tonti's account of the Chevalier La Salle's enterprise, in one of the volumes of its first series. It is since known, however, that this account was a bookseller's compilation from, it is believed generally, correct sources, but it was disclaimed by Tonti. It is at least but an abbreviation, and cannot be regarded as an original work.

In 1820, the American Antiquarian Society published in their first volume of collections, an account of Hennepin's discoveries, which is known to bibliographers to be also a translation of a mere abridgement of the original work, reduced to less than half its volume of matter. There was also an edition of this author, published in London in 1698; but still clipped of some of its matter, or otherwise defective; the tastes and wants of an English public being constantly consulted in the admission of continental books of this cast. The original work of Hennepin was published in French, at Amsterdam, in 1698. Being of the order of Recollects, and not a Jesuit, there was much feeling and prejudice against him in France, of which Charlevoix, the accomplished historian of New France, partook in no small degree. Yet whatever may have been the justice or injustice of these impeachments of the missionary's piety, there could be no motive for disagreement in a fact of this kind. As the original work has never been published in this country, I annex a translation of such parts of the journal as bear on this topic.

Hennepin was the camp missionary of the party on the way to Illinois, and the companion of La Salle on the occasion. By adverting to this narrative, the most satisfactory and circumstantial details will be found. The vessel, according to him, was built "two leagues above the falls," on the south banks. From every examination, there can be no doubt, that the spot selected was Cayuga creek, that is about three miles above the present site of Fort Schlosser.

On the 14th day of January, 1679, we arrived at our cabin at Niagara, to refresh ourselves from the fatigues of our voyage. We had nothing to eat but Indian corn. Fortunately, the whitefish, of which I have heretofore spoken, were just then in season. This delightful fish served to relish our corn. We used the water in which the fish were boiled in place of soup. When it grows cold in the pot, it congeals like veal soup.

On the 20th, I heard from the banks where we were, the voice of the Sieur De La Salle, who had arrived from Fort Frontenac* in a large vessel. He brought provisions and rigging necessary for the vessel we intended building above the great fall of Niagara, near the entrance into Lake Erie. But by a strange misfortune, that vessel was lost through fault of the two pilots, who disagreed as to the course.

The vessel was wrecked on the southern shore of Lake Ontario, ten leagues from Niagara. The sailors have named the place *La Cap Enragé*, (Mad Cape.) The anchors and cables were saved, but the goods and bark canoes were lost. Such adversities would have caused the enterprise to be abandoned by any but those who had formed the noble design of a new discovery.

The Sieur De La Salle informed us that he had been among the Iroquois Senecas, before the loss of his vessel, that he had succeeded so well in conciliating them, that they mentioned with pleasure our embassy, which I shall describe in another place, and even consented to the prosecution of our undertaking. This agreement was

\* Now Kingston.

of short duration, for certain persons opposed our designs, in every possible way, and instilled jealousies into the minds of the Iroquois. The fort, nevertheless, which we were building at Niagara, continued to advance. But finally, the secret influences against us were so great, that the fort became an object of suspicion to the savages, and we were compelled to abandon its construction for a time, and content ourselves with building a habitation surrounded with palisades.

On the 22d we went two leagues above the great falls of Niagara, and built some stocks, on which to erect the vessel we needed for our voyage. We could not have built it in a more convenient place, being near a river which empties into the strait, which is between Lake Erie and the great falls. In all my travels back and forth, I always carried my portable chapel upon my shoulders.

On the 26th, the keel of the vessel and other pieces being ready, the Sieur De La Salle sent the master carpenter named Moyse, to request me to drive the first bolt. But the modesty appropriate to my religious profession, induced me to decline the honor. He then promised ten louis d'or for that first bolt, to stimulate the master carpenter to advance the work.

During the whole winter, which is not half as severe in this country as in Canada, we employed in building bark huts one of the two savages of the Wolf tribe, whom he had engaged for hunting deer. I had one hut especially designed for observing prayers on holidays and Sundays. Many of our people knew the Gregorian chant, and the rest had some parts of it by rote.

The Sieur De La Salle left in command of our ship yard one Tonti, an Italian by birth, who had come to France after the revolution in Naples, in which his father was engaged. Pressing business compelled the former to return to Fort Frontenac, and I conducted him to the borders of Lake Ontario, at the mouth of the river Niagara. While there he pretended to mark out a house for the blacksmith, which had been promised for the convenience of the Iroquois. I cannot blame the Iroquois for not believing all that had been promised them at the embassy of the Sieur De La Motte.

Finally the Sieur De La Salle undertook his expedition on foot over the snow, and thus accomplished more than eighty leagues. He had no food, except a small bag of roasted corn, and even that had failed him two days' journey from the fort. Nevertheless he arrived safely with two men and a dog which drew his baggage on the ice.

Returning to our ship yard, we learned that the most of the Iroquois had gone to war beyond Lake Erie, while our vessel was being built. Although those that remained were less violent, by reason of their diminished numbers, still they did not cease from coming often to our ship yard, and testifying their dissatisfaction at our doings. Some time after, one of them, pretending to be drunk, attempted to kill our blacksmith. But the resistance which he met with from the smith, who was named La Forge, and who wielded a red hot bar of iron, repulsed him, and together with a reprimand which I gave the villain, compelled him to desist. Some days after, a squaw advised us that the Senecas were about to set fire to our vessel on the stocks, and they would, without doubt, have effected their object, had not a very strict watch been kept.

These frequent alarms, the fear of the failure of provisions, on account of the loss of the large vessel from Fort Frontenac, and the refusal of the Senecas to sell us Indian corn, discouraged our carpenters. They were moreover enticed by a worthless fellow, who often attempted to desert to New York, (*Nouvelle Jorck*,) a place which is inhabited by the Dutch, who have succeeded the Swedes. This dishonest fellow would undoubtedly have been successful with our workmen, had I not encouraged them by exhortations on holidays and Sundays after divine service. I told them that our enterprise had sole reference to the promotion of the glory of God, and the welfare of our Christian colonies. Thus I stimulated them to work more diligently in order to deliver us from all these apprehensions.

In the meantime the two savages of the Wolf tribe, whom we had engaged in our service, followed the chase, and furnished us with roe-bucks, and other kinds of deer, for our subsistence. By reason of which our workmen took courage and applied themselves to their business with more assiduity. Our vessel was consequently soon in a condition to be launched, which was done, after having been blessed according to our church of Rome. We were in haste to get it afloat, although not finished, that we might guard it more securely from the threatened fire.

This vessel was named The Griffin, (*Le Griffon*) in allusion to the arms of the Count de Frontenac, which have two Griffins for their supports. For the Sieur De La Salle had often said of this vessel, that he would make the Griffin fly above the crows. We fired three guns, then sung the *Te Deum*, which was followed by many cries of joy.

The Iroquois who happened to be present, partook of our joy and witnessed our rejoicings. We gave them some brandy to drink, as well as to all our men, who slung their hammocks under the deck of the vessel, to sleep in greater security. We then left our bark huts, to lodge where we were protected from the insults of the savages.

The Iroquois having returned from their beaver hunt, were extremely surprised to see our ship. They said we were the *Ot-kon*, which means in their language, *penetrating minds*. They could not understand how we had built so large a vessel in so short a time, although it was but sixty tons burthen. We might have called it a moving fort, for it caused all the savages to tremble, who lived within a space of more than five hundred leagues, along the rivers and great lakes.

I now went in a bark canoe, with one of our savage hunters, to the mouth of Lake Erie. I ascended the strong rapids twice with the assistance of a pole, and sounded the entrance of the lake. I did not find them insurmountable for sails, as had been falsely represented. I ascertained that our vessel, favored by a north or northeast wind, reasonably strong, could enter the lake, and then sail throughout its whole extent with the aid of its sails alone; and if they should happen to fail, some men could be put on shore and tow it up the stream.

Before proceeding upon our voyage of discovery, I was obliged to return to Fort Frontenac, for two of our company to aid me in my religious labors. I left our vessel riding at two anchors, about a league and a half from Lake Erie, in the strait which is between that lake and the great falls. I embarked in a canoe with the Sieur de Charon, and a savage; we descended the strait towards the great falls, and made the portage with our canoe to the foot of the great rock of which we have spoken, where we reëmbarked and descended to Lake Ontario. We then found the barque which the Sieur de la Forest had brought us from Fort Frontenac.

After a few days, which were employed by the Sieur de la Forest in treating with the savages, we embarked in the vessel, having with us fifteen or sixteen squaws, who embraced the opportunity, to avoid a land passage of forty leagues. As they were unaccustomed to travel in this manner, the motion of the vessel caused them great qualms at the stomach, and brought upon us a terrible stench in the vessel. We finally arrived at the river *A-o-ou-e-gwa*,\* where the Sieur de la Forest traded brandy for beaver skins. This traffic in strong drink was not agreeable to me, for if the savages drink ever so little, they are more to be dreaded than madmen. Our business being finished, we sailed from the southern to the northern shore of the lake, and favored by fair winds, soon passed the village which is on the other side of Keute and Ganneousse. As we approached Fort Frontenac the wind failed us, and I was obliged to get into a canoe with two young savages, before I could come to land.

\* \* \* \* \*

A few days after, a favorable wind sprung up, and fathers Gabriel de la Bibourde, and Zenobe Mambre, and myself, embarked from Fort Frontenac in the brigantine. We arrived in a short time at the mouth of the river of the Senecas, (Oswego river), which empties into Lake Ontario. While our people went to trade with the savages, we made a small bark cabin, half a league in the woods, where we might perform divine service more conveniently. In this way we avoided the instrusion of the savages, who came to see our brigantine, at which they greatly wondered, as well as to trade for powder, guns,

---

\* Probably the Genesee river.

knives, lead, but especially brandy, for which they are very greedy. This was the reason why we were unable to arrive at the river Niagara before the thirtieth day of July.

On the 4th of August I went over land to the great falls of Niagara with the sergeant, named La Fleur, and from thence to our ship yard, which was six leagues from Lake Ontario, but we did not find there the vessel we had built. Two young savages slyly robbed us of the little biscuit which remained for our subsistence. We found a bark canoe, half rotten, and without paddles, which we fitted up as well as we could, and having made a temporary paddle, risked a passage in the frail boat, and finally arrived on board our vessel, which we found at anchor a league from the beautiful Lake Erie. Our arrival was welcomed with joy. We found the vessel perfectly equipped with sails, masts, and every thing necessary for navigation. We found on board five small cannon, two of which were brass, besides two or three arquebuses. A spread griffin adorned the prow, surmounted by an eagle. There were also all the ordinary ornaments, and other fixtures, which usually adorn ships of war.

The Iroquois, who returned from war with the prisoners taken from their enemies, were extremely surprised to see so large a vessel, like a floating castle, beyond their five cantons. They came on board, and were surprised beyond measure, to find we had been able to carry such large anchors through the rapids of the river St. Lawrence. This obliged them to make frequent use of the word *gannoron*, which in their language signifies, how wonderful. As there were no appearances of a vessel when they went to war, they were greatly astonished now to see one entirely furnished on their return, more than 250 leagues from the habitations of Canada, in a place where one was never seen before.

I directed the pilot not to attempt the ascent of the strong rapids at the mouth of Lake Erie until further orders. On the 16th and 17th, we returned to the banks of Lake Ontario, and ascended with the barque we had brought from Fort Frontenac, as far as the great rock of the river Niagara. We there cast anchor at the foot of the *three mountains*, where we were obliged to make the portage caused by the great falls of Niagara, which interrupt the navigation.

Father Gabriel, who was sixty-four years old, underwent all the fatigues of this voyage, and ascended and descended three times the three mountains, which are very high and steep at the place where the portage is made. Our people made many trips, to carry the provisions, munitions of war, and other necessaries, for the vessel. The voyage was painful in the extreme, because there were two long leagues of road each way. It took four men to carry our largest anchor, but brandy being given to cheer them, the work was soon accomplished, and we all returned together to the mouths of Lake Erie.

I have heretofore remarked that the Spaniards first discovered Canada, and the Recollects first went there with the French colonies.

These good fathers were great friends of the Hurons, who told them that the Iroquois went to war beyond Virginia, or New Sweden, near a lake, which they called *Erige* or *Erie*, which signifies the *Cat*, or *nation of the Cat*, and because these savages brought captives from the nation of the Cat, in returning to their cantons, along this lake, the Hurons named it, in their language, *Erige* or *Erike*, the *Lake of the Cat*, and which our Canadians, in softening the word, have called Lake Erie.

We endeavored several times to ascend the current of the strait into Lake Erie, but the wind was not yet strong enough. We were therefore obliged to wait until it should be more favorable.

During this detention, the Sieur de La 'Salle employed our men in preparing some ground on the western side of the strait of Niagara, where we planted some vegetables for the use of those who should come to live in this place, for the purpose of keeping up a communication between the vessels, and maintaining a correspondence from lake to lake. We found in this place some wild chervil, and garlic, which grow spontaneously.

We left father Melithon at the habitation we had made above the great falls of Niagara, with some overseers and workmen. Our men encamped on the bank of the river, that the lightened vessel might more easily ascend into the lake. We celebrated divine service on board every day, and our people who remained on land could hear the sermon on holidays and Sundays.

The wind becoming strong from the northeast, we embarked, to the number of thirty-two persons, with two of our order who had come to join us. The vessel was well found with arms, provisions and merchandise, and seven small cannon.

The rapids at the entrance into the lake are very strong. Neither man, nor beast, nor ordinary bark can resist them. It is therefore almost impossible to stem the current. Nevertheless, we accomplished it, and surmounted those violent rapids of the river Niagara by a kind of miracle, against the opinion of even our pilot himself. We spread all sail, when the wind was strong enough, and, in the most difficult places, our sailors threw out tow lines, which were drawn by ten or twelve men on shore. We thus passed safely into Lake Erie.

We set sail on the 7th of August, 1679, steering west south west. After having chanted the *Te Deum*, we fired all the cannon and arquebuses, in presence of many Iroquois warriors, who had brought captives from *Tintonha*, that is to say, from the *people of the prairies*, who live more than 400 leagues from their cantons. We heard these savages exclaim, *gannoron*, in testimony of their wonder.

Some of those who saw us did not fail to report the size of our vessel to the Dutch at New York, (*Nouvelle Jorck*), with whom the Iroquois carry on a great traffic in skins and furs, which they exchange for fire arms, and blankets, to shelter them from the cold.

The enemies of our great discovery, to defeat our enterprises, had reported that Lake Erie was full of shoals and banks of sand, which rendered navigation impossible. We therefore did not omit sounding, from time to time, for more than twenty leagues, during the darkness of the night.

On the 8th, a favorable wind enabled us to make about forty-five leagues, and we saw almost all the way, the two distant shores, fifteen or sixteen leagues apart. The finest navigation in the world, is along the northern shores of this lake. There are three capes, or long points of land, which project into the lake. We doubled the first, which we called after St. Francis.

On the 9th, we doubled the other two capes, or points of land, giving them a wide berth. We saw no islands or shoals on the north side of the lake, and one large island, towards the southwest, about seven or eight leagues from the northern shore, opposite the strait which comes from Lake Huron.

On the 10th, early in the morning, we passed between the large island, which is toward the southwest, and seven or eight small islands, and an islet of sand, situated towards the west. We landed at the north of the strait, through which Lake Huron is discharged into Lake Erie.

Aug. 11. We sailed up the strait and passed between two small islands of a very charming appearance. This strait is more beautiful than that of Niagara. It is thirty leagues long, and is about a league broad, except about half way, where it is enlarged, forming a small lake which we called Sainte Claire, the navigation of which is safe along both shores, which are low and even.

This strait is bordered by a fine country and fertile soil. Its course is southerly. On its banks are vast meadows, terminated by vines, fruit trees, groves and lofty forests, so arranged that we could scarcely believe but there were country seats scattered through their beautiful plains. There is an abundance of stags, deer, roe-bucks and bears, quite tame and good to eat, more delicious than the fresh pork of Europe. We also found wild turkeys and swans in abundance. The high beams of our vessel were garnished with multitudes of deer, which our people killed in the chase.

Along the remainder of this strait, the forests are composed of walnut, chestnut, plum and pear trees. Wild grapes also abound, from which we made a little wine. There are all kinds of wood for building purposes. Those who will have the good fortune some day to possess the beautiful and fertile lands along this strait, will be under many obligations to us, who have cleared the way, and traversed Lake Erie for a hundred leagues of a navigation before unknown.

## WHO WERE THE ALLEGHANS?

This is an inquiry in our aboriginal archæology, which assumes a deeper interest, the more it is discussed. All the republic is concerned in the antiquarian knowledge and true etymology and history of an ancient race, to whom tradition attaches valor and power, and who have consecrated their name in American geography upon the most important range of mountains between the valley of the Mississippi and the Atlantic. But the inquiry comes home to us with a local and redoubled interest, from the fact that they occupied a large portion of the western area of the state of New York, comprising the valley of the Alleghany river to its utmost source, and extending eastwardly an undefined distance. Even so late as 1727, Colden, in his History of the Five Nations, places them, under the name of *Alleghens*, on his map of this river. It is not certain that they did not anciently occupy the country as far east and south as the junction of Allen's creek with the Genesee. A series of old forts, anterior in age to the Iroquois power, extends along the shores of Lake Erie, up to the system of water communication which has its outlet into the Alleghany through the Conewongo. There are some striking points of identity between the character of these antique military works, and those of the Ohio valley; and this coincidence is still more complete in the remains of ancient art found in the old Indian cemeteries, barrows, and small mounds of western New York, extending even as far east as the ancient Osco, now Auburn.

The subject is one worthy of full examination. Who this ancient race were, whence they came, and whither they went, are inquiries fraught with interest. We should not be led astray, or thrown off the track of investigation by the name. All the tribes, ancient and modern, have multiform names. This one of the Alleghans, probably fell upon the ears of the first settlers, but it is far from certain that it was their own term, while it is quite certain that it was not of the vocabulary of the bold northern race, the Iroquois, who impinged upon them. It has the character of an Algonquin word. Their descendants, whoever their ancestors were, may yet exist, under their own proper name, in the far west, or their blood may mingle in Iroquois veins. The Iroquois, who pushed their conquests down the Alleghany and Ohio rivers, did not found a claim to territory further south, on the Ohio river, than the mouth of the Kentucky. They pushed their war parties to the Cataba and Cherokee territories across the Alleghanies, and as far west as the Illinois. They swept over the whole region included between lakes Ontario, Erie and Huron, north. In the latter case we know it was a war against the tribes of the Algonquin stock, including one branch of another, and that their own generic stock, namely, the Quatoghies or Hurons.

The following communication on this subject addressed, in the year 1845, to the secretary of the Maryland Historical Society, is added in this connection. Although written to vindicate a question of antiquarian research, in a sister society, and partaking perhaps a little of a polemic cast, the facts are of permanent interest, and are thrown together in a brief and concentrated form.

Gentlemen: My attention has been called by a literary friend, to a notice of Mr. Brantz Mayer's report on the subject of a national name, or distinctive synonyme for our country. Mr. Mayer having chosen to reflect upon the antiquarian value of the historical research involved in the inquiry, I feel called upon, as a member of the committee of the New York Historical Society, before whom this question was discussed, to say a few words in reply.

The following quotation from my Glossary of Anglo-Indian Words, will best set forth my personal connection with the subject as a member of the society, and a humble laborer in the field of aboriginal antiquities, who is ready at all suitable times, to give authority for the use of whatever Indian terms he may employ.

"*Alleghan*, an obsolete aboriginal noun proper, applied adjectively both in French and English, to an ancient and long extinct people in North America, and likewise to the most prominent chain of mountains within the regions over which they are supposed to have borne sway."

Our authorities respecting the ancient Alleghans, are not confined to the very late period, that is, 1819,* which is alone quoted, and exclusively relied on by the learned secretary of the Maryland Historical Society. Nor do they leave us in doubt, that this ancient people, who occupy the foreground of our remote aboriginal history, were a valiant, noble and populous race, who were advanced in arts and the policy of government, and raised fortifications for their defence.† While they held a high reputation as hunters, they cultivated maize extensively, which enable them to live in large towns;‡ and erected those antique fortifications which are extended over the entire Mississippi valley, as high as latitude 43°, and the lake country, reaching from Lake St. Clair§ to the south side of the Niagara ridge (the old shore of Lake Ontario), and the country of the Onondagas and Oneidas.‖ Towards the south, they extended as far as the borders of the Cherokees and Muscogees.¶ From the traditions of Father Raymond, they were worshippers of the sun, had an order of priesthood, and exercised a sovereignty over a very wide area of country.**

\* Trans. Hist. and Lit. Com. Am. Phil. Soc., vol. 1, Philadelphia, 1819.
† N. Y. Hist. Col., vol. 2, p. 89, 91.
‡ Davies' Hist. Car. Islands.   § Am. Phil. Trans.
‖ Clinton's Discourse, N. Y. Hist. Soc., vol. 2.
¶ Seneca Tradition, N. Y. Hist. Col., vol. 2.
\*\* Hist. Carib. Islands, Paris, 1658. London ed. of 1666, p. 204, et. seq.

At what era the Alleghan confederacy, thus shadowed forth, existed and fell in North America, we do not know. Our Indian nations have no certain chronology, and we must establish data by contemporaneous tradition of the Mexican nations, or by internal antiquarian evidence.

The old fort discovered by Dr. Locke in Highland county, Ohio, in 1838, denoted a period of 600 years from its abandonment,* that is, 284 years before Christopher Columbus first sailed boldly into the western ocean. The trees on Grave-creek mound denote the abandonment of the trenches and stone look-outs in that vicinity to have been in 1338.† The ramparts at Marietta had a tree decayed in the heart, but the concentric outer circles, which could be counted, were 463.‡ The live oaks on the low mounds of Florida, where one of the Algonquin tribes, namely, the Shawnees, aver that they once lived and had been preceded by a people more advanced in arts, denote their abandonment about 1145.§ But even these data do not, probably, reach back sufficiently far to denote the true period.

If we fix upon the twelfth century as the era of the fall of the Alleghan race, we shall not probably over estimate the event. They had probably reached the Mississippi valley a century

* Cincinnati Gazette.
† Trans. Am. Ethnological Soc., vol. 1, N. Y., 1845.
‡ Clinton's Discourse.
§ Vide Arch. Am., vol. 1.

or two before, having felt, in their original position, west and south of that stream, the great revolutionary movements which preceded the overthrow of the Toltec and the establishment of the Aztec empire in Mexican America.

There are but two words left in our geography, supposed to be of the ancient Alleghan language.* These are *Alleghany,* and *Yioghiogany,* the latter being the name of a stream which falls into the Monongahela, on its right bank, about twenty miles above Pittsburgh.

Tradition, not of the highest character, gives us the words *Talligeu,* or *Talligwee,* as the name of this ancient nation, although it is nearly identical in sounds with the existing and true name of the Cherokees, which, according to the late Elias Boudinot (a Cherokee), is *Tsallakee.* Col. Gibson, a plain man, an Indian trader and no philologist, who furnished Mr. Jefferson with Indian vocabularies of the dialects of his day, to be used in answer to the inquiries of Catharine the Great,† expressed an opinion that this ancient people did not use a *T* before the epithet, but were called *Allegewee.* Tradition has, however, strictly speaking, preserved neither of these terms, although both appear to have strong affinities with them. The word Alleghany has come down to us, from the earliest times, as the name of the

---

* Other names have been subsequently found, and may be hereafter brought forward, as vestiges of the *Alleghan* language.

† Vide Trans. Royal Academy, Petersburgh.

great right-hand fork of the Ohio, and also as the name, from the same remote period of antiquity, of the chain of mountains of which the stream itself may be said to be the most remote northeasterly tributary. In this form it is evidently a local term, applied geographically, according to the general principles of the Indian languages, like *hanna* in the Susquehanna, and *hannock* in the Rappahannock, which appear to denote, in each case, a river, or torrent of water. By removing this local inflection, we have Alleghan as the proper term for the people, and I have felt sustained by this inductive process, in regarding Alleghan as the original cognomen of the *mound builders* of North America.

Having thus given my views with respect to the particular word which awakened this discussion, permit me now to turn to the other matters, so confidently brought forward by the secretary of the Maryland Historical Society.

The Iroquois affirm that they formerly lived in the area of the Cherokee country.* Captain Smith met a war party of this nation, in exploring one of the rivers of Virginia in 1608. So late as the era of the settlement of North Carolina, they brought off to the north the last of their cantons, in the tribe of the Tuscaroras. They sold the lands as far south as Kentucky river.† They *quitclaimed* the soil in northern Virginia and Maryland, and they quite forbid all sales of

* Clinton's Discourse, N. Y. H. Soc.
† Imlay's Hist. Kent.

land by the Delawares. All authorities, indeed, concur in showing the track of their migration, prior to 1600, to have been from the south to the north and northeast. Affiliation of language is also thought to denote their origin in the south.* The Hurons, who are of the same stock, affirm that they were originally the first of all the nations, and call the Lenapees, who have assumed the same distinction, *nephews*, denoting inferiority in the chronological and ethnological chain. In this term of nephews, so applied to the Delawares, all the Iroquois tribes concur.†

Algonquin tradition, recorded by Mr. Heckewelder in the Am. Phil. Trans. in 1819, on the part of the Lenapees, denotes that a confederation of these two stocks, namely, the political uncles and nephews, defeated the Alleghans, and drove them from the country. This tradition is referred to a time when the Delawares or Lenapees, were shorn of all power and consequence, "having been degraded," according to their phrase, to assume the petticoat, and found a refuge in a new country, to them, on the Muskingum, where they were taken under the care, as they had previously been east of the mountains, of the Moravain brethren. In their reminiscences they would consequently be prone to give prominence to such events as would reflect the most favorable lights on their history. They are speaking of events which, we see by the

* Vide Gallatin, 2 vol. Archa. Amer.
† Vide Oneota.

preceding references, must have transpired 500 or 600 years before, and in a very distant quarter of the Union. Yet they add some particulars which written history alone could preserve; and they ascribe to themselves such a degree of foresight, prudence, wisdom, valor and sense of Christian justice, as no Indian tribe in America ever evinced. These traditions are recorded by Mr. Heckewelder in a spirit of Christian kindness on his part, but he does not vouch for them; they are to be judged, like other traditions, by their probabilities and their conformity to other and known traditions. It is on this account that I have adduced the preceding data. Every Indian nation is prone to exalt itself, and if we would admit fully the claims of each, the rest would be sorry persons indeed.

The first thing to be borne in mind is, that the tradition is a very ancient one, and must have come down shorn of many particulars, which there appears to have been great carefulness to restate. The scene also is remote from the place of narration. No such fact as the principal one of the crossing, on which great stress is laid by Mr. Mayer, on the part of the Maryland Historical Society, could have taken place in the Ohio valley, or within one thousand miles of Pittsburgh, where alone, it must be remembered, we have any evidence, in the existing names of the country, of the residence of the Alleghans.

The Algonquins (we include the Lenapees in their proper groupe), attempting to cross the

Mississippi, into the territories of a foreign nation, with a large body of men, are defeated and driven back. They show themselves pacifically, in a moderate number, and the foreigners say, come! but turning out a multitude, are assailed. Whether this was an original stratagem, or an after thought, we are left to infer; but in either case, it would be quite conformable to Indian policy. For the sake of clearness, we will locate this event in the section of this great river between the Chickasaw bluffs and Natchez, its probable site. On this defeat they form an alliance with their uncles, the Iroquois, who were already east of the Mississippi, and were located north of the Alleghans. A long war begins, in the course of which the latter erect the fortifications which have excited so much curiosity in the Mississippi and Ohio valleys, and after proving themselves valiant men, are finally overpowered and driven off. The Lenapees are in 1819 the historians of their enemies, and berate them as faithless. The Maryland Historical Society, twenty-six years later, endorse the whole story, and pronounce the Alleghans pusillanimous, not so much it would seem for their heroic struggle and defence, as for the cause of it, namely, not letting the Algonquin hordes march into or through their country, as the superior forecast and judgment of the latter might, on further progress, dictate.

Does any sound historian, does any one acquainted with Indian life, character, or history, as it exists, and has always existed in North America, believe that the pacific and Christian request, put forth by Mr. Heckewelder, as the chronicler of his Delaware converts at Gnadenhutten, namely, that they might be allowed to explore a country east of them, to select it out and dwell therein, or that they had previously had the prudence, energy and forecast to send spies, like Moses, to spy it out—as if they were seeking a country for an agricultural settlement, with flocks and implements of husbandry—I repeat it, does any one, who reads this detailed part of the tradition, as told to and believed by the good old missionary, credit a syllable of it? If he does, his good-natured credulity must be greater than that of the committee of the New York Historical Society, whose suggestive report on the discussion of a distinctive national name has been the theme of so much misconception— may I not add, of so truly Pickwickian a degree of patriotism.

The truth is, this suggestion of a peaceful passage for the great Algonquin army, is to be found originally in the 20th chapter of Numbers, in the demand made by divine direction, by the Jewish leader, for a safe passport through the land of Edom, for the faithful performance of which there was a divine guaranty. And when the kind father had taught this historical lesson to his peaceful disciples on the banks of the Muskingum, he did not perceive, in afterwards putting down the traditions of his favorite Delawares, how completely they had adapted a sacred event to the exigencies of savage life, in a host of lawless invaders in the American wilderness, in the 12th century.

But we are not only to take this entire tradition of 1819, of an event happening 600 years before, *in extenso*, with all its moral exactness of motive, in the original actors, without any abatements or corrections required by other traditions or history, but the good father, whose moral excellence is pure and unimpeachable, but who was no philologist, aims to make the existing lexicography of the Delaware *prove* the tradition; and we have, in a foot note, a forced etymology of the name of the river Mississippi, to demonstrate that this is a Delaware name. Now, the name of this river is not *Namæsa sepu*, that is, Sturgeon, Trout, or as he gives it, Fish river, but *Missi-sippi*—a derivative from the adjective *great*, in an aboriginal sense, and *sippi*, a river. Mr. Gallatin[*] is inclined to believe that it should be translated *the whole river*, or a unity of waters; but neither he nor any other commentator, has been able to make *fish* out of *missi*. The merest tyro in the Indian languages, must perceive that the etymology does not bear the meaning of Fish river; and if it did, it would prove, contrary to their reputation, that the Indians give the most inappropriate geographical names, of all men in existence. Fish river would be the most mal-appropriate name for the Mississippi. Its

[*] Archa. Am., vol. 2.

turbid waters and rushing channel, surcharged with floating trees, and subject to a thousand physical mutations every season, is absolutely forbidding to the larger number of species, and favorable only to the coarser kinds, which are rejected from the table of the epicure.

A single remark more. The Delawares have never lived, or, if we examine Indian treaties, held an acre of land on the Mississippi, in its whole course between Itasca lake and the Balize. When Penn came to America, they lived on the Delaware river, in central Pennsylvania. They were ordered to quit the sources of the Delaware river by the Iroquois in 1742, and go to Wyoming or Shamoken.* They found their way across the Alleghanies in time to burn Col. Crawford at the stake,† and oppose the settlement of the Ohio valley, prior to the revolution; they settled on the Muskingum, and after some afflictions and mutations, chiefly brought upon themselves, they accepted lands, and first began to recross the Mississippi in 1818.‡ They are now located on the west banks of the Missouri, on the Konsas. Yet the etymology adverted to attributes to this tribe not only the naming of the river upon which they never lived, and never held any lands, but presupposes that the

* Colden's Hist. Five Nations, vol. 1, p. 31.

† Metcalf's Indian Wars in the West.

‡ This is the first time that this tribe ever, by history or tradition, other than their own, saw this river.

Illinois and other Algonquin nations living on its banks, above the influx of the Ohio and the Missouri, to whom, with the influence of the French, the actual name is due, preserved the Delaware term, *Namæsa sepu,* although it is neither used by their descendants, nor by Europeans.

## WAR WITH THE KAH-KWAHS.

Some inquiries have been made, in a prior paper, on the strong probabilities of this people being identical with the Ererions or Eries. While this question is one that appears to be within the grasp of modern inquiry, and may be resumed at leisure, the war itself, with the people whom *they* call Kah-kwahs, and *we* Eries, is a matter of popular tradition, and is alluded to with so many details, that its termination may be supposed to have been an event of not the most ancient date. Some of these reminiscences having found their way into the newspapers[*] in a shape and literary garniture which was suited rather to take them from the custody of sober tradition, and transfer them to that of romance, there was the more interest attached to the subject, which led me to take some pains to ascertain how general or fresh their recollections of this war might be.

[*] See Buffalo Commercial Advertiser, July 12, 1845, article Indian Traditions.

My inquiries were answered one evening at the mission house at Buffalo, by the Alleghany chief, *Ha-yek-dyoh-kunh*, or the Wood-cutter, better known by his English name of Jacob Blacksnake. He stated that the Kah-kwahs had their chief residence at the time of their final defeat, on the Eighteen-mile creek. The name by which he referred to them, in this last place of their residence, might be written perhaps with more exactitude to the native tongue, *Gah Gwah-ge-o-nuh*— but as this compound word embraces the ideas of locality and existence along with their peculiar name, there is a species of tautology in retaining the two inflections. They are not necessary in the English, and besides in common use, I found them to be generally dropt, while the sound of *g* naturally changed in common pronunciation into that of *k*.

Blacksnake commenced by saying, that while the Senecas lived east of the Genesee, they received a challenge from the Kah-kwahs, to try their skill in ball-playing and athletic sports. It was accepted, and after due preliminaries, the challengers came, accompanied by their prime young men, who were held in great repute as wrestlers and ball-players. The old men merely came as witnesses, while this trial was made.

The first trial consisted of ball-playing, in which, after a sharp contest, the young Senecas came off victorious. The next trial consisted of a foot race between two, which terminated also in favor of the Senecas. The spirit of the Kah-kwahs was galled by these defeats. They immediately got up another race on the instant, which was hotly contested by new runners, but it ended in their losing the race. Fired by these defeats, and still confident of their superior strength, they proposed wrestling, with the sanguinary condition, that each of the seconds should hold a drawn knife, and if his principal was thrown, he should instantly plunge it into his throat, and cut off his head. Under this terrible penalty, the struggle commenced. The wrestlers were to catch their hold as best they could, but to observe fair principles of wrestling. At length the Kah-kwah was thrown, and his head immediately severed and tossed into the air. It fell with a rebound, and loud shouts proclaimed the Senecas victorious in four trials. This terminated the sports, and the tribes returned to their respective villages.

Some time after this event, two Seneca hunters went out to hunt west of the Genesee river, and as the custom is, built a hunting lodge of boughs, where they rested at night. One day, one of them went out alone, and having walked a long distance, was belated on his return. He saw, as he cast his eye to a distant ridge, a large body of the Kah-kwahs marching in the direction of the Seneca towns. He ran to his companion, and they instantly fled and alarmed the Senecas. They sent off a messenger post haste to inform their confederates towards the east, who immediately prepared to meet their enemies. After about a day's march they met them. It was near sunset when they descried their camp, and they went and encamped in the vicinity. A conference ensued, in which they settled the terms of the battle.

The next morning the Senecas advanced. Their order of battle was this. They concealed their young men, who were called by the narrator *burnt-knives*,\* telling them to lie flat, and not rise and join the battle until they received the war cry, and were ordered forward. With these were left rolls of peeled bark to tie their prisoners. Having made this arrangement, the old warriors advanced, and began the battle. The contest was fierce and long, and it varied much. Sometimes they were driven back, or faltered in their line—again they advanced, and again faltered. This waving of the lines to and fro, formed a most striking feature in the battle for a long time. At length the Senecas were driven back near to the point where the young men were concealed. The latter were alarmed, and cried out, "Now we are killed!" At this moment, the Seneca leader gave the concerted war-whoop, and they arose and joined in battle. The effects of this reinforcement, at the time that the enemy were fatigued with the day's fight, were instantaneously felt. The young Senecas pressed on their enemies with resistless energy, and after receiving a shower of arrows,

\*A term to denote their being quite young, and used here as a cant phrase for prime young warriors.

beat down their opponents with their war-clubs, and took a great many prisoners. The prisoners were immediately bound with their arms behind, and tied to trees. Nothing could resist their impetuosity. The Kah-kwah chiefs determined to fly, and leave the Senecas masters of the field.

In this hard and disastrous battle, which was fought by the Senecas alone, and without aid from their confederates, the Kah-kwahs lost a very great number of their men, in slain and prisoners. But those who fled were not permitted to escape unpursued, and having been reinforced from the east, they followed them and attacked them in their residence on the Deoseowa (Buffalo creek), and Eighteen-mile creek, which they were obliged to abandon, and fly to the *Oheeo*, the Seneca name for the Alleghany. The Senecas pursued them in their canoes, in the descent of this stream. They discovered their encampment on an island, in numbers superior to their own. To deceive them, the Senecas, on putting ashore, carried their canoes across a narrow peninsula, by means of which they again entered the river above. New parties appeared, to the enemy, to be thus continually arriving, and led them greatly to overestimate their numbers. This was at the close of day. In the morning not an enemy was to be seen. The Eries had fled down the river, and have never since appeared. It is supposed they yet exist west of the Mississippi.

Two characteristic traits of boasting happened

in the first great battle above described. The Kah-kwah women carried along, in the rear of the warriors, packs of moccasins, for the women and children whom they expected to be made captives, in the Seneca villages. The Senecas, on the other hand, said as they went out to battle, "Let us not fight them too near for fear of the stench," alluding to the anticipated heaps of slain.

It may here be inquired, perhaps, whether the Kah-kwahs were not a remnant, or at least allies of the ancient Alleghans, who gave name to the river, and thus to the mountains. The French idea, that the Eries were exterminated, is exploded by this tradition of Blacksnake, at least if we concede that Erie and Kah-kwah, were synonyms. A people who were called Ererions by the Wyandots, and Kah-kwahs by the Iroquois, may have had many other names, from other tribes. It would contradict all Indian history, if they had not as many names as there were diverse nations to whom they were known.

### ANTIQUE INSCRIBED STONE OF MANLIUS.

It is some six and twenty years since a farmer in the town of Manlius, in Onondaga county, in gathering stones out of his field, turned up one, which had an inscription of a rude character, on its under side, with a date. It appeared to be a boulder, which had been appropriated to the purpose of a grave stone, by some European person or party of the adventurous era of wild discovery and gold hunting, which began with 1492. Several notices of this relic have appeared, differing, however, in their accounts of parts of the inscription. The stone itself has been, some years, deposited in the museum of the Albany Institute, where it is open to inspection. The following is a fac simile of it.

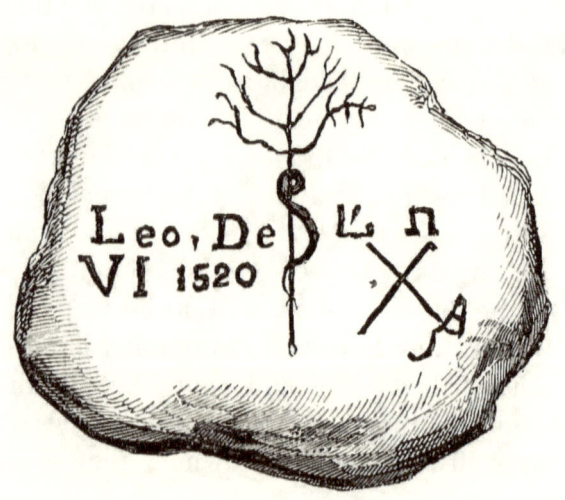

The disposition to exalt every antiquarian discovery of the country into a wonder, is one of the characteristics of the era. As the authenticity of this monument has not been questioned, and the fact it discloses does not put reason and probability to the stretch, there would not appear to have been a necessity for the multiplicity of speculations, which it has given rise to. But as such speculations have been made, it is proper to allude to them, in order truly to understand the question.

The discovery itself had all the simplicity which generally marks the narration of accidental incidents of the kind, by plain persons, who are intent on their own practical affairs, and are not set on theories, or discoveries of any sort. In the year 1820 or 1821, a farmer of Manlius, a Mr. Philo Cleaveland, determined to extend his meadow lands over a previously uncultivated part of his farm, and, after felling and removing the trees, began to prepare it, by picking up the larger stones. This inscription stone was found among them. It rested *on*, and was partly imbedded *in*, a moist piece of ground. It was toward evening, at the closing of his day's labors, when he raised the stone with his iron bar and turned it on its edge. Mr. C. being weary, leaned against a stump near by, with his hands resting on the top of the bar. While musing in that position, with his eyes fixed upon the stone, he observed something remarkable about it; and upon taking a nearer view, discovered some of the characters and letters above described. He removed it to a pile of stones not far distant, and at the time thought but little of it. Several days afterward he made another visit to the stone, when he found that the rain had washed the dirt clean from it, and the rude engraving was much more distinctly to be seen. This induced him to invite some of his neighbors to examine it, whereupon it was decided to remove it to a blacksmith's shop at Watervale, a small settlement near by. It remained there six months or more, and became the subject of much talk and speculation at the time.

Every person who came to the shop would of course examine the stone. It was not uncommon for some of them to take a horse nail, or old file, and scrape the cracks, seams and carvings, till all the parts of the inscription were freed from dirt. The stone was found with the inscription downward, about one-third buried. It was subsequently removed to Manlius village, and was visited by several gentlemen of science, most of whom were disposed to admit that it was genuine. It remained in this village nearly a year, and was finally deposited in the museum of the Albany Institute, now under the care of Dr. T. Romeyn Beck. The nature and objects of the inscription will best appear by a minute examination of the engraving. The stone is about fourteen inches, by twelve, and eight inches in thickness. It is a hard, oval shaped boulder, of a gneisoid character, and bears the evidence of attrition common to all the "erratic block groupe." By the figure of a serpent climbing a tree, a well known passage in the Pentateuch is clearly referred to. By the date, the sixth year of the reign of the Roman pontiff, Leo X, has been thought to be denoted. This appears to be probable, less clearly from the inscriptive phrase, Leo de Lon VI, than from the plain date, 1520, being six years after this pontiff took the papal chair.

It has been stated in newspaper notices, that Mexico had been fully explored and settled previous to 1521. In the appendix to Stone's Brant, this is narrowed down to the declaration that Mexico was "settled" at that date. Neither is strictly true. Cortez first attacked the city in 1519, whence he was expelled under the short but energetic reign of Guatamozin, but he finally prevailed, after taking the troops of Narvaez, and carried the city and razed it to the ground, as he entered it, in 1521. His army entered it finally on the 13th August. No exploration of the territory, far less "settlement," was made, or attempted, until after this date. We cannot look, indeed, to Mexico, as having originated any measure which led to a visit, however isolated, of the Iroquois country, a region possessed then, as afterwards, by brave muscular warriors, very different, in these respects, from the mild and luxurious Aztecs.

Gaspar Cotereal, a Portuguese, had explored nearly the whole coast of North America in 1501. The fishing grounds of Newfoundland were well known, and were occupied by the French as early as 1505. The Italian navigator Verrizani, examined the shores of the United States in 1525. Jacques Cartier reached Hochelaga, the present site of Montreal, in 1535.

It has been said that the inscription is due to persons connected with the celebrated expedition of De Soto. This explorer, who set out with the spirit of a Cortez, and who had the brilliant success of the latter to stimulate him to deeds of heroism, examined both banks of the Mississippi, for some leagues, and penetrated as far north as latitude 36°. It has been related by some that he with his party rambled over a considerable part of Florida, which then embraced nearly all the country now known as the southern states. During their travels, it is said, they fell in with a party of northern Indians, having with them a Spaniard taken from the party of Narvaez, who had proceeded over much of Florida ten years before; and that by their guidance, the captive Spaniard was led to this spot. It is further suggested by Sandford, in his Aborigines, in which he is followed by Stone, in his Life of Brant, that De Soto had probably gone as far north as the Susquehanna, from the analogies to this name found in the word "Saquechama," which is employed by the historian of the expedition. But it is quite overlooked, that De Soto did not set out on his expedition till 1538, eighteen years after the date of the Onondaga inscription. Florida had, however, then been known to the Spaniards for many years, having been discovered by De Leon in 1512, the very year that Leo X. assumed the papal chair. Its coasts and bays were known, as far west, at least, as the mouth of the Mississippi, which was evidently discovered by the Spaniards from Cuba in 1527. It was De Leon, however, who first visited the interior, and his visionary search for *the spring endowed with the property of restoring perpetual youth*, would hardly be credited, did it not rest on the best historical testimony. It is far more likely that some straggling party had reached the Iroquois country, from this Quixotic era of exploration, than from the mouth of the St. Lawrence, where the Cotereals were in 1501. And with this idea in view, it may be thought that the name De Leon is intended, by the words De Lon. The date, VI, would tally exactly with the sixth year after his landing in, and discovery of Florida, in 1512; the Onondaga country being then, *as much a part of Florida as any other part of the Atlantic and interior coasts.* If by the prefix of Leo, or Lion, a compliment to a brave and hardy explorer was designed to have been expressed, it would have well corresponded with the chivalric character of that age. As a mere historical question, a claim to the discovery of the interior of New York, by the Spanish crown, might, in this view, find something to base itself on.

ORIGINAL DISCOVERY OF THE ONONDAGA COUN-
TRY BY THE FRENCH.

If it is some abatement to the high conceptions which have been formed of a certain prominent class of antiquarian remains, existing in the general area of the Onondaga country, to find that they correspond with the Trans-Alleghany epoch of early occupancy, it is at the same time satisfactory to know, from authentic sources, that the vestiges of *European art*, scattered so widely through that quarter of the country, are due, almost exclusively, to the missionaries, fur traders, and early military commanders of France and Holland, and do not reach back beyond the opening of the sixteenth century. These powers first set foot in North America within about a year of the same time, Champlain having preceded Hudson perhaps a little; but the year 1609, is as early as either of them, actually, penetrated into the interior, or outskirts of the present area of western New York. It was western New York which was generally comprehended, at the several early eras, by the terms *Oneida Castle, Onondaga Country*, that excited their early rivalry. Both powers regarded it, as the store house of the wealth of the fur trade, and the prop of their political power. And they manouvred and fought for it, in a long series of years, and subtile negotiations, like a strong and wise man, who has much at stake. The conversion and civilization of the Indian tribes was put forth as a prominent object, and was not disregarded, by either power; but it is pretty evident, in scanning the history of the times, that, whatever other good the plan effected, it became the prominent means of carrying on a peculiar branch of inland diplomacy, and furnished the apology, at first, to the French, for entering into new territories, and afterwards, for remaining in them.

It is remarkable, however, when we examine

the ancient records, to find, that the Dutch possessed the entire and sole trade and control of the Iroquois cantons, during the whole period of the supremacy of the States General, in New York. This enterprising people, had gathered wisdom in the extension of their commerce in the East Indies, China and Japan. They went to that part of the world to extend their commerce. It was a business left exclusively in the hands of the merchants, who had chartered privileges; and the functionaries of the stadtholder submitted, as being a mere question of etiquette, to all the ceremonies and prostrations imposed by those pompous and semi-barbarous oriental courts. They applied the same policy here, and pleased the Iroquois so well, and adhered so faithfully to their compacts with them, that the French missionaries and emissaries, although they were active, made but little impression upon the Iroquois cantons, and did not draw them into a public alliance until 1667, being three years after the first surrender of New Amsterdam to the Duke of York.

It is interesting to trace the early movements of the French to gain an entrance into the Iroquois cantons, and serves to show the strength of the grasp, which the early colonists had on them, when it is perceived, that it was not till after the middle of the seventeenth century, that the Onondaga country was first successfully explored from the direction of Canada, or New France, as it was then denoted. Time has given an interest to the early details, on this head, which invests mere private, or at least, missionary adventure, with the importance of history. And it is from this consideration that I have inserted, in a translation, the journal of Father Le Moine, a Jesuit, who appears to have been one of the earliest, if not the first ecclesiastic of his order, who entered the country. This exploratory journey was commenced at Montreal, in July 1653, and completed in that month, and August and September following. The Iroquois gave their new visitor the name of *Ondessonk*. He was very respectful of their customs in conducting public councils; a good observer of character and motives, as well as of the natural features of the country; and his visit appears to have been well taken. The notice he gives of the salt springs at Onondaga lake, is probably the earliest for which we are to look to French authors. His allusion to the war with the Eries, an obscure subject, in some respects, is important in adjusting the chronology of their final defeat and expulsion; and the notices which appear, incidentally, of the quadrupeds, and the crops of zea maize, raised by this people, denote the substantial independence of the early Iroquois means of support. The journal commences in the following words.

On the 17th day of July, 1653, I set out from Montreal, and embarked for a land, as yet unknown, accompanied by a young man of piety and courage, who has long been a resident of the country.

July 18th. Following the course of the 'Saint Laurens,' we found nothing but breakers and impetuous rapids, full of rocks and shoals.

19th. We passed into a beautiful lake, eight or ten leagues long. At evening an army of importune musquitoes gave us warning of a storm, by which we were drenched the whole night.

20th. Islands, more beautiful than any in the world, here and there divide the placid stream. The land on the north side is excellent. Towards the west there is a chain of high mountains, which we named after St. Maguerite.

21st. The islands continue. In the evening we broke our bark canoe. It rained all night. The naked rocks served us for bed, covering and all. He who has faith in God, sleeps sweetly every where.

22d. The rapids, which for a season are not navigable, compelled us to carry our baggage and canoe on our shoulders. On the opposite side I perceived a herd of wild cattle, feeding at their ease, in the greatest security. Four or five hundred are sometimes seen in this neighborhood in one drove.

23d and 24th. Our guide being wounded, we were forced to encamp, a prey to the musquitoes. We took it patiently. A task the more difficult from there being no cessation from this inconvenience, day nor night. One could rest more at ease with death staring him in the face.

25th. We found the river so rapid, we were compelled to cast ourselves into the water, and drag our canoe after us among the rocks, as a dismounted cavalier leads his horse by the bridle. In the evening we landed at the mouth of Lake St. Ignace, where the eel abounds in prodigious quantities.

26th. A storm of wind and rain obliged us to land this morning, after four hours' journey. We soon made a shelter. Stripping some neighboring trees of their bark, we cast it on poles placed in the ground in a circle, the ends of which we brought together in the form of an arbor. This done, behold the house is finished. Ambition finds no door in such a palace—more delightful to us than if the roof was all gold.

27th. We coasted along the banks of the lake, which are high and rocky on all sides, presenting the frightful and picturesque. It is wonderful how such large trees can find root among so many rocks.

28th. A storm of thunder and lightning, and deluge of rain, obliged us to remain under the protection of our canoe, which, being inverted, served for our shelter.

29th and 30th. A continued storm of wind arrested us at the entrance of a great lake, named *Ontario*. We called it Iroquois lake, because the Iroquois nation have their villages on its southern borders. The Hurons are on the northern side, more in the interior. This lake is about twenty leagues broad, and forty long.

31st. We were this day obliged to make up for the time we lost by the storm. We traversed long islands, carrying our baggage, provisions, and canoe on our shoulders. It made the way seem long to us, poor weary voyagers.

August 1st. We landed this day at a small village of Iroquois fishermen.

2d. We began our march in the forest, and after travelling twelve or fifteen leagues, encamped about sunset.

3d. At noon we found ourselves on the banks of a river, one hundred or one hundred and twenty paces wide, on the other side of which there is a village of fishermen.

An Iroquois, whom I had befriended at Montreal, set me across in his canoe, and kindly bore me to the shore on his shoulders, being unwilling that I should put my feet into the water. Every one received me with joy, and these poor people enriched me with their poverty. They conducted me to another village, about a league distant, where a young man of consideration made a feast for me, because I bore the name of his father, *Ondessonk*. The chiefs, one after another, came to harangue us. I baptized some dying children, who perhaps were just spared for that sprinkling of the precious blood of Christ.

4th. They inquired of us why we were clothed in black. I embraced the opportunity to speak to them of the mysteries of our religion. They brought me a dying infant, which I named *Dominique*. They no longer conceal these little innocents from us. They took me for a great *medicine*, though I had for my prescription, only a pinch of sugar to give my patients. We pursued our journey. At noon we found a dinner waiting for us. The nephew of the principal chief of the country is to lodge us in his cabin, being commissioned by his uncle to escort us, and furnish us with every delicacy the season affords, especially bread from new Indian corn, of a kind which we roasted by the fire. We slept this night in the open air.

5th. We travelled four leagues before arriving at the principal Onondaga village. I passed many persons on the way who wished me a good day, one calling me brother, another uncle, and another cousin. I never before had so many relations.

At a quarter of a league from the village I began a speech in a solemn and commanding tone, which gained me great credit. I named all their chiefs, families and distinguished persons. I told them that peace and joy walked with me, that I scattered war among the distant nations.

Two chiefs addressed me as I entered the village, with a welcome I had never experienced among savages. Their women and children all treated me in a friendly and respectful manner. In the evening, I called the principal chiefs together, to make them two presents. One to wipe their faces, that they might regard me with kindness, and never show traces of sadness in their countenances. The second to clear away the little distrust that might remain upon their minds.

After considerable discourse, they retired to consult together, and then responded to my presents by two other gifts, richer than mine.

6th. I was called to-day in different directions to administer my medicine to dying children. Some I baptized. I also confessed our old Huron Christians, and found that God is every where, that he is pleased to labor silently in the hearts where faith has reigned. He there builds a temple, where he is worshipped in spirit and in truth, that he may be forever blessed.

In the evening my host took me one side, and told me with much affection that "he had always loved me; that he was now content, seeing that all the tribes of his nation desired nothing but peace; that recently the Senecas had requested negotiations for peace to be commenced, and for that object had made several beautiful presents; that the Cayugas had brought three belts for that purpose; that the Oneidas were gratified in having been, through his intervention, relieved from a bad position, and wished only for peace; that without doubt, the Mohawks would fall in with the others; that I must take courage, for I had the good wish of all."

7th. I baptized a young captive taken from the Neuter nation, fifteen or sixteen years old, who had been instructed in the mysteries of our faith by a Huron convert. This was the first adult baptism made at Onondaga, for which we are indebted to the piety of a Huron. The joy I experienced, was an ample compensation for all past fatigues. When God disposes a soul, a way of safety is soon provided.

9th. This day at noon a dismal cry arose, occasioned by the massacre of three Iroquois warriors by the nation of the Cat,* which took place about a day's journey from the latter. This amounts to a declaration of war.

10th. The deputies having arrived from the neighboring nations, after the customary proclamations by the chiefs, that "all should assemble in the cabin of Ondessonk," I opened the council by a public prayer, on my knees, in a loud voice, in the Huron tongue. I astonished them exceedingly by mentioning them all by nations, tribes, families and individuals, which amounted to no small number. This I was enabled to do from my notes, and it was to them as astonishing as it was novel. I told them I had nineteen messages to deliver.

The first was from Onnontio, (Monsieur de Lawson, governor of New France,) who spoke by my mouth, in behalf of the Hurons, Algonquins and French, since all these nations acknowledge

* The French apply the term *Chât*, to the Shawnees, at the present time.

him as their great captain. A large belt of wampum, a hundred small beads of green glass, which are the diamonds of the country, and an elk skin, accompanied my words.

The second was to cut the bonds of eight Seneca captives, taken by our allies and carried to Montreal.

The third was to break the bonds of some captives of the Wolf nation,* taken about the same time.

The fourth was to thank the people of Onondaga for having restored to us a captive.

The fifth was to thank the Senecas for having saved him from the torture.

The sixth was to thank the Cayugas for having acquiesced in his deliverance.

The seventh was to thank the Oneidas for having broken the bonds that held him captive.

The eighth, ninth, tenth and eleventh, were for those four Iroquois nations, a tomahawk to each, for their new war with the nation of the Cat.

The twelfth was to replace the lost head of the Senecas, (alluding to the capture of their chief by the Eries†).

The thirteenth was to strengthen their defences against their enemies.

The fourteenth was to paint their warriors for battle.

* The French apply this name to the Delawares.
† Erie, is from *Ererion*, a Wyandot name, for the nation elsewhere called the nation of the Cat.

The fifteenth was to unite all their counsels. Three presents for that object, a belt of wampum, two small glass beads and an elk skin.

By the sixteenth I opened the door of *Annonchiasse*, to all their nations. This was equivalent to a declaration they would be welcome among us.

By the seventeenth, I exhorted them to become instructed in the truths of our faith, and for that object I made three presents.

By the eighteenth I required them, henceforth, never to lay in ambush for the Algonquin or Huron nations who might be on their way to visit our French habitations. This I accompanied with three presents.

Finally, by the nineteenth present, I wiped away the tears from all the young warriors, shed for the death of their great chief, *An-nen-cra-os*, lately taken prisoner by the nation of the Cat.

On the delivery of each present, they uttered, from the bottom of their chests, a profound exclamation, in testimony of their gratification. I was about two hours in delivering my speech, in which I assumed the tone of a chief, walking about, as is their custom, like an actor on the stage.

After I had concluded, they assembled by nations and tribes, having called in a Mohawk, who by good chance happened to be there.

After consulting together for two hours more, they called me among them, and seated me in a place of honor.

The chief who is principal spokesman and orator of the country, repeated faithfully the substance of my whole speech, and after all had sung, in testimony of their joy, he directed me to pray to God, which I did very willingly. These exercises being finished, he addressed me in behalf of his nation.

First, he thanked Onnontio for his good wishes. Two large belts of wampum.

Second, in the name of the Mohawks, he thanked us for having restored five of their allies of the nation of the Wolf. Two other belts. .

Third, in the name of the Senecas, he thanked us for having rescued from the fire five of their people. Two other belts. Each present being followed by exclamations from the assembly.

Another chief, an Oneida, arose, and delivering four large belts, thanked Onnontio for having generously encouraged them to combat against their new enemies of the nation of the Cat, and for having exhorted them never to wage war against the French. "Thy words are admirable, Onnontio. They produce in my heart two contrary emotions. You animate me for war, and calm my heart with thoughts of peace. You are both a great warrior and peace-maker. Kind towards those you love, but terrible against your enemies. We all wish you love, and we will love the French for your sake."

In conclusion, the Onondaga chief commenced speaking. "Hear, Ondessonk," said he; "five nations speak through my mouth. I have in my heart the sentiments of all the Iroquois nations, and my language is faithful to my heart. Tell Onnontio four things, which are the substance of all our councils.

First, we will acknowledge him of whom you have spoken, who is the master of our lives and to us unknown.

Second, our national tree is this day planted at Onondaga; henceforth it will be the place of our councils, and treaties for peace.

Third, we request you to select, on the banks of our great lake, a convenient place for a French habitation. Place yourself in the heart of our country, since you have possessed our inmost affections. There we can go for instruction, and from thence you can spread yourselves everywhere. Have for us the care of fathers, and we will entertain for you the respect of children.

Fourth, we are engaged in new wars. Let Onnontio animate us for the scene. For him we will have no thoughts but peace."

Their most valuable presents were reserved for the last four speeches.

On the 15th of August we set out on our return, with a goodly company.

On the 16th we arrived at the entrance of a small lake.* In a large basin, half dry, we tasted the water of a spring which the Indians are afraid to drink, saying that it is inhabited by a demon who renders it stinking. I found it to

* Onondaga lake.

be a fountain of salt water, from which we made salt as natural as from the sea, some of which we shall carry to Quebec. This lake abounds in salmon, trout and other kinds of fish.

On the 17th we entered the outlet of the lake and passed the river of the Senecas on the left, the addition of which enlarges the stream. It rises, they say, in two streams among the Cayugas and Senecas. After three leagues more of pleasant travelling we passed on our right the river Oneida, which seemed quite deep. A league farther we encountered some rapids, which gave the name to a village of fishermen.

On the 18th my companions were engaged in putting their canoes in order.

Aug. 19th. We journeyed on, upon the same river, which is of fine width, and everywhere deep, except some rapids, where we found it necessary to get into the water and draw the canoe to prevent its being broken by the rocks.

20th. We arrived this day at the great Lake Ontario, called the Lake of the Iroquois.

21st. The lake is rough to-day by reason of a violent wind which succeeded a storm of rain.

22d. Coasting pleasantly along the shore of the lake, my companions shot a large stag. We contented ourselves with seeing it broiled; it being Saturday, a day of abstinence with us.

23d. We arrived at a place they have destined a French habitation, where there are beautiful meadows, also fine fishing, and convenient access for the different nations.

24th and 25th. We were detained by the wind.

26th. Having embarked before the tempest had abated, our canoe upset, and we expected to be drowned, but finally gained an island, where we dried ourselves at leisure.

27th. A temporary calm enabled us to reach the main land.

28th and 29th. Our companions were detained by hunting. They were put in excellent spirits by the abundance of flesh, which is their paradise.

30th and 31st. We experienced nothing but wind and rain. They are sadly inconvenient to the poor voyager, who, having labored all day, is poorly lodged at night.

Sept. 1st. I never saw so many wild deer; we have no desire to hunt them. My companions could not resist killing three. What waste, for we left the whole, except the skins and the tenderest pieces.

2d. Travelling through large meadows, we saw in many places immense droves of cattle; their horns in some respects resemble the antlers of a stag.

3d and 4th. We still found game in abundance. It seemed to follow us every where. A herd of twenty cows cast themselves into the water as if to meet us.

5th. This day we descended the same distance which took us two days to ascend, in consequence of the rapids and shoals.

6th. The falls of St. Louis so frightened my companions, that they landed me four leagues above Montreal. But God gave me sufficient strength to reach it before noon, and celebrate the holy mass, of which I had been deprived during all my voyage.

7th. I passed on and descended to the *Trois Rivieres*, where my companions desired to go, and on the 11th of September, 1653, arrived safely at Quebec.

## BURNING OF SCHENECTADY BY THE FRENCH IN 1690.

The ancient Mohawk village, which stood at this place, was called *Connocharie-guharie*, or as Benson writes it, *Oronowaragouhre*, in allusion to the vast piles of flood-wood which were left every spring on the flats. The term Origoniwontl,* appears to have been applied, at a later period, to the village at the same place; perhaps the site was a little varied in its particular location, and perhaps both names were applied, at the same time, to the same place, being different modes of describing the position of the village. When the Dutch obtained a patent, embracing the site in 1661, from Gov. Stuyvesant, the Indian name of the Vlachte, or flats, was mentioned therein, and it does not appear from any author, that Schenectady—the original Mohawk name for the site of Albany—was applied to it till after the first surrender of the colony to England, *four*

* Bleecker, vide Mitchell, N. Y. Hist. Coll.

*years after the date of this patent.* The temporary retaking of the colony by the Dutch in 1675, did not affect the inland names generally, as the province was soon restored by treaty.

The house of Stuart was now drawing to its close. Thirteen years after the last and final surrender of the province to the English crown, that crown passed, by a violent revolution, the great revolution of 1688, to another line. James the Second, who, as Duke of York and Albany, had given names to the two leading cities of the colony, was expelled, and William of Orange, who had ceded the New Netherland province, called to the British throne. To France, however, this great change was, in the highest degree, unwelcome. She regarded it as a double triumph of the spirit of liberty and protestantism. That remote colonies, in another quarter of the world, and less than all, an obscure and unimportant town, in one of the remotest of these colonies, had any influence, even the slightest, on these events, is most unlikely, and improbable. But the effects of the change appeared to fall most heavily on this little town. Small and remote as it was, it was a frontier, exposed to attack; and the barbarity of this attack, and the shock it gave to the moral sense of the country, were such as to leave a deep and lasting impression. And it is hence, and not from the strength or political importance of the place, that the burning of Schenectady has ever been a sensitive point in our early history.

In the researches made by Mr. Brodhead, in the French state offices, he discovered the following letter from an officer under Count Frontenac, giving an account of this expedition, which is interesting, as being an official document, from the pen of the secretary of the very man who had planned and organized the expedition. The cold-blooded and cowardly barbarity of the massacre itself, is unworthy of a Christian nation; while the expedition, in its general object, may find an excuse, if not a justification, in the threatening, arrogant, and triumphant position of the Iroquois cantons, at this particular time. These cantons had, it will be recollected, landed on the island of Montreal, with fifteen hundred men, in the month of August, 1689, and completely sacked and ravaged the island, killing men and cattle, and carrying blood and terror in their track. The very existence of the French colonies was a problem unsolved, and without some greater measure of energy than they had yet shown, these colonies were in danger of annihilation. Count Frontenac landed in Canada with the commission of its governor-general, in September, 1689, *within forty days after this inroad*, and the first news he met, on entering the St. Lawrence, was the account of it. He determined to retaliate, not by marching against the bold cantons, who had thus bearded the government, but against the English colonists who had furnished them arms, and were their allies and supporters. The result of this plan may be given in the writer's own words, premising, that Count Frontenac had passed some three or four months in his new governorship, and then selected the winter season to execute his schemes.

"He allowed no more time to elapse before carrying them into execution, than was required to send off some despatches to France, immediately after which he determined to organize three different detachments, to attack those rebels at all points at the same moment, and to punish them, at various places, for having afforded protection to our enemies, the Mohawks. The first party was to rendezvous at Montreal, and proceed towards Orange (Albany); the second at Three Rivers, and to make a descent on New York, at some place between Boston and Orange, and the third was to depart from Quebec, and gain the seaboard between Boston and Pentagouet, verging towards Acadia. They all succeeded perfectly well, and I shall now communicate to you the details. \* \* \* \*

"The detachment which formed at Montreal, may have been composed of about two hundred and ten men, namely; eighty savages from the Sault, and from La Montagne; sixteen Algonquins; and the remainder Frenchmen, all under the command of the Sieur Le Moyne de Sainte Helene, and Lieutenant Daillebout de Mantet, both of whom were Canadians. The Sieurs le Moyne d'Iberville and Repentigny de Montesson commanded under these. The best qualified Frenchmen were, the Sieurs de Bontepos and de

La Brosse, Calvinist officers, the Sieur la Moyne de Blainville, Le Bert du Chene, and la Marque de Montigny, who all served as volunteers. They took their departure from Montreal at the commencement of February.

"After having marched for the course of five or six days, they called a council to determine the route they should follow, and the point they should attack.

"The Indians demanded of the French what was their intention. Messieurs de Sainte Helene and Mantet replied, that they had left in the hope of attacking Orange (Albany), if possible, as it is the capital of New York and a place of considerable importance, though they had no orders to that effect, but generally to act according as they should judge, on the spot, of their chances of success, without running too much risk. This appeared to the savages somewhat rash. They represented the difficulties and the weakness of the party for so bold an undertaking. There was even one among them who, with his mind filled with the recollections of the disasters which he had witnessed last year, inquired of our Frenchmen, "since when had they become so desperate?" It was our intention, now, to regain the honor of which our misfortunes had deprived us, and the sole means to accomplish that, we replied, was to carry Orange, or to perish in so glorious an enterprise.

"As the Indians, who had an intimate acquaintance with the localities, and more experience than the French, could not be brought to agree with the latter, it was determined to postpone coming to a conclusion until the party should arrive at the spot where the two routes separate, the one leading to Orange, and the other to Corlear (Schenectady). In the course of the journey, which occupied eight days, the Frenchmen judged proper to diverge towards Corlear, according to the advice of the Indians; and this road was taken without calling a new council. Nine days more elapsed before they arrived, having experienced inconceivable difficulties, and having been obliged to march up to their knees in water, and to break the ice with their feet, in order to find a solid footing.

"They arrived within two leagues of Corlear about four o'clock in the evening, and were there harangued by the great Agniez, the chief of the Iroquois from the Sault. He urged on all to perform their duty, and to lose all recollections of their fatigue, in the hope of taking ample revenge for the injuries which they had received from the Mohawks at the solicitation of the English, and of washing themselves in the blood of the traitors. This savage was, without contradiction, the most considerable of his tribe; an honest man; as full of spirit, prudence and generosity as it was possible, and capable at the same time of the grandest undertakings. Shortly after, four squaws were discovered in a wigwam, who gave every information necessary for the attack on the town. The fire found in this hut served to warm those who were benumbed, and they continued their route, having previously detached Giguieres, a Canadian, with nine Indians, on the look out. They discovered no one, and returned to join the main body within one league of Corlear.

"At eleven of the clock that night, they came within sight of the town, resolved to defer the assault until two o'clock of the morning. But the excessive cold admitted of no further delay.

"The town of Corlear forms a sort of oblong square, with only two gates; one opposite the road we had taken; the other leading to Orange, which is only six leagues distant. Messieurs de Sainte Helene and de Mantet were to enter at the first, which the squaws pointed out, and which in fact was found wide open. Messieurs d'Iberville and de Montesson took the left, with another detachment, in order to make themselves masters of that leading to Orange. But they could not discover it, and returned to join the remainder of the party. A profound silence was every where observed, until the two commanders, who separated, at their entrance into the town, for the purpose of encircling it, had met at the other extremity. The wild Indian war-hoop was then raised, and the entire force rushed simultaneously to the attack. M. de Mantet placed himself at the head of a detachment, and reached a small fort where the garrison was under arms. The gate was burst in after a good deal of difficulty, the whole set on fire, and all who defended the place were slaughtered.

"The sack of the town began a moment before the attack of the fort. Few houses made any resistance. M. de Montigny discovered some, which he attempted to carry sword in hand, having tried the musket in vain. He received two thrusts of a spear—one in the body and the other in the arm. But M. de Sainte Helene having come to his aid, effected an entrance, and put every one of the garrison to the sword. The massacre lasted two hours. The remainder of the night was spent in placing sentinels, and in taking some rest.

"The house belonging to the minister was ordered to be saved, so as to take him alive, to obtain information from him. But as it was not known, it was not saved any more than the others. He was slain and his papers burnt before he could be recognized.

"At day-break, some men were sent to the dwelling of Mr. Coudre, who was major of the place at the other side of the river. He was not willing to surrender, and began to put himself on the defensive with his servants and some Indians; but as it was resolved not to do him any harm, in consequence of the good treatment which the French had formerly experienced at his hands, M. d'Iberville and the great Agnicz proceeded thither alone, promised him quarter for himself, and his people, and his property, whereupon he laid down his arms, on parole; entertaining them in his fort, and returned with them to see the commandant of the town.

"In order to occupy the savages, who would otherwise have taken to drink, and thus rendered themselves unable for defence, the houses had already been set on fire. None were spared in the town but one house belonging to Coudre, and that of a widow who had six children, whither M. de Montigny had been carried when wounded. All the rest were consumed. The lives of between fifty and sixty persons, old men, women and children, were spared, they having escaped the first fury of the attack. Some twenty Mohawks were also spared, in order to show them that it was the English and not they, against whom the grudge was entertained. The loss on this occasion in houses, cattle and grain, amounts to more than four hundred thousands *livres*. There were upwards of eighty well-built and well-furnished houses in the town.

"The return march commenced with thirty prisoners. The wounded, who were to be carried, and the plunder, with which all the Indians and some Frenchmen were loaded, caused considerable inconvenience. Fifty good horses were brought away. Sixteen only of these reached Montreal. The remainder were killed for food on the way.

"Sixty leagues from Corlear, the Indians began to hunt, and the French not being able to wait for them, being short of provisions, continued their route, having detached Messieurs d'Iberville and Du Chesne with two savages before them to Montreal. On the same day, some Frenchmen, who doubtless were very much fatigued, lost their way. Fearful that they should be obliged to keep up with the main body, and believing themselves in safety, having eighty Indians in their rear, they were found missing from the camp. They were waited for next day until eleven o'clock, but in vain, and no account has since been received of them.

"Two hours after, forty men more left the main body without acquainting the commander, continued their route by themselves, and arrived within two leagues of Montreal one day ahead, so that there were not more than fifty or sixty men together. The evening on which they should arrive at Montreal, being extremely fatigued from fasting and bad roads, the rear fell away from M. de Sainte Helene, who was in front with an Indian guide, and who could not find a place suitable for camping, nearer than three or four leagues of the spot where he expected to halt. He was not rejoined by M. de Mantet and the others, until far advanced in the night. Seven have not been found. Next day on parade, about ten o'clock in the forenoon, a soldier arrived, who announced that they had been attacked by fourteen or fifteen savages, and that six had been killed. The party proceeded, somewhat afflicted at this accident, and arrived at Montreal at 3 o'clock P. M.

"Such, madame, is the account of what passed at the taking of Corlear (Schenectady). The French lost but twenty-one men, namely, four Indians and seventeen Frenchmen. Only one Indian and one Frenchman were killed at the capture of the town. The others were lost on the road."

Colden remarks, that the Mohawks sent a hundred warriors in pursuit, who fell upon the rear of the retreating army, and killed and took twenty-five persons. They also sent an embassy of condolence to Albany, assured the inhabitants of their friendship, and ability to defend the frontier, and inspired a renewed feeling of confidence, from the bold style and ennobling sentiments of their address. It was, it is clear from this author, the renegade *Caughnawagas*, with Agniez at their head, that led the way in this sanguinary attack.

### ANTIQUE CURRENCY OF THE MANHATTANESE AND THEIR NEIGHBORS.

There were two kinds of wampum in early use by the Indians, as a standard of value; the *purple* or black, and the *white*. The purple was made from the interior portions of the Venus mercenaria, or common conch. The white was wrought out of the pillar of the periwinkle. Each kind was converted into a kind of bead, by being rounded and perforated, so as to admit of being strung, on a fibre of deer's sinew. This was replaced, after the discovery, by linen thread. These beads were of unequal length, but were worked down, by the Atlantic-coast tribes, to very nearly the same size and thickness—which was about that of a crow's quill, or a pipe stem. The article was highly prized as an ornament, and as such constituted an object of traffic between the sea-coast and interior tribes. It was worn around the neck; also as an edging for certain pieces of their garments; and when these strings were united, they formed the broad wampum belts,* by which solemn public transactions were commemorated.

The article was also called by the Manhattanese, *seawan*, and Long Island, which yielded the crude shells abundantly, was hence denominated by the sobriquet of Seawanacky,† or land of seawan shells. Its permanent name, however, appears to have been Metöac, from the particular type of the sea-coast Algonquins, who occupied it. By the more northerly tribes who spread over New England, this treasured article was called *peag* and *wampeag*. The labor of making it by hand, without the use of iron or

* The last belt of this kind, is believed to have been made to commemorate a grand pacification of the tribes, who assembled at Prairie du Chien, in 1825, to settle their boundary lines, under invitations from the government of the United States. The commissioners were the late General William Clark, of St. Louis, and Gen. Cass, of Michigan.

† The termination *acky*, in this word, is the same, which in the Odjibwa of the present day, is generally written *ackee*, land or earth. In both the *a* is broad, and the sound, as well as the sense, so far as we can judge, is identical.

steel instruments, must have made it very costly, before the discovery. The old wampum was, indeed, a rude article, and the specimens disinterred, now-a-days, from old Indian graves, and from the distant mounds of the west, denotes an article which in shape and size resembles, often, a horn-button mould, and at others, a heart-shaped, or an oval bead of large size. The Dutch introduced the lathe in making wampum, polished and perforated it with exactness, and soon had the monopoly of the supply of this article for the whole Indian trade.*

It appears from the Dutch records at Albany, which abound in details of the Indian trade, that three purple beads of wampum, or seawan, or six of white, were equal to a styver, among the Dutch, or a penny among the English. Some variations, however, existed in its value, according to time and place. A single string of wampum of one fathom, rated at five shillings in New England, and is known, in New Netherlands, to have reached as high as four guilders, or one dollar and sixty-six cents. Lands and merchandise were alike purchased of the natives for this oceanic kind of coin, which they esteemed more valuable than the precious metals, and it continued to be in vogue after the surrender of the colony to the English. It is stated on undoubted authority, that the first

* The principal place of its manufacture is still at Hackensack, in New Jersey.

church built on the (now) Jersey shore, opposite New York, was constructed out of funds contributed, from sabbath to sabbath, in grains of *seawan*, by the Dutch people. Coin was scarce, and paper money unknown.

Colden tells us, that the Mohawks and their allies imposed a tribute on the Manhattanese and Metöacs, which was paid annually in the conchological currency of their sea coasts. Whether they *ate* the shell-fish, or took the *shells* as ornaments, may be questioned.

### CHEROKEE TRADITION OF THE DELUGE.

Cherokee tradition preserves an allegoric version of the deluge which is quite peculiar. The following outline of it, was communicated to me, in the summer of 1846, by Mr. Stand Watie, a respectable and intelligent chief of that tribe, who was attending at the seat of government, as one of the delegates of his people, to compromise certain difficulties which had arisen, between separate parties of the Cherokee nation, and the government. It is affirmed by Cherokee tradition, said my informant, that the water once prevailed over the land, until every person was drowned, but a single family. The coming of this calamity was revealed by a dog to his master. This dog was very pertinacious in visiting the banks of a river, for several days, where he stood gazing at the water, and howling piteously. Being sharply spoken to, by his master, and ordered home, he revealed to him the coming evil. He concluded his prediction by saying, that the escape of his master and family from drowning, depended upon their throwing *him* into the water; that to escape drowning himself, he must make a boat, and put in it all he wished to save; that it would then rain hard, a long time, and a great overflowing of the land would take place.

The dog then told his master to look for a sign of the truth of what he had said, to the back of his neck. On turning round, and doing so, the dog's neck was raw and bare, the bone and flesh appearing. By obeying this prediction, one man and his family were saved, and from these rescued persons, the earth, they believe, was again peopled.

Stand Watie, who communicated this tradition, is a brother of the late Elias Boudinot, who fell a victim to the desperate feud which grew out of the treaty of *New Echota*,—a treaty by which the Cherokee lands, east of the Mississippi, were ceded, in 1835, to the United States.

The Cherokees, according to the same authority, have also a tradition of their crossing a large water, apparently a river, which was done by tying grape vines together,\* and making a sort of vine-bridge, over which they walked.

When questioned of their origin and progressive migrations of an ancient date, their traditions are narrowed down, very nearly, to the

---

\* This tradition of a vine-bridge, will also be observed among the traditions of the Iroquois.

above outlines; they add only, that they came from the *east*, and that their ancient progress was, uniformly, from the *east*. (*Mr. John Wheeler.*)

## ASIATIC ORIGIN OF THE AONIC, OR INDIAN RACE OF AMERICA.

Observation and discovery have not, as yet, prepared ethnographers confidently to decide on the origin of certain remote nations. Neither geography nor philology has achieved the highest points at which they aim. But their progress, in late years, is of the most flattering kind. No age has equalled the present, in its spirit of discovery, and the track of useful and scientific inquiry is annually becoming broader and deeper. In this labor, the American element of the world's population has but just begun to assume efficiency, while the spirit of literary and commercial enterprize is transporting to our shores the results of the researches and discoveries of the nations of the old world, who have done the most to advance the study of the knowledge of the original dispersion and affinities of the human family.

Of the original and wide-spread stock of the red race, who have filled Asia, and no small part of Africa, there are certain leading physical traits, which are readily recognized, although the highest and lowest points, in the physiological chain, exhibit very marked differences. But, in proportion as inquiries are pushed, there appear to be general coincidences, which mark their ancient affiliation, in the mental structure and tendencies of the several tribes and nations. Language, while it constitutes the most fixed and precise points of the mental peculiarities and progress of nations, also furnishes, at the same time, the most certain and irrefragible clue to affinities; and it is hence that, in modern times, so much stress has been laid on the study and comparison of distant and barbarous languages, as helps to history.

That parts of the oriental stock of the red man should have reached the American continent, and expanded and flourished here, in early ages of the world, and ere history arose to take cognizance of the fact, is no cause of wonder or surprise. But it is a subject of unabated interest and curiosity, to seek to determine, as well as our growing materials will permit, from which division or generic subtype of the oriental race, the American tribes are descended. To us, who are placed in proximity with them, and whose sympathies and duties, in relation to them, are in the most active exercise, this inquiry is one of deep historical interest. Nor are the means we possess, of pursuing the subject, wanting. Our intercourse with nations, based upon the British element of civilization, and reinvigorated, in these sweeping latitudes, with all the prime sources of the added Anglo-Saxon and Anglo-Norman power, in letters, arts and arms, is extended, at this day, to the utmost parts of the world. China, the last nation to come into a free intercourse, on the basis of treaties, is now laid open to investigation, and we have seen museums of its curious and antique arts, and highly characteristic fabrics, displayed, even on these coasts. To study its history and antiquities, is one of the first labors that at this moment invites attention. A people who profess to have had the knowledge of the mariner's compass, the art of printing, and even the composition of gunpowder, ages before these discoveries were known to Europe, cannot present a barren field for study. Their literature alone, is an unexplored mine, and may throw a flood of light on the early or Indian epochs of American history. But there is a still more inviting, perhaps because a still more isolated and unknown people, who demand scrutiny. They are the *Japanese*. Keeping out of the family compact of nations, and yet, in many respects, eminently entitled to the inquisitive spirit of letters and commerce, this people hold an interesting position, as one of the families of the red races of Asia, who may have contributed an element to the early mechanical tribes who first entered the precincts of the sea coasts, and interior valleys of Mexico. The chain of islands which connects the larger Japanese group, directly with the peninsula of Okotsk, would have made, as it does at this day, an easy and ready transit, to that remarkable projection of the Asiatic coast. And it is just at the northern end of this chain, it will be recollected, that the Aleutian islands commence;

that elongated group, which connects the practical and easy navigation, in small vessels, of the Asiatic main, with the peninsula of Onalaska, on the American side. These two groups of islands, with the seas of Japan and Okotsk, are very indicative of the geological formation of those coasts, and their structure and susceptibility of change, by oceanic action, constitute in this view, an object of research. An object, allow me to say, which is yet more interesting, when it promises to denote the mode of solving our hardest problem, namely, how the various classes of American *quadrupeds* reached the coast. For we cannot, on any sound principles, admit that the armadillo, the ichneumon, the tapir, the jaguar, the lama, the monkey, and other tropical species, could ever have been attracted to or endured the extreme frigid latitudes of Behring's straits.*

Of the wide-spread stock of the *Ta-ta* type, who stretch over the vast plains of central and northern Asia, from the seas of Japan and Okotsk, across the coterminous latitudes of both Chinese and Independent Tartary, we are only informed with respect to their general manners and character. Of the exact elements from which ethnological conclusions are to be drawn, we are, as yet, certainly in America, almost wholly deficient. The Chinese type of the Tartaric stock,

* It must be recollected, that London, the garden of England, yielding the highest floral catalogue of the British isles, lies in 59°, the exact parallel of the Aleutian peninsula.

has prevailed over, and incorporated itself so readily with the *Chéna\** proper, as to leave it probable that their original relations, in a philological sense, were greater than has generally been supposed. Viewed by itself, the Chinese language appears to be the most remote from the American group, of any in all Asia. It is, as is well known, monosyllabic, and if we except the Otomi of Mexico, no language, on this plan of utterance, has been found in America, although it is to be remarked, that many of the North American languages, however compounded and concrete, in their present *spoken* character, are, without any doubt, founded on monosyllabic and dissyllabic roots. It is further to be remarked, in examining the Tata and Chéna families, that the latter have reduced their language to writing, on the symbolic plan, partly of picture writing, and partly of hieroglyphics: from which, we may draw two conclusions; *first*, that the people are a very ancient one, and *second*, that they have borrowed nothing, in their system of notation, from either the Hebrew, Egyptian, or Greek alphabets. With regard to the system itself, it appears to be the most cumbrous and jejune, and the least suited to advance the progress of the human mind, that could have been devised. With its tens of thousands of concrete characters, it is a most complete exemplification, in the *notation* of a language, of what the American tribes have arrived at, in the compounding of

\* The word is so pronounced in the celestial kingdom.

their *spoken* dialects. Each character of it, like each word of these dialects, is a congeries of abbreviated combinations. The syllabical system of the Cherokee, which expresses every combination of *that* language by eighty-six characters, is as far superior to it, on the score of ease and facility in learning it, as it is possible to conceive one system of recording articulate sounds, may be superior to another.

When we cast our view to the northern latitudes of Asia, spreading across the great valleys of the Lena, the Yenissi, and the Obe, quite to the gulf of Obe, on the Arctic ocean, and the foot of the Ural mountains, we have still less material, of an exact and ethnographic character, to judge how far, if to any extent, these higher latitudes furnished an early impulse, or contributed to the early peopling of this continent. Of all the divisions of Asia, we know, indeed, least, and are therefore the least prepared to judge, of the distinctive traits and character of the native inhabitants of Siberia. That the Samoides, the Ostiacs, the Tunguissians, and the Koriaks, roved over these vast steppes and defiles, making wars, and pursuing game, and plunder, is only an evidence of generic traits of barbarism, which are common to distant branches of the human family, under adverse, but similar circumstances, between whom, however, there may be no direct affinities.

An opinion has been expressed, unfavorable to the probability of strong affinities to the American tribes being found to exist among the race, so early and so generally known to the maritime states of Europe, who extend between the banks of the Indus and the Ganges. It was from this race, admitting that they had also possessed themselves, essentially, of the East India islands, that Columbus doubtless drew his conclusions of identity, from their physical type. But if he was, as is thought, in error, the opinion before advanced renders it the more desirable that the basis of our knowledge of the man of India proper should be enlarged, and more fully investigated. It is in this quarter of Asia, that England, our mother country, has strongly set her foot, and in which we may expect, in the proper course of events, that a great Anglo-Indian empire will arise, basing itself on letters, Christianity, and high civilization. Already, the archives of British and European letters have been greatly enriched from this quarter. The labors of Sir William Jones alone, are a monument to his genius. It is in this country that the dreadful slavery of casts is so inveterately fixed, that *widows*, under a mistaken view of duty, piety, or affection, mount the funereal pyre; that the dreadful infanticide of females is tolerated by public sentiment; that the blood of idol worshippers is poured out from streaming hooks of steel, fastened in the whirling body, and that the aged cast themselves into the Ganges, under the impression that its waters are sacred, and offer a pious solace for human woes. Ideas, which are so remote from all that characterizes the Indian mind here, as to leave but little probability of affiliation with that stock. Philologists perceive in the nations of Hindostan, the elements, *not* of the transpositive languages of our hunter races, but of an ancient, and wholly diverse stock, which, at an unknown period of migration, threw itself westward upon Europe, and has left indubitable traces of its effects in modifying human speech, in the great Indo-Germanic language.

To Arabia, the southwest corner of Asia, allusion has been made, as having opened recent negotiations of friendship and commerce, with the United States. Travellers, who have visited that remarkable country, and crossed its sandy deserts—among whom we recognize a distinguished countryman,* learned in the oriental languages—represent its inhabitants as clinging, with such fixedness, to their original customs and traits of character, even in minor points, that little change would seem to have supervened since the days of Abraham. The Arabic is one of the oldest written and cultivated languages. Inscriptions in the ancient Hymaritic character, recently found upon its rocks, and decyphered by Prof. Wm. W. Turner, go back to the patriarchal ages.† Europe owes to that people, some of its earliest elements of knowledge; the whole civilized world daily

---

\* Dr. Robinson.

† Trans. Am. Ethnological Society, vol. 1.

practises the use of its symbols for numbers; and it is impossible that it should have furnished any increment to the leading tribes of America, without some fixed traces of it being left in their languages, customs, and rites. None such are known to exist.

Palestine, together with Syria and the whole of ancient Asia Minor, has claims to investigation, not so much perhaps from its having been the original seat of mankind, and the cradle of nations, as from the early expressed, and oft-repeated opinion, that the American Indians are lineal descendants of the Jews. It is not intended to discuss this subject here, but merely to name it as one of the topics connected with the oriental origin of the Indians, which are not, perhaps, exhausted. But if the discussion be renewed, it requires to be conducted on principles of more exactness, philologically speaking, and less likelihood to be swayed by theory, than it has yet received. To examine it candidly, we must have the two elements of comparison, namely, the Hebrew and Indian, or Aonic, complete. We not only require to place the languages side by side, but also the striking and peculiar rites, religious ceremonies, and mental idiocrasy of each. Nor should we hold our judgments under so easy a rein, as to be satisfied with identity, where there is only resemblance.

The theory of the Hebrew origin of the Indian tribes, has been a popular one, from the very foundation of the colonies. It is as old, as we are told by Forster,\* in the time of Grotius, who advanced it. Nor is it, in one respect, namely, the general question of philology, as destitute of plausibility, as the weak proofs and over-strained resemblances of some writers have really shown it to be. If not of Jewish, they may be of Persian or Mesopotamian origin. Granting that they are of the Shemitic family, which appears quite manifest, they are more likely to have been cotribes of the stock from which the Jews were descended, than lineal descendants of this peculiar people. We may account for some of the linguistic coincidences, mentioned by Boudinot, as being of a generic character, and shall at the same time keep on grounds which take in coincidences of another kind. It is difficult to admit, that a people, whose history is, in all its phases, so peculiar and striking as that of the Jews, marked as its rites were, with blood, should have given origin to the American tribes, without having transmitted some unequivocal proofs of it. The cleaving of the sea — the delivery of the law, amid thunders and lightnings — the smiting of the rock for the out-flow of a river in a dry barren — the raising of the brazen serpent — the guiding pillar of cloud by day and fire by night, and the standing miracle of the manna, were acts and revelations of such a character, as never to have been likely to be completely obliterated from tradition. The tribes of Judah and Benjamin, who appear to compose all the known Jews

\* Northern Voyages.

of the world, have never forgotten these great events although dispersed among all nations, and it is reasonable to suppose that the tribes of the Israelitish monarchy, were not less tenacious of their customs and peculiar traits. Yet, what the eventual character of changes may have been, on a people who went forth under the judicial judgment of heaven, it might be rash and premature to decide. According to Esdras, the ten tribes carried away by the Assyrians, some seven hundred and twenty-one years before the Christian era, determined to cross the Euphrates, and seek a country where man had never dwelt, by which the central and interior parts of Asia, beyond the Euphrates, were doubtless meant.

We have thus cast a rapid glance over the varied surface of Asia, and its leading nations of the present era, omitting the Grecian element, which is of the Japhetic line, and a single other Shemitic element, namely, the Chaldean and Persic type of man, who, at an early day, relinquished the knowledge of the true God, adopted the dreamy and sublimated notions of a *soul of the universe*, or omnipresent first cause, which led to the philosophic religion of Zoroaster, and resulted in the priesthood of the magi, and the symbolic or real worship of the sun, moon and stars. It is to this portion of Asia, renowned as it is for its early history, the shifting panorama of its ancient political revolutions, and the subtile forms of its notions of a transcendental deity; that we would point, as one of the most interesting fields of ethnological study at the present time, in reference to the early American tribes; and particularly of the leading stocks, who from era to era, seated themselves in Mexico, and in Central and South America.

To Africa, it is only necessary to allude, to denote how important, in an illustrative point of view, the history of its discovery and progressive coast colonies are, in connection with the question of the first knowledge of mankind of the American continent. The Egyptian, the Grecian and the Roman element of its early colonies, offer the most profound topics of research to the ethnologist.

Wherever the early families of mankind went, however, it was in Europe that civilization was destined to rise to its highest forms. The impulse of migration, which rose in Asia, spread westward with a force which carried its current rapidly from the shores of the Mediterranean, until population had reached over its central latitudes to the farthest confines of Scandinavia and the north, from which it afterwards began to react against the seats of empire, whence it had, itself, taken its early rise. Such, at least, are the modern teachings of ethnography and comparative philology.

In this onrush of nations, there was carried westward from the starting point, a rude alphabet consisting of some sixteen primary characters, mostly composed of angular strokes, which bore, in its western phases, the names of Etruscan, Celtic, ancient Gallic, Celtiberic, Old Erse, Runic, and other terms. Each of these terms denoted peculiarities, either in the form of some of the characters, or in the sounds of which they were the symbols; but there is full and sufficient evidence to show that they, one and all, arose from the Mediterranean alphabetic ground forms. When the Roman alphabet followed the eagles of its power and civilization into central Europe, and became the medium of the expression of the European languages and early literature, they found inscriptions of this ancient angular alphabet, on rocks and precipices, designed, doubtless, generally, to record the names and deeds of their primary heroes. By far the greater part of the ancient Celtic records were made on smooth blocks of hard beech wood, called *buken*, in the Anglo-Saxon, and hence our term of *book*. The points of Europe in which the rock inscriptions, in this character, have been found and studied with most success, are its extreme westerly and northerly shores, islands and prolongations. It will be sufficient to denote, how interesting and important this topic becomes, among the incentives to the study of the ancient period of American history, when it is added, that an inscription in this antique character, consisting of twenty-four letters or figures, has been found, on a small stone, in one of the great mounds of the Ohio valley. It is thus to be regarded as an intrusive element of western civilization, thrust in among monuments, and a race of tribes, whose general traditions, and whose history, so far as it can be deduced, show them to be orientals. And the remark may here be made, assuming the discovery of the western inscription to be indisputable, that two leading types of the human race, starting at the original point of their separation, say in the valley of the Euphrates, and taking opposite points of the compass, have thus met, in the valley of the Mississippi, after having travelled by land and sea around the globe. How has this happened? And how, after the lapse of probably not less than three thousand years, are we to trace the evidences of this early, long protracted and extraordinary migration? Are we to sit down with hands folded, because there is no written history? Are we to disregard the strong and important points and declarations of the inspired volume? Can we gather nothing from monumental data? From astronomy? From the state of ancient arts and inscriptions, in both hemispheres? From the character of the mind, as evinced by ancient forms of worship? Or from language, the most enduring and characteristic of all evidences of the affiliation of nations?

## THE LOST COLONY OF KASONDA.

It is now one hundred and seventy-five years since there was a chief, named Karrakontea, living in the Onondaga country, who exercised the greatest influence over his people of the

Onondaga canton. This canton were then numerous, proud and warlike. They cultivated the zea maize in their rich valleys. They hunted the deer on their hills, and their war parties uttered their shouts of defiance on the distant Illinois, and under the walls of Quebec.

Karrakontea had communicated personally, or otherwise, with the European races who had settled respectively, on the waters of the Cohatatea or Hudson, and the St. Lawrence. His war parties had visited other shades of the white race of men, who had planted themselves, fearfully, on the waters of the Chesapeake, and at several points on the wide stretching shores of Virginia, and he was well acquainted with the several efforts at colonization, which had been made during the next preceding period of forty to fifty years, on the storm-beaten shores of New England.

He was a sachem of a wise and benevolent character. He saw himself and his people seated at very remote points from the seaboard, where these embryo colonies had planted themselves. They existed, moreover, in each case, among particular branches of the Indian race, against whom his people warred, and some of whom they had before partially conquered or laid under tribute. He had, therefore, no objections to see Europeans come among them. It gave neither himself, nor his fellow counsellors of the Iroquois league, pain to observe that the fierce Manhattans and Narragansetts, or the counselling Lenapees and Powhattans, were subject to dwindle away in numbers, and become less formidable enemies to themselves. He clearly saw and acknowledged the great benefits which they all, as a race, had derived from the introduction of foreign goods and manufactures, which they could readily obtain, at various points, in exchange for their furs. Nay, he pointedly saw the advantages to be reaped by them from the introduction of a superior type of arts and knowledge, to any which the red men possessed. And he came to the conclusion of asking the foreign race, to send some persons to come and "sit down" with them, that his people might learn some of those superior arts and practices, which he observed that the white race, everywhere, more or less, possessed. To this proposition his fellow sachems and people assented; and the invitation was given to the French, who had proved themselves, at a very early date, not only the most enterprising, in pushing their way from the mouth of the St. Lawrence westward into the interior of the continent; but who fell into the manners and customs of the Indian race with the best grace, and rendered themselves very acceptable to this people, wherever they went. One reason of this was, perhaps, to be found in the custom of taking wives of the red stock of men, wherever they settled or dwelt; another was, doubtless, in a trait of national comity, which forbade their ever turning to ridicule the religious and superstitious ceremonies of the Indian priests and metais. Whatever might be the causes, however, which led to the selection of the French, as the early teachers of the Onondagas, there can be no doubt of the fact. There are old traditions of Indians passed away—letters and allusions in the miscellaneous history of the times, and monuments and ruins, curious and wonder-provoking, in the Onondaga country, to attest the truth of this transaction, and to show that a colony was actually planted in that country; that it spread and flourished, for a few years; eventually gathered into it the gold-hunting element of the Spanish adventurers, which had overturned the empires of the Incas, and of the Montezumas, and that it finally and horribly perished in one night, in a field of blood. The rest of this extraordinary tale of colonization and wild adventure, I state in the words of the late Govenor De Witt Clinton; a man whose comprehensive mind and grasping literary tastes led him to enter as an efficient laborer into the field of American antiquities; a man, whose researches were always governed by the spirit of philosophy, reacting on the well-provided materials of history, which dwelt in his own mind; and who *ever* sought to make the solemn instructions of the past, admonitory to the present and future, particularly in our singularly prosperous political career of government, population and vast resources. Not only do the references to books sustain this passage of his early researches;

but so far as I could draw living tradition from its recesses in the Iroquois mind, they most satisfactorily cover the general incidents of the colony, and its utter and sudden extirpation—this only being added, to render the fury of the natives intense and most merciless, namely, that it was led on by the fanatical hatred of the Iroquois priesthood.

"From the Jesuits' journal, it appears, that in the year 1666, at the request of Karakontie, an Onondaga chieftain, a French colony was directed to repair to his village, for the purpose of teaching the Indians arts and sciences, and to endeavor, if practicable, to civilize and Christianize them.

"We learn from the sachems, that at this time the Indians had a fort, a short distance above the village of Jamesville, on the banks of a small stream, a little above which, it seems, the chieftain, Karakontie, would have his new friends *sit down*. Accordingly they repaired thither, and commenced their labors, which being greatly aided by the savages, a few months only were necessary to the building of a small village.

"This little colony remained for three years in a very peaceable and flourishing situation, during which time much addition was made to the establishment, and, among others, a small chapel, in which the Jesuit priest used to collect the barbarians, and perform the rites and ceremonies of his church.

"But the dire circumstance which was to bury this colony in oblivion, and keep their history in secret, was yet to come. About this time (1669), a party of Spaniards, consisting of twenty-three persons, arrived at the village, having for guides some of the Iroquois, who had been taken captive by the southern tribes. It appears evident that this party came up the Mississippi, as it has been ascertained that they passed Pittsburgh, and on to Olean point; where, leaving their canoes, they travelled by land. They had been informed by some of the southern tribes, that there was a lake at the north of them, whose bottom was covered with a substance shining and white,* and which they took, from the Indians' description, to be silver; and it is supposed that the idea of enriching themselves upon this treasure, induced them to take this long and desperate journey; for silver was the first thing inquired for, on their arrival, and on being told that none was ever seen in or about the Onondaga lake, they became almost frantic, and seemed bent upon a quarrel with the French, and charged them with having bribed the Indians, and even those who had been their guides, that they would not tell where the mines might be found. Nor dare they, finding the French influence to prevail, venture out on a search, lest the Indians might

* The salt crystallizes at the present time on the grass and upon the naked earth in the immediate vicinity of the springs, though the water of the lake is fresh.

destroy them. A compromise was however made, and both parties agreed that an equal number of each should be sent on an exploring expedition, which was accordingly done. But the effect of this, upon the minds of the Indians, was fatal. Upon seeing these strangers prowling the woods with various kinds of instruments, they immediately suspected some plan to be in operation to deprive them of their country.

"Nor was this jealousy by any means hushed by the Europeans. The Spaniards averred to the Indians that the only object of the French was to tyrannize over them; and the French, on the other hand, that the Spaniards were plotting a scheme to rob them of their lands.

"The Indians, by this time becoming equally jealous of both, determined in private council, to rid themselves of such troublesome neighbors. For aid in this, they sent private instructions to the Oneidas, and Cayugas, who only wanted a watchword to be found immediately on the ground. The matter was soon digested, and the time and manner of attack agreed upon. A little before day-break, on *All Saints'* day, 1669, the little colony, together with the Spaniards, were aroused from their slumbers by the roaring of fire-arms, and the dismal war-whoop of the savages. Every house was immediately fired or broken open, and such as attempted to escape from the flames met a more untimely death in the *tomahawk*. Merciless multitudes overpowered the little band, and the Europeans were soon either lost in death, or writhing in their blood; and such was the furious prejudice of the savages, that not one escaped, or was left alive to *relate the sad disaster.*

"The French in Canada, on making inquiries respecting the fate of their friends, were informed by the Indians that they had gone towards the south, with a company of people who came from thence, and at the same time showing a *Spanish coat of arms,* and other national trinkets, confirmed the Canadian French in the opinion that their unfortunate countrymen had indeed gone thither, and in all probability perished in the immense forests. This opinion was also measureably confirmed by a Frenchman who had long lived with the Senecas, and who visited the Onondagas at the time the Spaniards were at the village, but left before the disaster, and could only say that he had seen them there."

Thus lamentably perished the first Christian colony, which, so far as is known, was ever attempted to be settled in the interior of western New York. A plan, fearful in itself, for a moment's reflection must have made it evident to the French, that they were not going to plant themselves in the midst of a mentally broken down people, as were the races of Peru, or Mexico, who had long given up their personal freedom and rights to be vested in a hereditary sovereign; but among a people who retained all these rights in the fullest manner, who were proud, bold and jealous to a fault, esteeming themselves superior to all other men, and who had a fixed and numerous priesthood, bent on retaining their sway; in a word, among the Konoshioni, or indomitable Iroquois. It was a colony, founded in *love*, cursed by the spirit of *gold*, and extinguished in *blood*.

## CHAPTER XI.

### LANGUAGE.

STRUCTURE OF THE CLASS OF AMERICAN LANGUAGES — COMPARATIVE VOCABULARY OF THE IROQUOIS AND ITS COGNATE THE WYANDOT.

Languages are the slow growth of centuries. Words do not rapidly change. They are like coins and medals, and carry along evidence of the parental mint. A child, who has, from its infancy, heard the name for father and mother, earth and air, fire and water, will strongly receive these sounds, and not depart from them, while his association of ideas remains unchanged. Some defects of utterance, in kings or rulers, greatly beloved, may be supposed to have had imitators, and produced some effects, but they must ever be small. The first sensible effect in the generation of a new dialect, may be supposed to arise from a change of national residence to a remote quarter of the world. New associations here come in — objects of another kind present themselves, and other motives excite the mind, and tend to obliterate early impressions. Migration naturally treads in the steps of migration. One country is exchanged for another; and by hearing new languages spoken, the old may be supposed to stand in danger of some innovations.

We may suppose the interposition of seas to have had the greatest effect, in leading men to depart from vocal standards of pronunciation, and in producing permanent changes. The vowel sounds are mutable, and melt into each other, in proportion as they are shortened, or drawn out, or otherwise articulated. We know that barbarous nations *mouth sounds*, and exercise a great range of enunciation, producing changes. The consonants admit of some exchanges; but are generally fixed; and it is to these that we owe, more than to any other cause, the perpetuity of old pronunciations in utterance. Hebrew notation availed itself of this principle, and as it is well known, left out, in its earlier periods, any provision beyond at least two characters,* for recording the vowels. Still, it must require a very long epoch, before a radical change can be affected. This is very clearly demonstrated to the student of the English language, who perceives, at this day, the roots of many nouns and verbs in the Gothic, German, Icelandic and other northern languages, which appear to have thrown parts of their vocabularies into the great Anglo-Saxon or Thiudic stock.

* Aleph and Yoth.

Centuries have not been sufficient to obliterate these sounds, and the general evidences, which link together this great Indo-Germanic type of languages are clear and satisfactory, at this moment.

Could we obtain evidence, as clear as this, we should bring together in one generic family, the Iroquois and the Algonquin, the Dacotah and the Appalachian, and other northern stocks, which we are now obliged to regard as different languages, only because their actual vocabularies are so diverse. In other respects — in their grammatical principles — the transpositive character of words — the laws of concord which they establish between persons and objects, and the curious principles of their mode of compounding words — they are, in fact, one great generic group, to which Mr. Duponceau has applied the term polysynthetic. We have only to become better acquainted with the parent stocks, in the other hemisphere, to perceive analogies which appear now but feeble. The comparison of concrete vocabularies is not sufficent for this purpose, although it has been heretofore chiefly relied on. Philologists must look up and search out the principles by which vowels and consonants necessarily change. Their juxtaposition to an antagonistical letter, must affect them — the principles of euphony, in a savage tongue, are ill explained. But we see, everywhere, that these tribes lay great stress on them themselves. Of the laws of consonants, as effected by minute traits in the physical organization of the tongue and glottis, we have better cognizance. But above all, the inquiry should be directed to the formation of generic comparative tables of roots and radical particles, expressing the same general ideas, as thought, motion, sound. It must be evident, to observers in our aboriginal philology, that different nations, and even remote tribes of the same ethnographical family, do not designate all objects by the *same traits* or characteristics, where the *vocabulary* is admitted to be essentially the same, and consequently the words must differ. Thus one tribe calls a horse the beast that bears burthens; another merely *pack;* another the beast of solid, or unsplit hoofs; another simply by a word which we may translate servant, or dog. Before vocabularies can be rightly compared, we should be sure that the natives meant to express the same ideas, by the different names bestowed. It is important too, in making comparisons of the vocabulary of remote tribes, to know whether the name be generally adopted, or there be two or more names for the same object. And especially, whether words be used with, or without the pronouns, and other cumulative adjuncts. Without the analysis, and a very complete one of every word in the vocabulary, no true advance can be made.

There are two principles which prevail extensively in the grammars of the North American tribes, or rather of those of Algonquin origin, which dwell within the United States, east of the Rocky mountains, to which I will for a moment advert. And I do so, under an impression of their being both novel or indigenous, that is, novel to the Asiatic groups, and indigenous here.

1. The first characteristic rule in the syntax is, that every animate verb requires an animate substantive, and every inanimate verb an inanimate substantive. This rule, which is unknown to the Hebrew, or to any ancient or foreign language we are acquainted with, is of such universal and stringent application, in the Algonquin family of dialects, that its effect has been almost completely to annihilate the grammatical distinctions of sex, in words of that stock. There are no masculine or feminine genders, and but few neuter words in that important class of languages. Adjectives, as well as verbs, and nouns, are subject to this rule, and indeed the whole list of the numerous class of particles which perform in these dialects, the offices of prepositions and conjunctions, and even exclamations, obey this concord. So broad is the rule, and so important is its operation deemed, that in some cases entirely different ground elements are employed to express the qualities of objects.

2. Another leading and characteristic principle of the native languages of this continent, so far as they have been examined, consists in their power of amalgamation. Words are condensed and reformed by the introduction of ideographic roots, to which pronominal, tensal, and other appendages, are prefixed, or subjoined, to de-

scribe new objects or relations. It has long been known that these compound terms are replete with meaning. And when this meaning has been extracted, as in the case of their euphonious names for our hills and streams, it has seemed scarcely possible to our rigid Saxon syntax, that such full descriptive and expressive ideas should be thrown together in a single phrase. The principle is analogous to that which exists in their ancient system of picture-writing. By this system, symbols are chosen to represent ideas, or chains of ideas, both simple and complex. The figure of a bird, to illustrate the system of picture-writing, is drawn both for the *name* and *species* of a bird, and the act of its flight, or death, is a pure matter of inference, as denoted by the contiguity of a man, a sky, a tree, or an arrow. Yet the head or the claw of a bird may also represent both the name and class of the bird. So the syllabic increment of a compound, represents the generic trait of the whole word, and the syllable preceding or following it, governs and determines its particular meaning, in this new relation.

In the Indian compounds, or concrete derivatives, the ideographic syllable or particle to be introduced, is taken from the root of the disjunctive noun, or verb. It is invested with the whole and entire meaning of the word, as expressed when used disjunctively, and not a part of it only. It must be recollected, that by far the largest number of the primitives, when trimmed and clipped of their pronominal and other adjuncts, are chiefly monosyllables, or dissyllables. In these cases, sometimes the entire root is thrown in. It is, however, generally shorn of its full proportions. But whether a monosyllable or not, the intrusive particle or syllable is subject, in this new position, to the law of euphony. A letter may be thrown away for this purpose, either from the beginning or end of it. Two consonants or vowels coming together, would require one to be dropt. In this process of syllabic curtailment, and the readjustment and interfusion of new roots, sometimes, but a single letter out of the word to be introduced, is left in the compound; yet that letter is an ideographic sign, and represents, and carries the whole and full meaning of the parent word. In this latter case, however, the end or the beginning of the word annexed, or the word annexed to, supplies the sound thrown away, and thus guides the native ear in its nice perceptions of the etymology. Thus to give an example of the rule, the two vowel sounds, *io*, in the Iroquois terms, Ohio and Ontario, which denote a water landscape, are from the same radical, and bring before the mind the entire landscape of woods and water denoted. They are qualified exclusively by the prefixed or appended syllables, *o*, *on*, *oh*, and *tar*. *Oh*, denotes beautiful, *on* hills or mountains, and *tar* rocks or cliffs, as heard in the name of Ontario, which is a Wyandot word, being applied to the first prospect of the lake, on the issue from the old portage of Cadaracqui. A still further cause of the ability of happy and truthful geographical description, possessed by our native languages, is owing to a stock of generic particles, of an adjective character, which are used as separable prefixes and suffixes to the substantive. Thus, *na* denotes excellent, *ish* is derogative, *ees* diminutive, *ing* local, &c. With a language purely transpositive in its rules, and with a magazine of these generic particles at his command, the native orator is never at a loss to give a turn, a piquancy, or beauty to his expressions. While the words poured out by an orator, enchain the mere casual hearer as an out pouring of well collocated sounds, they transport with their ideality, an audience of glowing foresters, to whom these felicities of thought, and capacities of expression, have been familiar from their cradles.

These traits of the native languages, although apparently indigenous, may be developements of ancient grammars and vocabularies. Correspondences may be found, in portions of the globe, with whose philology we are as yet but little acquainted. Before true comparisons can be well made with foreign languages, we should have vocabularies of both the foreign and domestic languages, collected on uniform principles, with such notices of their grammars as shall tell us, not merely how they conjugate a verb, how they denote tenses and number, but what provisions there are in the texture of the word itself, for regulating this principle of compounds. Do any tribes of the old world view the globe, as the Algonquins do, as existing in two grand animate and inanimate classes, equivalent to genders? Do they compound their words by ideographic increments of preëxisting roots, or ground forms of words, which retain the original meaning of whole words? Do they possess, like the tribes of the western hemisphere, an original vocabulary of primitive generic particles, which, under the use of free transposition, principles can be employed, with almost the facility of men on a chess board, to form new combinations, making new forms, at every evolution of the mind, to express meanings the most recondite, graphic, or admirable?

In applying these remarks to the Iroquois language, we may take the Algonquin, of which more has been written, as a point for comparison. Like this leading language of the *north* and *west*, the Iroquois abounds in the power of geographical description, forming derivative and compound terms, as an evidence of which, it may be mentioned, that it has actually covered the ancient domain of their residence in western New York, with many euphonous names for the streams and other features of its topography, which constitute the most permanent monument to their memory. Like it, also, its verbs and nouns receive the pronouns as inseparable prefixes or suffixes, which become essential parts of the words. Like it, also, they are mutually transferable into each other, nouns becoming verbs and verbs nouns, *ad libitum*. They are inflected, like the Algonquin, 1, for locality; 2, for general quality, as size, texture, color, weight, form, beauty or deformity; 3, for a character of particular hurtfulness or destructiveness, which may be called the *derogative* inflection; 4, for diminution. They have inseparable particles, as we observe in the Algonquin dialects, to denote propositions, which render the use of both nouns and verbs precise; and the language has a full provision to denote number. At this point, it passes beyond the Algonquin, in its capacities of exact expression, denoting number, not only in some cases, in the conjugation of verbs, where the other language often fails, but it gives us a dual, as well as a general plural. It also gives us a masculine, a feminine and a neuter gender, and does not fall under the more barbaric and certainly anomalous grammatical rule of classes of animate and inanimate words, requiring concords of that character. The Iroquois count, like all our known United States or Alleghanic stocks, by the decimal system. Their numerals denote a stronger degree of analogy between the languages of the cantons, reaching to the Tuscaroras and Wyandots, than any other class of their words. The actual differences in the Iroquois vocabulary of the different cantons, are very considerable and rather striking. In all, however, a law of combination is obeyed, which, giving the speaker the general meaning of the primary, or root forms, allows great latitude and independency in bestowing names on things, or rather in the choice of traits or qualities in the thing to be named; whence it happens that the several diverse names of the cantons, for the same thing or object, are well known and understood by each, proving a general and original unity, in those very points where philology, guided alone by orthoëpy and orthography, finds the greatest discrepancies. The Iroquois has no labials; it rolls from the tongue and glottis, with lips unclosed. And although it has some of the deepest gutturals, it abounds in long and open vowel sounds, along with its liquids and aspirates, which fall musically on the ear, and give it a manly, and dignified flow. Its nasal vowel sounds and dipthongs, as heard so often in the Oneida and Onondaga dialects, have a peculiar softness and melody.

LANGUAGE. 393

## COMPARATIVE VOCABULARY OF THE IROQUOIS.

| English | Mohawk (1) | Oneida (2) | Onondaga (3) | Cayuga (4) | Seneca (5) | Tuscarora (6) | Wyandot (7) |
|---|---|---|---|---|---|---|---|
| God | Niyoh | Louee | Hawaneuh | Niyoh | Honianeyuh | Yawuruueyuh | Tamainrlezui |
| Devil | Onesohrono | Onislauh,'omuh | Onishonluainmuh | Onesoono | Honishaiwwinuh | Onnasaroonuh | Deglishorenoh |
| Man | Rongwe | Longwee | Hningwee | Nujina | Hongweh | Elukweh | Aingahou |
| Woman | Yongwe | Yongwee | Watboonwixsus | Konherghtie | Yeao | Hohwulunuh | Uteluke |
| Boy | Raxaa | Lakisalyyeksah | Huxsaha | Aksaa | Huxsaa | Kunelukweh'r | Omunisentehah |
| Girl | kaxaa | Lakisaliyeksah | Ixesaha | Exaa | Yixsaa | Yatcahchayeuh | Yaweetsenthe |
| Child | Exaa | Kumcixsada | | Exaa | Yakesauh* | Kutsuli | Cheahhah |
| Infant | Owiraa | | | | Godonn-ahah* | | |
| Father | [my] Rakeriha | [my] Knhenecha | [my] Knehah | Ouoekwataa | [my] Hahnee | Ealukrehn | Hayesta |
| Mother | " Istenha | " Akhanodha | [my] Uknohah | Hanni | Noyeh | Eunuh | Anehch |
| Husband | " Teyakenitero | Loma | [my] Haiwnah | Iknoba | Dayakni | Euayahkeahwunhtekchmreannhn | |
| Wife | " Teyakenitero | Tehmedion | Telinetaiw | Iouknuiago | Yo* | (The same as at-we,) [nehah] | [my] Azutunoloch |
| Son | " Iyeaha | [his] Loyansh | [his] Hohawa | Iouginhsoko | [his] Houwuk | Trahwuhuruh, nuhnuim, a | [his] Hoomekauk |
| Daughter | " Keyeaha | " Sayoyeh | [his] Sagohawa | Ihihawog | [my] Kauwuk | [his] | Ondequien |
| Brother | " Akyatarekeaha | Teluchdianoulal | Taukeadanouda | Ikhchawog | [his] Dayadanouda | Ealukeahtkeup | [my] Aenyeha |
| Sister | " Akzatatoscaha | Onndadagonh | Taokeadanouda | Irekyatehmonte | Dayadanouda | [my] Ealukeahnhnpoah'r | [my] Acnyeha |
| An Indian | Ongwehowe | Onewahoawe | Lugwahongwa | Kekeaha | Ongweeongwe | Reukkwelhebunweh | Iomwheen (pl.) |
| Head | Ononti | Ouondj | Ouuwa | Ougwchowe | Omouga | Yairch [wuha] | Skotau |
| Hair | Osonkwis | Ouokwish | Ouoikwich | Ouowsa | Kogauga | [his] Trahwuhuruh, rahwchrah | Arochu |
| Face | Okonsa | Y-goouksaa | Ogrooksah | Onoukia | [his] Hagoossaga | Trahwuhuruh, rahkenhseuhkeh | Aouchia |
| Scalp | Onora | Onhuntah | Olouhtali | Okonsa | Onoah | Trahwuhuruh, rahunireh | |
| Ear | Ohonta | Ozah | Ograhah | Ohoha | Ooltah | Trahwuhnrahkunhonuhkeh | Hoontseuh |
| Eye | Okara | Oxen hs | Quin-sah | Heuta | Ogah | Trahwuhurnhokolreuhken | Yochgniondoch |
| Nose | Onyohsa | Telsesagalun | Ojsah | Okaeluha | Ogonduh | Trahwuhnrahoheutsentihkeh | Yumzah |
| Mouth | Jirasekarune | Ovnsa | Ouahsah | Onyokxia | Ksaugaaud | Trahwuhnrahskahrenh | E-skanhereeh |
| Tongue | Aweaughsa | Ohuwee | Onoshia | Sishakaeni | Wamahsah | Trahwuhnreuhtohneahkeh | Undanehsherua |
| Tooth | Onawi | Ogeosta | Onodia | Aweanaghsa | Oaqah | Trahwuhnrentralitwohhtseh | Uskonndeenu |
| Pearl | Oketescara | Ouiawl | Onueska | Ouojia | Oguostwea | Trahwulnureuhseohkcheh | Orhquieroot |
| Neck | Onyara | Onnuts | Ouhalı | Okosteaa | Kanusa | Trahwuhnrahkunhhahtseh | Ohoura |
| Arm | Ononbsa | Ouuxt | Onenatsha | Onyaz | Ouiashah | Trahwuhnrahmentheherahkeuh | |
| Shoulder | Oginehsa | Veesheouhit | Ouehsah | Ouemsa | Ouehsah | Trahwuhnrumrahmmlneh | |
| Back | Ognagea | Veeawonga | Olsunkwah | Orhnesia | O-wauuah | Trahwuhnrohrenhwrunikeh | |
| Hand | Osnsa | [ore] Yosntsada | Ohnix | E-shoghute | Ooltuh | Trahwuhnruhruhralrclouhkch | Vareesaw |
| Finger | Osnsa | | | E-shoghtage | Ohia | Trahwuhuhrooikweh | Eyingia (plural.) |

51

## HISTORY OF THE IROQUOIS.

| English | Mohawk (1) | Oneida (2) | Onondaga (3) | Cayuga (4) | Seneca (5) | Tuscarora (6) | Wyandot (7) |
|---|---|---|---|---|---|---|---|
| Nail | Ojera | Ojeail | Oata | Ojeighta | Ohta | Trahwuluruhskeahkahreh | Obetta (plural.) |
| Breast | Aonakweaa | Ontsahkwa | Oalisah | Oalsia | Odohsa | Trahwulnrulahsmhkeh | |
| Body | Oyeronta | Oyeoleondah | Oiatah | Oyeona | Oyahdah | Trahwulnruhketstheuhkeh | |
| Leg | Oghsina | Ohsenah | Ononutah | Ogiscna | Ohseenah | Trahwuluruhrenlseuhkeh | |
| Navel | Oaentsta | Onietah | Orguatah | koishetot | Hoke-sadote* | Trahwuluruinse-seuhrenhkeh | |
| Thigh | Ojunitsa | Ohneetsah | Ohnectshah | Onhoska | Oyahtah* | Trahwuluruluteheuhkeh [e'] | Ochsheetau (do.) |
| Knee | Oktwitsa | Yagwontshalga | Okahenah | Okonisha | Yoshah* | Trahwuluruhreuhkeuhruht' smhk | |
| Foot | Oghsita | O-seetah | Ohseetah | Oshita | Oseedah* | Trahwuluruhrahneuhkeh | |
| Toe | Ozhyakwe | Oneagwelah | Obeagwia | Oghyakwea | Oyahgweeyeh* | Trahwuhnrulrahsoohkweh | |
| Heel | Orata | Yelahdane | Oattah | Iyatage | Oadatsuh* | Trahwuhrohutehhenhcheh | Onuaonda |
| Bone | Ostica | Ostia | Ostiautah | Ostienda | Ouaeyoh | Trahwulurulskeulreh | Yootooshaw |
| Heart | Aweri | Ahwaleh | Ahwauasa | Kawaghsa | Owyngawshaw | Trahwuluruhrarealseh | |
| Liver | Otwealisa | Ootwansah | Ouahkwa | Gotwesa | Otwelsaia* | Trahwulnruhraht'wuhiseh | |
| Windpipe | Ratoryelata | Ohsongwah | Ohnuwa | Ouekreauda | Ouhweii* | Trahwulnruhrahmkt'seh | |
| Stomach | Onekereanta | Yeyadagooh [insides] | Oyouvrah | Obowa | Yadoeshgoh* | Trahwuhruhkehrhaheauh | Ingoh |
| Bladder | Ouuleaghlata | Odinisaduk | Inhahakwah | Ouhcha | Salaundagrnah* | Trahwuluruloteahueh | |
| Blood | Onegweasa | Oneewuhsuh | Outkwalseh | Ogrweasa | Tiqueusa | Trahwonruluharra | |
| Vein | Ogunolyaghtough | Ojenohyahrun | Otlshentulata | Ojnohyada | Ogeenodyahdah* | Trahwuhrulnuuhyahtseh | |
| Sinew | Ogenoiyaghtough | Ojenohyahtun | Otlshentulata | Ojnohyada | Onuhyah* | Tra.wuhnruhnuuhyahtseh | |
| Flesh | Owarough | Owahlan | Weinuta | Owaho | Owahau* | Ekawareh | |
| Skin | Oghua | Omahgwalah | Komhwa | Ogonegliwa | Oshoda* | Ekannuhkeh | |
| Scat | Outskwara | | Oolnaasa | Ondadakwa | Gaunhsah* | Eaktak | |
| Ankle | Osnegotta | | | Ojilongwa | Ogeeaogwah* | | [ate |
| Town | Kanata | Kunadiah | Kumadaia | Kanetae | Innekanaudaa* | Katuhnahyenh | Onhaiyearhataaud |
| House | Kanosa | Kanusoda | Kunosaia | Kanosiod | Gansote* | Yalukeahmuh | [big] Yeaneghshu |
| Door | Kauhoha | | | Kauhoha | Galogaant* | Onekahreh | [wana |
| Lodge | Teyrtasta | Yagodus kwahele | Wuskwaka | Teyetasta | Gamohasetah* | Waluktahnahyeuhoalogh | |
| Chief | Rakowana | Loganil | Houscnowahn | Agisseanewane | Aeluslaunane | Yakowanauh | |
| Warrior | Roskeahrageloc | Loskanlagete | | Osgeagehta | Ooskingehtaw [aase | Rooskenhrahkehreh | Trazue |
| Friend | Atearoscra | Hunawianitu | Untslee | Ateroleera | Gachce | Ehhunuhrooh | Neatarugh |
| Enemy | Shagoswease | Aaleoska | Kihuniagwasa | Ondateswaes | Dayahdahuegoaseow | Yenhchooktseh | Nematrerue |
| Kettle | Onta | Ooudak | Kunatia | Kanadsia | Konnowynn | Osmuhwch | Yayanetih |
| Arrow | Kayoakwere | Kiowilla | Kahanka | Adota | Canah | Ootch | |
| Bow | Aeana | Haahna [high | Akainda | Kajiwaodriohta | Oonaw* | Nahchreh | |
| Warclub | Yeanterjyohtakanyoh | Yuuleohtakwagun | Kajeehkwa | Kaghswah | Gajeewah* | Oschekweh | Otoyaye |
| Spear | Aghsakwe | Hoshgweh | Ajudishuah | Kagluigrwa | Gahzeegwra* | Claurets | Whoranuua |
| Axe | Atokea | Adegun | Askwasa | Atokra | Otioyeh | Nokeuh | |
| Gun | Kagaore | | | Kaota | Gahaodah* | | |

# LANGUAGE. 395

| English | | | | | | |
|---|---|---|---|---|---|---|
| Knife | Asare | | Hasha | Kainara | Obsalkeulneh | Weneashra |
| Flint | Kainhia | Hashale | Kmeaetah | Aurakwenda | Ahtigwendale* | Taweghskera(plu) |
| Boat | Kahoweya | Kahoawveia | Kahoonisanah | Kaowa | Kanoowau | Gya |
| Ship | Kahoweyakowa | Kahoonweiagoo | Ahtahkwa | Kaowarowa | Gaowohgrowah* | Araghshu |
| Shoe | Aghta | Ahta | Kais | Ataghkwa | Aulroyuawohwa (pl | Yaree (plural.) |
| Legging | Karis | Katis | Adasdawehtsa | Atyatawitra | Garesheh* | |
| Coat | Atyata wii | Adiadawehi | Kagahha | Nikabelia | Ahdeadalwisheh* | Catureesh |
| Shirt | Onyatnraaatyatawit | Kanyagahadus | Ajenuhkahkwa | Kairotoa | Ahdendahwssheh* | |
| Breechcloth | Kahare | Ojunka | Kagaitah | Teaunigwistrista | Gahkarah* | |
| Sash | Atyataaha | Adnnkwrnaha | Kaissiowah | Todnaawonhasta | Galigatiah* | |
| Headdress | Onowarori | Olaoouqua | Kononawehta | Atsiokwaghta | Gustoweh* | (Belt or sash) Ooehehaht'ehra |
| Pipe | Kanonawea | Konanawuh | | Otkoa | Osagnawtuw | Yahah?hsoohstoh |
| Wampum | Onegorina | | Oyaikwa | Oyeangwa | Oatgoeh* | Hednokweh |
| Tobacco | Oyeangwa | Kalonia | Ksaiwia | Oisdata | Oyagua | Chah?rshoobstoh |
| Sky | Oi-hata | Kakonia | Kaniwiaga | Kaohyage | Kinnyage | |
| Heaven | Karonghyage | Kokonhiagee | Anikka | Kaagikwa [wa | Gaoyageh* | Caghroniate |
| Sun | Karaghkwa | Wolneda | Asoheka | Soheghkakaaghk | Kaehgua | Oorenhyal'rs |
| Moon | Eghnita | Wolneda | Ojstunahkwa | Ojishonda | Kachgua | Oorenhyahkeuhf |
| Star | Ogsiok | Yugsiokwa | Wundada | Omisrate | Ogeshanda | Heteh |
| Day | Egluisera | Kwondegi | Aseohwa | Aeoie | Ijule | Aht'scutsyebah [shra |
| Night | Agisameane | Kwasandegi | Teohahiaih | Teyohuate | Nehsoha | Vaudehra |
| Light | Teyoswathe | Wanda | Teokaus | Tyotsontage | Teuhotta | Waughsamyaande |
| Darkness | Tyokaras | Tedhingallas | Haigahtsheek | Sedeisiha | Teudawsnnl'igo | Tezhehu (plural.) |
| Morning | Ohrhonkene | Osihusiiee | Oguisah | Okaasa | Teaueoendau | Ourhetha |
| Evening | Yokoraskha | Ugalhsunh | Kigwedchkee | Kagretijiha | Oralhshat | Asoutey |
| Spring | Keankwetene | Ktnngwedaleh | Kogeniagee | Kakentage | Ungsunikneh | |
| Summer | Akeuhage | Gwagoulage | Knnunaakee | Kananagene | Kaueynch | Asoaratoy |
| Autumn | Kanonage | Kunonagth | Kehsahgth | Kohsregiue | Gankneh | Tedeinret |
| Winter | Koghserage | Koisdagrh | Oah | Kawasoales | Oushat | Howeraguey |
| Wind | Owera | Uwelomlo | Tawomehwhns | Teweaudios | Gahah | Honenhet |
| Lightning | Tewerauerekarawas | Tawomkalawras | Kawnudotate | Kawcanotatias | Eeno | Anandge |
| Thunder | Kaweras | Gasagiunda | Osdta | O-inondion | Eechnung | Oxley |
| Rain | Yokesnorongh | Okanolabseeh | Okah | Ouleye | Oostafat | Izaquas |
| Snow | Oulyelate | Onenlna | Owesoroudiix | Ontriondio | Onyeiak | Timmendignas |
| Hail | Yo-soute | Wawizonde | Ojistia | Ojista | Oneryustouede | Heno |
| Fire | Yotekha | Oljista | Ohnagonnoos | Omikanos | Ojsista | Immndasc |
| Water | Ognneknnos | Ohnagonnoos | Ouceeso | Otre | Onekandus | Deuehta |
| Ice | Oi-e | Howiseee | Owhaingeah | Denaja [nc | Owesah | Ondehia |
| Earth, land | Owehetsia | Ogwuugeah | Raneadaewah | Kanyateowaregh | Lenjah | Sea-sa |
| Sea | Kanyaterakekowa | Kaweadaiaokoa | Kuneada | Kanyataeni | Caniowdage | Saudnstee |
| Lake | Kanyatare | Kanc adatahk | | | Conutic | Des-hra |
| | | | | | | Uuatsegh |
| | | | | | | Giontarouemne |
| | | | | | | Voontauray |

396  HISTORY OF THE IROQUOIS.

| English | Mohawk (1) | Oneida (2) | Onondaga (3) | Cayuga (4) | Seneca (5) | Tuscarora (6) | Wyandots (7) |
|---|---|---|---|---|---|---|---|
| River | Kaihoghha | Kehwad'adee | Kinadadee | Kihade | Kceehoade | Keunh | Yeaudawo |
| Spring | Yohnaweronte | Kuniqiohaa | Nekayunwahia | Oginawaot | Odushote* | Halis'nunhyeuhtih | |
| Stream | Yohyohonto | Kohmawkh | Kagus-wenusa | Oghyeaunto | | Ahwmhrahsothkenh | Quieunontouin |
| Valley | Teyohrowe | Ynundoos | Kunadota | Teyostowemo | Jennusha | Yununuit'heh | Ononah |
| Hill | Yonante | Yenout | Onundowrahurah | Onontea | Iheoudate | Yuuuniyeuhtih | Ohonnah |
| Mountain | Yonettickowa | Kothadahk | Odngwunzhiqrwio | Onontowanea | Oonumdawouna | Walukeulnahyeuh | |
| Plain | Kahcanta | Kahisoau | Kahhagro   [shoo | Kahagro | | Oohr'hahnahkeuhf | |
| Forest | Karhago | Yngunigileaht | Stowlaoktah | Ostondriakta | Yaatyarktah* | Yahareohtoli | Aboindo |
| Meadow | Yeheautykta | Kunawuk-h | Kunawakouh | Oweaupanawe | Aloumozeh* | Yuneh'reuht'sahnereauh | Arie-ta |
| Bog | Yonauawea | Kahwranood | Kahwanae | Kaweghnoa | Kawanoot | Yuhwelanoeh | Reiuda |
| Island | Kawenote | Onjia | Onia | Kaskwa | Kosgua | Ooreihneh | |
| Stone | Oneliya | Osta | Usitaha | Osteaha | Oceteheh* | Ooetenhreh | |
| Rock | Ostcara | Kahwishtomolung | Kahwishtonoo | Kawistanoo | | Kahkwistahnoreuh | |
| Copper | Karistanora | Kwenis | Okwaneet | Ogwenida | Yuinnish | Kwzansnees | Nayhah |
| Iron | Oginigwark-aristaji | Kalisnteh | Otakatshah | Kaniawasa | Kawneuhshah | Oowannni | |
| Silver | Karistaji | Kowisiatomawnhs | Onionsa | Kanzkanawis | Omuldtah* | Nahwade'steh | |
| Lead | Kawistanawis | Ounst | Oudnah | Onehn | Onaa | Oounuhheh | |
| Maize | Onea-ii | | Onntla | Onajia | Onaijah* | Ootoos | |
| Wheat | Eanckeri | | Onndia | Oats | Onuhjunt* | O'ch | |
| Oats | Youehonte | Yunahoont | Oponuhkwa | Onatt | Ononuhdah* | Oonunhtseh | Yearonta |
| Potato | Oghuranata | Ohnunnaht | Kainta | Krael | Garouta | Ocreuheh | Onaghta |
| Tree | Kherine | Kellheet | Wenndah | Oycauda | Garouta | Oxyeuhkwereh | Exrohi |
| Wood | Oyeante | Oyunt | Onailitah | Otaa | Ooseuah | Holteh | |
| Pine | Oghnehta | Ohnait | Kiondagra | Kakata | Kankauuau | Rahrosh | |
| Oak | Tokeraha | Otokuhha | Konicw | Koboweya | Gahnyoh* | Wloh't | |
| Ash | Eznesa | Kumilh | Kayurkwa | Osakra | Galunuga* | Kahraht'kwoh | Ourata |
| Elm | Akaraji | Ogunlawsh | Holiosa | Oheotra | Oosa* | Odoosaroh | Eruta |
| Bass-wood | Oheecra | O.co-za | Ohunta | Ohonda | Oeoclote* | Kwerohkeuh | |
| Shrub | Nikakwerasa | Ogwile | Onattah | Ouraghta | Ouechta | Oeeuhreh | |
| Leaf | Oneraglite | Oonlat | Kasoontah | Owajsta | Kashua | Skeulnoireh | |
| Bark | Owajste | Askoout | Owinoka | Owenioghkra | Okeoju | Yuharuhkweh | |
| Grass | Ohonte | Onekee | Onnhkwabsa | Owheatra | Oecktah* | Yalkoobaroliroh'r | |
| Nettle | Ohrhes | Olhooht | Owemhkasoeeh | Owenokrasod | Oatah* | Chuwakahlharahka | |
| Weed | Kahontaxa | Onariuicshoo | Oraisa | Oweha | Aiwaoh* | Ooe-heelee-treli | Dataruh |
| Flower | Ojiia | Yuljnount | Ohakwuh | Onada | Oaquah* | Ootainalureh | |
| Bread | Kanstarok | Kaudarook | Tshekwigrostaits | Onehaotetra | Jitgwaehataseh* | Odatunalureli | |
| Indian meal | Oneaeiothesera | Ogwaluuweneholaijce | | Otetra | Otaseh* | Ootene'hrali | |
| Flour | Othesera | | | | | Ooteuc'hrali | |

# LANGUAGE. 397

| English | | | | | | |
|---|---|---|---|---|---|---|
| Meat | Owarough | Owalloo | Owaleh | Owahon | Oowaha* | Ohwagloha |
| Fat | Yoresea | Tshomeht | Oakayahke | Osra | Odohseh | Sootaie |
| Beaver | Jonitough | Uskounot | Skanodo | Akaniago | Nungeancawgrung | Oughsanoto |
| Deer | Oskoueantia | Okwa-e | Ohwaie | Wahontes | Naegah | Aune |
| Bear | Oghkwan | Toween | Skwaaea | Yekwai | Yucury | Tawenleh |
| Otter | Tawine | Skunux | Skahuxa | Intedro | Oidalwraunlub* | Thenaintouto |
| Fox | Jisho | Orahue | Hohyone | Ishaie | Onungwratyuaw | Ticanne |
| Wolf | Okwaho | Aithol | Tsleethia | Tahioni | Ticaune | Cheryke |
| Dog | Eluriar | Tshukwedoh | Talukatakee | Sluoas | Cheyke | Ogtuch |
| Squirrel | Arosea | Tshoonkotlo | Ogonowitah | Jonsskro | Ukiaako | |
| Hare | Taloutunegea | Nogi | Onoji | Toutaend | Tuudient | |
| Muskrat | Anokyra | Onrdus | Nrdash | Teoni | Geenadalgah* | Quisquesh |
| Polecat | Takoskowa | Kuskus | Kweaskweas | Kane wagcha | Gergohsaoch* | Uglashntte |
| Hog | Kwiskwes | Vagesadus | Kosudus | Kwiskwis | Gwisgws* | |
| Horse | Vagesateas | Gwunladakwas | Teuuloskwi | Karundanenkwi | Gaenalanchgwee* | |
| Cow | Kanona | Taudenagatuntanha | Teedinakaimia | Tidoskwaemt | Gannhgwart* | |
| Sheep | Teyotinakuromoha | Tnowul | Tipowhahl | Teyedimekaoudea | Dayadenuhgaunt | |
| Turtle | Anowara | Tshunskagwaloud | Nooskwakwiauto | Kaningchtengowa | Tanyatehgowah* | Tuengenseeh |
| Toad | Jighanaatah | | | Naskwagaotta | Nogwagwraundoh* | Ognonchia |
| Inseet | Ostruown | Olcheneo | Osiuishta | Osisnwa | Ogenhwith* | |
| Snake | Onyare | Otk | Kayatoali | Ozasta | Osishetaw | |
| Bird | Jitrahn | Tshola | Onhtuska | Jiteae | Ochretaw | |
| Egg | Onhonsa | Onlush | Ouahkwa | Omhonsia | Oholsiaw | |
| Feather | Ostesera | Oatoze | Oilihuh | Ostotra | Oainh* | Yathhouk |
| Claw | Ogiera | Ogail | Oeuta | Osiouhta | Oothrehsch | Aroissan |
| Beak | Ojikeweyeanta | Owennl | Ocata | Kannontasa | Osunokre | Tareu |
| Wing | Oweya | Oweahooms | Kronk | Kawaontes | Ouhalahehseh* | Oritey |
| Goose | Onasakeara | Olosagonlat | Oueagiche | Itonkah | Oneidahsah* | Dughlontah |
| Partridge | Oglikwesea | Okwas | Soak | Kawesea | Ouyenhwets'neh | |
| Duck | Sora | Ihollongoo | Tshula | Ohezo | Ungezauk | |
| Pigeon | Orite | Oleek | Netahninchwa | Jakawa | Jahyangrne | |
| Turkey | Skawernwane | Skowrolowah | Kahkah | Sohout | Sonvek | |
| Crow | Jokawe | Kaga | | Kagika | Jeehkuan | |
| Robin | Jiskoko | | | Jiskoko | Oosoneant | |
| Eagle | Orangea | Adonitol | Skaujeolumnh | Nataongowra | Galgrah* | |
| Hawk | Karhalohui | Kidnghoo | Tagiahtahkwah | Tekayatakwa | Geeoyike* | Yeem-o |
| Snipe | Tawistawis | Kawemelusko | Tawishtawish | Tawisdewi | Dmyondoti* | |
| Owl | Ohowra | Skaunulano | Kakhoa | Owa | Galgredars* | |
| Woodpecker | Kwarre | Ojeesokwolanoo | | Kwaa | Oowah* | |
| Fish | Kranisea | Kintshe | | Osisouda | Qnnah* | |
| Trout | Tyoryaktea | Bodiahto | | Tiadatsea | Kennck | |
| | | | | | Dyaweh* | |

# HISTORY OF THE IROQUOIS.

| English | Mohawk (1) | Oneida (2) | Onondaga (3) | Cayuga (4) | Seneca (5) | Tuscarora (6) | Wyandot (7) |
|---|---|---|---|---|---|---|---|
| Bass | Ojkakwara | Ahwadj | | Onoksa | Gahquali* | Keuhcheahheuhs'che | |
| Pike | Jikonsis | Skugahlux | | Jikonsis | Geegwase* | Koowaluk | |
| Sturgeon | Nikeanjiakowra | kuneageoch | | Kajhista | Gahsaseetah* | Hahrah | |
| Fin | Odare | Owcasluouuts | | Owaia | Odayate* | Ootooneh | |
| Scale | Osta | Yu-stait | | 'asta | Osetah* | O s'ueh | |
| White | Kearakea | Owiska | Owikaishta | Gwaankea | Noandaun | Oowahreahkeuh | Oneienta |
| Black | Kahouji | Aswant | Osuutah | Sweandaea | Jenshtau | Kahhunhs'ehe | Cheestaheh |
| Red | Onegweantara | Onegwata | Tutkwaihta | Otkwenjia | Queehtaha | | Orsichaye |
| Blue | Oronya | Olooh | Owiuhea | Drinaea | Unrau | Oothheuhreeh | |
| Yellow | Oginigwur | Ojeenkwulh | Otiaainda | Jrakwa | Jetgnau | Thkalechet?kahnahyeuh | |
| Green | Ohoute | Owonlh(la) | Tsheeckwa | Draltaea | Kounehtikoh | Oobareh | Obsinguarae |
| Great | Kowanea | Kwan | Kuan | Kowanea | Kowah | Weyu | Ouen |
| Small | Niwaa | Kunewuh | Newnah | Niwaa | Newaa | Wastteuh | Okrye |
| Strong | Kashauste | Katshaust | Kahwheesea | Kashaste | Kawhosta | Ootereuh | |
| Weak | Yoyatakeaheyea | | | Oyatakeaheyo | Dagahhusteh* | | |
| Old | Oksteaha | Agti | Ogayoongbe | Osten | Kawgehehee | Oauuhhahah | |
| Young | Niyoyeaha | Odoee | Ustwasali | Ongwetasea | Catwasah* | Oo?toh | (he is) Hauwohstee |
| Good | Yoyawere | Yuyonteh | Yanlee | Oyanri | Usekoss | Wahkwast | |
| Bad | Waherkea | Wiaheet-h | Wahaitkee | Waetgea | Tauraookos | Wabsunh | Hauste |
| Handsome | Yorase | Yuyustung | Agoule | Oyanri | Weoh | Yuyahtahyeuhsunh | |
| Ugly | Wahetkea | [lia?] Waheetkh | Wahaitka | Waetkea | Tautaweoh | Kohseuh | |
| Alive | Yonhe | Aeonha | [life] Oonha | O,he | Eohuay | Wunhleh | (he lives) Eronteh |
| Dead | Yaweaheyea | Lawanhayum | [he is alive] Owahaioo | Aweaheyea | Aluwaayoh* | Y-alwunihayeuh | |
| Life | Yonhe | Yun'sa | Haiuha | Oube | Yuhhleh* | Nayalwunht?kwah | |
| Death | Keaheyea | Yawuhsayah | Owahaiyut | Keaheyea | Guayart* | Keuhhayeuh | |
| Cold | Yotore | Yathola | Uthove | Otowi | Ootoe | Aht'hnh | Turea |
| Hot | Yotaribea | Yutalehan | Odaehah | Otaiho | Oouaino | Yuhnahrehin | |
| Sour | Teyohyojis | Yayoyogis | Oshewagza | Teyohyojis | Ojeewahgeh* | Nayuhcheranohneh | |
| Sweet | Yaweko | Yawazeon | Wunwaundah | Okao | Orahah* | Yahwakenh | Deeh |
| Bitter | Yotskara | Yutskalot | Uskast | Odjwage | Dayoganis* | Yuchewahkenh | Sah |
| I | Iih | Ee | Ech | I | Eee | E | Howomohah |
| Thou | Ise | Eesa | Ee-sahhe | Ise | Ees | Eis | |
| He | Raonha | Laonha | H-ourti | Aoha | Alwha | Trahyanueltch | |
| She | Aouha | Aoonha | Ovkah | Kaoha | Conwha | Ayaunehteh | |
| They | Ronouha | Lanohah | Onunhage | Onoha | Anawioha | Kahyayehsunhteh | Newmohah |
| You, Ye | Jiyoha | Eesa | Iskalugwuh | Johhu | Ees | Thwahyasunheh | |
| We | Oikyohi | Tannejaloo | Ongeunhage | Onkyohia | Diwaguago | Eahkwahyasunhteh | |
| This | Keatkea | Kakekah | Naungahah | Neaugea | Namgeh | Keh'unun | |

# LANGUAGE.

| English | | | | | | | |
|---|---|---|---|---|---|---|---|
| That | Toikea | Toeknh | Thogee | Shigea | Nashekeh | Hanuh | |
| All | Agwegon | Agnakon | Ugwahe | Gwegon | Kawknago | T'wa'hn | |
| Who | Onka | Honka | | Sonaot | Sloah | Kohna | |
| Near | Niyorea | Aetah | Tuscaha | Niyorea | Tooskanh* | Nooskenh | |
| Far off | Ino | Enon | Ecnoo | Ino | Wach* | Emh | Pseruoeh |
| To-day | Keaweante | Kawauada | | Wanewauisade | Nawau | Halwuuhyah?rheukenh | |
| Yesterday | Tetcare | Tatau | | Tethea | Tateh | Tehunh | |
| To-morrow | Eayiorheane | Ayulhana | Iorhana | Iyohea | Youehent | Enhyah?rheuh | |
| By and by | Owagchascaha | | | Swegeha | Iegweew* | Kawulotheuhrah | |
| Yes | Ea | Ifa | | Eathea | Um | Enhhenh | |
| No | Yahtea | Yahten | Jachte | Trah | Taun | Kwuhs | Heh |
| Perhaps | Toktl | Togauonah | | Tokatgisa | tisheh* | Ahreuhkwehe | Tayauh |
| Above | Enegra | Anahkan | | Hetgea | Hetegeh* | Stralkwe | |
| Under | Onagon | Nagon | | Nagon | Afahgeh* | Enhtohkreuh?f | |
| Within | Omagounmonga | Asta | | Nagongwadi | Nulgult* | Oonuhskeuh | |
| Without | Aistenongrati | Kalnale | | Atstegwadi | Osteh* | Th'arhteh | |
| On | Ednorh | Othokaohota | | Ednogth | Galia* | Hohheh'n | |
| Something | Onhemo | Yahatanon | | Tikaweaniyoh | Hahgwisteh* | Stoekenh | |
| Nothing | Yaghotheno | Anscot | | Peaskoutea | Datahgwisteh* | | |
| One | Easka | Daganee | Skata | Skat | Skant | Pauche | Seat |
| Two | Tekeni | Hason | Tekina | Tekni | Tirknee | Nakte | Tuulee |
| Three | Aghsea | Kiyalee | Aehso | Segh | Shegh | Absunk | Shaiglit |
| Four | Kieri | Wisk | Gajeri | Kei | Kace | Kunhtoh | Auhaght |
| Five | Wisk | Yahyak | Wsk | Wis | Wish | Weesk | Weesh |
| Six | Yayak | Jadak | Achiak | Yei | Yace | Oolyok | Wauslauu |
| Seven | Jatak | Takalon | Tschoatah | Jatah | Jawduek | Cheohnoh | Sootaie |
| Eight | Sategro | Wailon | Tekiro | Tekro | Tikkuhg | Nakreuh | Autarai |
| Nine | Tiyohto | Oyalee | Watiro | Tyohto | Tentongh | Nereuh | Aurne |
| Ten | Oyeri | | Waeshestangachera | Waghsea | Wushagh | Wahlh'sunk | Aughseeth |
| Eleven | Easkayaweare | Auscolyawala | Tekeni | Skatskuie | Scotskaaaewusheh* | Pauchesknhhah | Asanraaieesearhet |
| Twelve | Tekunjaweare | Daganayawala | | Teknnskaie | Delmenewusheh* | Nahtuhskahhah | Assauueauexearhet |
| Thirteen | Aghseayaweare | Hasonyawala | | Aghsegliskaie | Sehmewusheh* | Absunskahhah | |
| Fourteen | Kaijeriyaweare | Kiyaluyawala | | Keiskaie | Gainnewusheh* | Hnuhtohskahhah | |
| Fifteen | Wiskyaweare | Wiskyawala | | Wiskaie | Wisnewusheh* | Weeskskahhah | |
| Sixteen | Yayakyaweare | Yayuhyawala | | Yeiskaie | Yailnewusheh* | Oolyokskahhah | |
| Seventeen | Jatakyaweare | Jadakyawala | | Jataskaie | Jahluknewusheh* | Oolyokskahhah | |
| Eighteen | Sategoyaweare | Takalonyawala | | Tkroskaie | Dreohanewusheh* | Nakreuh | |
| Nineteen | Tiyohtoyaweare | Watlonyawala | | Tyohtoskaie | Tyntolanewusheh* | Nereuh | |
| Twenty | Tewasera | Ta washon | Twasshe | Tewagisea | Tawushah | Nawahth'sunk | Teuheitawaughsa |
| Thirty | Aebseranwaghsea | Hasomewashon | Aehsonewasshe | Seniwaghsea | Shinewushah | Absunhewahh'sunk | Shaighkawaughsa |
| Forty | Kaieninnaghsea | Kiyaluewas | | Keinwaghsea | Gainnewushah* | Hunhtohtewahh'sunk | Audaghkawaughsa |

# HISTORY OF THE IROQUOIS.

| English | Mohawk (1) | Oneida (2) | Onondaga (3) | Cayuga (4) | Seneca (5) | Tuscarora (6) | Wyandot (7) |
|---|---|---|---|---|---|---|---|
| Fifty | Wiskniwaghera | Wishawas | | Wisunaghsea | Wisnewusheh* | Weestewahth'sunk | Weeishawaughsa |
| Sixty | Yayakniwaghera | Yahyakuewas | | Yeiuwaghsea | Yaihnewusheh* | Oohyoktewahth'sank | Waushawwaughsa |
| Seventy | Jatakniwaghsera | Jatakhuewas | | Jatakniwaghsea | Jadohgewusheh* | Cheotnoltewahth'sunk | Soouarewaughsa |
| Eighty | Sateconwaghsera | Takahuewas | | Tekroniwagh-ra | Dogeohneewusheh* | Nakrenhtewahth'sunk | Antararawaughsa |
| Ninety | Tyothonwaghsua | Watronewas | | Tyohouwaghsea | Tyotohnewushel¹* | Naraulnewahth'sunk | Aintrawaughsa |
| One hundred | Enskatewanhware | Auscetawancawa | Wasshenewasshe | Skatewanuawe | Tawenyoha | Hadyokstre | Setuemaingarwe |
| One thousand | Oyerheweanyawe | Oyalectawaurawa | Wasshenewoemiawe | Waghsonnatewrani | Wu-hainnntawcu | Euheheooyokstre | Assenatheuogoanoy |
| To eat | Teayouakahou | Youtakehorme | Wauuterout | Eyondkoui [awe | Wauuntakone | Ahrcnhehureek | Honçautiosh |
| To drink | Eayehnekira | Yatmakeelah | Echnekiehre | Ejelmekiha | Wawanigaah | Ah'rweh'treuhk | Erayhrah |
| To run | Teayoraghtate | Yadakna | | Tescatal | Out-ahtaute | Ahkahteahs'hink | |
| To walk | Eayouteanti | Eeyou | | Eyohtcanti | Ech¹ | Ahrenhrakwunk | Erch |
| To dance | Trayegnayakwe | Traynutqua | | Teyoutkwa | Tcoantyuoh | Nahrenh'tt'kwunk | |
| To burn | Eawatsa | Liekia | | Ewatsia | Ayodaihe* | Yachoohrodnahrehiu | |
| To love | Eayenarnoronhkwe | Eenolouqua | Schnugarastencloh | Teyoudauwonk | Ouseot | Alikahueorenhkwrunk | Eenkoorobqnoh |
| To go | Eayouteaut | Walsousale | Agohawissare | Eyouteanti | Wauohtanete | Nahrenttahhahkink | Ecreh |
| To strike | Eayeycanti | Eayeonick | | Eyegoheg | Agayenht* | Ahkahkeuhkwahrets'enk | |
| To kill | Eayoutatcryo | Wagouakew | | Eyoudatryo | Watn-aunlolo-o | Ahrahkwunkanhk | Anrezhue |
| To sing | Eayontereanoeca | Kateunota | Joruelwaelqua | Eyoutreanote | Wauuntamidah | Ahreanhwuharcnhk | Torone |
| To speak | Eayoutati | Yagoehala | | Iyeghnaca | Stoshreot | Ahkahwehrehk | Atakia |
| To die | Eatayighheye | Waaccluaya | | Iyahhe | Agehch* | Ahwunihayeuhk | |
| To see | Eayoukagiuho | Waroukot | | Iyomkaghto | Waunmtkothoo | Ahkahkenk | Eehayeuk |
| To hear | Eayeronkie | Yagotloouday | | Ayohouk | Aolunk* | Alkahkoolunksa'henhk | |
| To give | Eayoutatea | Wabaauladou | | Eayoutatea | Aonloh* | Ahkahyenkahmhmauh | |
| To carry | Eaychhawe | Vayhawe | | Eyeha | Haoloi* | Alkalilahk | |
| Walking | Yagoheantyohatyea | Eeyou | | Goghneaulahaudia | Eweh | Eweh | |
| Singing | Yeroane | Halouuosa | | Eeanot | "denote* | Rohuwunharenk | |
| Dancing | Teyakowanyakwa | Tahlatqta | | Yeyagotkwea | Dayoegweh* | Naualat'kah | |
| To be or exist | Eghnoyotea | Yagouha | | Nethonuayohtohaag | | | |
| I am | Inglse | Eguaha | | Si | | | |

(1) By Rev. Adam Elliot, Canada.
(2) By H. R. S. to the word Cold, p. 398, the remainder by Richard Updike Shearman of Oneida county, N. Y.
(3) By H. R. S. and Mr. Gallatin's Vocab., in Archæologia Americana.
(4) By Rev. Adam Elliot, Canada.
(5) All words marked by a star, by Ely S. Parker, Tonawanda Reservation; remainder by H. R. S. and Arch. Amer.
(6) By Rev. Gilbert Rockwood and William Chew, Tuscarora, Niagara county, N. Y.
(7) By John Johnson, Arch. Amer., and H. R. S.

## CHAPTER XII.

### MORAL AND SOCIAL CONDITION, AND PROSPECTS.

The gospel was preached to the Iroquois, as well as to the several tribes of Algonquin origin, who, under various names, lined the banks of the Hudson and Delaware rivers, early in the seventeenth century. The Reformed church of Holland does not appear to have underrated its duties in this respect. While the Holland states, under a hereditary president or stadtholder, were extending their civil jurisdiction and commercial power on this continent, the ecclesiastical courts of Amsterdam took cognizance of the incipient religious wants of the newly founded colony,* and sent out preachers and catechists, to their settlements, who sought the conversion of the Indian tribes. It was in this quality that Pyrlaus and Romeyn, labored respectively, at different eras, among the

* Vide Proceedings of the New York Hist. Society for a notice of the Rev. Thomas De Witt's visit to the classis of Amsterdam, and other ecclesiastical bodies of Holland, 1846.

Mohawks and Oneidas. It was eminently the policy of the Dutch West India Company, to introduce the arts dependant on commerce, and it is observed, in early records of the times, that their servants and agents were alert in pushing the fur trade, among the interior tribes, to the farthest points, and used their utmost influence to convince them of the superior advantages of cultivating the arts of peace. And they left the teacher and missionary to tread in their tracks, as time and circumstances dictated. It was the common impression of those times, not only in Holland, the centre of theological discussion, where Erasmus, Arminius, and Bœmgærten contended, but in the reformed churches of the continent generally, that civilization and the arts must *precede* the introduction of Christianity among barbarous and idolatrous tribes. It was under such impressions that the gospel was first carried to India and to Iceland, by the pious zeal of the early German reformers, and the same theoretical views governed the exertions of the New England colonists and divines in this behalf. Their earliest efforts were directed to wean the tribes from the arts of war and the chase, and to fix their minds and habits on the maxims and practices of an agricultural life, as the basis of Christianity.

A different, a wider, wilder and more sweeping spirit, arose in Europe, with almost the first successful dawnings of the reformation; and while Luther thundered against errors in the

Christian church, maintaining a deeply purposed, yet conservative theology, respecting the conversion of men, the spirit of enthusiasm burst out from the pale of admitted orthodoxy, leading to deeper and more searching views of the power of truth on the heart, and its capacities to regenerate the mind, and to curb and regulate human action, even in the wildest and most uncivilized conditions of society. The excess of this feeling led to fanaticism, and the wildest errors of pietism, and the brief rebellion of Munzer, his death and overthrow, sounded out to the church, as a warning voice against the imminent danger of zeal, without the sober aid of judgment, and the sustaining influences of a peaceful, well ordered and fixed state of industrial society.

The fears and the policy of the Christian or Romish church, as organized at this period, say A. D. 1500, regarded, or chose to regard, the outbreaks and episodes of the reform, and reformation itself, sanctioned and adopted as it was by states and synods, as parts of one and the same system, and as constituting an indivisible effort by the protestants to overthrow her power and hold on the wide-spread masses and orders of the European and Christian world. Hence the origin of the Jesuit order — an order of priesthood excelling all others in its boldness, zeal, and indomitable efficacy, in presenting and enforcing the claims of that type of the church, on the notice of distant and barbarous tribes and nations. It is one of the remarkable facts of history, that America was discovered at the same general period of the origin and first establishment of the reformation. And it resulted, naturally, that when colonies were sent out to the new world, the same religious strifes and acrimony, which had marked the discussion and progress of Christian reform in the European branches of the church should be transferred to the forests of America. It often became, indeed, to some extent, a contest of no little moment between the missionaries of the gospel, whether the new found tribes should acknowledge the Romish or Protestant doctrines; and there was sometimes more zeal, apparently, shown in an anxiety to secure external conformity in matters of belief, and church discipline, than the actual opening of the savage mind to the simple intellectual truths of revelation, or the steady and consistent advance of the tribes in order, morals, industry, and the essentials of civilization.

The impulse which had been imparted to the subject of the conversion of the natives through the zeal and devotion of Xavier and Loyola, and the energetic spirit of making proselytes and converts, which characterized the particular order of the church which they founded, impressed the rulers of Spain, France and Portugal, with a deep sense of the importance of carrying the gospel to the aborigines of the countries which they discovered. Hence it was put forth and really became one of the cardinal points of attention in their early attempts to found new colonies. And while the governors and servants of these countries did not prosecute the objects of trade and politics with less determination and success, nay, with a more unscrupulous disregard of the means, as the history of South America alone testifies, they carried missionaries in every early enterprise, and set forth to the world the conversion of the native inhabitants as the great object of their aim, as it was indeed often the shield and cover to the reckless avarice and ambition of the Cortezes and the Pizarros who carried their flags.

It was not consonant to the genius of Christianity, as interpreted by the reformed churches, to proceed in the work of spiritual conquest with so noisy and gorgeous a display, or with arm locked in arm with the state; and if the states of Holland did not put forth the object, in their first charters and commissions to the new world, it was, perhaps, because the church was actuated in, and was guided by, the general policy of the protestant European churches. England and Sweden, who planted colonies here, did the same.

It was not, indeed, until the new impulse which arose in the middle of the seventeenth century, and which brought Oliver Cromwell to the English throne, that different views and a deeper obligation of national duties in this respect began to prevail. And hence, when the English pilgrims, who had been sheltered awhile in the tolerant domains of Holland, set their faces towards the new world, it was with a predetermination not only to carry out the principles of the gospel, in their own settlements, but to extend its benign influences among the aborigines. This was averred, and the well known prominency of the fact stamps their efforts to convert and civilize the North American Indians, with a moral force and grandeur, which cannot be claimed for England, in her royal capacity as administrator of patents and honors here, or for any other protestant king or potentate, who sent her bold or enterprising children to the American wilds.

This much can be said, without disparagement to the piety of the Netherland church, which had her pastors and teachers at Manhattan, Fort Orange, and various other incipient points of her settlements at an early day. Whatever had been her policy, (and we have paid but little attention to this,) in sending teachers among the Mohegans, the Maquaas, and other tribes, who resorted to her forts and factories at Albany, and other points of early contact with these simple and warlike men; the English, after the conquest of 1664, appear to have followed in her footsteps, and pursued the same general, gradual and persuasive means, attaching high and deserved value at all points to the influence of European arts and the value of fixed industry.

Churches were founded at an early day, among the Mohawks at Caughnawaga, and at Dionderoga, at the mouth of Schoharie creek, better known as Fort Hunter, the latter of which received a present of a set of plate for the communion service, from Queen Anne.

Unfortunately for the conversion and civilization of the Indians, they had not a fixed population — they drew their supplies mainly from the chase, gave up a large portion of their time and means to war, and besides moving periodically, at least twice a year, *from* or *to* their hunting and planting grounds, they were in a general progress of recession before a civilized population. They shrank before the determined spirit of progress of the civilized arts and industry, which elicited resources where the Indian had seen none, and made an industrious use of every acre of tillable ground. But while the silent influence of this progress did much to teach him, by denoting the use of tools and implements of art and agriculture, to improve him in his domicil and its fixtures, and in his costume, and to harmonize and fix his mental habits and character, he was not proof against the leading temptation of the times, namely, the free and inordinate use of ardent spirits. From the partial paroxysms of this pernicious indulgence, he rose with less energy to pursue the chase, or follow the war path. The policy of land sales, the acceptance of presents as boons from the crown, and the distribution of small sums of coin to the heads of families in the shape of annuities—a system founded, in all but the last feature, under James VI, and confirmed under the old confederation, stepped in, as it were, to aid and reinforce him in his means of living, but which in effect held him away from his hunting grounds, paralyzed his home industry, and supplied him new means of indulging his propensities for liquor and luxuries. That the gospel should not have made a very marked progress under these circumstances, is not surprising.

Some years before the breaking out of the American revolution, Mr. Kirkland planted the gospel standard among the Oneidas, at a time when the broad and sylvan fields and glades of *Kun-a-wa-loa*, or Oneida Castle, were still beyond the pale of European civilization.* And he may be regarded as the apostle to the Iroquois. For many years, in perils and dangers, he preached the gospel to the Oneidas, at their once celebrated castle; and by the purity, firmness, and excellence of his character, won the confidence and the heart of their leading sachem. Skenandoah gave his attention to this new scheme of acceptance with his Maker, admitted it, and became a consistent professor and practiser of its precepts; and of him, it can be confidently said, that he lived and died in the faith. To gain the influence of the most powerful man in the canton, was to gain the whole canton; and when the war broke out, the tribe, wavering, as it did for a time, and assailed with all the arts of British

* Herkimer, the nearest point east, was about forty miles distant.

intrigue and promise, so profusely put forth, adhered to the colonies. Kirkland, in the inception and progress of these movements, became the principal agent in disseminating the doctrines of peace and neutrality among the six cantons. Washington and the continental congress reposed the highest trust in his virtue, judgment, and intelligence. He took from the lips of the father of his country, words of peace and good counsel, which coincided admirably with the precepts of the gospel. He traversed the then wilderness of Genesee and Niagara on this mission, and has left enduring monuments of his faithfulness and zeal.

But the spirit of war prevailed—that spirit which the great body of this people had so long served, under the guidance of their native priesthood. All but the Oneidas, some few of the Tuscaroras, who were then settled in their western precincts, and some one or two individuals from St. Regis, joined the ranks of the mother country, under their bold and politic leader, Brant. Seven years of battles, expeditions, ambushes, and murders, terminated not only in their political overthrow as a confederacy, but plunged many of them who had before listened to the voice of Christianity, back into the arms of their native priests and forest habits. The Mohawks, part of the Cayugas, and some Onondagas and Tuscaroras, fled the country, and settled chiefly in Canada. The Oneidas, the body of the Onondagas and Senecas, and some parts of the Cayugas and Tuscaroras, remained. But they had fought for a phantom. All the rich promises of glory and conquest, emanating from Johnson Hall and Fort Niagara, and the Canadas, had failed; and their delegates came to the treaty of Fort Stanwix in 1784, poor, crest fallen, and defeated; and by their first public act, after the drama of the revolution, they put their hands to a treaty, ceding away the larger portion of their ancient domain. Thus they were thrown back an immeasurable distance in the work of civilization and Christianity, and the effort to introduce the gospel was to be commenced almost anew.

Time will not permit any notice in detail, of this second period in their history. Kirkland, true to his original purpose, continued his ministry and useful labors, and died in the Oneida country. The venerable Skenandoah followed him at some few years later, and requested to be buried by his side. New missions were projected and carried into effect, at distinct times among the remaining cantons. A review of these, it is impossible to make within the space allotted to this work. Letters from the Rev. Gilbert Rockwood and Rev. James Cusick of Tuscarora; from the Rev. Asher Bliss at Cattaraugus, and from Rev. William Hall at Alleghany, will be found in the appendix, and are referred to as giving the latest and most authentic information on the progress of Christianity, letters, and morals among these respective tribes. So far as relates to their progress in agriculture and the arts, the results of the census, hereto prefixed, although they denote striking depopulation, afford the most definite, and at the same time, most favorable view of the remains of these cantons, which has, perhaps, ever been presented, of a whole Indian nation in America. The reluctance, which was felt in some quarters, in imparting statistics, has rendered it less complete than it might have been made. Still, with every proper abatement and qualification, applicable to the reservations as departmental bodies, and to the whole as a mass, there are strong encouragements to the friends of Christianity to persevere. The seeds of industry are well sown; letters have been generally introduced, and, in some instances, they have produced men of talents and intelligence, who have taken an honorable part in the professional and practical duties of life. Very gratifying evidences exist of the adoption, on a large scale, of the improved arts and conveniences of polished life. In manners, costume and address, the Iroquois people offer a high example of the capacities and ready adoptive habits of the race. It only needs a reference to the statistical tables mentioned, to show that they are not behind hand in implements of husbandry, vehicles, work cattle, horses, and the general features of their agriculture. They are abundantly able to raise sufficient for their own consumption, and some of the communities have a surplus which is added to the productive resources of the state. From those who have done so well, and who have shown such unequivocal capacities for improvement, we may expect more. From the tree, which has produced blossoms, we may expect fruit; and from the bearing tree which has produced grafts, we may expect an abundant harvest. Under all circumstances, we may regard the problem of their reclamation as fixed and certain. They have themselves solved it. And whatever an enlightened people and legislature should do to favor them, ought not to be omitted. Churches and societies who have granted their peculiar aids, should continue those aids; and the heart of the philanthropist and the statesman has cause to rejoice, that after all their wars and wanderings, mistakes and besetments, the Iroquois, made wise by experience, are destined *to live*. The results of the census, herewith submitted, demonstrate this. The time is indeed propitious for putting the inquiry, whether the Iroquois are not worthy to be received, under the new constitution, as *citizens of the state*.*

* This question was debated in the convention for revising the constitution of New York, which assembled at Albany, in May, 1846, but the provision to this effect, recommended and adopted by the committee, was decided in the negative by the convention.

## CHAPTER XIII.

### MISCELLANEOUS TRAITS, ETC.

SOIENGARAHTA, OR KING HENDRICK—INFANT ATOTARHO OF THE ONONDAGAS — RED JACKET AND THE WYANDOT CLAIM TO SUPREMACY— POCAHONTAS — ANECDOTE OF BRANT — UNIVERSAL SUFFRAGE, THE IROQUOIS CONSIDERED — COUNTY CLERK AND THE WOLF SCALP — FAMILY OF THE THUNDERERS.

### SOI-EN-GA-RAH-TA.

Such was the name, in his own dialect, according to the researches of Mr. Yates, of the celebrated sachem, usually called King Hendrick, who during the middle of the eighteenth century, stood at the head of the proud Mohawk canton. A chief who, at the head of two hundred picked Iroquois, by his name and valor, on the day of Count Dieskau's defeat, gave his powerful influence, at a single blow, to exalt to honor one of the greatest friends to America in Gen. William Johnson; and at the same time, to humble her constant and most strenuous enemy, the French of Canada. It was a crisis which turned the scale in favor of the colonists, after a long and severe struggle for political supremacy, and paved the way for the heavier, and final defeat, which but four years afterwards, marked the total downfall of the French power, under Montcalm at Quebec.

We should not, in our reminiscences of the past, and our felicitations of the present, forget the stalwart warriors who raised their weapons faithfully for the colonies; nor feel averse to giving our tribute of applause to the manly race of brave men and orators, who figure conspicuously alike in *their* and *our* history.

The great Mohawk sachem, *Soi-en-ga-rah-ta*, lived through the entire reigns of Queen Anne and George I, and nearly to the close of George II. He was therefore a cotemporary with Pope and Addison, as well as with the heroic Duke of Marlborough, with some of whose veteran regiments, after their triumphs on the continent, he fought against the French on the frontiers of New York; at first, as a youthful scout, and afterwards as an approved war captain. There was a time, in our settlements, when there was a moral force in the name of *King Hendrick* and *his Mohawks*, which had an electric effect; and at the time he died, his loss was widely and deeply felt and lamented, even in Great Britain. And were the time and occasion pertinent, it is believed that a search of the colonial records, and of cotemporary papers, respecting him, would well reward the pen of his biographer.

"A Mohawk he, by Tiondoga stood,
And fell, the mighty monarch of the wood."

Mr. Giles F. Yates, to whose manuscripts and gleanings of the "olden times in the Mohawk valley," we are indebted for the following details, traces him to the reign of William III. "The precise time," he observes, "of Hendrick's birth, cannot be ascertained, but several circumstances conspire to induce the belief that it took place sometime between the years 1680 and 1690. If he was in London at the time Addison wrote his account of the *Mohocks*, 1713 I think, then Hendrick may have been nearly seventy years old when he was slain in battle, 1755. He was then and before called *old* King Hendrick. The aboriginal name of this celebrated chieftain has never, to my knowledge, been known, since the days he flourished, and in all contemporaneous notices of him, he was always called by his English name Hendrick. It is therefore the duty of his biographer to give his authority for the name he may use as the true original one. My authority is the release to King George II, of which the reader will find a notice in the sequel.

"It is said that he, on two occasions, visited his British sovereign. On one of these occasions, doubtless the last, which is conjectured to have been about the year 1740, his majesty presented him a rich suit of clothes—a green coat, set off with brussels and gold lace, and a cocked hat, such as was worn by the court gentry of that period. In these, he sat for his portrait, which was executed by a London artist. From this portrait, which has no date, engravings were made, of a large 'cabinet size,' and colored in conformity with the original. I saw one of these engravings in the family of a relative at Schenectady, which has, however, been long since destroyed by fire; and recently I have seen another, which had been for nearly a century, preserved in the family of the late Jeremiah Lansing, Esq., of Albany. The prosopological indicia of his countenance, denote a kind disposition, honesty of purpose, and an order of intellect, much above mediocrity. Although his complexion was 'the shadowed livery of the burnished sun,' his figure and countenance were singularly prepossessing and commanding. The concurrent testimony of every traditionist, awards to him great natural talents, judgment, and sagacity. As a diplomatist and orator, he was greatly distinguished, and divided the palm only with his brother Abraham, of pious memory, who was exclusively devoted to civil pursuits.

"In the early part of his life, he lived at the upper castle of the Mohawks, Canajoharie; but afterwards his residence was, for the most part, on the north side of the Mohawk, and a little below the residence of Major Jellis Fonda, near a place then and now called the Nose.

"Hendrick's greatest speech was delivered on the 2d July, 1754, 'in the name and behalf of the Six Nations' in answer to a speech made by the lieutenant-governor of New York, 'in the name of the king of Great Britain, and in the name and behalf of the American colonies,' which were all represented on the occasion. This speech, with several others, is reported at full length in the London Gentleman's Magazine, the editor whereof speaks of these speeches in the following terms. "They contain strains of eloquence which might have done honor to Tully or Demosthenes." The speeches of Hendrick and his brother Abraham, made the same day above named, in the name and behalf of the Mohawks of the upper castle (Canajoharie) to the governor of New York, attended by several sachems of the other (Six) nations, were also evincive of much talent and eloquence.

The journalists of the day paid our chief the following high compliment, which I have every reason to believe was not undeserved or exaggerated praise. "For capacity, bravery and vigor of mind, and immovable integrity united, he excelled all the aboriginal inhabitants of whom we have any knowledge."

Soiengarahta is the identical chief who granted to Gen. (afterwards Sir Wm.) Johnson, "the dream land," as it was significantly called. At an entertainment given by the general, which lasted several days, our chief was one of the guests. Johnson had recently received from his royal master, several military dresses, resplendent with scarlet and gold, which were temptingly displayed in the view of the guests. One morning, before the close of the entertainment, Hendrick told his pale-faced friend and patron, that he had had a dream the night previous.

"Indeed," said the general, "and what did my red brother dream?" "I dreamt" replied the chief, "that you presented me with one of those dresses," pointing to them. "You shall have it," was the prompt response, and in a few moments the person of the majestic chief was ensconced in the splendid uniform he had coveted. It is necessary, in this connection, to observe, that one of the prevailing superstitions of the Iroquois, was an implicit faith in dreams, which, they said, were sent by the Great Spirit for wise purposes, and that if a dream is not fulfilled, at whatever hazard or sacrifice, some evil may fall upon the dreamer. At a subsequent entertainment, given by Gen. Johnson, Hendrick was invited as before. On this occasion it was the general's turn to dream, and he dreamt, or pretended to Hendrick to have dreamt, that the Iroquois chief had made him a present of three thousand acres of land, describing its locality. The chief replied, "You shall have it, but I will never dream with you again. Your dreams are too hard for me." The conveyance of this tract of land, afterwards received the royal sanction or confirmation, and is, at the present day, known as "the Royal Grant."

I have been induced particularly to describe the parties in whose behalf, and to whom our hero spoke, and also to relate the foregoing anecdote, as affording evidence of the high official standing, power and influence he held among his people. He was their great embassador and minister plenipotentiary, while at the same time, he was the great war chief of the Iroquois, as will presently appear. It is not, however, to be inferred, that he had power in his own right, and without the assent of his own nation, in council assembled, to convey the 3000 acres referred to. The Mohawk nation, like a sovereign state in our own republic, had the right to dispose of their own territory, without the assent of the grand assembly of the whole confederacy of the Iroquois, whose council fires were lighted annually in the valley of the Onondaga.

In a release dated 18th November, 1753, which I find recorded in the office of the secretary of state of this state, conveying a tract of land ("20 miles above Schenectady, purchased by Dow Fonda and others") to King George II, twelve chiefs are named as "the sole proprietors of the Mohocks'country." Of these, the only names, given in the Iroquois tongue, are Soiengarahta, Kanadagoies (Destroyer of Towns), and Kaheoana (Great Turtle.)

Hendrick was, in his day, esteemed the bravest of the brave, among the Iroquois. His spirit, energy, and martial prowess, were the subjects of much laudation. He was the leader in behalf of the British, in several expeditions of parties of his red warriors against the Canadian French and their tawny associates; for he and his people were ever the fast friends and uncompromising allies of the British on this important frontier. The last and principal of these expeditions was to Lake George, in which our hero fell mortally wounded at the memorable battle of September 8, 1755. According to the official despatch of the commander in chief of the British forces (Gen. Johnson), these forces consisted of 1000 whites, and 200 Iroquois under the command of their great captain, Hendrick. The French troops, under Baron Dieskau, were composed of 200 grenadiers, 800 Canadians, and 700 Indians. The French general was taken prisoner, and 900 of his soldiers killed, while on the side of the British only 120 were killed and 80 wounded. Of the Iroquois 38 were killed and 12 wounded. Gen. Johnson, in his report, gives Hendrick and his warriors great praise. He says, "they fought like lions." Hendrick was seen leading his warriors in the thickest of the fight, "to glory or the grave." Gen. Johnson, in reward of his merit on this occasion, was created a baronet, and parliament voted him a present of £5000.

From the New York Mercury, under date of September 22, 1755, I glean the following additional particulars. The whole body of the Iroquois in alliance with the English were greatly exasperated against the French and their Indians, more particularly on account of the death of "the famous Hendrick, a renowned warrior among the Mohocks, and one of their sachems, or kings. His son, on being told that his father was killed, gave the usual groan on such occasions, and suddenly putting his hand on his left breast, swore that his father was still alive in that place, and stood there in his son. It was with the utmost difficulty Gen. Johnson prevented the fury of their resentment taking place on the body of the French general, Dieskau, whom they would have sacrificed without ceremony, but for the interference of Gen. Johnson."

## INFANT ATOTARHO OF THE ONONDAGAS.

While I was engaged in taking the census of the Onondagas, at their council house, at the castle, where a large number of all ages and both sexes were assembled, the interpreter, who spoke English very well, taking advantage of a pause in the business, said to me, pointing to a fine boy who sat on a bench, near a window, "that is our king!" I had, a short time before, requested that this boy should be sent for His mother had now, unperceived by me, brought him, dressed out in his best clothes, and evinced by the expression of her eyes and bearing a conscious pride in bringing him to my notice. And truly, she had every reason to be proud of so finely formed, bright and well-looking a boy. In addition to these advantages, it is to be remembered that descent, amongst the Onondagas and the other Iroquois, is counted by the female, which constituted a further motive of satisfaction and pride to the mother, in showing her pretty *hux-sa-ha*, or boy. She made no remark, however, on my noticing him, but sat with modesty and ease near him, but with an eye beaming with too much pride and self-complacence to be concealed.

The lad was but three years old, but tall for that age, and offered a fine model of form. I could not help noticing, what had often impressed me in similar instances, that the infusion of European blood, derived from his grandfather by the father's side, had served to heighten and improve physical development, and fullness and beauty of muscle. His eyes were full, large, black and sparkling. His dark hair also was a true trait of his race. His countenance was of a bright brown, showing the blood, and rather formed on the Grecian mould, with a good nose and pretty lips. Yet, over all, there was a physiological dash of the muscular expression, hue and air of the true Konoshioni.

There was nothing peculiar in his dress, which was of good materials and well made, agreeably to the nation's fashion for boys, except it might be the lining of the under brim of a light straw hat, which the mother had carefully decorated with a piece of light figured cotton goods, looking as if it had been cut from a printed handkerchief.

I did not think to ask the name of this promising young candidate for the seat and honors of the Atotarho, or chief magistracy of his nation. His father's name is *T'so-ha-neeh-sa*, which, according to the curious principles of naming persons, and the still more curious rules of the Indian syntax, means a road, the receding parallel lines of which intermingle by atmospheric refraction. This, apparently to them, mysterious uniting and separating of the lines in such a vista, is the idea described by this compound term. The boy, however, inherits, or has the right of inheritance of the Atotarho, not "a king," through the mother, who was a daughter of the principal *ho-ai-ne*, or chief. This daughter was married to Ephraim Webster, an American, a New Englander, a Vermonter, I think, who either by freak, taste or fortune, wandered off among the Iroquois soon after the close of the American revolution, and finally fixed himself in the Onondaga valley, where he learned the language, established a trade in the gin-seng root, and became a man of note and influence in the tribe. He died in old age, and is buried in this valley, where he has left sons and daughters, all of whom, however, are recognized as members of the ancient Onondaga canton, or People of the Hills.

### RED JACKET AND THE WYANDOT CLAIM TO SUPREMACY.

At a great council of the western tribes, assembled near Detroit, prior to the late war, the celebrated Seneca orator, Red Jacket, was present, when the question of the right of the Wyandots to light the council fire, was brought up. This claim he strenuously resisted, and administered a rebuke to this nation in the following terms:

"Have the Quatoghies forgotten themselves? Or do they suppose we have forgotten them? Who gave you the right in the west or east, to light the general council fire? You must have fallen asleep, and dreamt that the Six Nations were dead! Who permitted you to escape from the lower country? Had you any heart left to speak a word for yourselves? Remember how you hung on by the bushes. You had not even a place to land on. You have not yet done p——g for fear of the Konoshioni. High claim, indeed, for a tribe who had to run away from the Kadarakwa.*

"As for you, my nephews," he continued, turning to the Lenapees, or Delawares, "it is fit you should let another light your fire. Before Miquon came, we had put out your fire and poured water on it; it would not burn. Could you hunt or plant without our leave? Could you sell a foot of land? Did not the voice of the Long House cry, go, and you went? Had you any power at all? Fit act indeed for you to give in to our wandering brothers—you, from whom we took the war-club and put on petticoats.†"

* Hon. Albert H. Tracy.
† For similar language to this, addressed to the Delawares, see Colden's Five Nations, for a speech of an Iroquois chief, in council, at Lancaster.

Sarony & Major Lith.  117 Fulton St New York

### PO CA-HON-TAS.
1618

## POCAHONTAS.

It appears from a letter written by Richard Randolph Esq., of Virginia, dated April 1, 1842, that Pocahontas and her husband, Mr. Rolfe, arrived at Plymouth on the 12th of June, 1616. Whilst in England, where their son Thomas was born, their portraits were taken at the request of Mr. Rolfe's relatives. In the act of returning to America, when they had reached Gravesend, on the Thames, Pocahontas was seized with the small-pox, and died at that place, early in the year 1617, being then, according to the best accounts, in her twentieth year.

Her husband continued his voyage, and returned to Virginia, after having left her son Thomas with his brother, Mr. Henry Rolfe, to be brought up and educated. When Thomas Rolfe junior had completed his education, he also went to Virginia, where he married, and had a daughter named Jane. Jane Rolfe, the granddaughter of Pocahontas married Col. Thomas Bolling, by whom she had a son named John. John Bolling, the great-grand-son of Pocahontas, marrying, had a daughter, bearing his mother's name, Jane, who married Richard Randolph of Curles, Henrico county, Virginia. Ryland Randolph, a son by this marriage, being the fourth remove in a direct line from Pocahontas, was educated in England, and having learned after his return that portraits of Pocahontas and of

Mr. Rolfe existed in England, wrote for them, and offered to purchase them. But when the kinsman of Mr. Rolfe in Warwickshire, learned that Mr. Randolph was a descendant of Pocahontas, he presented both the portraits to him, through Mr. Randolph's correspondent, who sent them out to Virginia, where they were received by Mr. Ryland Randolph, and hung up in his mansion on Turkey island. Mr. Ryland Randolph died in 1784, and on closing the estate, the portraits were publicly sold, after a valuation of them had been made. There were four bidders, but it was agreed that they should be bid off by Mr. Thomas Bolling, of Cobbs, in the county of Chesterfield, Virginia, a lineal descendant of Jane Rolfe.

This is the history of the portrait. David Mead Randolph Esq., father of the writer of the letter here quoted, was the executor of the estate of Ryland Randolph, and in this capacity sold the pictures, as mentioned, and filed an inventory of the sales, along with other property, in the office of the county court of Henrico, where it is open to examination.

The engraving presented of Pocahontas, is reduced from a copy of the original, in the possession of Mr. Bolling, which was painted by Mr. R. M. Sully, prior to 1830; testimonials are given in the Philadelphia Indian Portrait Gallery,* of the faithfulness of the copy which ap-

---

* The History of the Indian Tribes, &c. &c. Rice & Clark, Philad. 1844. Vol. 3, No. 20.

pears in that work, and of the costume in which Pocahontas appears: which are entirely satisfactory, and leave no doubt that we possess, in these lineaments, the sweet and merciful traits, which prompted the noble daughter of Powhattan, at the impulsive age of ten, to save the life of the virtual founder of Virginia.

### ANECDOTE OF BRANT.

When this chief was in London, he received ten pounds sterling, to be given on his return to America, to any person or persons, among his people, whom he found to be doing most to help themselves. On coming to the Seneca reservation on Buffalo creek, they had just finished the church, at an expense of seventeen hundred dollars. He gave the money to these Indians to buy stoves to warm it, which are still used for this purpose. He said he had seen no people who were doing so much to help themselves.

### UNIVERSAL SUFFRAGE — THE IROQUOIS CONSIDERED.

In reconstructing our constitution, under circumstances favorable to the rights of all classes of a varied population, the occasion is presented for asking the question, *whether justice to the Iroquois of New York, does not demand that they also should be admitted to the rights of citizenship?* This people have some strong claims to such a distinction. They were not only the owners of the soil, at the era of the founding of the colony early in the seventeenth century, but they defended it manfully during the whole of that, and the greater part of the succeeding century, against the efforts of the crown of France to colonize and wrest it from our grasp. A portion of them fought with us in the contest for independence. The Mohawks, who took adverse grounds, fled and took shelter at its close in Canada. Such of the tribes and parts of tribes as remain, have devoted themselves to agriculture, and continue, to the present time, to show themselves as peaceable and orderly inhabitants. As such they are regarded in the western and northern counties, where they are very well liked.

The recent census exhibits them in a favorable light. This is the view in which they are presented in the governor's message to the legislature. They cultivate wheat, oats and corn. They raise cattle, horses, hogs and sheep. They are, generally, good farmers and herdsmen. There are some mechanics and a few professional men. All the cantons have made respectable advances in morals and education. Their social organization exhibits schools, churches and temperance societies. They have gone through the severe and scathing ordeal of the settlement of the state; and it is believed that such as remain upon these reservations, could now be incorporated into our system, as separate towns, left to their own organization, to the great benefit of themselves, and without detriment to us. To give them the right of suffrage and a representation in our legislature, would act as a seal to all prior means to exalt them, and would accomplish more, in this respect, than a *house full of legislative acts* without it.

### THE COUNTY CLERK AND THE WOLF-SCALP.

A Seneca hunter killed a wolf just within the bounds of Cattaraugus county, close to the Pennsylvania line, and took the scalp to Meadville, Pennsylvania, for the bounty. Being questioned where the animal was killed, he honestly told the officer that he had come across it and shot it, as near as he could tell, within the territory of New York, very near the state and county lines. On this, the clerk told him that it would be contrary to law to pay him the bounty. "That is a *bad* law!" replied the red man. "Why?" said the magistrate; "we cannot pay for scalps taken out of the county." "It is bad," replied the hunter, "because you require that the wolf should know the county lines. Had this wolf seen a flock of sheep just within the Pennsylvania lines, I dare say he would not have stopped for the county lines." On this, the magistrate paid him the bounty of five dollars.

### THE FAMILY OF THE THUNDERERS.

Iroquois tradition affirms that a great family of the Thunderers lived under Niagara falls. According to the Senecas, (who have from the days of the lost Eries inhabited the country around the cataract,) the residence of this family of Thunderers was discovered in this manner. When this tribe lived on the *Gue-yo-gwa* creek, (a stream which empties into the Niagara river above the falls, and between the brink of water, and the inlet of the Tonawanda,) there happened a time of great mortality and famine among the people, their corn-fields dwindled away, as if a spell had been cast over them, and there was a most signal mortality. Men were buried daily, and while their numbers grew thinner and thinner, their grave-yards grew larger and larger. There was a young married couple living there at this time, who felt the strongest attachment to each other. The woman was very handsome, and the man an expert hunter. One day he determined to go on a hunting excursion, and to take his wife with him far inland, where they might be safe from all danger. Accordingly they went, and built a lodge in the woods, where game was abundant, and they lived in perfect harmony, and felt that all their wishes were realized. Every day he went into remote parts of the forest and killed game, while she remained to take care of the lodge. Once when he returned from the chase he found his wife asleep, and he saw that a rattle-snake had crawled into her womb; he woke her up, and proposed that they should return to their former home; he told her nothing of what he had seen. When they got back to the village he divided with her the game, and told her to go home to her mother's lodge, as he did not wish to have any thing more to do with her. She did not know the cause of such cruel conduct, but being compelled, she was forced to obey. Nothing that either her father or mother could do, would induce him to tell the secret of his sudden dislike in sending her away. There was a final separation between them, and not long after she married again, but her husband died immediately, being bit by the rattle-snake. Again and again she married, and again and again her husbands died, from the same cause. The rapid deaths of her husbands soon began to create much suspicion and village talk; her first husband therefore exposed the secret of her condition, and assigned that singular misfortune as the only reason of his sending her away. She was fair to look on, he said, but to touch her, was to touch the poisoned tooth of the serpent. The discovery overwhelmed her with horror, and finally she got into a state of mind bordering on despair. She was young, and very handsome, and the admiration of all who saw her, but she loathed herself, and after great conflicts and lamentations, determined to put an end to her existence. She dressed herself in her gayest attire, and taking her light painted cedar paddle in her hand, she stepped into her bark canoe, and pushed it out into the stream. The roar of Niagara was in her ears, but no one saw her leave the shore, on her voyage of death, until she was far down the river; gliding into the tumult of the stream, she seemed resigned and determined to end her life by plunging down the falls. The boat was seen to descend the roaring rapids and the precipice, and of course all her friends gave her up as lost; but one of the before mentioned Thunderers spread a blanket and caught her as she swooned away. When she opened her eyes, she saw a man reclining over her, and he held her in his arms. He took her into a room, and there sat the old Thunderer, who gave her a very kind salutation. He gave her some medicine, which healed her complaint, and then told her that it had been in accordance with his will and purpose that the rattle-snake should enter her womb, in order that he might be able to secure her in his family for a season. He then gave her in marriage to him who had spread out the blanket and saved her life. She remained there one year, when the old Thunderer told her she must now return to her home, and tell her people that a great snake poisoned their water once a year, and that there was a giant, named Famine, who lived under ground, and ate up all their corn-fields, which caused so much mortality and starvation among the people. He advised them to remove in order to give the Thunderers an opportunity to destroy these enemies of man. She returned home, and in compliance with the instructions she brought, the Senecas removed to Buffalo creek. Within ten days the Thunderers had killed Famine, and in one year they killed the great snake on Buffalo creek. In a certain season of the year he poisoned their waters, and then crawled into their grave-yards and ate up their dead bodies. But now he found none, and coming out of the ground to learn the cause, he found that the settlement had been abandoned. He then tracked them, and found that they had gone up the river. He followed them, and was not attacked until he had reached the shallow waters of Buffalo creek, where they killed him. His home was subsequently found by the Indians at Black Rock.

# ORIGINAL NOTES.

### LETTER FROM THE SECRETARY OF STATE.

The following letter indicates the origin and motive of these notes and memoranda. Such parts only of them are retained, as have been referred to as original materials, of which there is yet some particular fact or statement which has not been exhausted. Sometimes the note itself was chiefly of a mnemonic character, and designed to recall further particulars entrusted to the memory.

Secretary's Office,<br>
Albany, June 25, 1845.

Henry R. Schoolcraft, Esq.:

Sir—I have deemed it proper to appoint you to take the enumeration of the Indians residing on the following reservations, to wit: the Oneida, Onondaga, Tuscarora, and the reservations of the Senecas, one or more in each of the counties of Alleghany, Cattaraugus, and Erie, and also of the Tonewanda Indians in the county of Genesee. Your duties are summarily defined in the fifteenth section of the act of the legislature, which authorizes me to make this appointment, and to which I invite your attention.

On calling at this office you will be furnished with the proper blanks to enable you to perform the duties of the important trust committed to your hands, which will indicate with sufficient precision the method of ascertaining the numbers, ages, sex, condition, and classification of the remnants of this interesting race. You will find, on running through and examining the blanks, for these returns, full scope for all the information that can be of any practical use.

I desire that you will be very particular and minute in your inquiries in respect to every matter which relates to agricultural and statistical information, as well as of all other information called for by the returns, which will be furnished to you.

It is believed, from the information which has been received at this office, that there may be found, at the different reservations, Indians who were not originally of the tribe or stock to which they now profess, perhaps, to belong. You will, as far as may be in your power, and without exciting the jealousy and distrust of the Indians, endeavor to ascertain the number of their people, now living at the different reservations, who are not of the original stock or tribe with whom they are now sojourning.

It is important that you do not consolidate or bring into one return, any more than the inhabitants of one reservation, and a sufficient number of blank returns will be furnished to enable you to accomplish this object without any difficulty, and you can use some one of the columns which will otherwise be found useless, to denote or mark the number who derive their subsistence from the chase.

It is expected that you will complete the enumeration and file the several returns in the Secretary's office by the first day of September next, that I may be able to prepare abstracts and copies to be submitted to the legislature at the next session.

You will no doubt experience some difficulties in the performance of the duties devolved upon you, owing to the jealousy of the Indians, and the novelty of these proceedings; this, it is believed, being the first effort of the kind ever attempted by the state. You will assure our red brethren that, in taking this enumeration of them, and making the inquiries into their present condition and situation, the legislature, the governor of the state, or any of the officers, have no other objects in view but their welfare and happiness.

The Indians within our state are under its guardian care and protection, and it is a high duty that is now to be performed of sending a competent and well-qualified citizen to visit them, and inquire particularly into their situation. We have no connection with the government of the United States, or any land company, which prompts to these inquiries into their present social condition.

You will be at liberty to extend your inquiries to the early history and antiquarian remains of the Indians in the central and western parts of the state, but it is desired that these may be as brief as the nature of these inquiries will allow.

With these views of the subject, I commit this important trust to your hands, confidently expecting and anticipating a very satisfactory result.

I have the honor to be, with great respect,
Your ob't ser't,
N. S. BENTON.

## INDIAN RESERVATIONS IN NEW YORK.

*Cattaraugus county.*—Reservation on the Alleghany river; Oil Spring reservation (one mile square, no Indians).

*Erie county.*—Buffalo creek reservation (sold to Og. co.); part of Cattaraugus reservation.

*Alleghany county.*—Part of Oil Spring reservation in this county.

*Genesee county.*—The Tonawanda reservation is principally in this county (sold, yet in litigation).

*Onondaga county.*—Onondaga reservation.

*Niagara county.*—Tuscarora Indian reservation.

*Oneida county.*—Oneida reservation (dwindled away now, to a few individual rights).

## MEMORANDA, LOCALITIES TO BE EXAMINED, &C.

Pompey, Onondaga county.—Vestiges of a town, five hundred acres; three circular walls, or elliptical forts, eight miles apart; these formed a triangle, enclosing the town.

Camillus.—Two forts; one, three acres on a high hill; east, a gate; west, a spring ten rods off; shape elliptical; ditch deep; wall ten feet high: second fort, half a mile distant; lower ground; constructed like the other; about half as large; shells, testaceous animals, plenty; fragments, pottery; pieces of brick; "other signs" of ancient settlement, found by first settlers.—(*Clinton.*)

East Bank of Seneca River.—Six miles south of Cross and Salt lakes; forty miles south of Oswego; discovered 1791 (New York Magazine, 1792), with picture writing, on a stone five feet by three and a half, and six inches thick, evidently sepulchral; two hundred and twenty yards length; fifty-five yards breadth; bank and ditch entire; two apertures middle of parallelogram, one towards the water, other land; second work half a mile south; half-moon; outwork; singularity, extremities of the crescent from larger fort; bank and ditch of both, large old trees; pottery well burned, red, indented; these works traced eighteen miles east of Manlius square.

Oxford, Chenango county.—East banks Chenango river; great antiquity; north to Sandy creek, fourteen miles from Sackett's Harbor, near one which covers fifty acres; fragments of pottery west in great numbers.

Onondaga Town: Scipio: Auburn, two forts: Canandaigua, three forts; between Cayuga and Seneca lakes, several.

Ridgeway, Genesee.—Several forts and places of burial.

Allen's Residence, 1788.—Two miles west; a flat; deserted Indian village; Junction of Allen's creek with Genesee; eight miles north of Kanawageas; five miles north of Magic spring; six acres; six gates; ditch eight feet wide, six deep; circular on three sides; fourth side, a high bank; a covered way, near two hundred years old; second, half a mile south, on a greater eminence; less dimensions, but deeper ditch; more lofty and commanding.

JOAIKA.—Twenty-six miles west of Kanawageas; six miles further; Tegatainedaghgwe, or double fortified town; a fort at each end; first about four acres; two miles distant another, eight acres; ditch about first five or six feet deep; small stream one side; traces of six gates; dug way to the water; large oaks, two hundred years old or more; remains of a funeral pile, bones; mound six feet by twenty, thirty diameter (sixty to ninety).

PATH TO BUFFALO CREEK.—Heights, fortified.

WEST OF TONAWANDA.—Still another.

ON BRANCH OF THE DELAWARE.—A fort one thousand years old, by trees.

SOUTH SIDE OF ERIE.—Cattaraugus creek to Pennsylvania line, fifty miles; two to four miles apart, some half a mile; some contain five acres; wall and breast-works of earth; appearance of ancient beds of creeks; note the geological change; Lake Erie retired from two to five miles.

FURTHER SOUTH.—A chain of parallel forts; two table grounds; recession of lake.

All these vestiges denote long periods of time, and probably different eras of occupation. Who preceded the Iroquois? Who preceded their predecessors? Do these vestiges tell the story? How shall we study them? By antiquities; by language; by comparison with other races of America, Asia, Africa, Europe.

ALBANY.—Examine the site of ancient Mohawk residence, in 1609, on the island and its vicinity, at the mouth of Norman's kill; look for their ancient burial places; bones, pieces of pottery, and other objects of art may tell something bearing on their history. Is the oasis opposite the turnpike gate, the site of their ancient burial ground? Is this the spot denoted by their name of Tawasentha, or is it to be sought in other places, at the mouth, or up the valley of this stream?

UTICA.—The Mohawk valley appears to have no monumental or other evidences of its having been occupied by races prior to the Mohawks.

VERNON.—Who were the original race that first set foot in Oneida county? When did the Oneidas come? Where did they originate, and how? They are said to be the youngest of the Six Nations.

L. Hitchcock Esq. says that he was present, when a boy, some forty years ago, when the last executions for witchcraft among the Oneidas took place. The suspected persons were two females. The executioner was Hon Yost. They were dispatched unawares, by the tomahawk.

*Sachan*, a strong wind, or tempest, was the Oneida name for Col. L. Schoolcraft, whose monument is on the banks of the Scanado.

The principal tributary to the Oneida creek which traverses this rich grazing town, is called after the noted chief, to adopt the common pronunciation, *Scanado*. It means a deer. The old orthography for this word is *Skenandoah*.

*Forced Etymology.*—*Ot*, Judge J. says, means water, in the Oneida tongue. Otsego, he adds, is from *ot*, water, and *sago*, hail, welcome, how d'ye do. This I don't believe. It is not in accordance with Indian principles of combination.

ONEIDA LANGUAGE.—The Oneidas call a man *lon-gwee;* a woman, *yon-gwee;* God, *Lonee;* Evil Spirit, *Kluneolux*. Some of their words are very musical, as *ostia*, a bone; *ahta*, a shoe; *kiowilla*, an arrow; *awiali*, a heart; *loainil*, a supreme ruler. The French priests, who filled the orthography of this language with the letter *r*, committed one of the greatest blunders. There is no sound of *r* in the language; by this letter they constantly represent the sound of *l*.

ONEIDA CASTLE.—In a conference with Abraham Denne, an aged Oneida, he stated that Brant was brought up by his (Denne's) grandfather, at Canajoharie; that he was a bastard, his mother Mohawk; and did not come of a line of chiefs. Says, that Scanado was a tory in the war, notwithstanding his high name; that he acted against us at the siege of Fort Stanwix. The anecdote of an Indian firing from a tree, he places, while they were repairing the fort; says that after the man got up, he drew up loaded rifles with a cord; that both Scanado and Brant were present. Says Scanado was adopted by the nation when quite young; came from the west; does not know of what tribe, but showed himself smart, and rose to the chieftaincy by his bravery and conduct. Says, that the (syenite) stone on the hill, is the true Oneida stone, and not the white stone at the spring; was so pronounced by Moses Schuyler, son of Hon Yost, who knew it forty years ago; that the elevation gave a view of the whole valley, so that they could descry their enemies at a distance by the smoke of their fires; no smoke, he said, without fire. They could notify also, from this elevation, by a beacon fire. The name of the stone is O-ne-a-ta; auk, added, renders it personal, and means an Oneida. The word Oneida is an English corruption of the Indian.

*Origin of the Oneidas.*—Abraham Schuyler, an Oneida, says that the Oneidas originated in two men, who separated themselves from the Onondagas. They first dwelt at the outlet of Oneida lake. Next removed to the outlet of Oneida creek, on the lake, where they fortified. Williams says he was born there, and is well acquainted with the old fort. They then went to the head of the valley at the Oneida stone, from which they were named. Their fourth remove was to the present site of the Oneida castle, called a skull on a pole, where they lived at the time of the discovery of the country, and settlement of the colony by the Dutch; that is, 1609 to 1614.

*Etymology of the Oneida Stone.*—Asked several Oneidas to pronounce the name for the Oneida stone. They gave it as follows: O-ni-o-ta-aug; O-ne-u-ta-aug; O-ne-yo-ta-aug. The terminal syllable, aug, seems to be a local particle, but carries also with its antecedent, ta, the idea of life or existence, people, or inhabitants. Oniu is a stone. The meaning clearly is, people of the (or who have sprung from the) place of the stone.

Adirondak, Jourdain pronounces *Lod-a-lon-dak*, putting *l*s for *r*s and *a*s. It means a people who eat trees—an expression ironically used for those who eat the bark of trees. For Cherokees, he gives *We-au-dah;* for Delawares, *Lu-na-to-gun.* What a mass of fog philologists are fighting with, who mistake, as the eminent Vater and Adelung have, in some cases done, the different *names* of the same tribes of American Indians for different *tribes.*

*Antique Corn Hills.*—Counted one hundred cortical layers in a black walnut; centre broke so as to prevent counting the whole number, but by measuring estimated one hundred and forty more. If so the field was deserted in 1605.

The present proprietor of the farm comprising the Oneida stone, spring, butternut grove, &c., is Job Francis. He first hired the land of Hendrik's widow; afterwards he and Gregg were confirmed by the state. The white stone at the spring, a carbonate of lime, is not the *true* Oneida stone. The Oneida stone is a *syenite,* a boulder.

ONONDAGA CASTLE.—Abraham Le Fort says, that Ondiaka was the great chronicler of his tribe. He had often heard him speak of the traditions of his father. On his last journey to Oneida he accompanied him. As they passed south by Jamesville and Pompey, Ondiaka told him that in ancient times, and before they fixed down at Onondaga, they lived at these spots. That it was before the Five Nations had confederated; but while they kept up a separate existence, and fought with each other. They kept fighting and moving their villages often. This reduced their numbers, and kept them poor and in fear. When they had experienced much sickness in a place, they thought it best to quit it, and seek some new spot, where it was hoped they would have better luck. At length they confederated, and then the fortifications were no longer necessary and fell into disuse. This is the origin, he believes, of these old works, which are not of foreign origin.

Ondiaka told Le Fort that the Onondagas were created by *Ha-wä-ne-o*, in the country where they lived. That he made this entire island, *Ha-who-nao*, for the red race, and meant it for them alone. He did not allude to or acknowledge any migrations from foreign lands.

Their plan, after the confederation, was to adopt prisoners and captives; that fragments of tribes were parted amongst them, and thus lost. They used the term *We-hait-wa-tsha*, in a figurative sense, in relation to such tribes. This term means a body cut and quartered and scattered around. So they aimed to scatter their prisoners among the other nations. There is still blood of the Cherokees in Onondaga. A boy of this nation became a chief among the Cherokees.

I called Le Fort's attention to the residence of the Moravian missionary, Zœisberger. He said there was no tradition of such residence; that the oldest men remembered no such mission; that they were ever strongly opposed to all missionaries after the expulsion of the Jesuits, and he felt confident no such person, or any person in the character of a preacher, had lived at Onondaga Castle; that there must be some mistake in the matter.

ONONDAGA.—Ondiaka told Le Fort that the Onondagas formerly wandered about without being long fixed at a place, frequently changing their villages from slight causes, such as sickness, &c. They were at war with the Iroquois bands. They were also at war with other tribes. Hence forts were necessary, but after they confederated, such defensive works fell into disuse. They lived in the present areas of De Witt, Lafayette, Pompey and Manlius, along Butternut creek, &c. Here the French visited them, and built a fort, after their confederation.

Ezekiel Webster stated that the Indians were never as numerous as appearances led men to think. This appearance of a heavy population happened from their frequent removals, leaving their old villages, which soon assumed the appearance of ancient populous settlements.

Nothing is more distinct or better settled in the existing traditions of the Iroquois, than their wars with the Cherokees. I found this alluded to at Oneida, Onondaga, &c., in the course of their traditions, but have not been able to trace *a cause* for the war. They seemed to have been deeply and mutually exasperated by perfidy and horrid treachery in the course of these wars, such as the breaking of a peace pledge, and murder of deputies, &c. Their great object was, as soon as young men grew up, to go to war against the Cherokees. This long journey was performed without provisions, or any other preparation than bows, clubs, spears, and arrows. They relied on the forest for food. Thousands of miles were not sufficient to dampen their ardor, and no time could blot out their hatred. The Oneidas call them *We-au-dah*.

Jeremiah Gould went with me to view the twin mounds. They exhibit numerous pits or holes, which made me at once think of the *Assenjigun*, or hiding pit of the western Indians. Gould, in answer to my inquiry, said that it was a tradition which he did not know how much value it was worth, that the Tuscaroras were brought from the south by the Oneidas, and first settled in this county. They warred against the Onondagas. The latter, to save their corn, buried it in these mounds or hills, then hid by the forest. In one of these excavations, dug into forty years ago, they found a human skull, and other bones belonging to the human frame.

James Gould went with me over the Butternut stream, to show me a mound. It is apparently of geological formation, and not artificial. Its sides were covered with large trees, the stumps of which remain. There was a level space at the top, some four or five paces in diameter, trees and bushes around. The apex, as paced, measures one way seventeen, the other twelve paces; is elongated. It seemed to have been the site of the prophet's lodge. Near it is the old burying ground, on an elongated ridge, where the graves were ranged in lines.

*Pottery.*—Webster gives the tradition of this ancient art thus. The women made the kettles. They took clay and tempered it with some siliceous or coarse stone. This they first burnt thoroughly, so as to make it friable, (probably they plunged it while hot into water,) and then pounded it, and mixed it with blood.

*Charred Corn, &c.*—In Ellisburgh is found much charred corn beneath the soil, and numerous remains of occupancy by the natives. Is this the evidence of Col. Van Schaack's expedition into the Onondaga country during the revolutionary war? His battle with the Indians, tradition here says, took place near Syracuse. Bones, supposed to be of this era, were discovered in ditching the swamp, near Cortland House.

Kasonda.—Mr. I. Keeler says that he cut a large oak tree near the site of the old fort, two and a half feet through. In recutting it at his door, a bullet was found, covered by 143 cortical layers. It was still some distance to the centre. If this tree was cut in 1810, the bullet was fired in 1667. Consult Paris Documents, 1666, treaty with the Onondaga Iroquois.

The Goulds say that the fort was a square, with bastions, and had streets within it. It was set round with cedar pickets, which had been burnt down to the ground. Stumps of them were found by the plough.

Nearly every article belonging to the iron tools of a blacksmith shop have been ploughed up at different times—an anvil, horn, vice, screw, &c.; Indian axes, a horse shoe, hinges, the strap hinge. A pair of these hangs the wicket gate to his house.

A radius of five to six miles around the old fort, would cover all the striking remains of ancient occupancy in the towns of De Witt, Lafayette, and Pompey.

Webster told the Goulds that the French who occupied this fort, and had the nucleus of a colony around it, excited the jealousy and ire of the Onondagas, by the hostility of some western tribes in their influence. Against these the Onondaga warriors marched. The French than attacked the red men, &c. This led to their expulsion and massacre. All were killed but a priest, who lived between the present towns of Salina and Liverpool. · He refused to quit peaceably. They then put a chain around a ploughshare, and heating it, hung it about his neck; he was thus, with the symbol of agriculture, tortured to death. His hut was standing when the country was settled.

The attempt to settle western New York by the French was in the age of western chivalry, (the 16th century,) and was truly Quixotic.

*Tradition.*—Pompey and its precincts were regarded by the Indians as the ground of blood, and it brought up to their minds many dark reminiscences, as they passed it. Some twenty years ago, there lived an aged Onondaga, who said that many moons before his father's days, there came a party of white men from the east in search of silver. From the heights of the Onondaga hills, they descried the white foam of Onondaga lake, and this was all the semblance they ever found of silver. One of the men died, and was buried on Pompey hill, and his grave was marked by a stone.\* The others built a fort on the noted ground, about a mile east of Jamesville, where they cultivated the land; but at length the Indians came in the night and put them all to death. But there was a fearful and bloody strife, in which the Indians fell like leaves before the autumn wind. This spot is the field of blood. This was told me by Lucien Birdseye, Esq.

AURORA.—Called on the Rev. Mr. Mattoon; vestiges of the Cayugas; villages; orchards; old forts. Get a vocabu-

---

\* Query, is not this the inscription stone now deposited in the Albany Institute.

lary of their language from Canada; get diagram of forts. *Karistagea*, or Steeltrap, thought to have been unfairly dealt with at his death; buried in the road. Fish Carrier's reserve at the bridge; four miles square. Red Jacket born on the opposite banks of the lake at Canoga; historical reminiscences of Mr. Burnham; letter stating the first settlements on the Military tract at Aurora; address before the G. O. I.; folly of keeping the society secret; intelligence, moral tone, hospitality of the place; cars at Cayuga bridge; Logan was the son of a Cayuga; did the Cayugas conquer the Tutelos of Virginia, and adopt the remnant? Cayugas scattered among the Senecas, in Canada and west of the Mississippi; how many left? what annuities?

GENEVA.—Ancient site of the Senecas; origin of the word Seneca; is it Indian or not Indian? examine old forts said to exist in this area; are there any vestiges of Indian occupancy at the Old Castle, at Cashong, Painted Post, Catherinestown, Appletown?

CANANDAIGUA.—In visiting Fort hill on the lake, see what vestiges; another site bearing this name, exists to the north of Blossom's; what antiquities? what traditions? ask old residents; inquire of Senecas west.

ROCHESTER.—Nothing left here of the footprints of the race; all covered deep and high with brick and stone; whole valley of the Genesee worthy examination, in all its lengths and branches; wants the means of an antiquarian society to do this.

Truly the Iroquois have had visited upon them the fate with which they visited others. They destroyed and scattered, and have, in turn, been destroyed and scattered. But their crime was the least. They destroyed as *heathens*, but *we* as *Christians*. In any view, the antiquarian interest is the same, the moral interest the same. The Iroquois had noble hearts. They sighed for fame. They took hold of the tomahawk as the only mode of distinction. They brought up their young men to the war-dance. They carefully taught them the arts of war. We have other avenues to distinction. Let us now direct their manly energies to other channels. The hand that drew a bow can be taught to guide a plough. Civilization has a thousand attractions. The hunter state had but one. The same skill once devoted to war would enable them to shine in the arts of peace. Why can not their bright men be made sachems of the pen, of the press, of the pulpit, of the lyre?

BATAVIA.—There are still traces of a mound on Knowlton's farm, a mile from Batavia, up the Tonewanda. Bones and glass beads have been ploughed out of it. Other traces of former aboriginal occupancy exist in the vicinity, a stone pestle, axes, &c., having been found. The Indian name of Batavia is *Ge-ne-un-dah-sais-ka*, meaning musquito. This was the name by which they knew the late Mr. Ellicott.

The Tonewanda falls forty feet at a single place, within the Indian reservation. It heads on high ground about forty miles above Batavia. On the theory of the former elevation of Lake Erie, Buffalo itself would be the highest ground, between Batavia and the lake, in a direct line. Attica is, perhaps, more elevated in that direction.

TONEWANDA RESERVATION.—The Senecas call themselves *Nun-do-waw-ga*, or people of the hill. The term *Seneca* is taken from the lake, on the banks of which they formerly lived, and had their castle. It is *not* a name of Indian origin. They are called *Nun-do-waw-ga*, from the eminence called Fort hill, near Canandaigua lake.

They call the Cherokees *O-yau-dah*, which means a people who live in caves. Their enmity against this people, the tradition of which is so strong and clear, is stated to have originated from the contact of war and hunting parties, in the plains of the southwest. The Senecas affirm that the Cherokees robbed and plundered a Seneca party and took away their skins. Retaliation ensued. Tragic scenes of treachery and surprise followed. The Five Nations took up the matter in all their strength, and raised large and strong war parties, who marched through the country to the Cherokee borders, and fought and plundered the villages, and brought away scalps and prisoners. There are now descendants of Cherokees in the third degree, living on the Tonawanda reservation, (*Ho-ho-ee-yuh*). Some years ago, a chief of this blood, pure by father and mother, lived among them, who had been carried off captive when a boy. The fact being revealed to him, after he had obtained the chieftaincy, he went south to seek his relations and live and die among them, but he was unable to find them. He came back to the Senecas, and died among them, (*Le Fort*).

The most curious trait, of which we know but little, is that respecting *Totems*. Asked the chief called Blacksmith, his name in Seneca. He replied *De-o-ne-hoh-gah-wah*, that is, a door perforated, or violently broken through, not opened. Says he was born on the Tonawanda reservation, and wishes to die there; will be 60 years old, in the winter of 1846.

Says the Senecas call the fort Stanwix or Rome summit, *De-o-wain-sta*, meaning the place where canoes are carried across the land from stream to stream; that is, a carrying place.

Says, *Te-to-yoah*, or William Jones of Cattaraugus, can relate valuable Seneca traditions.

He says there are eight Seneca clans; they are the Wolf, Bear, Turtle, Deer, Plover, Beaver, Hawk and Crane. He is of the Wolf clan. This was also Red Jacket's clan. These clans may be supposed to have arisen from persons who had greatly distinguished themselves at an early period as founders, or benefactors, or they may have held some such relation to the original nation, as the Curatii and Horatii, in Roman history. It is not only the Iroquois, who ascribed this honor to the clans of the Bear, the Turtle and the Wolf. They are equally honored among most of the Algonquin tribes.

*Osteological Remains.*—In the town of Cambria, six miles west of Lockport, a Mr. Hammon, who was employed with his boy in hoeing corn in 1824, observed some bones of a child, exhumed. No farther thought was bestowed upon the subject for some time, for the plain on the ridge was supposed to have been the site of an Indian village, and this was supposed to be the remains of some child, who had been recently buried there. Eli Bruce, hearing the circumstance, proposed to Mr. H. that they should repair to the spot, with suitable instruments, and endeavor to find some relics. The soil was a light loam, which would be dry and preserve bones for centuries without decay. A search enabled them to come to a pit, but a slight distance from the surface. The top of the pit was covered with small slabs of the Medina sandstone, and was twenty-four feet square, by four and a half in depth—the planes agreeing with the four cardinal points. It was filled with human bones of both sexes and all ages. They dug down at one extremity and found the same layers to extend to the bottom, which was the same dry loam, and from their calculations, they deduced that at least four thousand souls had perished in one great massacre. In one skull, two flint arrow heads were found, and many had the appearance of having been fractured and cleft open, by a sudden blow. They were piled in regular layers, but with no regard to size or sex. Pieces of pottery were picked up in the pit, and had also been ploughed up in the field adjacent. Traces of a log council house were plainly discernible. For, in an oblong square, the soil was poor, as if it had been cultivated, till the whites broke it up; and where the logs of the house had decayed, was a strip of rich mould. A maple tree, over the pit, being cut down, two hundred and fifty concentric circles were counted, making the mound to be A. D. 1574. It has been supposed by the villagers that the bones were deposited there before the discovery of America, but the finding of some metal tools with a French stamp, places the date within our period. One hundred and fifty persons a day visited this spot the first season, and carried off portions of the bones. They are now nearly all gone, and the pit ploughed over. Will any antiquarian inform us, if possible, why these bones were placed here? To what tribe do they belong? When did such a massacre occur?

None of the bones of the men were below middle size, but some of them were very large. The teeth were in a perfectly sound state.

*Present Means of Living on the Reservation.*—These are: 1. Rent of land from twelve shillings to three dollars per acre; 2. Sale of timber, fire wood, hemlock bark, staves, saw logs; 3. Fishing and hunting, very little now; 4. Raise corn, cattle, horses, hogs, some wheat, &c., &c., cut hay; young men hire themselves out in harvest time.

*Human Bones.*—At Barnegat is an ancient ridge, or narrow raised path, leading from the river some miles, through low grounds; it is an ancient burial ground, on an island, in a swamp. Bones of the human frame, bone needles, and other ancient remains, are ploughed up at an ancient station, fort or line, in Shelby. A human head, petrified, was ploughed up by Carrington, sen., in a field in Alabama, Genesee county, and is now in the possession of Mr. Grant, at Barnegat. These are believed to be remains of the ancient Eries. Petrified tortoises are said to be ploughed up in many places.

*Opinion of a Chief of the word Seneca.*—De-o-ne-hoh-gah-wah is the most influential chief of the Tonawandas. He is of the Wolf tribe, born on the forks of the Tonawanda, and is 59 years old. Being interrogated as to the Seneca history, he says that the tradition of the tribe is clear; that they lived on the banks of the Seneca and Canandaigua lakes. They were called Dun-do-wau-onuh, or People of the Hill, from an eminence now called Fort hill, at the head of Canandaigua lake. They are now called, or, rather, call themselves, Nun-do-wau-gau. The inflection *onuh*, in former times, denoted residence, at a hill; the particle *agau*, in the latter, is a more enlarged term for locality, corresponding to their present dispersed condition.

The word Seneca, he affirms, is not of Indian origin. While they lived in Ontario, there was a white man called

Seneca, who lived on the banks of the lake of that name. Who he was, where he came from, and to what nation he belonged, he does not know. But wherever he originated, he was noted for his bravery, wisdom and strength. He became so proverbial for these noble qualities, that it was usual to say of such, and such a one, among themselves, he is as brave as Seneca, as wise as Seneca, as noble as Seneca. Whether the lake was called after him, or he took his name from the lake, is not known. But the name itself is of European origin. The tribe were eventually called Senecas from their local residence. The idea, he says, was pleasing to them, for they thought themselves the most brave and indomitable of men. Of all the races of the Ongwe-Honwe, they esteemed themselves the most superior in courage, endurance and enterprize. He refers to Te-to-yoah of Cattaraugus for further information.

On reference to Te-to-yoah, some time afterwards, he had no tradition on this particular subject. The probability is, that Blacksmith meant only to say, that the name was not of his tribe or *Nundowaga.* So far is true. What he says of a great man living on Seneca lake, &c., in older times, is probably a reproduction, in his mind, of an account of Seneca, the moralist, which has been told him, or some Indian from whom he had it, in days by-gone. As the name of Seneca is one of the earliest we hear, after 1609, it was probably a Mohawk term for that people. It is spelt with a *k* in old French authors.

LEWISTON.—The Tuscarora clans are the following: the Turtle, the Wolf, the Bear, the Beaver, the Snipe, or Plover, the Eel (this is not an Iroquois totem), the Land Tortoise. They have lost the Falcon, Deer, and Crane, perhaps in their disastrous wars of 1713. By this, it appears they have lost one clan entirely—probably in their defeat on the Taw river, in North Carolina. Two others of the clans are changed, namely, the Falcon and Deer, for which they have substituted the Land Tortoise and Eel.

Descent is by the chief's mother and her clan, her daughter or nearest kin, to be settled in council. The adoption of chiefs was allowed, where there was failure of descent.

Curious barrow, or mound, on Dr. Scovill's place; to be examined;* two others, near the old mill and orchard; old fort of Kienuka, to be visited, (see plate, p. 210); get vocabulary of Tuscarora to compare. This tribe has gone through a severe ordeal; their history is full of incident. The following list shows their number in North Carolina, and all other Indians of that colony in 1708:—Tuscaroras living in fifteen towns, 1,200 men; Waccons, in two towns, 120; Maramiskeets, 30; Bear Rivers, 50; Hatteras, 16; Neus, in two towns, 15; Pamlico, 15; Meherrin, 50; Chowan, 15; Paspatank, 10; Poteskeets of Carrituk, 30; Nottoways, 30; Connamox, in two towns, 25; Jaupim, 2: total, 1,608.

Visited James Cusick, the brother of David the Indian archæologist, preacher to the Tuscs; pictures in the house; old deeds from Carolina.

Sunday, attended Mr. Rockwood's meeting; admirable behavior of all; dress well, good singing; W. Chew interprets; females, however, adhere to their ancient costume; women more pertinacious in their social habits and customs than men.

Tuscaroras raise much wheat, cattle, horses, quite in advance of the other tribes in agriculture. They own the fee simple of about five thousand acres, which they purchased from the Holland Company, besides their reservation.

NIAGARA FALLS.—This name is Mohawk. It means, according to Mrs. Kerr, the neck; the term being first applied to the portage or neck of land, between lakes Erie and Ontario. By referring to Mr. Elliot's vocabulary, (chap. xi,) it will be seen that the human neck, that is, according to the

---

* Subsequently opened by the doctor, but nothing of much note found; a rude heap of the Niagara gorge stone.

concrete vocabulary, *his* neck, is *onyara*. Red Jacket pronounced the word Niagara to me, in the spring of 1820, as if written *O-ne-au-ga-rah*.

Buffalo.—Whence this name? The Indian term is *Te-ho-so-ro-ro* in Mohawk; and *De-o-se-o-wa* in Seneca; Ellicott writes it *Tu-she-way*; others, in other forms; in all, it is admitted to mean the place of the linden, or bass-wood tree. There is an old story of buffaloes being killed here. Some say a horse was killed by hungry *Frenchmen*, and palmed off for buffalo meat at the camp. How came a horse *here?* A curious bone needle was dug up this year, in some excavations made in Fort Niagara, which is, clearly, of the age prior to the discovery. Bones and relics must stand for the chronology of American antiquity. America is the tomb of the red men. All the interest of its anti-Columbian history, arises from this fact.

Eries.—By a letter, Father Le Moyne's, of 1653, (vide *Relacions*,) the war with the nation of the Cat or Eries, was then newly broken out. He *thanks* the Onondagas, Senecas, Cayugas, and Oneidas, for their *union* in this war. " On the 9th of August, 1653, we heard," says he, " a dismal shout among the Iroquois, caused by the news, that three of their men had been killed by the Eries." He condoles with the Seneca nation, on the capture of their great chief, *Au-ren-cra-os*, by the Eries. He exorts them to strengthen their defences, or forts, to paint their warriors for battle, to be united in council. He requires them never to lay in ambush for the Algonquin or Huron nations, who might be on their way to visit the French. We learn, from this, that the Eries or Cat nation were not of the Wyandot or Huron, nor of the Algonquin nations. It would seem that these Eries were not friends of the French, and that by exciting them to this new war, they were shielding their friends, the Algons and Hurons, from the Iroquois club and scalping knife. That they were the same people called the Nenter Nation, who occupied the banks of the Niagara, there is not a little reason to believe. The Senecas call them *Gawgwa* or *Kah-kwah*.

Cusick states that the Senecas fought against a people, west of the Genesee river, called Squakihaw, that is, Kah-kwah, whom they beat, and after a long siege took their principal fort, and put their chief to death. Those who recovered were made vassals and adopted into the tribe. He states that the banks of the Niagara river were possessed by the *Twa-kenkahor*, or Missasages, who, in time, gave it up to the Iroquois peaceably. Were not these latter, firm allies of the Neuter Nation?

To discuss the question of the war with the Eries, it is necessary to advert to the geographical position of the parties. The Senecas, in 1653, as appears by French authorities, lived in the area between the Seneca lake and the Genesee river. The original stock of the Five Nations appears to have entered the area of western New York in its central portions; and, at all events, they extended west of the Genesee, after the Erie war, and possessed the land conquered from the latter.

*Mission Station, Buffalo Reservation.*—Seventy-four Seneca chiefs attended the general council held here. Putting their gross population at 2,500, this gives one chief to every thirty-three souls.

The Seneca language has been somewhat cultivated. Mr. Wright, the missionary, who has mastered the language, has printed a spelling book of 112 pages, also a periodical tract for reading, called the Mental Elevator. Both valuable philological data.

The Senecas of this reservation are on the move for Cattaraugus and Alleghany, having sold out, finally, to the Ogden company. They leave their old homes and cemetery, however, with " longing, lingering looks."

Here lie the bones of Red Jacket and Mary Jemison. Curious and interesting reminiscences the Senecas have;

can't always separate fiction from fact; they must go together; for often, if the fiction or allegory be pulled up, the fact has no roots to sustain itself.

*Philology.*—The Seneca language has a masculine, feminine and neuter gender. It has also an animate and inanimate gender, making five genders. It has a general and dual plural. It abounds in compounds descriptive and derivative terms, like the Algonquin. They count by the decimal mode. There are names for the digits to ten. Twenty is a compound of two and ten, and thirty of three and ten, &c. The comparison of adjectives is effected by prefixes, not by inflections, or by changes of the words, as in English. Nouns have adjective inflections as in the Algonquin. Thus *o-a-deh* is a road, *o-a-i-yu* a good road. The inflection in this last word, is from *wi-yu*, good.

IRVING, Mouth of Cattaraugus.—This is a fine natural harbor, and port of refuge. Its neglect appears strange, but it is to be attributed to the influence of capitalists at Silver Creek, Dunkirk, Barcelona, &c.

It is a maxim with the Iroquois, that a chief's skin should be thicker than that of the thorn locust, that it may not be penetrated by the thorns. Indian speakers never impugn each other's *motives* when speaking in public council. In this, they offer an example.

INDIANS IN CANADA.—It is observed by a report of the Canadian parliament, that the number of Indians now in Canada is 12,000. Of these, 3,301 are residing in Lower Canada, and the remainder 8,862, in Canada West. The number of Indians is stated to be on the increase, partly from a numerous immigration of tribes from the United States. This report must be taken with allowances. It is, at best, but an estimate, and in this respect, the Canadians, like ourselves, are apt to over estimate.

The Indian is a man who has certainly some fine points of character; one would think a man of genius could turn him to account. Why then are Indian tales and poems failures? They fail in exciting deep sympathy. We do not feel that he has a heart.

The Indian must be *humanized* before he can be loved. This is the defect in the attempts of poets and novelists. They do not show the reader that the red man has a feeling, sympathizing heart, and feeling and sympathies like his own, and consequently he is not interested in the tale. It is a tale of a statue, cold, exact, stiff, but without *life*. It is not a man with man's ordinary loves and hopes and hates. Hence the failure of our *Yamoydens*, and *Ontwas*, and *Escallalas*, and a dozen of poems, which, although having merits, slumber in type and sheepskin, on the bookseller's shelf.

HORTS' CORNERS, Cattaraugus county.—One seems here, as if he had suddenly been pitched into some of the deep gorges of the Alps, surrounded with cliffs and rocks and woods, in all imaginable wildness.

COLD SPRING, Alleghany river, Sept. 3.—Reached the Indian village on the reservation at this place, at 9 o'clock in the morning. Indians call the place *Te-o-ni-gon-o*, or *De-o-ni-gon-o*, which means Cold Spring. Locality of the farmer employed by Quakers, at the mouth of a creek, called *Tunasassa*; means a clear stream with a pebbly bed. Alleghany river they call *Oheo*, making no difference between it, and the stream after the inlet of the Monongahela. Gov. Blacksnake absent; other chiefs, with his son Jacob, meet in council; business adjusted with readiness. Alleghany river low; very different in its volume of water and appearance from what it was twenty-seven years before, when I descended it, on my way to the *west*. Lumbering region; banks lined with shingles, boards, saw logs. Indians act as guides and lumbermen. Not a favorable location for the improvement of the Senecas; steal their timber; cheat them in bargains; sell whiskey to them. Had the imaginative Greeks lived in Alleghany county, they would have pictured the Genesee and Alleghany rivers, as two girls, who having shaken hands, parted, the one to skip and leap and run eastward to find the St. Lawrence, and the other to laugh through the Ohio valley, until she gradually melted into the ocean in the gulf of Mexico.

NAPOLI CENTRE.—The counties of Cattaraugus, Chautauque and Alleghany, and part of Wyoming and Steuben, constitute a kind of Switzerland. The surface of the country resembles a piece of rumpled calico, full of knobs and ridges and valleys, in all possible shapes and directions. It is on the average elevated. Innkeepers and farmers encountered on two trips over it, say that there is considerably more moisture in the shape of rain, and dews and fogs, than in the Genesee country. It is less valuable for wheat, but good for corn, grass, and raising stock. Nothing can be more picturesque. The hills are often cultivated to their very tops. It is healthy. Such a region is a treasure in a state so level and placid as much of western New York; and had it the means of ready access to markets, and to the Atlantic, it would, in a few years, be spotted with gentlemens' seats from the seaboard. There are some remarkable examples of the east and west, and north and south fissures of rocks (a trait also noted at Auburn,) in these counties. At one place, the fissures are so wide, and the blocks of rock between so large, that the spot is sometimes called *city of rocks*. The rock here is conglomerate, that is, the bed of the coal formation; a fact which denotes the elevation of the country. It is to be hoped, when this country is further subdivided into counties and towns, that some of the characteristic and descriptive names of the aborigines will be retained.

LODI.—This bright, busy, thriving place, is a curiosity from the fact, that the Cattaraugus creek, (a river it should be called,) splits it exactly or nearly so, in two parts, the one being in Erie, the other in Cattaraugus. Efforts to get a new county, and a county seat, have heretofore been made. These conflict with similar efforts, to have a county seat located at Irving, at the mouth of the creek.

EIGHTEEN MILE CREEK.—Here are vestiges of the Indians' old forts, town sites, &c. Time and scrutiny are alone necessary to bring out its antiquities.

BATAVIA.—The Tonawandas at length consent to have their census taken.

AUBURN.—Go with Mr. Goodwin to visit Owasco lake; Gov. Throop's place; Old Dutch church overlooking the lake, &c.; extensive vestiges of an elliptical work exist on Fort ill; curious rectangular fisures of the limestone rock on the Owasco outlet, north and south. The Indian name of this place, as told by an Onondaga chief, is *Osco;* first called by the whites, Hardenburgh's Corners; finally named from Goldsmith's Deserted Village; so that the poet may be said to have had a hand in supplying names for a land to which he once purposed to migrate. It would have pleased "poor Goldsmith" could he have known that he was the parent of the name for so fine a town — a town thriving somewhat on the principle laid down in the concluding lines of the poem —

> "While self-dependent power can time defy,
> As rocks resist the billows and the sky."

SYRACUSE.—Pity a better name could not have been found for so fine, central, capital a site. The associations are now all wrong. What had Dionysius or Archimedes to do here? It was Atotarho, Garangula, Dekanifora, Ontiyaka, and their kindred, who made the place famous. Onondaga would have been a far better appellation. The Indians called the lake and its basin of country together, *Gan-on-do-a.* Salt point, or the saline, sounded to me as if it might be written *Ka-di-ka-do.*

UTICA.—There was a ford in the Mohawk here. It was the site of Fort Schuyler—a fort named after Major Schuyler, a man of note and military prowess in the olden time, long before the days of General Philip Schuyler. Some philological goose, writing from the Canadas, makes Utica an Indian name.

ALBANY, Mouth of the Norman's Kill, or Tawasentha.—
Mr. Brayton says, that in digging the turnpike road, in
ascending Kiddenhook hill, on the road to Bethlehem, many
human bones, supposed to be Indian, were found. They
were so numerous that they were put in a box and buried.
This ancient burial ground, which I visited, was at a spot
where the soil is light and sandy. On the hill, above his
house, is a level field, where arrow-heads have been found in
large numbers. Mr. B., who has lived here sixteen years,
does not know that the isolated high ground, east of the
turnpike gate, contains ancient bones; has not examined it
with that view. Says Mr. Russell, in the neighborhood, has
lived there fifty years, and will ask him. Nothing could be
more likely, than that this oasis on the low land should have
served as the cemetery for the Mohawks, who inhabited the
island, where the Dutch first landed and built a fort in 1614.

The occupancy of this island by the Indians could never
have been any thing but a summer residence, for it is subject
to be inundated every year by the breaking up of the river.
This was probably the cause why the Dutch almost immediately abandoned it, and went a little higher, to the main
land, where Albany now stands. The city, however, such
are the present signs of its wealth and progress, has extended
down quite half way to the parallel of the original site of
*Het Casteel*, under Christianse, and should these signs continue, within twenty years South Pearl street will present
lines of compact dwellings and stores to the bridge over the
Tawasentha, and Kiddenhook be adorned with country seats.

FRANCHISE.—Whatever else can be done for the red race,
it is yet my opinion, that nothing would be as permanently
beneficial, in their exaltation and preservation, as their admission to the rights and immunities of citizens.

## SKETCHES OF AN INDIAN COUNCIL.

A grand council of the confederate Iroquois, writes Mr. G. S. Riley, of Rochester, was held Oct. 1, 1845, at the Indian Council House, on the Tonawanda reservation, in the county of Genesee. Its proceedings occupied three days. It embraced representatives from all the Six Nations; the Mohawk, the Onondaga, the Seneca, the Oneida, the Cayuga, and the Tuscarora. It is the only one of the kind which has been held for a number of years, and is, probably, the last which will ever be assembled with a full representation of all the confederate nations.

The Indians from abroad arrived at the council grounds, or in the immediate vicinity, two days previous; and one of the most interesting spectacles of the occasion, was the entry of the different nations upon the domain and hospitality of the Senecas, on whose ground the council was to be held. The representation of Mohawks, coming as they did from Canada, was necessarily small. The Onondagas, with the acting *todo-dahhoh* of the confederacy, and his two counsellors, made an exceedingly creditable appearance. Nor was the array of Tuscaroras, in point of numbers at least, deficient in attractive and imposing features.

We called upon and were presented to Blacksmith, the most influential and authoritative of the Seneca sachems. He is about sixty years old, is somewhat portly, is easy enough in his manners, and is well disposed, and even kindly towards all who convince him that they have no sinister designs in coming among his people.

Jemmy Johnson is the great high priest of the confederacy. Though now sixty-nine years old, he is yet an erect, fine looking, and energetic Indian, and is both hospitable and intelligent. He is in possession of the medal presented by Washington to Red Jacket in 1792, which, among other things of interest, he showed us.

It would be incompatible with the present purpose, to describe all the interesting men who there assembled, among whom were Captain Frost, Messrs. Le Fort, Hill, John Jacket, Dr. Wilson and others. We spent much of the time during the week in conversation with the chiefs and most intelligent Indians of the different nations, and gleaned from them much information of the highest interest, in relation to the organization, government, and laws, religion, customs of the people, and characteristics of the great men, of the old and once powerful confederacy. It is a singular fact, that the peculiar government and national characteristics of the Iroquois, is a most interesting field for research and inquiry, which has never been very thoroughly, if at all, investigated, although the historic events which marked the proud career of the confederacy, have been perseveringly sought and treasured up in the writings of Stone, Schoolcraft, Hosmer, Yates, and others.

Many of the Indians speak English readily, but with the aid and interpretations of Mr. Ely S. Parker, a young Seneca of no ordinary degree of attainment, in both scholarship and general intelligence, and who, with Le Fort, the Onondaga, is well versed in old Iroquois matters, we had no difficulty in conversing with any and all we chose to.

About mid-day on Wednesday, Oct. 1, the council commenced. The ceremonies with which it was opened and conducted, were certainly unique—almost indescribable; and as its proceedings were in the Seneca tongue, they were in a great measure unintelligible, and in fact profoundly mysterious to the pale faces. One of the chief objects for which the council had been convoked, was to fill two vacancies in the sachemships of the Senecas, which had been made by the death of the former incumbents; and preceding the installation of the candidates for the succession, there was a general and dolorous lament for the deceased sachems, the utterance of which, together with the repetition of the laws of the confederacy—the installation of the new sachems—the impeachment and deposition of three unfaithful sachems—the elevation of others in their stead, and the performance of the various ceremonies attendant upon these proceedings, consumed the principal part of the afternoon.

At the setting of the sun, a bountiful repast, consisting of an innumerable number of rather formidable looking chunks of boiled fresh beef, and an abundance of bread and succotash, was brought into the council house. The manner of saying grace on this occasion was indeed peculiar. A kettle being brought, hot and smoking from the fire, and placed in the centre of the council house, there proceeded from a single person, in a high shrill key, a prolonged and monotonous sound, resembling that of the syllable *wah* or *yah*. This was immediately followed by a response from the whole multitude, uttering in a low and profoundly guttural but protracted tone, the syllable *whe* or *swe*, and this concluded grace. It was impossible not to be somewhat mirthfully affected at the first hearing of grace, said in this novel manner. It is, however, pleasurable to reflect that the Indian recognizes the duty of rendering thanks to the Divine Being, in some formal way, for the bounties and enjoyments which he bestows; and were an Indian to attend a public feast among his pale faced brethren, he would be affected, perhaps to a greater degree of marvel, at witnessing a total neglect of this ceremony, than we were at his singular way of performing it.

After supper, commenced the dances. All day Tuesday, and on Wednesday, up to the time that the places of the deceased sachems had been filled, every thing like undue joyfulness had been restrained. This was required by the respect customarily due to the distinguished dead. But now, the bereaved sachemships being again filled, all were to give utterance to gladness and joy. A short speech from Capt. Frost, introductory to the enjoyments of the evening, was received with acclamatory approbation; and soon eighty or ninety of these sons and daughters of the forest—the old men and the young, the maidens and matrons — were engaged in the dance. It was indeed a rare sight.

Only two varieties of dancing were introduced the first evening; the trotting dance and the fish dance. The figures of either are exceedingly simple, and but slightly different from each other. In the first named, the dancers all move round a circle, in a single file, and keeping time in a sort of trotting step to an Indian song of *yo-ho-ha*, or *yo-ho-ha-ha-ho*, as sung by the leaders, or occasionally by all conjoined. In the other, there is the same movement in single file round a circle, but every two persons, a man and a woman, or two men, face each other, the one moving forward, the other backward, and all keeping step to the music of the singers, who are now, however, aided by a couple of tortoise or turtle shell rattles, or an aboriginal drum. At regular intervals, there is a sort of cadence in the music, during which a change of position by all the couples takes place, the one who had been moving backward taking the place of the one moving forward, when all again move onward, one-half of the whole, of course, being obliged to follow on by *advancing backwards!*

One peculiarity in Indian dancing would probably strongly commend itself to that class among pale faced beaux and belles denominated the bashful; though perhaps it would not suit others as well. The men, or a number of them, usually begin the dance alone; and the women, or each of them, selecting the one with whom she would like to dance, presents herself at his side as he approaches, and is immediately received into the circle. Consequently, the young Indian beau knows nothing of the tact required to handsomely invite and gallantly lead a lady to the dance; and the young Indian maiden, unannoyed by obnoxious offers, at her own convenience, gracefully presents her personage to the one she designs to favor, and thus quietly engages herself in the dance. And moreover, while an Indian beau is not necessarily obliged to exhibit any gallantry as towards a belle, till she has herself manifested her own good pleasure in the matter, so, therefore, the belle cannot indulge herself in vascillant flirtations with any considerable number of beaux, without being at once detected.

On Thursday the religious ceremonies commenced; and the council from the time it assembled, which was about 11 o'clock, A. M., till 3 or 4 o'clock, P. M., gave the most serious attention to the preaching of Jemmy Johnson, the great high priest, and the second in the succession under the new revelation. Though there are some evangelical believers among the Indians, the greater portion of them cherish the religion of their fathers. This, as they say, has been somewhat changed by the new revelation, which the Great Spirit made to one of their prophets about forty-seven years ago, and which, as they also believe, was approved by Washington. The profound regard and veneration which the Indian has ever retained towards the name and memory of Washington, is most interesting evidence of his universally appreciated worth; and the fact that the red men regard him not merely as one of the best, but as the very best man that ever has existed, or that will ever exist, is beautifully illustrated in a singular credence which they maintain even to this day, namely, that Washington is the only white man who has ever entered Heaven, and is the only one who will enter there, till the end of the world.

Among the Senecas, public religious exercises take place but once a year. At these times Jemmy Johnson preaches hour after hour, for three days; and then rests from any public discharge of ecclesiastical offices the remaining three hundred and sixty-two days of the year. On this, an unusual occasion, he restricted himself to a few hours in each of the last two days of the council. We were told by young Parker, who took notes of his preaching, that his subject matter on Thursday abounded with good teachings, enforced by appropriate and happy illustrations and striking imagery. After he had finished, the council took a short respite. Soon, however, a company of warriors ready and eager to engage in the celebrated corn dance, made their appearance. They were differently attired. While some were completely enveloped in a closely fitting and gaudy colored garb; others, though perhaps without intending it, had made wonderfully close approaches to an imitation of the costume said to have been so fashionable in many parts of the state of Georgia during the last hot summer, and which is also said to have consisted simply of a shirt collar and a pair of spurs. But in truth, these warriors, with shoulders and limbs in a state of nudity, with faces bestreaked with paints, with jingling trinkets dangling at their knees, and with feathered war-caps waving above them, presented a truly picturesque and romantic appearance. When the centre of the council house had been cleared, and the musicians with the shell rattles had taken their places, the dance commenced; and for an hour and a half, perhaps two hours, it proceeded with surprising spirit and energy. Almost every posture of which the human frame is susceptible, without absolutely making the feet to be uppermost, and the head for once to assume the place of the feet, was exhibited. Some of the attitudes of the dancers, were really imposing, and the dance as a whole, could be got up and conducted only by Indians. The women, in the performance of the corn dance, are quite by themselves; keeping time to the beat of the shells, and gliding along sideways, without scarcely lifting their feet from the floor.

It would probably be well, if the Indian every where could be inclined to refrain at least from the more grotesque and boisterous peculiarities of this dance. The influence of these cannot be productive of any good; and it is questionable, whether it will be possible, so long as they are retained, to assimilate them to any greater degree of civilization, or to more refined methods of living and enjoyment, than they now possess. The same may be said of certain characteristics of the still more Vandalic war dance. This, however, was not introduced at the council.

A part of the proceedings of Friday, the last day of the council, bore resemblance to those of the preceding day. Jemmy Johnson resumed his preaching; at the close of which the corn dance was again performed, though with far more spirit and enthusiasm than at the first. Double the numbers that then appeared, all hardy and sinewy men, attired in original and fantastic style, among whom was one of the chiefs of the confederacy, together with forty or fifty women of the different nations, now engaged, and for more than two hours persevered in the performance of the various, complicated and fatiguing movements of this dance. The appearance of the dusky throng, with its increased numbers, and of course proportionably increased resources for the production of shrill whoops and noisy stamping, and for the exhibition of striking attitudes and rampant motions, was altogether strange, wonderful, and seemingly superhuman.

After the dance had ceased, another kind of sport, a well contested foot race, claimed attention. In the evening, after another supper in the council house, the more social dances, the trotting, the fish, and one in which the women alone participated, were resumed. The fish dance seemed to be the favorite; and being invited to join it by one of the chiefs, we at once accepted the invitation, and followed in mirthful chase of pleasure, with a hundred forest children. Occasionally the dances are characterised with ebullitions of merriment and flashes of real fun; but generally a singular sobriety and decorum are observed. Frequently, when gazing at a throng of sixty or perhaps an hundred dancers, we have been scarcely able to decide which was the most remarkable, the staid and imperturbable gravity of the old men and women, or the complete absence of levity and frolicsomeness in the young.

The social dances of the evening, with occasional speeches from the sachems and chiefs, were the final and concluding ceremonies of this singular but interesting affair. Saturday morning witnessed the separation of the various nations, and the departure of each to their respective homes.

The writer would like to have said a word or two in relation to the present condition and prospects of the Indians, but the original design, in regard to both the topics and brevity of this writing, having been already greatly transcended, it must be deferred. The once powerful confederacy of the Six Nations, occupying in its palmy days the greater portion of New York state, now number only a little over 3,000.* Even this remnant will soon be gone. In view of this, as well as of the known fact that the Indian race is every where gradually diminishing in numbers, the writer cannot close without invoking for this unfortunate people, renewed kindliness, sympathy and benevolent attention. It is true that with some few exceptions, they possess habits and characteristics which render them difficult to approach; but still, they are only what the Creator of us all has made them. And, let it be remembered, it must be a large measure of kindliness and benevolence, that will repay the injustice and wrong that have been inflicted upon them.

## THE INDIAN FORT AT POMPEY.

Agreeably to your request, (says Mr. J. V. H. Clark of Manlius, in a letter to the author), I have been upon the grounds in our vicinity once occupied as forts and places of defence. So devastating has been the hand of time and the works of civilized men, that little can now be possibly gleaned by observation. Our main reliance in these matters must depend almost entirely upon the recollections of early settlers and traditions. Many of these accounts, as you are aware, are differently related by different individuals, and not unfrequently in material points contradictory. A locality in the town of Cazenovia, Madison county, near the county

---

* 3,753, vide preceding census, p. 32, et. seq.

line, and on lot 33, township of Pompey, Onondaga county, has been called the *Indian Fort*. It is about four miles southeasterly from Manlius village, situated on a slight eminence, which is nearly surrounded by a deep ravine, the banks of which are quite steep and somewhat rocky. The ravine is in shape like an ox-bow, made by two streams, which pass nearly around it and unite. Across this bow at the opening, was an earthen wall running southeast and northwest, and when first noticed by the early settlers, was four or five feet high, straight, with something of a ditch in front, from two to three feet deep. Within this enclosure may be about ten or twelve acres of land. A part of this ground, when first occupied in these latter times, was called the *Prairie*, and is noted now among the old men as the place where the first battalion militia training, was held in the county of Onondaga. But that portion near the wall, and in front of it, has recently, say five years ago, been cleared of a heavy growth of black oak timber. Many of the trees were large, and were probably one hundred and fifty or two hundred years old. Some were standing *in* the ditch, and others *on the top* of the embankment. There is a considerable burying place *within* the enclosure. The plough has already done much towards leveling the wall and ditch; still they can be easily traced the whole extent. A few more ploughings and harrowings and no vestige of it will remain. The specimens of dark brown pottery I send with this are from this locality. I picked them up at this visit. These specimens are somewhat numerous upon this ground now. Almost every variety of Indian relic has been found about here, but so fastidious are the holders of them, that I have not been able to procure any for you, and cannot, except *at a price.* However, they can be of little consequence, as they are described in the article above referred to. One fact, will, I think, apply to this locality, that does not belong to any other of the kind in this region, that I know of. Two cannon balls, of about three pounds each, were found in the vicinity, showing that light cannon were used, either for defence, or in the reduction of this fortification. There is a large rock in the ravine on the south, on which are inscribed the following characters, thus, *IIIIIX*, cut three-quarters of an inch broad, nine inches long, three quarters of an inch deep, perfectly regular, lines straight. Whether it was a work of fancy, or had significance, I know not.

On the site of the village of Cazenovia, I am told there was a fort or embankment; some persons say it was roundish; others that it was angular, with sides at right angles. Recollections respecting it are very imperfect. Many relics have been found here, indicating an earlier occupancy than those usually found in this county. This was on the Oneida's territory. There is a singular coincidence in the location of these fortifications which I have never observed until my recent visit. They are nearly all, if not quite all, situated on land rather elevated above that which is immediately contiguous, and surrounded, or partly so, by deep ravines, so that these form a part of the fortification themselves. At one of these (on the farm of David Williams, in Pompey), the banks on either side are found to contain bullets of lead, as if shot across at opposing forces. The space between may be about three or four rods, and the natural cutting twenty or twenty-five feet deep. This only goes to show the care these architects had in selecting the most favorable situations for defence, and the fear and expectation they were in of attacks.

I do not believe any of the fortifications in this neighborhood are more ancient than the period of the French settlement of missionaries among the Onondagas, during the early part of the seventeenth century. But the more I investigate, the more I am convinced that there were many more of the French established here among the Indians, by far, than has been generally supposed, and their continuance with them longer.

The nature of the articles found, utensils of farmers and mechanics, hoes, axes, horse shoes, hammers, &c., go to prove that agriculture was practised somewhat extensively, as well as the mechanic arts. The Indian name by which it was anciently called, and is now, by the natives, I think goes to substantiate this fact: *Ote-que-sah′-ĕ-ĕh*, an open place, with much grass, an opening, or prairie. The timber has a vigorous growth, and although in many places large, there is a uniformity in the size and age, which shows that it has all grown up *since* the occupancy; because under the trees are not only found the relics, but among them in many instances, corn hills can be traced in rows at considerable distances.

The presentation of medals, I believe to have been a very common custom among the missionaries and traders. Several have been found. A valuable cross of pure gold, sold for $30, was found on the farm of Mr. David Hinsdale, west part of Pompey. The significant IHS was upon it. Brass crosses are frequently found, and so are medals of the same metal. One recently found on the last named farm, about the size of a shilling piece. The figure of a Roman pontiff in a standing position, in his hand a crosier, surrounded with this inscription, *B. virg. sin. P. origi. con.*, which I have ventured to write out, *Beata virgo sine peccato originali concepta;* or as we might say in English, the blessed virgin conceived without original sin. On the other side was a representation of the brazen serpent, and two nearly naked figures, looking intently upon it. This is by far the most perfect one I have seen. The letters are as perfect as if struck but yesterday. It was undoubtedly compressed between dies. It is oval in shape, and bored, that it might be suspended from the neck. A silver medal was found near Eagle village, two miles east of this, about the size of a dollar, but a little thinner, with a ring or loop at one edge to admit a cord, by which it might be suspended. On one side appears in relief, a somewhat rude representation of a fortified town, with several tall steeples rising above its buildings, and a citadel, from which the British flag is flying. A river broken by an island or two, occupies the foreground, and above, along the upper edge of the medal, is the name Montreal. The initials, D. C. F., probably those of the manufacturer, are stamped below. On the opposite side, which was originally made blank, are engraved the words Canecya, Onondagas, which are doubtless the name and tribe of the red ruler, on whose dusky breast this ornament was displayed. A valuable token of friendship of some British governor of New York, or Canada, to an influential ally among the Six Nations. There is no date on this, or any of the medals. But this must be at least older than the revolution, and probably an hundred snows at least, have fallen on the field where the plough disinterred it, since the chief whose name it has preserved, was laid to rest with his fathers.

I have sent with this, such relics and Indian trinkets, as I could prevail upon our people here to part with. They are less than I expected to obtain. The gun lock, spear head, axe, piece of gun barrel, and lead ball, are all of the size and patterns usually found. They are from the farm of Mr. David Hinsdale, in the town of Pompey, west part. All the gun barrels, or parts of them, are found flattened similar to this. Not a perfect one has been found. The two parts of the axe, want about two inches between the broken portions to make the *bit* of the ordinary length. The stone axes, I thought might interest you. I have no doubt they were used in flaying animals slain in the chase, as well as in cleaving wood. I did intend to send you a beautiful gouge of hornblende, but to my surprise, it is not to be found; the like are frequently found here. It proves conclusively, that the natives were at an early day acquainted with the virtues of the maple, and possessed the art of making sugar. I have sent, as you will see, fragments of pipes of many varieties. The patterns are as various as the articles are numerous. The specimens of glass are different from any I have seen from any other quarter. I think some of the beads may have been used in rosaries, for the native proselytes. I have lately seen a fragment of a bell, which, when whole, would have weighed probably two hundred pounds, the metal is very fine, and from appearance, this article must have been of considerable value; time and exposure has not changed it in the least. When found some twenty years since, it was broken up, and the pieces found, enough to make it nearly entire.

## MR. JAMES CUSICK, ON THE TUSCARORAS.

It appears to me, says Mr. Cusick, very great difficulties are in the way of finding out and becoming acquainted with the discovery of all ancient traditions, and what original stock we came from. So far as our recollections extend, according to our traditions of many centuries, the aborigines who inhabited the vast wilderness in this great continent, now North America, were guided and led by a certain man, who stood highest in dignity, and next to the Supreme Being, who is called *Tharonyawago*, that is to say, being interpreted, the Holder of Heavens. He was the great leader of the red men, and he regulated and taught how to divide the country and rivers, and mode of their living, and manners of costume and ceremonies, in many centuries. The Tuscaroras were descended from the Iroquois; they emigrated from the Five Nations to the southern country in North Carolina, and when the Iroquois used to send expeditions and war parties to go to war with other Indian tribes in that quarter, these parties went to the Tuscarora towns in North Carolina, and found a resting place and refreshment, and they used to be in the habit of intermarriage with each other; they have never been to war against each other, and they were always on terms of good friendship and connexion. And therefore we considered that the Tuscarora nation belonged to the Six Nations from ancient times. Before the discovery by Columbus, the Tuscaroras consisted of six towns, and they were a most powerful nation, numbering more than twelve thousand warriors. But many combinations and causes fell upon the Tuscarora nation, and they became diminished in their numbers, by wars and pestilence, and were poisoned by ardent spirits. The Tuscaroras had many years of enjoyment and peaceful possession on the Roanoke river, until the colony was planted near the settlement; something brought up disturbances, and their right was disputed to their territory. In 1712 the Indians of the Tuscaroras in North Carolina, with their accustomed secrecy, formed a design of exterminating in one night, the entire white population; the slaughter on the Roanoke was great; Capt. Barnwell appointed and sent troops, who suddenly attacked the Tuscaroras; he killed 300, and took 100 prisoners; the survivors retreated to Tuscarora town, within a wooden breast-work, where at last they sued for peace.

The Tuscaroras soon after abandoned their country, and united themselves with the Iroquois, and became the Sixth Nation. When we first came into this country, we lived with the Oneida nation, (now Oneida county,) and we called the Oneidas the elder brother, the second is the Cayugas, the youngest brother Tuscaroras.

When the first missionary was sent to the Tuscarora nation, 1807, Eld. Elkanah Holmes, from the New York Missionary Society, labored several years with success, among them. This Mr. Holmes belonged to the Baptist Missionary Society. Afterwards, when Mr. Holmes was removed, another missionary was sent to the Tuscaroras by the American Foreign Mission, namely, the Rev. Mr. Grey, who remained until last war. After his dismissal in 1816, another missionary was sent by the Board of the New York Missionary Society, the Rev. James C. Crane. I will state briefly those missionaries who afterwards came to the Tuscaroras; Rev. B. Lane, Rev. John Elliot, Rev. Joel Wood, Rev. Mr. Williams; the last, who is now missionary, was the Rev. Gilbert Rockwood. In 1836, a portion of the Tuscarora nation thought expedient to become Baptists, according to the dictates of their own conscience, and free enjoyment of their religion in this republican government. And consequently a Baptist church was built and organized among the Tuscaroras; and they were called in council with several Baptist churches in this county. In 1838, they were admitted into the Niagara Baptist Association at Shelby, and have now in good standing fifty members of the church. In a ministerial council, June 14th, 1838, Mr. James Cusick was examined touching his Christian experience, and called to preach the gospel by Providence and the council; they decided on that question, and gave him ordination as a native preacher, deciding that he was well qualified by a knowledge of theology. And now he has labored with several tribes among the Six Nations. Under his instrumentality, three Baptist churches have been formed, numbering 200 members, and he established a temperance society in 1830 of more than 100 members. In 1845 he established another temperance society among the Indians, numbering 50 members. Intemperance is one of the greatest and most destructive evils, and many more begin to be intemperate, especially among the young men. Among the females of the Tuscarora nation there is more virtue and sobriety and good morals than among the males. I hope the white citizens will try to assist them and promote the melioration of the Indian condition, in order to qualify him for life, and lead him to appreciate its true end, and to encourage intermarriages in their future generations, and to advance in civilization, Christianity and industry.

At the Rev. Mr. Vrooman's, in Queenston, you will find a copy of my late brother David's book on the Indians.

## DAVID CUSICK'S BOOK.

The following extracts are made from the curious publication referred to, in the preceding letter. It appears to have been first printed at Lewiston, in 1825. As the work of a full blooded Indian, of the Tuscarora tribe, it is remarkable. In making these extracts, no correction of the style, or grammar is made, these being deemed a part of the evidence of the authenticity of the traditions recorded.

*Account of the Settlement of North America.*—In the ancient days the Great Island appeared upon the big waters, the earth brought forth trees, herbs, vegetables, &c. The creation of the land animals: the Eagwehoewe people were too created and resided in the north regions; and after a time some of the people became giants, and committed outrages upon the inhabitants, &c.

*Ancient Shipwreck.*—After many years a body of Eagwehoewe people encamped on the bank of a majestic stream, and was named *Kanawage*, now the St. Lawrence. After a long time a number of foreign people sailed from a port unknown; but unfortunately, before they reached their destination the winds drove them contrary; at length their ship wrecked somewhere on the southern part of the Great Island, and many of the crews perished; a few active persons were saved; they obtained some implements, and each of them was covered with a leather bag, the big hawks carried them on the summit of a mountain and remained there but a short time. The hawks seemed to threaten them, and were compelled to leave the mountain. They immediately selected a place for residence and built a small fortification in order to provide against the attacks of furious beasts; if there should be any made. After many years the foreign people became numerous, and extended their settlements; but afterwards they were destroyed by the monsters that overrun the country.

*Origin of the Five Nations.*—By some inducement a body of people was concealed in the mountain at the falls named *Kuskehsawkich*, (now Oswego). When the people were released from the mountain they were visited by *Tarenyawagon*, that is, the Holder of the Heavens, who had power to change himself into various shapes; he ordered the people to proceed towards the sunrise, as he guided them and came to a river and named *Yenonanatche*, that is, going round a mountain (now Mohawk), and went down the bank of the river and came to where it discharges into a great river running towards the midday sun; and named *Shaw-nay-taw-ty*, that is, beyond the Pineries, (now Hudson), and went down the bank of the river and touched the bank of a great water. The company made encampment at the place and remained there a few days. The people were yet in one language; some of the people went on the banks of the great water towards the midday sun; but the main company returned as they came, on the bank of the river, under the direction of the Holder of the Heavens. Of this company there was a particular body which called themselves one household; of these were six families and they entered into a resolution to preserve the chain of alliance which should not be extinguished in any manner.

The company advanced some distance up the river of *Shaw-na-taw-ty* (Hudson), the Holder of the Heavens directs the first family to make their residence near the bank of the river, and the family was named *Te-haw-re-ho-geh*, that is, a speech divided (now Mohawk), and their language was soon altered; the company then turned and went towards the sunsetting and travelled about two days and a half, and come to a creek* which was named *Kaw-na-taw-te-ruh*, that is, Pineries. The second family was directed to make their residence near the creek, and the family was named *Ne-haw-re-tah-go*, that is, Big Tree, now Oneidas, and likewise their language was altered. The company continued to proceed towards the sunsetting under the direction of the Holder of the Heavens. The third family was directed to make their residence on a mountain named Onondaga (now Onondaga), and the family was named *Seuh-now-kah-tah*, that is, carrying the name and their language was altered. The company continued their journey towards the sunsetting. The fourth family was directed to make their residence near a long lake named *Go-yo-goh*, that is, a mountain rising from water (now Cayuga), and the family was named *Sho-nea-na-we-to-*

---

* The creek now branches of the Susquehanna river at the head generally called Col. Allen's lake, ten miles south of the Oneida Castle.

*wah*, that is, a great pipe, their language was altered. The company continued to proceed towards the sunsetting. The fifth family was directed to make their residence near a high mountain, or rather nole, situated south of the Canandaigua lake, which was named *Jenneatowake,* and the family was named *Te-how-nea-nyo-hent*, that is, Possessing a Door, now Seneca, and their language was altered. The sixth family went with the company that journeyed towards the sunsetting, and touched the bank of a great lake, and named *Kau-ha-gwa-rah-ka,* that is; a Cat, now Erie, and then went towards between the midday and sunsetting, and travelled considerable distance, and came to a large river which was named *Ouau-we-yo-ka,* that is, a principal stream, now Mississippi; the people discovered a grape vine lying across the river by which a part of the people went over, but while they were engaged, the vine broke and were divided, they became enemies to those that went over the river; in consequence they were obliged to disperse the journey. The Holder of the Heavens instructs them in the art of bows and arrows in the time of game and danger. Associates were dispersed and each family went to search for residences according to their conveniences of game. The sixth family went towards the sunrise and touched the bank of the great water. The family was directed to make their residence near *Cau-ta-noh,* that is, pine in water, situated near the mouth of Nuse river, now in North Carolina, and the family was named *Kau-ta-noh,* now Tuscarora, and their language was also altered; but the six families did not go so far as to lose the understanding of each other's language. The Holder of the Heavens returns to the five families and forms the mode of confederacy, which was named *Ggo-nea-seab-neh,* that is, a long house, to which are: 1st. *Tea-kaw-reh-ho-geh;* 2d. *New-haw-tch-tah-go;* 3d. *Seuh-nau-ka-ta;* 4th. *Sho-nea-na-we-to-wah;* 5th. *Te-hoo-nea-nyo-hent.*

## ANCIENT WORK ON FORT HILL, AUBURN.

This enclosure, Mr. James H. Bostwick informs me, is situate on the highest point of land in the vicinity of Auburn, and is in the form of an ellipsis; and measures in diameter, from east to west, (from the outside of the base of the embankment,) four hundred and sixteen feet, and from north to south, three hundred and ten feet; the circumference, twelve hundred feet; present height of the highest part of the embankment on the west side, from the bottom of the ditch, four feet; the thickness at the base, fourteen feet; from the centre of the enclosure the ground has a gentle slope to the north, east, and west, and is nearly level towards the south. The openings on the south, one of sixty, and the other of seventy-eight feet, are directly opposite or against deep ravines, separated by a narrow steep ridge, access through which would be difficult, being on an angle of nearly forty-five degrees. The opening on the north measures one hundred and sixty-six feet, opposite to which, the ground continues to slope to the north for the distance of seventy feet, from which point the descent is very abrupt. The opening on the east measures sixty-six feet, opposite to which, the ground continues on a gentle descent to the east for several hundred feet. The opening on the southwest measures fifty feet, and is opposite to a ridge gently descending to the southwest. There are no less than ten deep ravines, and as many steep ridges surrounding and leading to this ancient fortification.

McAuley in his History of the State of New York, vol. 2d, pages 111 and 112, gives a minute and interesting description of this fortification, which, however, contains some inaccuracies; and also of another fortification, situate in the northeast part of Auburn. The large chestnut stump described by him as standing in the moat on the west side of the enclosure, is still to be seen; there are still to be seen the remains of two large oak stumps, which seem to have escaped his notice, situate on the southeast side of the enclosure; one of them on the top of the embankment, and the other in the ditch, some twelve feet distant. There are scarcely any traces remaining of the fortification described by McAuley as being in the northeast part of Auburn, from the fact that the ground upon which it stood has been under cultivation for many years. (See page 192, et. seq.)

## ACCOUNT OF FORT HILL, LE ROY.

The following letter is from Frederick Follet, Esq., of Batavia, who visited the ancient fortification he describes, in the fall of 1845.

The ground known as Fort hill, is situated about three miles north of the village of Le Roy, and ten or twelve miles northeast from Batavia, the capital of Genesee county. The better view of Fort hill, is had to the north of it, about a quarter of a mile, on the road leading from Bergen to Le Roy. From this point of observation it needs little aid of the imagination to conceive that it was erected as a fortification by a large and powerful army, looking for a permanent and almost inaccessible bulwark of defence. From the centre of the hill, in the northwesterly course, the country lies quite flat—immediately north, and inclining to the east, the land is also level for one hundred rods, when it rises nearly as high as the hill, and continues for several miles quite elevated. In approaching the hill from the north it stands very prominently before you, rising rather abruptly, though not perpendicularly, to the height of eighty or ninety feet, extending about forty rods on a line east and west, the corners being round or truncated, and continuing to the south on the west side for some sixty rods, and on the east side for about half a mile, maintaining about the same elevation at the sides as in front; beyond which distance the line of the hill is that of the land around.

Fort hill, however, is not a work of art. The geological character of it shows it to be the result of natural causes.

Nevertheless, there are undoubted evidences of its once having been resorted to as a fortification, and of its having constituted a valuable point of defence to a rude and half civilized people.

It is probable that at a period of time very far distant, the ground about Fort hill was, for some considerable distance around, entirely of the same level, and that by the action of water, a change took place, which brought about the present condition. The low land immediately in front to the north, is only the remains of a water course, which was made up of a stream coming down the gorge of the west side, and the present Allen's creek, which flows through a portion of the gorge of the east side, the stream of the west having been a branch of that of the east side. Through the west gorge now flows, in a wet season, a moderate stream, coming from the lands above the gorge, and having an interrupted fall of some forty or fifty feet; while Allen's creek occupies a portion of the eastern gorge, much broader, at the extremity of which, some half a mile from the hill, there is a beautiful fall of eighty feet perpendicularly. The structure of the hill bears out this construction; it being composed of the same rock—with the exception of the upper strata—as the falls. At the falls the upper strata of rock, and that which forms the bed of the creek for some two miles or more east, is the *corniferous limestone;* underlaying which are *hydraulic* and *Onondaga limestones.* The two latter are only seen at Fort hill, covered by a few feet of soil and several small masses of stone, a part out of place, among which are a few of *Medina sandstone.* The strata are, therefore, continuous from the falls, and at some former periods, extended over the gorges, and formed a regular and nearly level surface, the action of water having removed, which has left the broad and conspicuous point of Fort hill, as memorable monuments of the earlier condition of the country.

When Fort hill was used as a fortification, the summit was entrenched. Forty years ago, an entrenchment ten feet deep and some twelve or fifteen wide, extended from the west to the east end, along the north or front part, and continued up each side about twenty rods, where it crossed over, and joining, made the circuit of entrenchment complete. At this day, a portion of this entrenchment is easily perceived for fifteen rods along the extreme western half of the north or front part, the cultivation of the soil, with other causes, having nearly obliterated all other portions. It would seem that this fortification was arranged more for protection against invasion from the north, than from any other quarter, this direction evidently being its most commanding position. Near the northwest corner have, at different times, been found collections of rounded stones, of hard consistence, which are supposed to have been used as weapons of defence by the besieged against the besiegers.

Arrow heads, made of flint or horn stone, gouges, pestles, hatchets, and other weapons formed from stone, have been found about the hill, and throughout this section. Of the rarer articles, are pipes and beads, a few of the latter of which I have been able to obtain. The gouges, pestles, and hatchets, are, I think, frequently made of compact limestone, probably what is now known in Mr. Hall's State Report, as the *one foot limestone* at Le Roy, though many of them seem to be formed of primitive rock, and very likely were worked out from boulders scattered about the country.

Skeletons found about Fort hill and its vicinity, sustain the impression that the former occupants of this military station, were of a larger and more powerful race of men than ourselves. I learned that the skeletons generally indicated a stouter and larger frame. A humerus or shoulder bone, of which one has been preserved, may safely be said to be one-third larger or stouter than any now swung by the living. A resident of Batavia, Thomas T. Everett, M. D., has in his cabinet, a portion of a lower jaw bone, full one-third larger than any possessed by the present race of men, which was found in a hill near Le Roy, some two years since. From the same hill, arrow heads and other articles have been removed for many years.

The articles I send you are as follows: No. 1, an Indian gouge, made of very hard stone, found at Fort hill; No. 2, is a stone tomahawk, presented to me by Jerome A. Clark, Esq., of this village, found on his premises half a mile south of this place; No. 3, arrow heads, of flint; No. 4, beads; No. 5, a bead, evidently formed from a tooth, as the enamel and other distinctive marks indicate; No. 6, a bead, apparently of bone.

The following paper is from the Rev. C. Dewey of Rochester, on the same subject:

This is celebrated as being the remains of some ancient work, and was supposed to have been a *fort*. Though the name is pronounced as if *hill* was the name of some individual, yet the place is a fort on a hill, in the loose use of the word. The name designates the place as *Fort*-hill, to distinguish it from the hills which have no fort on them. Neither is it *a hill*, except as you rise from the swale on the north, for it is lower than the land to which it naturally belongs.

As you pass towards Fort hill in the road from Le Roy village, which is about three miles to the south, you descend a little most of the distance to this place. The road passes a little west of the middle of the space nearly north and south.

The shape is quadrangular, and is shown in the diagram or ground plot. On the right and east side is the deep water course of Allen's creek, cut down through the rocks for a mile or more, perhaps one hundred and thirty feet deep; on the north is that of Fordham's brook, of nearly the same depth, which drains a wide swale from the north and northwest; and on the west is a short and deep ravine, which is a water course in some seasons of the year, where the waters fall over a precipice a litte south of the quadrangular space, or fortification. This ravine is not so deep as the water courses on the east and north. The descent is quite steep on these three sides. At the northeast Allen's creek turns to the east and receives the waters from Fordham's brook.

The quadrangular space, D, A, B, C, (see plate, p. 199) was enclosed by a trench, D, A, nearly a north line on the east, by A B on the north, and B C on the west.

A B is the north trench about sixty rods long, and nearly east and west. A D is about thirty rods, and B C is fifteen rods, and terminates at the ravine at C. The trench D A, and A B, lies on the brow of the descent to the streams below. At D the bend of the ravine stops the trench. At the northwest corner B, a trench is continued about 15° to the right and down the declivity 15 rods to a spring; fifty feet perhaps below A B, and B G, is the brow of the descent west of the trench at B, and G C is the edge of the ravine on the west. Q W is Allen's creek on the east; H I K is Fordham's brook on the north, and L P M is the water course on the west to the precipice at M, over which the water falls at some seasons, and the surface at M is only a few feet lower than the general level of the quadrangle. The space F was a burying ground, as bones, skulls, pipes, beads, have been ploughed up there. The road R N passes through the middle nearly of the space enclosed by the trench, and at N turns to the right to descend to the flat below; but formerly the road turned to the right at U, and passed down at the right of the trench at D to T.

The place was pointed out to me by H. M. Ward, Esq., who was familiar with it when it was covered with the forest. He states that the trench must have been eight to ten feet deep and as many wide; that the earth was thrown either way, but much of it inwards; that the forest trees were standing in the trench and on the sides of it, and of the same apparent age and magnitude as on the ground generally; that the heart-wood of black cherry trees of large size was scattered over the ground, evidently the remains of a forest anterior to the then growth of maple and beech, and that this black cherry was used by the settlers for timber; that the road, when first made, crossed the trench at N by a *bridge ;* that the trench at D and A was cut down the bank a few feet, or else in time water had worn a passage from the trench downwards; that there was no tradition heard of among the Indians of the country, in respect to the use or design of the work.

The underlying rock is the hydraulic limestone of this section, which is fully exposed at the falls of Allen's creek, half a mile south of Fort hill. This rock was struck in digging the trench on the north line in some places, and portions of it were thrown out with the earth.

Of the pipes found at F, one was formed from granular limestone; one was of baked clay, in the form of the rude outlines of a man's head and face, nose, eyes, &c., and it reminds one of the figures in some of Stephens' plates of the ruins of Palenque. It has the hollows for the ears to be fastened on, and shows no little effort. The top of the head is surrounded by a fillet or wreath, and behind are two more fillets. At the bottom of the neck is a similar ornament, and on the front is another below it. This is the most curious. (See p. 204, et seq.)

## MORAL AND RELIGIOUS STATE OF THE TUSCARORAS.

The Rev. Gilbert Rockwood writes as follows:

This mission was commenced about fifty years since, under the care of the New York Mission Society. It was transferred to the United Foreign Missionary Society, in 1821, and to the American Board of Commissioners for Foreign Missions, in 1826.

The church was organized in 1805, with five persons. The whole number of native members who have united since its organization is one hundred and twenty-three. The present number of native members is fifty-three; others five, total fifty-eight.

Between July 1st, 1844, and July 1st, 1845, there were

only three admissions, two by profession and one by letter. About one-third of the population attend meeting on the sabbath. Their meeting house was built by themselves, with a little assistance from abroad.

They have also a school house, the expense of which was nearly all defrayed by themselves. There is but one school among them, which is kept the year through, with the exception of the vacations. The teacher is appointed by the American Board. The number of scholars the past year, is not far from fifty.

I have been among these Indians now nearly eight years. I can see that there has been an advance, both in their moral and physical condition.

It is within the memory of many now living among them, when drunkenness was almost universal; now, comparatively, few are intemperate. A majority of the chiefs, are decidedly temperance men, and exert a salutary influence. They have a temperance society, and hold frequent meetings. They utterly forbid the traffic in intoxicating drinks on their own soil.

The marriage relation is being better understood by them, and more appreciated. More of the young men and women, enter into the marriage relation, in the regular Christian way, than a few years ago. Four couple have been regularly married the past year. Number of deaths, eight; an unusual number since I have been among them.

There is besides the church, above referred to, a Baptist church, organized a few years since, the particulars of which, I am unable to give. For any information you may wish respecting it, I would refer you to James Cusick their minister.

On the whole, there is much to encourage the philanthropist and the Christian in labors for the good and well being of the Indians here, although we meet with many obstacles and difficulties in the way.

They are becoming more and more industrious in their habits, as the appearance of their farms, and the amount of produce, and their personal appearance, will testify.

## TUSCARORA VOCABULARY.

*Man lives.* Euh queh, yah kenh hek 'gh.
*God exists.* Ya wunh ne yuh, yah kenh hek 'gh.
*Fishes swim.* Kenk chinh, keuh hoh nuk, wah nah wuhn's.
*Birds fly.* Che nunh, keuh hoh neuh, na yuh nunh hah n'yeh.
*A fish swims.* Skenh che aht, wah nah wuhn's.
*A bird flies.* Skah che nunh e'shrah.
*One man.* Enh che, a ne hah.
*Twenty men.* Na wah th'sunh, kah ya ne hah.
*A little man.* Renh thras s'tenh, a ne hah.
*A little dog.* A re's.
*A good man.* Renh kweh, strah kwah'st.
*A bad man.* Renh kweh, struh k'senh.
*A good bow.* Wah nah kwah'st.
*A bad bow.* Wah nah k'senh.
*Good.* Kah re whah ya nih.
*Evil.* Kah re whah k'senh.
*Blessedness.* Kah yenh wah nunk.
*Mankind.* En noo keuh'f.
*The world.* Wah'f nah kwa kenh.

There is nothing answering to the infinitive and participle. I have therefore used the present indicative in the translation. I have divided the words into syllables, whether they are simple or compound. Where two or more words occur in the translation of a phrase, I have separated them by a comma. I have used the English alphabet with natural powers so far as Tuscarora sounds could be indicated by them. It is impossible to give, in many cases, a correct sound. *A* alone, has the sound of *a* in hate. Ah, like our interjection ah. The sound I intend to indicate by sunh, keuh, heuh, would be given, very nearly, by the Seneca alphabet used by Mr. Wright, thus, sah, kah, or kah, ha. The emphasis is, almost invariably, on the penultimate. Often a slight emphasis on some others. There is also often a prolongation of sound not indicated by any mark, as I supposed you would not need it.

Nicholas Cusick, the father of James and David, was about eighty-two when he died. I have not been able to learn where he was born. He died at this place October, 1840. I do not know that there was any thing very peculiar about him. He never was a "priest or juggler in his earlier days," that I can learn.

*Inquiries.*—There are several words in your vocabulary of the Tuscarora, in which the sound of *f* is used, always, however, as a terminal sound, as in *eh-noo-keuh'f*, mankind. Is this to be understood as denoting the ordinary sound of the letter? Does it occur in other positions in words? What is to be understood by the comma, which is invariably put before it?

*Mr. Rockwood's Reply.*—In reference to the vocabulary of Indian words we furnished you, I have further to remark, that the language having never been reduced to writing, each individual undertaking to reduce any portion of it, will have a system in part, at least, of his own. I have tried three different ways myself. It is difficult, if not impossible, to represent all the Tuscarora sounds by any combination of the English alphabet. I presume a stranger to the language would not, with the use of the vocabulary we have furnished you, give the correct sound in many instances.

The letter *f* terminating a word, has the sound of *f* in *chief*. I do not know as the comma before it, as in the word *eh-noo-keuh'f*, is of any use. In common conversation, or at any time when they speak rapidly, the sound of *f* is not distinguished, as a general thing. Yet when they speak a word entire, there is this *f* sound, slowly and distinctly; it seems to be a distinct sound, or very nearly so. It appears to be a little separated from the main part of the syllable, as though another syllable was to follow immediately beginning with *f*; but as soon as the sound of *f*, as in find, is given, the person stops short. Thus instead of *eh-noo-keuh* find, (I use the

English word *find*, because the power of *f* in this word is the power of the letter intended in the Indian word given,) we say *eh-noo-keuhf*, breaking off when you have given the sound of *f*, without proceeding to give the sound of *ind*. Perhaps if a comma is used at all, it would be more proper to place it *after* the *f*, thus *f'* or the *f* might join the syllable thus, *keuhf*.

I do not recollect that the sound of *f* is heard in any other part of a word than as a terminating sound.

Sometimes an *r* occurs separated, you will observe, by a comma from the rest of the syllable. It matters not much whether the *r* is joined to the preceding or following syllable. There is the sound of an *r* between them when the word is spoken. I have been puzzled to know where to place it. It seems to answer either way. Thus, in the word for to-morrow, *euh-yuh'r-heuh*, or *euh-yuh'-rheuh*. If joined to the syllable *yuh*, without being separated by the comma, you would pronounce it very nearly like the English word *your*. As it is, thus, *yuh'r*, its sound is very nearly like the English word *use*, and I am not sure but that would be a preferable way of writing it, thus, *euh-use-heuh;* yet there is a twirl or *r* sound you do not get as in the other mode of writing it. Terminating in *r*, a word has much the same sound.

Instead of using the word *find* above, I might have used any other word beginning with *f*. It has its ordinary sound.

## THE SENECAS OF CATTARAUGUS.

The following facts were communicated by the Rev. Asher Bliss, of the Cattaraugus Mission:

Agreeably to your request I forward you some facts in regard to the establishment and progress of the gospel among the natives of this reservation. The Cattaraugus Mission Church was organized July 8th, 1827, (which is a little more than eighteen years). It consisted of Mr. Wm. A. Thayer, the teacher, his wife, and twelve native members. There have been additions to it from time to time, until the whole number who have held a connection with this church is one hundred and eighteen. Thirteen of these have been white persons and most of them connected with the mission family. Of the one hundred and five native members, seven or eight have come by letter from other reservations, so that the number who have united on profession of faith is a little short of one hundred. Twenty-five of these have gone to their final account. Some have died in the triumphs of faith, and we humbly hope and trust that they are among the blessed, in the kingdom of our common Father. A number (as it was natural to expect from converts out of heathenish darkness), have apostatized from Christianity, and returned to their former courses. The proportion of these is not probably more than one in ten. Between sixty and seventy are now connected with some of the mission churches. A few only have removed to Alleghany, Tuscarora, while the remainder still live on this reservation.

The effect of the gospel in promoting morality and civilization, may be learned in part from the fact that the public worship of God has been steadily maintained ever since the organization of the church, with members ranging from fifty to one huurdred, and sometimes one hundred and fifty and two hundred, as regular hearers of the word. A sabbath school has been sustained a considerable share of the time. Many copies of the Holy Scriptures, and the New Testament, together with tracts, sabbath school books, temperance papers, and religious periodicals, have been circulated among the children and youth. Temperance societies have been patronized by nearly all the chiefs and leading men on the reservation. Pledges have been circulated, and received the signatures of a large majority of the population, of all parties, on the Washingtonian plan.

Day schools for teaching the English language have been kept in operation almost without interruption for more than twenty years, under the patronage of the American Board of Commissioners for Foreign Missions.

During the thirteen years that I have superintended these schools, nearly thirty different persons have engaged for a longer or shorter time, as teachers. For the past year there have been four schools under the patronage of the American Board, and one under the Society of Friends. The whole number who have been instructed in the five schools is probably not far from one hundred and twenty-five. The attendance of a part has been very irregular, sometimes shifting from one school to another, and sometimes attending no school at all. Several of the early pupils in the mission schools are now heads of families, well informed, industrious, temperate and religious, and in good circumstances. Some are interpreters, some teachers of schools, and others engaged in transacting the business of the nation.

You can, sir, best judge of the influence of the gospel in promoting worldly prosperity, when you have fully completed the census which is now being taken. When you count up the framed houses and barns, the horses, cattle, sheep and hogs, the acres of improved land, with the wagons, buggies and sleighs, clocks and watches, and the various productions of agriculture, you can easily conceive the difference between the present, and thirty years ago. I suppose there was not then a framed building of any description, and scarcely a log house, properly so called; no teams, no roads, no ploughed land, and but small patches of corn, beans and squashes. What an astonishing change!

As to the capacity of Indian children for improvement, my own impression is that there is no essential difference between them and white children. The fact that Indian children usually make slow progess in studying English books, can be accounted for in three ways: 1. They generally have little or no assistance from their parents at home; 2. They are irregular in their attendance on schools, for want of order and discipline on the part of parents; 3. Being ignorant of the

English language, it is a long time before they comprehend fully the instruction of their teachers.

These circumstances operate to make the school room a very dull and uninteresting place to the scholar, and the reflex influence gives the scholar the same appearance. When they can once rise above these circumstances, and overcome these obstacles, they make good proficiency in their studies.

## THE SENECAS OF ALLEGHANY.

Rev. William Hall, of the Alleghany mission, writes:

Your inquiries in relation to the state of religion, education, &c., among the Indians of this reservation, if I rightly understand them, are briefly answered as follows:

Christianity very much prospered here during the four years next preceding that of 1845. The number of church members during that period, was nearly tripled, and very encouraging additions were made to their knowledge and zeal. But the past year has been one of stupidity and drought. There have, however, been four additions from the Indians, made to the church, by profession of faith, and two whites.

The present number of Indian members, is about one hundred and fifteen. The number of whites is eight. Seven of the Indian members are under censure.

I have sustained three schools during the past summer, in which about eighty Indian children have been more or less taught. One of these schools, whose whole number is only about thirty, gives an average attendance of nearly twenty-five. In this neighborhood the population is sufficiently compact for a farming community, and the younger parents are partially educated.

In the other neighborhoods, the population is very sparse, and the parents very ignorant. The consequence is, that the daily attendance falls short of one-half the whole number of scholars, and cannot be called regular at that. Many do not get to school earlier than half past eleven, and very few carlier than ten, and half past ten. Those who attend regularly, evince a capacity to acquire knowledge, equaling the whites, and one of our schools will suffer nothing, in comparison with common country schools.

## MOHAWK AND CAYUGA VOCABULARIES.

Letter from Rev. Wm. McMurray, communicating Mr. Elliot's vocabularies of the Mohawk and Cayuga:

I have just received the vocabularies, with the Indian words, from the Rev. Adam Elliot, of Tuscarora, to whom I sent them for the translation. The cause of the delay, was his severe illness, and the difficulty of getting suitable persons to give him the Indian.

## STATISTICS OF THE ONEIDAS.

The following letter was received from Mr. Richard U. Shearman, communicating the Oneida vocabulary.

I completed the enumeration of the Oneida Indians some days ago, but delayed sending a return to you to ascertain the Indian names. Several families are included in the marshal's enumeration of the inhabitants of the town of Vernon. The remainder reside in Madison county.

The houses of these Indians are generally much better than the *log* houses of the whites, being constructed of hewn, even jointed logs, with shingle roofs and good windows. There are three good frame houses belonging to them; one of these is a very handsome one, belonging to Skenado. I noticed in it some tasty fringed window curtains and good carpets. The Indians whom you met at Oneida were the *flower* of the tribe, being mostly farmers, who raise a sufficiency of produce for their comfortable support. There are several heads of families in my list, who cultivate no land of their own, but gain a subsistence by chopping wood and performing farm labor for others.

The whole number of families, I make, as you will perceive, 31. The whole number of houses I believe is but 28, but in each of these houses I found two families. The number of persons is 157. The count of last winter, which made 180 souls, was made with reference to retaining a certain amount of missionary funds, and Mr. Stafford, the Indian attorney, tells me it was made too high. Skenado says the tribe in this state numbers just 200 souls, of whom 40 are with the Onondagas.

I have filled up your Indian vocabulary to-day. I wrote down the words as they were given to me by one Johnson, a pretty intelligent man, who sometimes acts as interpreter. My orthography may be somewhat at fault, owing to my limited knowledge of the Indian manner of sounding the letters of the English alphabet. In general, I have endeavored to spell the words according to their sound in English, though the letter *a* is used often as in the English, and often to express the sound of *ah!* With this exception, and the use of *hon, han* and *hun,* to express a sound of which nothing in the English can convey an accurate impression, the spelling accords with the pronunciation. The Indian from whom I obtained the information informs me he knows of no words in his language to express such large numbers as *thousands* and *millions.* I have, therefore, in the cases of those numbers, filled the blanks with the Indian for *ten hundred* and *ten hundred thousand;* that is, in the latter case, *ten hundred ten hundreds.*

I hope the table will be satisfactory, and that it may aid you in making the comparison between the languages which you desire.

## IROQUOIS LAWS OF DESCENT.

L. Morgan, Esq., in a letter, dated Rochester, Oct. 7, 1845, furnishes the following particulars on this subject:

You have doubtless seen a notice of the great council of the Six Nations, recently held at Tonawanda. We call it great because we never saw any thing of the kind before, and perhaps never will again. Three of us started in season, and spent the whole of last week in attendance, and were also joined by Mr. Hurd, a delegate from Cayuga. We were there before the council opened, and left after the fire was raked up. Our budget of information is large, and overthrows some of our past knowledge, and on the whole, enlarges our ideas of the vastness and complexity of this Indian fabric. We are a great way from the bottom yet; we may never reach it, but what we do bring up to the surface, remunerates richly for the search.

We learn that at the establishment of the confederacy, fifty sachemships were founded, and a name assigned to each, which they are still known by, and which names every sachem of the several sachemdoms, from the beginning to the present time has borne. There were also fifty sub-sachems, or aids; that is, to every sachem was given a sub-sachem to stand behind him—in a word to do his bidding. These sachemships are still confined to the Five Nations; the Tuscaroras were never permitted to have any. They are unequally divided among the Five Nations, the Onondagas having as many as fourteen. The eight original tribes or families still hold to be correct as we had it, but each tribe did not have a sachem. In some of the tribes were two or three, in others none. As the English would say the Howard family had a peerage in it, so would the Indians say that a certain tribe or clan had one or two or no sachemships running in it. The idea seems to be that the sachem did not preside over a tribe as that would leave some tribes destitute; but the nine Oneida sachems, for instance, ruled the Oneida nation conjointly, and when the nations met in council, would represent it. The fifty sachems were the only official characters known at the councils of the confederacy. The sub-sachems and chiefs had nothing to say. And unanimity, as in the Polish diet, was always necessary. Over this council, the *tha-do-da-hoh*, or great sachem of the confederacy, presided. He was always taken from the Onondagas, as we heretofore supposed; but what is very important, it is denied that there was any such officer as a *tokarihogea*, or military chieftain over the confederacy. They recognize no such office, and deny that Brant was any thing but a chief, or an officer of the third and lowest class. I sifted this matter thoroughly, in conversations with Blacksmith, Le Fort, Capt. Frost, and Dr. Wilson, a Cayuga, and am satisfied, that the *tha-do-da-hoh*\* was the chief ruler of the Iroquois, and that they had no other. We fell into this error by following Stone, who in the life of Brant, pretends to establish in him the title of war chieftain or *tokarihogea* of the confederacy. In relation to the head warriors or military leaders of the nations, there is still some obscurity. The Seneca nation has two, but the other nations none. The truth is, the learning, if we may so call it, of the Iroquois, is in the hands of a few, and it is very difficult to reach it, as those who are the most learned are the most inveterate Indians, and the least communicative.

Their laws of descent are quite intricate. They follow the female line, and as the children always follow the tribe of the mother, and the man never is allowed to marry in his own tribe, it follows that the father and son are never of the same tribe, and hence the son can never succeed the father, because the sachemship runs in the tribe of the father. It really is quite surprising to find such permanent original institutions

\* This is a Seneca pronunciation of the name written *Atotarho*, by Cusick, and *Tatotarho*, by another and older authority. For a figure of this noted primary ruler, as it is given in Iroquois picture writing, see page 91.—S.

among the Iroquois, and still more surprising that these institutions have never seen the light. If I can construct a table of descents with any approach to accuracy, I will send it down to the Historical Society. The idea at the foundation of their law of descent, is quite a comment upon human nature. The child must be the son of the mother, though he may not be of his mother's husband—quite and absolutely an original code.

The object of this council was to " raise up sachems" in the place of those who had died. It would require more room than twenty letters would furnish to explain what we saw and heard—the mode of election and deposition—the lament for the dead—the wampum—the two sides of the council fire, &c., &c., and the other ceremonies connected with raising up sachems; also the dances, the preaching, and the feast.

We were well received by the Indians, and they seemed disposed to give us whatever information we desired on the religious system of the Iroquois, their marriage and burial rites, &c.

### KING HENDRICK.

The following note in relation to King Hendrick, was received from G. F. Yates, Esq., dated Albany, July 17, 1847, after the sketch on page 413 had gone through the press.

Dear sir: In the hurried notice I gave you of King Hendrick, not having turned my attention to the subject for many years, several things escaped my memory with which I had been once familiar. In my notes I had a mem., referring to Mrs. Grant's American Lady. That work I have not perused since a mere youth, and it was not at hand when I penned my notice of Hendrick. I perused it yesterday, and deem it of importance to give you the testimony on certain points mooted in my notice, which this authoress furnishes. She wrote these memoirs more than thirty years after her return to Scotland, " unassisted by written memorials," and as she herself says, may have mistaken dates and misplaced facts. She was herself born in 1755, two years after old Hendrick's death, and fixes the date of his visit, with three other sachems and Col. Schuyler, to England, in 1708 and 1709. With these data in the reader's mind, he may be able to understand the following passage from Mrs. Grant's memoirs.

"It was the fortune of the writer of these memoirs more than thirty years after, to see that great warrior and faithful ally of the British crown, the redoubted King Hendrick, then sovereign of the Five Nations, splendidly arrayed in a suit of light blue, made in an antique mode, and trimmed with broad silver lace, which was probably an *heir loom in the family*, presented to his *father* by his good ally and sister, the female king of England."

She here evidently speaks of the *son* of old King Hendrick, as arrayed in a suit of his father. This leads us to infer, that the son succeeded to the titles and dignity of his father, and must have enjoyed the same until his death, which was followed by the installation of Thayendanegea or Brant, as his successor; for it was him we find at the commencement of the revolution, acknowledged as the chief captain of the Mohawks, and minister plenipotentiary of the said Five Nations.

www.ingramcontent.com/pod-product-compliance
Lightning Source LLC
Chambersburg PA
CBHW030258080526
44584CB00012B/359